ENGLISH FILMING, ENGLISH WRITING

ENGLISH FILMING WRITING

JEFFERSON HUNTER

Indiana University Press

Bloomington & Indianapolis

This book is a publication of

Indiana University Press
601 North Morton Street
Bloomington, IN 47404-3797 USA

www.iupress.indiana.edu

Telephone orders   800-842-6796
Fax orders   812-855-7931
Orders by e-mail   iuporder@indiana.edu

⊗ The paper used in this publication
meets the minimum requirements of
American National Standard for Information Sciences—Permanence of Paper
for Printed Library Materials, ANSI
Z39.48-1992.

Manufactured in the United States of
America

**Library of Congress Cataloging-in-
Publication Data**

Hunter, Jefferson, date-
English filming, English writing /
Jefferson Hunter.
    p. cm.
Includes bibliographical references
and index.
    ISBN 978-0-253-35443-3 (cloth : alk.
paper) — ISBN 978-0-253-22177-3
(pbk. : alk. paper) 1. Film adaptations—
History and criticism. 2. Television
adaptations—History and criticism.
3. English literature—Film and video
adaptations. 4. Motion pictures—Great
Britain—History. 5. Motion pictures
and literature. I. Title.

PN1997.85.H86 2010
791.430942—dc22

2009033652

1 2 3 4 5 15 14 13 12 11 10

CONTENTS

PREFACE

This is a book about English films and television dramas, as works of art of compelling interest in themselves, and as works related to the larger culture of England in the twentieth century, especially its literary culture. Hence the book's title, which is meant to suggest not so much a double subject as a double approach to one subject—the expression, whether on the page or the screen, of certain significant themes, of certain ways of seeing and understanding. I have used the term "English" rather than "British" in the title partly because we still usually speak of English rather than British literature, but mostly because the screen works I consider, along with the literary works influencing or influenced by them, were in fact produced in England rather than in Scotland or Wales.

A great many screen works are mentioned in the following pages; I examine a dozen or so at length, from Gracie Fields's *Look Up and Laugh* in 1935 to Alan Bennett's *The History Boys* in 2006. That examination, I have found, is obliged to take literary connections into account, some of the connections being obvious (*The History Boys* was a stage play before it was a film), some not (*Look Up and Laugh* derives stylistic cues, as well as its screenplay, from the novelist J. B. Priestley). For all the distinctiveness of its visual and auditory operations, its purely cinematic qualities, English filming turns out to have a great deal to do with writing, especially English filming in the period of its greatest achievement. Michael Powell, a very literary filmmaker indeed, signaled as much with his 1944 fantasia *A Canterbury Tale,* a film with a Chaucerian title and a Kiplingesque village setting, with lettered signs in a bombed street, portentous inscriptions by a doorway, repeated close-ups of books on a study table.

Readers of this book should be aware that it is a kind of close-up itself, a look at films sometimes shot by shot, or sound by sound. Many pages are devoted to careful formalist analysis, to the end of achieving a *detailed* understanding of what filmed sequences mean and how that meaning is conveyed—to the end, that is, of doing justice to works which have been written, photographed, and edited with a detailed genius—and ultimately to the end of gaining the greatest possible pleasure from them. I urge readers to compare my analyses against their own viewings of the sequences in question, just as they would read and think about quoted passages if this were a book on the twentieth-century English novel.

Neither literary contextualizing nor formalist analysis is particularly the method of film studies as currently practiced in the academy (though both are the methods of serious film reviewing), and for that reason I begin the book with a brief introduction setting forth arguments for proceeding in the way I do, taking as examples for analysis *My Beautiful Laundrette* and *Sammy and Rosie Get Laid,* two films with script by Hanif Kureishi and direction by Stephen Frears. I would never contend that mine is the only way to approach English screen works, only that it is a valid way, and I believe a rewarding way, given some oddities of the development of film studies as a discipline, and given the richness of screen works which have received nothing like the attention due them. *The Third Man* has been analyzed to a fare-thee-well, but other ganglord-on-the-run films, for example John Mackenzie's *The Long Good Friday,* have not. Two of the works I focus on are not films at all, but television series written by Dennis Potter, *Pennies from Heaven* and *The Singing Detective.* My rationale for considering television together with film, in spite of the manifest differences (industrial, technical, budgetary) between the two media, is also given in the introduction.

After the introduction, in a chapter largely historical in orientation, I look at two films from World War II, *A Canterbury Tale* and Humphrey Jennings's avant-garde documentary *Listen to Britain,* both selected for their representative as well as their idiosyncratic qualities. These are what-we-are-fighting-for works, only to be fully comprehended in a broader context of patriotic films and writings, as also in the pleasingly eccentric context of village pageants and wartime political shows, and finally in two seemingly opposed literary contexts, Kipling's nostalgia and T. S. Eliot's Modernism.

The third chapter, focusing on genre, examines crime films, chiefly because crime as a subject is linked so inextricably with a nation's understanding of itself, its countenancing of certain kinds of violence and its insistence on certain forms of morality. I concentrate on a limited number of examples—among them *No Orchids for Miss Blandish, Stormy Monday, The Long Good Friday,* and *Get Carter*—particularly in their relation, imitative or combative, to American models. The main writer involved here is George Orwell, author of two important 1940s essays about crime, and the screen work considered at greatest length is *The Singing Detective,* in my view the culmination of a distinctively English tradition of domestic crime dramas.

Following that, the fourth chapter considers literary adaptation—the most obvious sort of involvement of film with writing. This is a topic much analyzed theoretically, but perhaps narrowly, with regard only to the transition from page to screen, its success or failure, its fidelity to or betrayal of an original. I am just as interested in the influence of screen on page, or more generally the intellectual entanglement of the two kinds of storytelling, and I examine that entanglement in the Merchant-Ivory *Remains of the Day* and in the 1985 BBC television serialization of Dickens's *Bleak House.* The latter version stands as an exemplary visualization—a more exemplary visualization, in my view, than the BBC *Bleak House* of 2005—of Dickens's fog-soaked images and as an enactment of his dark characterizations.

The next chapter considers a technique—music in screen works. Here my examples are orchestral scores in older works like the famous *Brief Encounter* and the almost unknown *The Captive Heart;* upbeat production numbers in *Look Up and Laugh;* jazz in *Look Back in Anger;* popular songs in *Pennies from Heaven* and other Potter works; and a mixture of popular and classical music in two art-house films by Terence Davies, *Distant Voices, Still Lives* and *The Long Day Closes.* What all these filmed performances have in common is summed up in a line from Noël Coward about the strange potency of cheap music—a much repeated cliché that finally has more to convey about the strangeness of musical effects than about their cheapness.

In a conclusion, I follow the history of involvement between English writing and filming out to its late twentieth- and early twenty-first-century culmination in the work of the poet Tony Harrison and the playwright Alan Bennett. Harrison's "film/poems," like *Prometheus* or *Crossings*, a remake of the 1936 documentary *Night Mail*, merge writing and filming into what Harrison considers a thematic (and even rhythmic) hybrid form, while Bennett's *The History Boys*, if demonstrating a more modest sort of hybridity, is nevertheless developed from an extraordinary range of dramatic, filmed, and televised productions. Twentieth-century English playwrights have routinely undertaken screen work (Coward, Tom Stoppard, Harold Pinter), but Bennett has done more than most, and been more influenced by the cinema and television—and for that reason he seems representative of where the national culture stands at this moment in its history.

Dates given for English screen works are those of initial exhibition or broadcast in England; when possible, these have been taken from Denis Gifford's *British Film Catalogue*, third edition (London and Chicago: Fitzroy Dearborn, 2001). Dates of American or other screen works are as given in the Internet Movie Database (www.imdb.com). Quotations from dialogue are taken directly from soundtracks, not from published screenplays, unless otherwise specified. Bibliographical information for critical and biographical publications which I have consulted is given in the endnotes.

Any American writing about modern English culture, in the form of its films and television programs, ought to feel a decent sense of trepidation. I certainly do. No doubt I have misconstrued actions or phrases which English viewers would instantly comprehend, belabored the obvious, missed jokes, erred about a tone or two; in short, gotten things wrong. My rationale for proceeding anyway is that sometimes approaches from afar may be useful precisely because they come from afar, not from within. They engage with a subject freshly and curiously, are drawn to interesting details but also willing to generalize, with an outsider's daringness. Joseph Losey (born La Crosse, Wisconsin) saw the English class system from afar and so was able to direct an extraordinarily perceptive film about it, *The Servant,* admittedly with Robin Maugham's novel and Harold Pinter's screenplay to guide him. I have not emulated Losey's creative achievement, of course, but at least been encouraged by his example.

Such understanding of English screen culture as I have, I owe in part to my good fortune in being able to do research in England, particularly in the National Film Library at the British Film Institute in London, and in the BFI's viewing facilities, where works from the National Film and Television Archive, otherwise unavailable, can be seen. I am grateful to many librarians and to staff at the BFI, Janet Moule and Kathleen Dickinson in particular, for their help.

Smith College funded more than one research trip to London and made possible the writing of much of this book with the granting of a year's leave from teaching. For that help, and for generosities extended by the associate provost, Charles Staelin, I am very thankful. Librarians at Neilson and Josten Libraries at Smith were unfailingly energetic in answering queries, obtaining books, and suggesting research tactics. It is a pleasure to thank them: Pamela Skinner, Robin Kinder, Sika Berger, Bruce Sadjak, Janet Spongberg. My Smith colleagues William Oram, Michael Gorra, Luc Gilleman, and Michael Thurston read portions of the text in draft and made helpful suggestions for revision, as did John C. Elder of Middlebury College. They were an ideal audience, the sort of readership every writer would wish to have—generous, encouraging, usefully finicky. My son Andrew Hunter gave last-minute research help. Pamela C. Hunter gave such spousal support and encouragement as made the long labor of writing a book tolerable. Finally, I am indebted to my Smith research assistants, especially Mia Cabana and Jill Testerman, and to the Smith students to whom I have taught British film and television over a number of years. Naa-Adei Kotey, Noelle Lundgren, and Dawn Thornton in particular had good ideas and asked hard questions about the subject. This book is meant to give better, or at least more developed, answers than I was able to deliver on the spot.

Lines from W. H. Auden, "Night Mail," © 1938 by W. H. Auden, from *Collected Poems,* reprinted by permission of Random House, Inc., and by Faber & Faber Limited.

Lines from Noël Coward, "Twentieth Century Blues," from *Cavalcade*, and "Play Something Light," from *Shadow Play*, published in Coward, *Plays: Three* (London: Methuen, 1979), reprinted by kind permission of NC Aventales AG, successor in title to the Estate of Noël Coward, and by A & C Black Publishers.

Lines from T. S. Eliot, "Defense of the Islands," published in *Collected Poems 1909–1962* by T. S. Eliot, © 1936 by Harcourt, Inc., and renewed 1964 by T. S. Eliot, reprinted by permission of Houghton Mifflin Harcourt Publishing Company and Faber & Faber Limited.

Lines from Philip Larkin, "For Sidney Bechet" and "The Whitsun Weddings," published in Larkin, *Collected Poems* (NY and London: Farrar, Straus and Giroux, 1988, 1989), copyright © 2003 by the Estate of Philip Larkin, reprinted by permission of Farrar, Straus and Giroux, LLC and Faber & Faber Limited.

Lines from Dylan Thomas, "Our Eunuch Dreams," published in *The Poems of Dylan Thomas* (NY: New Directions, 1957 and London: J. M. Dent, 1954), © 1953 by Dylan Thomas, reprinted by permission of New Directions Publishing Corp., and David Higham Associates.

ENGLISH FILMING, ENGLISH WRITING

BY WAY OF HANIF KUREISHI AND STEPHEN FREARS

It is routine for a certain kind of contemporary scholarship to refer to the films it deals with as *texts,* that is, as sign-systems comparable in their operation to poems, novels, plays, reality programs on television, rock videos, advertising slogans, newscasts, or any of the other expressions of our culture which this scholarship has, for its own generalizing and theorizing purposes, lumped together. If I resist calling screen works texts, however useful the term might be to others, it is because doing so would seem to me to obscure the ways in which films actually work—*not* textually, in the ordinary sense of the word, or not textually in the main, but rather with images, with sounds, with simultaneity of image and sound, with rapid transitions from image to image and from sound to sound, with (usually) spoken dramatic dialogue and visible gestures, with the enactment of action, with a host of conventions we have learned to interpret in the century of moving pictures' existence; in short, with a language distinctive to itself. I can see why Dennis Potter once referred to his *Pennies from Heaven* as a "novel for television,"[1] but without wanting to take anything away from that work's ambitious scale and seriousness of purpose, or its fiction-like, ample characterizations, I would insist on noticing all the qualities that make it in fact what it is, a multi-part television series. It is, precisely, televisual—or cinematic even, though less cinematic than Potter's other major screen work, *The Singing Detective,* for reasons to be explained in a later chapter.

In one obvious sense, of course, films do resemble texts. They are interpretable, and complex films are interpretable in the same way as complex texts. They invite an attentiveness to detail and require an ability to arrange details into whole impressions, and then they grant a complex pleasure. This pleasure is partly intellectual, that of successful comprehending, of following the convolutions (and the straightaways) of a discourse, but in my experience it is also aesthetic, the pleasure of following the convolutions (and the straightaways) of a carefully shaped work, one given coherence by its artfulness. Explicated, analyzed formally, taken apart into their constituent elements, as poems by Donne or Marvell used to be taken apart in the heyday of New Criticism in the 1950s and 1960s, screen works paradoxically seem more whole than ever. At least, that is the critical position which I take, and which has governed the chapters that follow. Unlike a deconstructionist (such as Catherine Belsey: the "object of the critic is to seek not the unity of the work, but the multiplicity and diversity of its possible meanings"),[2] I am or attempt to be an assembler of parts into wholes. It is precisely the unity of a film or television series, even perhaps of a screen genre, which I am looking for. In a later chapter of this book, for example, I propose a single category ("domestic crime drama") for many screen works, *They Made Me a Fugitive* and *It Always Rains on Sunday, Traffik* and *Get Carter* among them.

Throughout the book, in discussions of individual films, I seek to identify unifying themes and, especially, formal consistencies—the relations of one part to another and to the whole, the sense of proportion among parts, and the management of tone throughout. Formal consistency is not always fully achieved, of course; no one could turn *They Made Me a Fugitive* into an *objet d'art* as perfectly realized as the best poems of Donne or Marvell, and in the following pages I have had to acknowledge formal shortcomings when they are there on the screen to be seen. Nor is full-scale analysis always the way to get at formal consistency when it *is* achieved, especially when analysis marches straight through an entire film, scene by scene or shot by shot. I have avoided that kind of relentlessness, dealing more with sequences than with whole works.

Serious criticism of the cinema in England has been practiced for seventy years or so (I am thinking of Charles Davy's *Footnotes to the Film,* from 1938, as a starting point, followed shortly by Roger Manvell's work in the 1940s), and in that time it might have been expected to give every significant screen work its aesthetic due, but that has not in fact happened. There is a backlog of works awaiting formalist appreciation. The reason is that such an appreciation requires seeing films carefully and repeatedly, in a way that was rarely possible until the spread of videocassette technology in the 1970s and 1980s, and which has now in the era of the DVD become even easier.[3] But by the 1970s, film scholarship had begun to discount aesthetics and emphasize other matters. Its projects became highly theoretical, poststructuralist interrogations (films as sign-systems, films as social codes), inquiries into industrial organization or cinema buildings or audience responses to film, histories of genres, gender studies and queer studies, examinations of stardom, and above all the political contextualizing of film, the assessment of the cinema's resistance to or acquiescence in, say, Tory policy under Margaret Thatcher. In other words, just when it became possible to watch the screen more closely than ever before, criticism tended to turn aside from close watching; away from a formalist interest in what exactly was happening on the screen, and away from the sorts of judgment—this film is worth watching, that one not—which generally accompany formalist criticism. This situation may now be beginning to change, for example with the arrival on the publishing scene of two different series of short critical books on individual films, several of which have an admirable care for aesthetic matters.[4] Still, Peter Wollen, the British film critic and scholar prominent since the publication of his groundbreaking book *Signs and Meaning in the Cinema* in 1969, has recently counseled a rethinking of the aims of film criticism:

> As I read through copious new accounts of British studios or genres or periods or representations of gender or national identity, I begin to wonder where aesthetics fits into the agenda of research and rediscovery. Perhaps the point has come when we need to step back for a moment and make some broad judgements about British cinema, to look at it again as an art form. Which are the films that really count, the films we wouldn't mind seeing again and again?[5]

This appeal, especially coming from a figure like Wollen, seems worth paying attention to. I have tried to pay attention to it throughout this book.

Among "the films that really count" for many scholars (and ordinary viewers) is *My Beautiful Laundrette,* directed by Stephen Frears, written by Hanif Kureishi, and produced by Tim Bevan and Sarah Radclyffe. It was released in November, 1985, after two festival screenings. *My Beautiful Laundrette* excited interest for many reasons. Its frank sex scenes between the two main characters, the ex-punk Johnny and his boyhood friend Omar, a young Anglo-Pakistani, drew admiration from gays and alarmed vigilance from would-be censors. The film depicts an arresting London, full of money and decay, with hustling Pakistani businessmen on one side and feckless white skinheads on the other. That is, it reconceives urban Englishness as a racially mixed, erotically charged, and economically determined state of being; as a condition of painful ambivalence ("this damned country, which we hate and love" says one immigrant); as a mode of life encompassing both violence and toleration, both cynicism and heartfelt commitment to "the new enterprise culture." *My Beautiful Laundrette* thus lent itself to a wide variety of political or historical interpretations, with "The Empire strikes back" being the usual formulation of its politics.[6] It was the first screenplay for Kureishi, who in 1985 was getting to be well known as a playwright (while revising *My Beautiful Laundrette* he was adapting *Mother Courage* for the Royal Shakespeare Company),[7] and only the third feature-length directorial assignment, after *Gumshoe* and *The Hit,* for Frears, who had first served as assistant director for Lindsay Anderson, then established a considerable reputation in television.

Let us take a look at a one short sequence from the film, as an example of the treatment of many film sequences in the pages to follow, and thus an introduction to the general critical method of the book. I will touch on theme, on the politics arising from theme, on film history, and above all on aesthetics—film "as an art form," as Wollen says. After the close reading, and only after it, we will be able to move on to other considerations, such as the larger cultural context to which Kureishi and Frears's film belongs.

Almost at the end of *My Beautiful Laundrette* a young woman named Tania makes her exit from the plot. Tania is a highly modern and secularized Anglo-Pakistani, the daughter of Omar's uncle Nasser and his aunt Bilquis, and so Omar's cousin. In the view of the older generation, especially Omar's vodka-soaked and despairing father, she ought by decent family tradition to become his son's wife. Omar drunkenly proposes to her, but he has committed himself fully to Johnny, as Tania has the intelligence to see, and besides Tania is attracted to Johnny, if she is attracted to any man. At the spiffy new laundrette she issues Johnny a teasing invitation ("I'm going, to live my life. You can come"), followed by a warning (her family will swallow him up "like a little kebab"), then strides out. A few moments of screen time later she departs for parts unknown by train, befitting the sense of restless movement—Pakistani travelers arriving from Heathrow with smuggled drugs, cars moving through dangerous, skinhead-infested construction sites, Johnny climbing in and out of squats, London visibly on its way to becoming something else—with which *My Beautiful Laundrette* is filled.

Tania's train station is visible from the meager balcony of Omar's papa's flat, a significant setting, in that it so much recalls the favorite mise-en-scène of 1950s or 1960s English films, domesticity linked with a tired industrialism, factory chimneys looming behind shabby rowhouses. The sky is gray (Frears liked shooting in February because in that month "England looked especially unpleasant"),[8] and the grayness gives the balcony a monochrome dreariness. The balcony also looks cramped. Frears puts Papa and his successful brother Nasser in each other's faces, framing them tightly, and allows their opening dialogue exchanges to be a little drowned out by train noises. In sum, the effect of the setting is to create a momentary pastiche of, and then show differences from, an older kind of filmmaking, namely the kitchen-sink realism of a Tony Richardson or a Karel Reisz. *My Beautiful Laundrette* is, let us say, a *Saturday Night and Sunday Morning* in which a wayward youth is finally *not* trapped into conformity by marriage with a beautiful young woman. (The filmmakers may have wanted to acknowledge this. In Karel Reisz's 1960 film, the young wife is played by Shirley Anne Field, who twenty-five years later played Rachel, Nasser's English mistress, in *My Beautiful Laundrette*.)

As Kureishi originally conceived it, Tania's departure was to be conventionally filmed:

> *A train is approaching, rushing towards* NASSER. *Suddenly it is passing him and for a moment, if this is technically possible, he sees* TANIA *sitting reading in the train, her bag beside her. He cries out, but he is drowned out by the train.*

> *If it is not possible for him to see her, then we go into the train with her and perhaps from her POV in the train look at the balcony, the two figures, at the back view of the flat passing by.*[9]

In the scene as actually shot, however, the handling is quite different. We glimpse Tania in a point-of-view shot from Papa and Nasser; she is standing with her suitcase on the distant station platform, wearing a chic and rebellious red scarf. Nasser calls out in surprise, but Tania fails to hear him, already being in departure mode. An Intercity express goes by fast in one direction, blocking his view of her, then another train equally fast in the other direction. Neither train stops or slows, but when the second has passed we see that Tania has vanished, as if by magic— gone off on her journey, presumably, but not in any way that makes realistic sense, not in any way that might have been photographed for *Saturday Night and Sunday Morning*.

How do we explain this odd set-up? In production, it presumably saved money and time, but it also belongs to an overall conception. It seems to involve magic; so do other parts of the story—in keeping with "the tradition of magic realism associated with postcolonial literatures,"[10] the jealous Bilquis gathers herbs, mutters arcanely over them, and so from afar gives her husband's mistress Rachel a painful skin rash. Furthermore, Tania's disappearance is cinematically cheeky, a way for the director to "say" something like "you know and I know that all we're doing here is removing the character from the scene, so let's not bother with a slowing train and a halt for passengers, etc., let's just remove her as expeditiously as possible"; cheekiness runs all the way through *My Beautiful Laundrette*. As Leonard Quart has noted, the film disrupts our sense of order and affirms the value of spontaneity. As Christine Geraghty has noted, it conveys throughout a "sense of cinema as a place for the unexpected," and it drew reviewers' praise for being "entertaining, zany, fresh and quirky."[11] It is playful, allusive (a Bollywood poster stuck on a wall next to a *Some Like It Hot* poster), and provokingly mixed in tone: brutal violence comes out of nowhere, then suddenly stops, and seriousness gives way to farce, as when earlier in the film Tania bares her breasts at a party, to tease Omar, while "Rule, Britannia" in a back-beat version sounds on the house stereo system. In *My Beautiful Laundrette* a drug-dealer commands no more attention than a "fluff-drying spin-drier," as Kureishi puts it in the screenplay. Both writer and director obviously wanted their film to amuse, to employ the "modern mode" of irony in order to comment on "bleakness and cruelty without falling into dourness and didacticism."[12] It is a sad irony, admittedly, which caps Tania's exit. Just before she appears on the platform Papa has said something wistful about his son's marriage and asked if Tania is a possibility, to which Nasser nods yes, enthusiastically and unconvincingly; but then her sudden and total disappearance makes her an obvious impossibility, and sends Papa glumly back to the bottle.

By exiting, Papa ends the scene, after having begun it with his entrance onto the balcony, though the first thing we actually see is the window beside the balcony door: a match to the laundrette window through which the immediately preceding shot has been framed. A few seconds after the entrance, Frears—or the film's editor, Mick Audsley—matches shots in the direction of Tania's train station with reverse shots in the direction of Nasser's disbelieving face; both perspectives include out-of-focus, fast-moving trains, in the foreground and in the background respectively. The spatial organization of the scene is in fact a little hard to read, a little disorienting, but the filmmakers seem to have accepted disorientation as the price of filling this minute of screen time with balanced visuals and symmetrical movements (all told, we see six trains in motion, three from left to right, three from right to left). In other words the scene has a careful design of its own, something tidy and predictable to set against the strangeness of Tania's unaccountable disappearance. This design is unobtrusive. It does not get in the way of the natural-looking staging (train sounds make Nasser and Papa turn their heads toward the tracks, the camera follows the turn in a gentle pan and then continues on to what they are seeing) or of the dialogue. It does not fully compensate for the unpleasantness of February and the shabbiness of the setting. But the design is there in the sequence. To a film which after all has the word "beautiful" in the title it contributes a touch of pleasing orderliness, a modest cinematic beauty.

The funds to make *My Beautiful Laundrette* came from television, the Channel 4 program *Film on Four*. Shot inexpensively on 16mm film and originally intended for broadcast, Frears's and Kureishi's film was only later released theatrically, after its success at the Edinburgh Festival.[13] *Film on Four* financing was essential to many other successful films; in the early 1980s alone it produced such works as *Prick Up Your Ears, Experience Preferred, But Not Essential, The Ploughman's Lunch, Dance with a Stranger, A Private Function,* and *Letter to Brezhnev.* And the involvement of television with independent filmmaking has not been merely financial. Filmmakers and scriptwriters have been profoundly influenced by work seen on the small screen. Kureishi specifically acknowledged his indebtedness to television writers like Alan Bennett, Dennis Potter, Alan Plater, and David Mercer, most of them authors of scripts for the famous BBC series *Play for Today.*[14] Stephen Frears, who got his directorial start with *Film on Four,* was no less indebted to the medium.

These are all reasons why in this book I have followed an emerging trend in current academic criticism and written about television together with film—the practice, for example, of the gathering of essays in *The Cambridge Companion to Literature on Screen,* edited by Deborah Cartmell and Imelda Whelehan.[15] To older analysts, the differences between the industrial organizations of the two media (or between their budgetary resources, or their technical capacities) were paramount. Even so fine and generous-minded a critic as Penelope Houston, writing in 1984, felt a sharp sense of these differences. She approved of Channel 4 financing projects but thought there were still distinctions to be made between television and the "movie movie," which enjoyed "not only a wider vitality but the power to probe more deeply . . . there are crucial aesthetic differences, as well as differences in the quality of the experience . . ."[16] To me, however, the commonalities of the two media seem much more striking, their aesthetic ambitions and achievements—especially in the years since 1984—fully comparable, and accordingly I have discussed them as related components of a national screen culture. Did it matter to viewers in the 1980s if they saw *My Beautiful Laundrette* on a cinema screen or a television screen? Is there any significant difference, artistically speaking, between Tania's disappearance in the Frears-Kureishi film and an equally magic disappearance which figures, as we will see, in one of the scenes of Dennis Potter's television series *The Singing Detective*—two coal-miners in a working men's club, at first firmly in place and looking enigmatically at the protagonist, then a second later not there at all? Is there any significant difference between the tricks played with windows and mirrors, the coinciding of images or dissolving of face into face, which feature prominently in both *My Beau-tiful Laundrette* and *A Question of Attribution,* Alan Bennett's television drama of 1992? It seems to me that answers to questions like these should be sought not generally or theoretically, but in the kind of analysis that looks closely at particular films and television dramas, and at films and television dramas comparatively. At any rate that is how I have sought answers. In doing so, the one attitude toward television drama which I have flatly rejected, and which I hope all serious critics would reject, is simple snobbery: the disdain for the broadcast medium perfectly captured in the comment (by a literary agent): "What do you expect, darling? After all, small screens, small minds . . ."[17]

Film studies has tended from the start to disregard involvements of another sort, not of cinema with television, but of cinema with literature. As the distinguished cultural critic Raymond Williams observed in 1983, the young discipline wanted to draw "a hard line around the separated subject of film," defiantly rejecting the idea that theatre or literature could have anything significant to do with it, or claiming indeed that theatre and literature, if admitted to consideration, might have "diluted or destroyed the pure essence of 'Film' . . . then not a name for a body of actual practice and works but an idealized projection of supposedly pure and inherent properties." A prominent current practitioner from within the field, Andrew Higson, has sketched the same history: film studies "established itself as a distinct discipline precisely by breaking away from respectable middle-class English literary culture, by celebrating the central texts of political modernism, by exploring what was seen as the specifically filmic, and by embracing popular culture."[18]

This sort of intellectual exclusivity is an understandable phenomenon, part of the process which new disciplines invariably undergo as they circumscribe their subject areas and define their methods rigorously, ruthlessly even, against those of older and rival disciplines. And it has in some ways been a beneficial phenomenon. To learn how screen works are "specifically filmic" has been no mean or unimportant task. But intellectual exclusivity in the study of film has by now become a serious limitation in approach and a distortion of the subject, especially when, having trickled downward to the level of reviewing, it produces prejudicial misjudgments—say, condemnations of this or that English film, or possibly even the whole of the English cinema, for being word-driven, "literate," derived from some written source which allegedly has left its anti-visual (and "elitist") traces on the screen.

Here too, as with aesthetic concerns, attitudes in film studies are changing. In recent years a less purist, more comparative approach has arisen, producing, for example, discussions (by Wendy Everett) of the influence of T. S. Eliot's poetry on the cinema of Terence Davies; of analogies between seventeenth-century revenge drama and Mike Hodges' gangster film *Get Carter*, with the hard man Carter viewed as an avatar of the malcontents of those dramas (Steve Chibnall); of stylistic resemblances between Michael Powell and Emeric Pressburger's 1946 melodrama *A Matter of Life and Death* and the Jacobean court masque, two forms of spectacle comparable in the way they combine "verse drama, dance, music, scenery and costume" (Ian Christie); of the pastoral elements shared between Powell and Pressburger's *A Canterbury Tale* and Georgian poets like Rupert Brooke and Edward Thomas (Andrew Moor).[19]

In the case of *A Matter of Life and Death*, the yawning historical gap between World War II and Renaissance dramatic poetry might seem too great for even ingenious scholarship to bridge, but the fact is that Powell and Pressburger do some bridging of cinema and literature themselves. Consider the way their films often feature autocratic, action-provoking, visually creative, waywardly brilliant characters—in short, director figures, versions of Michael Powell; there is a particularly complex example in *A Canterbury Tale*, as we will see. Early on in *A Matter of Life and Death*, one of these directorial types, a famous consulting neurologist named Reeves, goes to his specially constructed *camera obscura* and in the oval mirror of its darkened chamber observes street life in his village, musing aloud about what he sees. In doing this, he is visibly acting like a filmmaker, perhaps a documentarian like Humphrey Jennings. After all, what is a filmmaker but a watcher of life through a mechano-optical apparatus, a connoisseur of moving images and a commentator on the meaning of those images? In his mirror Doctor Reeves watches June, a pretty American radio operator, approach, and if a Jacobean court masque does not come to his mind at this moment, Byron's love poetry does. He murmurs "She walks in beauty, like the night . . ." in appreciation. Conversation ensues:

JUNE   Surveying your kingdom?

REEVES   A village doctor has to know everything. You'd be surprised
how many diagnoses I've formed up here.

JUNE   I love looking at the village from here. Looks so different!

REEVES   (*Laughs*) That's because you see it all clearly and at once, as in
a poet's eye . . .

From *camera obscura* operator to filmmaker to poet: there is a straight line connecting all these creators, as Powell and Pressburger would have us believe.

What this moment of *A Matter of Life and Death* hints at, what critics like Everett, Chibnall, Christie, and Moor are responding to in their various ways, and what in this book I have undertaken to examine, are elemental qualities of English culture—its distinctive regard for the past, the pleasure it takes in continuities and reworkings, its resistance to creative specializations, its talent for collaborations, and especially the complex interrelatedness, in the twentieth century, of its major forms of expression. *A Matter of Life and Death* and *A Canterbury Tale* could not have been produced without the English books which furnished Michael Powell's and Emeric Pressburger's imaginations. To that extent, these two filmmakers *are* poets, or readers of poetry at least. Nor could *The Singing Detective* have been produced without books. Potter's television drama is the fusion of Raymond Chandler detective novels with Joycean verbal pyrotechnics and with the biblical description of Eden.

One may also come at the interrelatedness in the other direction. Philip Larkin's poem "Faith Healing," a meditation on sufferers from disease who file forward at a revival meeting to be blessed, could not have been written without the film documentary which put those sufferers before Larkin's skeptical gaze. Nor could Larkin's even better-known "The Whitsun Weddings" have been written without a film. In this 1958 poem about just-married provincial couples taking the train into London for the start of their lives together, the poet derived the extraordinary image of his last stanza,

> We slowed again,
> And as the tightened brakes took hold, there swelled
> A sense of falling, like an arrow-shower
> Sent out of sight, somewhere becoming rain,

from the arrows launched into the sky in the Agincourt scene of Laurence Olivier's filmed *Henry V.* In an act of the imagination which no one could have predicted, precisely, but which nevertheless seems fully understandable, the sturdy combativeness of English yeomen becomes, centuries later, the poet's cautious hope for renewal and regeneration. For Larkin, it is a plain matter of fact that the English cultural landscape includes film as well as literature, just as the literal landscapes—such as are scanned through the train windows by the bridal couples in "The Whitsun Weddings"—include cinemas along with other emblems of Englishness:

> A dozen marriages got under way.
> They watched the landscape, sitting side by side
> —An Odeon went past, a cooling tower,
> And someone running up to bowl . . .[20]

A whole history of direct influences from English film to literature and from English literature to film might be written, and to accompany it a history of other kinds of indirect involvement, such as the collaboration of writers and filmmakers, the employment of analogous themes or styles, and the straying of apparently purely literary types into the film world. Rudyard Kipling was one such type. His short story "Mrs. Bathurst" (1904) marks the entrance of the newly invented "cinematograph" into serious English fiction, the cinematograph here, projected on to the "big magic lantern sheet" of a variety program, capturing the arrival of the Western Mail in Paddington Station:

> First we saw the platform empty an' the porters standin' by. Then the engine come in, head on, an' the women in the front row jumped: she headed so straight. Then the doors opened and the passengers came out and the porters got the luggage—just like life. Only—only when any one came down too far towards us that was watchin', they walked right out o' the picture, so to speak. I was 'ighly interested, I can tell you.

Two decades later Kipling got into the business himself, to the extent of co-writing the original scenario for a documentary called *One Family,* the first venture of the Empire Marketing Board into filmmaking.[21] Some of Kipling's literary successors would be much more involved in the film world, creating, for example, a whole subgenre of satirical novels on the movie business. There are examples by Anthony Powell (*At Lady*

Molly's), John Mortimer (*Charade*), Christopher Isherwood (*Prater Violet*), and J. B. Priestley (*Bright Day*)—novels in some cases penned immediately after their authors had themselves strayed into film-studio work and based on the painful or enlightening experience gained there. For his part, the film director Bryan Forbes, who in the 1960s made *Whistle Down the Wind, The L-Shaped Room,* and *Séance on a Wet Afternoon,* strayed into literature with his 1972 novel *The Distant Laughter,* about an embittered 1960s director of films.

If the English cinema has for long been engaged in a back-and-forth with English literature, it is so in part because of the bookish twentieth-century society the cinema reflects. The tokens of bookishness are often enough to be seen in films' mises-en-scène—volumes lying on a study table, or being read by weary Londoners in wartime documentaries, or for sale in one of the market stalls of Gracie Fields's musical *Look Up and Laugh,* a film which, incidentally, could scarcely have been made without the prior example of J. B. Priestley's novel *The Good Companions.* In the Merchant-Ivory *The Remains of the Day* (itself, of course, the film adaptation of a novel), Stevens the butler reads an old-fashioned romance novel and then, when the woman he secretly loves walks in, clutches the book to his heart. Neatly ranged books line the walls of the "library," the fireplace-lighted, middle-class room to which Laura Jesson and her husband Fred retreat in the most iconic English film of all, David Lean's *Brief Encounter,* the screen version, it will be remembered, of a Noël Coward play.

Brief Encounter captures suburban England at the precise moment of its cultural history when its inhabitants feel equally devoted to the old medium of books and the new medium of films. Laura regularly visits the cinema. After a lunch with her intriguing new friend Alec Harvey, she goes with him there for a matinee:

> LAURA   We have two choices—*The Loves of Cardinal Richelieu* at the Palace, or *Love in a Mist* at the Palladium.
> ALEC   You're very knowledgeable . . .

They watch *Love in a Mist,* preceded by the trailer for the laughably exotic *Flames of Passion,* then a week later *Flames of Passion* itself, or part of it, walking out in disgust at its absurdity. However, in the midst of all this film-going Laura is apparently no less regular in her visits to the lending library at Boots. The critic Richard Dyer has written about the women's fiction someone like Laura might be expected to borrow there, and about parallels between that fiction and *Brief Encounter*.[22] Back in the book-lined library of their home, when Fred is doing the crossword and asks Laura ("You're a poetry addict") to supply the missing word in the verse line "Huge cloudy symbols of a high . . . ," she knows her Keats well enough to say, with a puzzled frown, "romance," and to refer him to *The Oxford Book of English Verse*.

Cinema-going and book-reading feature no less prominently in the cultural background of *The Third Man*, made two years after *Brief Encounter*. In Carol Reed's film, with its script by the novelist Graham Greene, Holly Martins and Anna Schmidt hide from police pursuit in a movie theatre—taking to a melodramatic extreme, one might say, the escapism offered by such places. Later, the English military policemen of the story discuss Martins's cheap novelettes, *Death at Double X Ranch, The Lone Rider of Santa Fe*. Sergeant Paine likes a good Western, while Major Calloway in his tough urban way despises them, for their outworn sentiments, for their belief in lone-riding kinds of justice. Five decades after these two films, one of Mike Leigh's melancholy comedies, *Career Girls*, examines a very different cultural world, one where books now seem to matter less than rock groups and are useful only in solacing a character's loneliness. But in a scene or two even *Career Girls* showcases one book, *Wuthering Heights*, consulted as an oracle by the main characters in their scruffy undergraduate digs. "Ms. Brontë, Ms. Brontë, will I find a fellow soon?" they ask ritualistically, then in a bedsit version of the *Sortes Virgilianae* they open the novel at random for an answer, investing the old Penguin Classics paperback with a lingering magic value.

That *Wuthering Heights* occupies some sort of niche in contemporary culture might seem anomalous enough, but consider the presence of an equally classic text in a film made exactly a decade before *Career Girls, Sammy and Rosie Get Laid*, the second of the Kureishi-Frears collaborations. This text is T. S. Eliot's *The Waste Land*, neatly inscribed in black letters on the white-painted side of a caravan parked under a west London motorway—pages of the poem enlarged and published as it were in twentieth-century broadside form. To the caravan the black man Danny and the married white social worker Rosie repair, intent on sex. They enter, passing Eliot's solemn Tarot-deck-reading mumbo-jumbo ("I do not find / The Hanged Man"), and make passionate love, while outside, strolling musicians, the "Ghetto-lites," serenade the union with a dance routine and a miming of Otis Redding's 1965 hit "My Girl." This is the notorious moment of cinematic ecstasy in *Sammy and Rosie Get Laid* when not just Danny and Rosie but the other interracial and passionate couples of the film, Anna and Sammy, Rafi and Alice, make love, with the screen momentarily splitting into three horizontal segments to accommodate their simultaneous climaxes.

Under that motorway, Danny's caravan is parked in an encampment of anarchists moving about in free-spirited dress, a tutu worn with combat boots, an academic get-up complete with mortarboard, several ostentatiously befrogged military jackets. There are also a roving jazz band and a chess game played with oversized, abstract-art pieces. In short, we are shown a visual farrago, as is true of the film generally. Earlier, a poster of Virginia Woolf depicts the novelist gazing sadly at a London coming apart into social violence—riots in the street, police crackdowns, crazies in the Tube, homeless people huddled in their cardboard shelters—not to mention into aesthetic chaos: Sammy eats fast food while snorting cocaine and simultaneously listening to Schubert's "Erlkönig" on his headphones. In all of this, *The Waste Land* might be thought only one more random element, a meaningless bit of high-toned décor, and yet on the screen it seems meaningful, more than a token of superannuated literariness. The film insists on our noticing the poem, and even on our reading it; the quotations on the caravan are invitingly clear.

Is it Hanif Kurieshi who is doing the inviting? He is certainly a literary kind of screenwriter, well educated, well read, the author of plays and prose journalism as well as film scripts. It is significant that he saw to the publication in book form of the scripts for both *My Beautiful Laundrette* and *Sammy and Rosie Get Laid,* together with an introduction for the first and a production diary for the second. So published, these texts beg for comparison with other texts. They assume a place in a recognized category of fictions, both reportorial and autobiographical, about London immigrants and London anger—novels by Doris Lessing in the 1960s (*The Golden Notebook*), by Margaret Drabble in the 1980s (*The Middle Ground*), by Zadie Smith and Monica Ali in the first decade of the twenty-first century (*White Teeth, Brick Lane*). A more direct contribution to this category would be Kureishi's 1990 novel *The Buddha of Suburbia,* later to be adapted in its turn for a 1993 BBC miniseries.

In other words, Kureishi purposely aligns himself with fellow authors. The "best screenplays," he has said, "are not written by people who call themselves screenwriters, but by good writers, writers who excel in other forms. . . . the substance of a decent screenplay, character, story, mood, pace, can only come from a cultivated imagination." It is such a cultivated imagination which puts into the published screenplay for *Sammy and Rosie* one allusion to Dickens's Miss Havisham, a second to Flaubert's *Sentimental Education,* from which Kureishi concedes he has lifted a scene involving an older woman's letting down her white hair. Apropos of a lesbian kiss in the film, Kureishi, no less poetry-minded than Doctor Reeves in *A Matter of Life and Death,* quotes Byron's *Don Juan,*

> Each kiss a heart-quake,—for a kiss's strength
> I think it must be reckon'd by its length,[23]

and he writes dialogue which if not Byronic and poetic is at least epigrammatic and literary. As for that anarchist encampment, the published screenplay renders its disorder in a collage style belonging as much to prose-poetry as to stage direction:

> *Next to one fire, on a crate, is a huge TV which the kids watch. On TV a headless man reads the news. . . . Nearby, two cars are half buried in the mud, as if they plunged over the rim of the motorway and nose-dived into the ground. A huge red Indian totem pole sticks up into the sky. A swing hangs down from under the motorway. A kid swings in it.*[24]

Throughout the screenplay Kureishi calls the encampment "waste ground"—but otherwise he makes no reference to Eliot or the quotations from *The Waste Land.* The caravan texts might not in fact have originated with Kureishi, but been the contribution of the art director David McHenry or the improvisation of a set dresser. Whatever their actual origin, they seem ultimately to come from the whole social and aesthetic world which the film creates. It is a particular 1987 London milieu, full of intellection and dismay, which *Sammy and Rosie* reproduces, and within this milieu dwell cultivated, ironic, bookish, and occasionally despairing characters not unlike Kureishi himself. Danny keeps a row or two of books in the caravan (the published screenplay pictures him as lying naked on his bed, reading a paperback, under pictures of Gandhi, Tolstoy, and Martin Luther King), but as London goes up in flames outside, the books do not appear to help him decide between angry rioting and standing peaceably by. The discontented Alice is described as having Jane Austen novels beside her bed. Meanwhile, many shelves of paperbacks are visible in Sammy and Rosie's flat, and a tattered copy of Raymond Chandler's *The Long Goodbye* appears in close-up as husband and wife dispute which of them owns what volumes. Sammy and Rosie like to chaff each other about authors: "If you had to choose between sleeping with George Eliot or Virginia Woolf, who would you choose?" "Virginia," Sammy says, "on looks alone," then asks Rosie to make a similar choice between De Gaulle or Churchill. In a montage of intellectual London activities—this is an homage to Woody Allen as *montagiste* of Manhattan—Sammy speaks of going to special bookstores to buy novels written by women, of attending plays at the Royal Court if they have been well reviewed by the *Guardian,* or sitting in on evening seminars on semiotics.

Some of this intellectual activity may be satirized in the film (Sammy is ironic as he voices the montage), but it is undeniably a part of Kureishi's overall conception, referred to constantly in the dialogue and made visible in the furnishings of the mise-en-scène. And in this conception, T. S. Eliot and *The Waste Land* have parts to play—so much so that a full discussion of *Sammy and Rosie Get Laid,* fuller than I can give here, would have to address the allusion in all its complexity.

I can at least sketch the outline of an interpretation. Eliot would seem to be a looming presence in the film, an outsider whose acculturation to England, like Kureishi's, involves both the sense of belonging and the sense of detachment. Quoted on the side of Danny's caravan, lines from Eliot's great poem serve to recollect an earlier period of English intellection and dismay, just as the dour prophets quoted in *The Waste Land* itself give monitory lessons about the past to a 1922 full of confusion. Surreal touches, sudden transformations and shock cuts, high-toned speeches next to popular songs, ironies in the "modern mode," a society shown to be sick with competing ideologies, sexual longing combined with sexual malaise, traditions broken or defaced but somehow vestigially there and rebuking the present—what does this description of *Sammy and Rosie* sound like but *The Waste Land*? In the film, there is a threatening ghost; specters also haunt the poem. Both works touch on the playing of a game of chess. Anna the photographer is planning an exhibition to be called "Images of a Decaying Europe," which would have served Eliot well as a subtitle. Rafi brings an Asian perspective to bear on contemporary London, along with some lines of Punjabi; Eliot looks east for moral principles (*Datta, Dayadhvam, Damyata*) expressed in Sanskrit. In Kureishi's city, violence seems to be coming from the periphery to the center, ever closer, ever more threateningly; so too with Eliot's nightmarish view of "hooded hordes swarming / Over endless plains" towards a city of angry voices and falling towers.[25] Coincidentally, it is even possible, as Hugh Kenner suggested, that those hooded hordes derive from crowds which Eliot saw in World War I newsreels: films influence a poem which in turn influences a film. . . .[26] In the end, there would be a good deal to say about two parallel visions of urban life, that of *The Waste Land* and that of *Sammy and Rosie Get Laid;* something to say as well about the subject I will address throughout this book, the significance of context, the forming of a common culture, the contiguities of English filming and English writing. If finally I do not think screen works should be called texts, I believe absolutely that screen works and texts have to be discussed together.

ONE

WARTIME PAGEANTRY

This late afternoon I sit & think of you & hear for you the sounds of
English summer: the buzz of the fly against the window pane—the bees
in the sun—the curious whine of the Spitfire high up in the blue—the
children shouting away down the valley.

HUMPHREY JENNINGS

Three-quarters of the way through Michael Powell and Emeric Pressburger's 1944 film *A Canterbury Tale,* the main characters find themselves on top of a windswept hill. Six centuries before, it was a vantage point on the Pilgrim's Way and gave travelers their first glimpse of
Canterbury and its cathedral in the distance. Now, towards the end of
the Second World War, it affords these new pilgrims equally sweeping
views. Back and down to the Kentish countryside where the characters
have been plotting and counter-plotting, ahead to the city or up to the
sky: at Powell's direction the camera turns every which way, sometimes
getting right down next to the characters beside the blackberry bushes
or in the long grass, sometimes taking them in from afar, to emphasize
their littleness against the landscape. With each point-of-view shot or
pan, the film comprehends more of the country.

With its restless energy and its commanding if vague sense of up-
lift, this scene belongs precisely to the historical moment in which it was
created, and contributes to the public rhetoric of that moment. It offers

as a visible prize the metaphorical landscape which Winston Churchill had promised in the most famous of all his wartime orations:

> The whole fury and might of the enemy must very soon be turned on us. Hitler knows that he will have to break us in this Island or lose the war. If we can stand up to him, all Europe may be free and the life of the world may move forward into broad, sunlit uplands.[1]

But the scene also looks forward to what would become a cliché in post-war English filmmaking—namely, the pastoral escape, when characters go for a walk up the local hill, gain some distance on whatever slum or bourgeois semi-detached existence is entrapping them, and then scan the view with their understandings temporarily liberated (there is a particularly clear example in Tony Richardson's *A Taste of Honey,* from 1961).

Equally, the hilltop scene looks backward to the elevated panoramas of early twentieth-century English writing. That is, Powell and Pressburger replicate in their film the overviews imagined in Thomas Hardy's epic poem *The Dynasts,* or the airborne surveys made from a primitive flying machine in H. G. Wells's novel *Tono-Bungay.* Or the moment in E. M. Forster's *Howards End* when the novelist turns essayist and displays his country from a hilltop:

> If one wanted to show a foreigner England, perhaps the wisest course would be to take him to the final section of the Purbeck Hills, and stand him on their summit, a few miles to the east of Corfe. Then system after system of our island would roll together under his feet. Beneath him is the valley of the Frome, and all the wild lands that come tossing down from Dorchester . . . the Stour, sliding out of fat fields, to marry the Avon beneath the tower of Christchurch. . . . Salisbury Plain itself . . . Nor is Suburbia absent. Bournemouth's ignoble coast cowers to the right . . . red houses and the Stock Exchange . . . Southampton, hostess to the nations . . . How many villages appear in this view! How many castles! How many churches, vanished or triumphant! . . . What incredible variety of men working beneath that lucent sky to what final end![2]

Forster inspects vastly more territory than Powell and Pressburger do, and advances the forthright opinions ("ignoble," "cowers") which the film medium can convey only by indirection. Still, the writer and the filmmakers are working beneath the same lucent sky and noticing the same details: a river valley, fat fields, a cathedral enacting the part of church triumphant. And the writer and the filmmakers are working to approximately the same end. At this key moment of their fictions they are presenting England visually, as an imagined whole, so that it may be properly valued, and thereafter inherited by those who seem best stewards of it (*Howards End*) or who are most willing to join in its traditions (*A Canterbury Tale*).

A Canterbury Tale is a film of audacious, screen-filling images— "cast your eye on that noble prospect," says the American sergeant in it, pointing to Canterbury Cathedral standing in the distance, surrounded by barrage balloons—and of some silly plot turns. It solves a series of minor crimes but leaves greater mysteries intact. In dramatizing a communal, allied-for-the-duration theme it recalls a number of other English wartime films, but also stands deliberately apart from them; it takes chances, makes mistakes, improvises solutions. The critics who saw it on its release treated it with cautious respect that turned quickly into bafflement ("remarkable . . . authentic . . . odd . . . untidy . . . queer . . . bewildering"), and in spite of recent critical rehabilitations it still raises questions.[3] In other words, it is like the England of Forster's passage, seen from afar; it stands in need of proper valuing.

What does that valuing entail? In the first place, finding a place for *A Canterbury Tale* in the cinematic culture of the 1940s, the sum total of films seen and screenplays read by Powell and Pressburger. Throughout their distinguished seventeen-year collaboration, these two filmmakers—"the Archers"—indisputably regarded themselves as being in and of this culture. The cinema shaped their understanding and ambition and gave them successes to imitate or failures to learn from (films in both categories were to hand for the shaping of *A Canterbury Tale*). The cinema also schooled them in what could be communicated to filmgoers by photography and a soundtrack: Canterbury glimpsed through a curtain of waving grass blades on the hillside, the laughter of a fourteenth-century pilgrimage suddenly sounding in an astonished land girl's ear, and much else in *A Canterbury Tale* which, as we will find, requires a close examination, if only to do justice to its makers' specifically cinematic workmanship.

But Powell and Pressburger also created films within a larger culture. Their filmmaking was profoundly influenced by a sensibility formed by books, as the similarity of the hilltop scenes in *Howards End* and *A Canterbury Tale* suggests. As it happened, neither filmmaker ever declared an affiliation with Forster,[4] but about other literary inspirations Powell in particular was emphatic. "Bunyan and Kipling have conducted me all my life, and they will conduct me into the other world, or that part of it reserved for me." Early in life, he was devoted to contemporary fiction: "every penny went on little editions of G. K. Chesterton, Hilaire Belloc and H. G. Wells, who, excitingly, was a fellow inhabitant of Hythe and could be seen cycling through the lanes of Romney Marsh, perhaps to call on Henry James at Rye, or on Joseph Conrad at his farmhouse." Later, the film business seemed to Powell no different from "ordinary story telling or writing plays"; one reason for his liking Kipling was that a Kipling character declared that "all art is one."[5] If we are to make any real sense of *A Canterbury Tale,* we will have to examine this aspect of it too: its unusual bookishness, its tendency to focus (sometimes in a strictly literal way) on texts of all sorts, of which Chaucer's *Canterbury Tales* is only the most obvious example. Making sense of the film will, in turn, lead to an awareness of how it belongs to a wider national context, how it is accompanied along the way to its hopeful and eccentric conclusion by a whole panoply of cultural productions which attempted to define Englishness and make Englishness seem worth defending in wartime. Constituting this panoply are pamphlets and narratives, anthologies and George Orwell essays, historical-political pageants put on by villages, and especially Humphrey Jennings's film documentary *Listen to Britain, A Canterbury Tale*'s only real rival in cinematic bookishness and sophistication.

THE ARCHERS ON PILGRIMAGE

The Archers famously insisted that their work be seen as fully collaborative. "Written, Produced, and Directed by Michael Powell and Emeric Pressburger," the final line in the credits always ran, and there is much evidence of extensive consultation between them before and during production. One of the best wartime film critics, Richard Winnington, thought their collaboration made possible the "only consistent unification of script, production and direction in British films."[6] In actual practice, however, Powell was clearly responsible for directing, Pressburger for scriptwriting, or more exactly for writing a basic draft which would be rewritten by both collaborators, alternately or together.[7]

As Pressburger remembered it, A Canterbury Tale was conceived, prosaically enough, in a car, where he and Powell had escaped to gain some privacy during the shooting of their 1942 behind-the-enemy-lines thriller One of Our Aircraft Is Missing. They started chatting: "I said to Michael, 'There is so much talk about the country and the people, about protecting the women and children, but who is going to think about the human values—the values that we are fighting for?' And we sat there and Michael said: 'That should be our next film.'"[8] From the start, then, A Canterbury Tale was meant to stand somewhat apart from the war and its propaganda, including the cinematic propaganda of such prior Archers productions as the The Lion Has Wings (1939), the five-minute short An Airman's Letter to his Mother (1941), and the Nazi-hunting thriller 49th Parallel (1941). A Canterbury Tale would also depart from the scale, and the color cinematography, to which the Archers were committed in the film which actually came next after One of Our Aircraft Is Missing—The Life and Death of Colonel Blimp (1943), a historical saga bringing David Low's famous cartoon figure to the screen, involving him with an eternal-feminine character played by Deborah Kerr, and putting him into semi-comical conflict with the urgencies of modern Total War. A Canterbury Tale, like the Archers' Highlands romance I Know Where I'm Going (1945), with which it has a great deal in common, would be intimate, photographed in black-and-white, in a "less combative register," and far more localized.

Though not propaganda, A Canterbury Tale could contribute to an important category of cultural work by teaching traditions, and so confirm everyone's sense of nationhood at the moment it was undergoing attack. This work, the discursive equivalent of panoramic views from hilltops, took many different forms in the 1940s, including the publication of histories like Arthur Bryant's English Saga (1941), Sir Ernest Barker's Britain and the British People (1942), and G. M. Trevelyan's English Social History (1944), or of more specialized studies like the illustrated volumes in the Britain in Pictures series (1941–1945)—British Education, British Ships and British Seamen, The Englishwoman, and so on.

T. S. Eliot contributed to the cause an unusually straightforward and patriotic poem, "Defense of the Islands," asking that "memorials of built
stone" and "music's enduring instrument" be enlisted to say to

> . . . the past and the future generations
> of our kin and of our speech, that we took up
> our positions . . .[9]

Falling into a considerably odder, more Archers-like category is Francis
Brett Young's *The Island* (1944), another history of the nation begun in
the "distressful days" of 1939, "when the very existence of Britain was
imperiled," but this time a book-length history in *verse,* with changing poetic modes to describe different eras of the past: alliterative lines
for the Anglo-Saxons, a poetic drama for the Renaissance, and so on.
Young's historical sweep and nearly hysterical patriotism allow him
to figure RAF pilots as having in their blood the valor of Drake and
Hawkins, or

> The fierce ancestral strains
> Of Caradoc's charioteers, who never quailed
> Before Rome's armoured legions . . .[10]

Patriotic anthologies were even more characteristic of and copiously produced in the period, some examples being J. B. Priestley's *Our Nation's
Heritage* (1939), Collie Knox's *For Ever England* (1943), and Clemence
Dane's quintessential period piece *The Shelter Book* ("A gathering of
tales, poems, essays, notes and notions for use in shelters, tubes, base-
ments and cellars"; 1940).[11]

The new Archers film would work in comradely solidarity with all
these publications but still have to be a fictional narrative, not historical
discourse or a compilation. What about a Shakespeare film? Powell and
Dane had met in early 1941 to talk about a possible script, but nothing
came of this.[12] Or a screen version of *The Pilgrim's Progress*? In spite
of Powell's veneration of Bunyan, Pressburger ultimately doubted the
"filmic potential" of Christian allegory and decided on a story of his
own, more up to date but still historically minded; current events seen
in the long perspective of time.

In later years Pressburger thought *A Canterbury Tale* the Archers
film that was most his own,[13] but it was Powell who led him to a setting

for the story in East Kent, where the director had been born. The village of Chilham, a few miles west from Canterbury, would with other Kentish villages become the "Chillingbourne" of the film, and since Powell had walked the nearby Pilgrim's Way many times, it was easy for him to conceive that the story should involve modern-day versions of medieval pilgrims. According to his later account, these updated pilgrims "crowded in on us, insisting to be used":

> There was a loony English squire, who was so anxious to preserve Britain's traditional virtues that he poured glue on girls' hair when they went out at night with soldiers. This traditionalist had to be given a good old English name, and we called him Thomas Colpepper. [In the film, spelled "Colpeper."] The modern pilgrims to Canterbury were three: a young British soldier, in civilian life a cinema organist, a virtuoso on the Wurlitzer, who combined ruthless materialism with sensitive musicianship; an observant young American soldier from a lumber town in Oregon; a young land-girl, one of the Women's Corps mobilised to take over fighting men's jobs on the farm, and who is trying to forget a tragic love affair. . . . For different reasons they have all alighted from the train in the dark at the little village of Chillingbourne. The English soldier is training there, Allison [the land girl, spelled "Alison" in the film] is going to work at a farm there, and the American thought it was Canterbury. They all chase the Glueman, but he escapes and they decide to spend the weekend hunting him down. . . . essentially the film is a morality play in which three modern pilgrims to Canterbury receive their blessings.[14]

In the parts of the loony squire and land girl Powell wanted to use the leading actors from *Colonel Blimp,* Roger Livesey and Deborah Kerr. But Kerr, with whom he had been romantically involved, went out of his life and off to Hollywood, and in the event Powell cast Eric Portman as the squire and the then unknown Sheila Sim as the girl. The equally unknown Dennis Price became the English soldier-organist Peter Gibbs, while an amateur actor from the American Army, Bob Sweet, whom Powell had seen in a performance of a play called *The Eve of St. Mark,*[15] became the film's American sergeant Bob Johnson. Powell unhesitatingly named two other non-Englishmen to key positions on the crew, both of them UFA-trained German émigrés with whom he had worked before, Erwin Hillier as his lighting cameraman, and Alfred Junge as the designer.

Production of *A Canterbury Tale* took place in the summer and autumn of 1943, half of the time on location in Kent—to which, in an irony which would have to be resolutely excluded from the finished work, Emeric Pressburger, then still technically an enemy alien, was denied access on the orders of the Chief Constable. Powell was present from the start, of course, and while in Kent spent his evenings doing research by reading a thick volume he remembered as *The History of British Civilization*. Presumably this was Esmé Wingfield-Stratford's standard work of 1930, and in spite of its snobbish dismissal of films ("the indiscrimination of a twentieth century mob, debauched by cinema . . . monstrously divorced from sense and reality") the filmmaker may have found it useful for historical background.[16]

During the day his first task was to scout locations. At the tiny village of Shottenden near Chilham he found two brothers, a blacksmith and a wheelwright, whose forge and shop ("a prop man's dream") would provide a center for Chillingbourne's traditional life. Shooting of exterior scenes took place in both villages, while scenes in Canterbury were photographed in the streets and among the blitzed ruins of the city. The Cathedral itself, however, the destined blessing-place for all the characters, could not be used, the Dean and Chapter having denied the Archers' request for filming, and in any case it was in a wartime state (organ dismantled, stained-glass taken out) unsuitable for filming. For interior sequences, Junge had to create a nave on the soundstage at Denham, where Olivier's *Henry V*, a historical drama of a different but equally patriotic sort, was concurrently being shot. Powell wanted to open and close *A Canterbury Tale* with a tracking shot through pealing bells, and because this could not be accomplished in the real bell-chamber at Canterbury, Junge made miniature bells out of fiberglass, which a team of real bellringers operated with tiny ropes as they listened to prerecorded ringing: "the kind of lark the Archers were always getting up to in those days."[17]

The film produced by these efforts begins, after those pealing bells, with a prologue which we will have to examine later, in considerable detail. The main plot gets under way with the arrival of Powell's three modern pilgrims at a station so dark that they can barely be seen. (What other filmmakers, the critic Chris Wicking has asked, would have dared to keep the stars' faces invisible for the first twelve minutes of a film?)[18]

As the trio walk into Chillingbourne, a shadowy figure wearing a uniform comes out of nowhere to pour glue on Alison's hair. The land girl and the two sergeants pursue the assailant to the village hall, where he disappears. Having gotten much of the mess out of her hair, and learned that she is the eleventh girl to have been attacked by the mysterious Glueman, Alison goes upstairs to report to Colpeper, whose farm she has been sent to work on. He expresses disdain for the help she, a young woman, could provide—or perhaps it is a fatherly concern for her virtue. Does she not know about the threat to chastity posed by the soldiers encamped nearby? Colpeper chats with Bob Johnson too, and when the American and the land girl confer later they realize that certain clues they have noticed—a hastily closed blackout curtain, a Home Guard uniform hanging in the closet—hint strongly that Colpeper is the Glueman. (Wartime viewers would not have been unduly shocked by such a revelation: two years previously, in Alberto Cavalcanti's *Went the Day Well?*, they had seen another authority figure, in this case, a Nazi-sympathizing squire, preying on his own village.)

Predictably, Alison and Bob decide to make a few inquiries into the goings-on at Chillingbourne, and in this effort they are joined the next day by the English sergeant Peter Gibbs. (Collaboration is thus emphasized in a film produced by the collaborating Archers.) Over the course of the August weekend, Alison talks to other victims of the attacks. Bob, working his American charm hard and dispensing quarters right and left, finds some local boys playing at war games, enlists them in the anti-Colpeper cause, and through them is eventually able to trace purchases of glue back to the magistrate. For his part, Peter pays a call on Colpeper and surreptitiously takes away the latter's fire-watching rota, which when examined reveals that the Glueman only strikes when the magistrate is on duty. Meanwhile the three amateur detectives have together attended one of the slide-illustrated lectures on local history which Colpeper likes to give to soldiers. The lecture aids the plot by suggesting a motive for the attacks—if girls are afraid of getting glue in their hair, then they will refuse to walk out with the soldiers, who in turn will fill up the long empty evenings learning history from Colpeper—but also allows listeners, the fictive ones in the lecture hall and the real ones in the cinema theatre, to begin to find the loony Colpeper faintly likable, to discover that his antiquarianism is genuine and infectious.

Powell and Pressburger present all the detecting with efficiency but not single-mindedness, since almost from the start their film takes as much interest in the investigators' personal problems as in their pursuit of the Glueman. The multiple and carefully paralleled plot lines (another constant feature of wartime cinema)[19] developed about the three characters are at the heart of *A Canterbury Tale*. Alison, we learn in the course of several tight-lipped admissions, visited Chillingbourne before the war. She spent an idyllic summer camping in a caravan with her fiancé Geoffrey, an archeologist excavating a part of the nearby Pilgrim's Way, and would have married him, except for his family's opposition to the match; now Geoffrey is in the RAF and missing in action. Bob also has a love problem, since his girl back in Oregon has not written to him in months. Peter is more generally dissatisfied with life. His "sensitive musicianship," as Powell's description has it, would seem to qualify him for a place behind a church organ, but in Civvy Street he has merely been playing the Wurlitzer in a cinema palace and growing more and more cynical about everything.

During the hilltop scene already glanced at, Alison tells the story of her lost love to the now sympathetic and apologetic Colpeper, and these two, withdrawing into the grass, watch Bob and Peter approach, then overhear them talking. The two soldiers know that Colpeper is the Glueman but simultaneously admit to liking the man. The various truths of the film now being out, and Canterbury looming in the distance, all is prepared for a final confrontation. This takes place when the three amateur detectives and Colpeper leave Chillingbourne for the city. Like a pilgrim making her way to the shrine of the martyr Thomas à Becket (the film makes the analogy possible without ever stating it directly), Alison is going to the garage where she has stored the caravan, the venerated relic of her summer on the Pilgrim's Way. Bob plans to meet another American soldier at the cathedral; Peter will attend a soldiers' service there before shipping out. In the carriage of the Canterbury train, challenged by the stares of three young people seated across from him, the magistrate implicitly confesses to his misdeeds and quite candidly speaks of the motives behind them: not only did he intend to attract an audience to his lectures, he wanted to help keep local girls faithful to their husbands and boyfriends overseas. But why *attack* the girls?, Alison sensibly asks. Why not simply invite the girls to the lectures too?

Colpeper fails to respond, possibly strengthening Peter's resolve—the other two are in favor of forgiveness—to report the Glueman to the police in Canterbury.

The last twenty minutes of the film follow these individual purposes to conclusions which seem, and are contrived to seem (for example, by special-effect lighting or abrupt appearances and disappearances), miraculous. Alison attends the caravan, weeping over all the dust which has settled on the homely items inside, but then is told by the garage-owner that her fiancé's father has been trying to reach her with news: Geoffrey is alive after all, safe in Gibraltar. Bob's army friend delivers the missing letters from his girl: they have been delayed because they have had to come all the way from Australia, where she is serving with the WACs. Finally, Peter the church-organist-manqué encounters a stray sheet of music in the cathedral. It flutters down the organ-loft staircase toward him as magically and invitingly as the theater program fluttering out of the sky at the opening of that other Denham-produced feature of 1944, *Henry V.* Peter follows the sheet-music's lead upwards to the great instrument of the cathedral, where the friendly old organist engages him in conversation. We hear the voices of choristers rehearsing somewhere in the distance, and at the moment when Peter sits down at the console of the organ they modulate into the ethereal theme which has been associated all along with the miracles of the film. He plays the Bach *Toccata and Fugue* in d minor, followed by "Onward Christian Soldiers" as the troops parade in; any remaining thought of a visit to the police is lost in the thundering chords. Bob wonders admiringly at the cathedral's architecture; Geoffrey's father puts a protective arm around Alison as he leads her into the service; and Colpeper stands solemnly and silently by, presiding in some unspecified way, his declaration, made on the hilltop, that "miracles still happen," proved true in the end.

Released early in 1944, *A Canterbury Tale* was unsuccessful at the box-office, the first real failure in the Archers' career. An older Michael Powell blamed the timing ("the centre of interest had shifted to the Continent") or the complication of Pressburger's plot ideas, which, he decided, he should have insisted on simplifying. Meanwhile, in 1949, in an attempt to make the film a hit in the States, the Archers recut it and gave it a new narrative frame. After the war, Bob Johnson and his new bride look down on Fifth Avenue from the top of Rockefeller Center, and he recalls his adventures in Chillingbourne in an extended flashback. This version too was unsuccessful.[20]

Complicated (and original, and tricky to make sense of) *A Canterbury Tale* may be, but its original audiences would have found in it one thing as unmistakable as Sergeant John Sweet's country-boy accent on the soundtrack: the wartime theme of Anglo-American cooperation. If an American soldier and two English people can work effectively together on the small scale of village crime-solving, then the Allies ought to be able to do the same on the large scale of a war; so the logic of the film runs. To make the idea of a successful alliance of equal partners as clear as possible, Powell repeatedly pairs the two sergeants, always in uniform, in tight two-shots. Standing shoulder to shoulder, they puzzle out the timing of the attacks or the business of Colpeper's glue purchases. On top of the hill, they amiably dispute the benefits of tea-drinking, eat blackberries, then race each other back to the village. One or two critics particularly approved of the fact that the Archers' American soldier was played by a real GI—Edgar Anstey thought Sweet "the best piece of propaganda for America which has yet reached our screens"[21]—as if authenticity somehow had predictive value, and Anglo-American collaboration in a film cast could give promise of the two armies' successful collaboration in the fighting to come.

The idea of Anglo-American solidarity was scarcely original in itself, of course. *A Canterbury Tale* was one among many 1940s proalliance films. Some of these were imports, like Paramount's *One Night in Lisbon* (1941), directed by Edward H. Griffith, which concocts a whirlwind London romance between an English ATS driver and an American pilot, then sets the pair improbably to defying Nazis and unmasking traitors in Portugal. *One Night in Lisbon* earned a savage rebuke from George Orwell, in one of the film reviews the journalist produced (quickly, for the money) for *Time and Tide* in 1940–41: "What rot it all is! What sickly, enervating rubbish! How dare anyone present the war in these colours when thousands of tanks are battling on the plains of Poland and tired aircraft workers are slinking into the tobacconist's to plead humbly for a small Woodbine?" With characteristic honesty Orwell went on to modify this political judgment on aesthetic grounds: "And yet as current films go this is a good film. It moves easily, there are no gaps or *longueurs* in it, and the photography is adequate. Its only fault is to be twenty years behind the times in outlook, and since that is almost general in films likely to have a wide appeal, I suppose one ought not to grumble."[22] Other pro-alliance films were home-grown, like the quasi-documentary *San Demetrio, London* (1943), with its shipload of British merchant sailors and one American crewmate, or British National's *Welcome, Mr. Washington,* directed by Leslie Hiscott, which entertained the same 1944 audience as *A Canterbury Tale* with the story of an American lieutenant who copes manfully with the prejudices of English villagers, falls for the local landowner, and eventually calls in his men to bring home the harvest.

The next year would see a much more considerable film, Anthony Asquith's *The Way to the Stars,* a generally realistic depiction of USAAF and RAF flying crews sharing an English airbase. Here, an initial display of national stereotypes (the Americans are brash and loud, the English stuffy and reserved) yields to the development of camaraderie, and at last to a merging of identities (the Americans grow sensitive, the English discover baseball) in the common cause. Finally, just after the war, with *A Matter of Life and Death,* Powell and Pressburger brought to the screen their own most ambitious treatment of the theme. Developing the film from its simple-minded origin in public relations (the Ministry of Information "wanted it laid down as to why we were all one family"),[23] they showed Americans and English working companionably together—for example, staging a performance of *A Midsummer Night's Dream*—but also having their cultural disagreements. Indeed, with typical Archers bravado they transformed the disagreements into a dreamy midsummer playlet of their own: the English pilot of their story, saved from death by a mistake in the divine bureaucratic machinery, falls in love with a beautiful American radio operator, then has to stand trial in heaven to justify his continued existence, which means countering the attacks of a rabidly anglophobe Yankee prosecutor. The national insults fly back and forth, focusing on the boring incomprehensibility of English cricket and the vulgarity of American jazz, until the pilot's and radio operator's selfless love finally ends the conflict.

For all its imaginativeness, in other words, *A Matter of Life and Death* is built around the familiar idea of an Anglo-American romance. This cinematic cliché and others *A Canterbury Tale* resolutely avoids.

No one is seen to fall in love with anyone else. Bob Johnson stays devoted to his girl at home, and the English, innocent of baseball to the last, stay firmly English. Such cultural disagreements as the villagers have with America are kept at a low-key, plausible, non-dramatic level: continued and irritated amazement that Bob's sergeant's stripes are turned the wrong way round on his uniform sleeve, mild resentment at his too bright GI flashlight. In outward demeanor the sergeant stays correspondingly American. He is invariably naïve, outgoing, impressed in an aw-shucks way by the quaintness of the village, and in one of the film's brief slapstick scenes comically frustrated by the arcane workings of Button A and Button B on the inn's public telephone.

Inwardly, however, certain changes do take place in Bob and the other major characters—personal changes, not adjustments of nationality. Thanks to the ministrations of Chillingbourne, they are led to discover qualities in themselves which they have forgotten, and the importance of that process to *A Canterbury Tale* sharply differentiates it from films like *One Night in Lisbon* or *Welcome, Mr. Washington*. In roundabout ways which would have been highly unsuited to propaganda the Archers set out to examine the spiritual damage which modernity has done to Americans and Englishmen alike. The allies of the film really do battle not with Nazis but "materialism," to use Pressburger's all-purpose term for the enemy.

To take Bob Johnson's experience first, during the early scene with Colpeper at the village hall, the American admits to a liking for the movies. "It's a great thing to sit back in an armchair and watch the world go by in front of you," he says, to which Colpeper responds: "people may get used to looking at the world in a sitting position . . . then when they really do pass through it they don't see anything." It seems a pity to the Englishman that Bob should make a pilgrimage to Canterbury and only go to a cinema. The next day the American has apparently taken the warning about a sitting position to heart. As he wanders around the village, noticing things and commenting amiably on them, he strolls at random past the blacksmith's forge and into the wheelwright's shop. There he notices some timber ("lumber," he insists) being stored and, remembering his father's sawmill business at home, pleasurably exchanges wood talk with the English workman. Their shared knowledge that "You can't hurry an elm" in the process of seasoning identifies them as fellows in the same craft, and an invitation to dinner with the wheelwright's family soon follows. In other words, the village accepts him, his American lingo notwithstanding. Moreover, rural England redeems the sergeant's rootless, movie-corrupted existence by making him feel at home abroad. In Canterbury, Bob visits the cathedral, as he promised his mother he would, and so takes another modest step toward being freed of cultural superficiality, of materialism. Wandering about once again, this time to the accompaniment of the Bach which Peter is playing on the organ, the American looks reverently about him; the camera, in a beautifully timed slow tracking shot, goes along with him through the organ screen and into the choir. The stone vaulting shown far overhead in the apse—the one real interior view of the cathedral we get, shot surreptitiously by a crew member, as Ian Christie has noted[24]—makes Bob murmur about the wooden Baptist church his grandfather built in Oregon in 1887. "Well, that was a good job too," he says loyally. This is the same grandfather, we learn from a scrap of dialogue, who visited Canterbury before him. Bob has simultaneously found beauty and repossessed his origin.

It takes no great leap of the imagination to link this fiction about following the right cultural cues, being accepted, getting to share a meal at the wheelwright's, to Emeric Pressburger's personal history. The scriptwriter could only have invented these warmhearted sequences in *A Canterbury Tale* in the course of recollecting and interpreting his own immigrant experience, no doubt with a certain wistfulness, as his biographer suggests.[25] Pressburger arrived in England in 1935 by way of the German UFA studios and then Paris, a Hungarian Jew exiled from his homeland and looking for a new national identity. By 1944 he had not quite found it. "England is a very, very difficult country for foreigners to come to," he noted, and after all he was still being excluded from the coastal zone in Kent.[26] But Pressburger could well imagine or hope what the experience of acceptance would be like, and he shaped Bob Johnson's experience accordingly. In later screenplays he continued to meditate on the theme, sometimes denying acceptance to his characters (the European nuns in *Black Narcissus,* for example, who never succeed in finding a place in their Himalayan community), sometimes allowing them to earn acceptance (as in *I Know Where I'm Going*, where the English heroine is cured of a fatal modern waywardness when she falls in love with an impecunious laird and devotes herself to their settled life in the Highlands). When he retired, with these fictions of outsiders-moving-in behind him, Pressburger could confidently deem himself fully accepted, and on his own terms. To the end he kept up a few Continental mannerisms (and his Hungarian accent: like Bob Johnson, he was always marked on the tongue) but settled comfortably into the life of a Suffolk village even smaller than Chillingbourne, and there filled his cottage bookshelves with the works of Charles Dickens and Winston Churchill.

As for Michael Powell, that member of the partnership had his own influence on the theme of an American coming to England if, as appears likely, he brought his devotion to Rudyard Kipling to bear on the script of *A Canterbury Tale*. Kipling came home to England from afar (India, travel through the Empire, a temporary sojourn in America) and once settled in Sussex produced a series of remarkable fictions about village life, local customs, and national history; some of these are transparent allegories of his own experience in rediscovering an English heritage. One Kipling story in particular, though never acknowledged as a source for the film (the Archers may have thought one allusion to English literature in the title was enough), seems nevertheless to have been just that. "An Habitation Enforced," the lead story in *Actions and Reactions* (1909), describes a married couple, moneyed Americans wandering about Europe as peevish tourists, who purchase a neglected English estate and bring it and themselves back to life. They wish to modernize, of course, but are taught lessons in patience and age-old traditions by their tenants. Wood lore features here as in *A Canterbury Tale*, a crucial lesson being that bridges ought to be built from long-seasoned oak. In the end, the Americans realize that in coming to Sussex they have only come home, so complete has their re-identification as country landowners been; their adopted village even turns out to be the place from which the wife's family left for the New World. They have repossessed their origin, like Bob Johnson.[27] Kipling liked to print companion verses immediately before or after his stories, and those following "An Habitation Enforced" memorably sum up its sentiments:

I am the land of their fathers.
In me the virtue stays.
I will bring back my children,
After certain days.
Under their feet in the grasses
My clinging magic runs.

This poem, "The Recall," could appropriately be delivered by Colpeper in his role as mystagogue, though even Colpeper might well demur at its last two lines—"They shall return as strangers, They shall remain as sons"—knowing as he does that visitors to Chillingbourne or Canterbury are not literally coming to settle there, but merely to recover their own pasts, then move on. In this sense *A Canterbury Tale* is marginally more realistic than "The Recall" or "An Habitation Enforced."

It is also more up-to-date and evenhanded, since it regards materialism as a problem, and cultural recovery as an obligation, for the English, not just the Americans. Alison Smith and Peter Gibbs, a shop assistant and a cinema organist, Londoners both, are initially as dispossessed as Bob Johnson of the things which Chillingbourne represents. (To make Peter's alienation from the village visible for the screen, Powell puts him in an armored Bren Gun carrier and sends him careening about the country lanes; the vehicle almost collides with Alison's horse-drawn farmcart.) The English characters have lessons to learn, and then to teach. They pay quiet attention at Colpeper's lecture; Peter slips briefly into the lecturer's mode himself when he points out the local river from the hilltop and informs his fellow sergeant "you'll be happy to tell your folks you've seen the River Stour." Admittedly, Peter follows this with the casual remark that in London he likes to spend his Sundays playing cards with the boys and waiting for the pubs to open. Powell and Pressburger have no illusions about this sergeant's cultural education happening overnight.

However much or little Peter and Alison may learn about their national heritage in a public lecture, the crucial lessons for them are private ones. They have to be encouraged to seek out their own redemptive pasts, and their mentor is again Colpeper. Asked at the lecture "What have we got to do with this old road and the people who traveled along it six hundred years ago?" the magistrate replies

There are more ways than one of getting close to your ancestors. Follow the old road, and as you walk, think of them and of the old England. They climbed Chillingbourne Hill just as you did. They sweated and paused for breath just as you did today. And when you see the bluebells in the spring and the wild thyme and the broom and the heather, you're only seeing what their eyes saw. You ford the same rivers, the same birds are singing.

The general theme here is continuity between ages in a long historical span, say that span which separates the present day of bombers coming on their runs from the day of pilgrims nearing Canterbury on horseback and believing in the miracles to be found there, but the actions manifesting the theme are noticeably unmystical and ordinary ones. If Colpeper instigates a pilgrimage, it is only up the hill and across the Stour. Instead of a transformation, he seems to be prescribing a kind of attentiveness to the constants of daily life, a historically informed exercise of everyone's quotidian Englishness. In accordance with this principle, Alison and Peter finish their education in the cathedral precincts by undertaking modest personal acts of recollection—of a summer in a caravan, of playing church music—and in the scheme of the film as a whole these are what count as truly valuable. The starting point of *A Canterbury Tale* may have been the Archers' wish to promote English traditions or communicate non-materialistic values, but the film was made by two incorrigible individualists with complex personal memories of their own to draw from and hint at, and it is as much interested in individuals' acts of remembering as in cultural teaching at large. "Think . . . of the old England" turns out to mean "think of what you used to be."

Audiences at homefront films in the 1940s could count on seeing a variety of settings, some of which they might recognize with pleasure, know as their own: a Welsh coalmining district and rural Scotland (both in *The Captive Heart*, 1946), an aircraft engine factory (*Millions Like Us*, 1943), a shipyard town (*The Demi-Paradise*, 1943), London south of the river (*Waterloo Road*, 1945), the capital's devastated but resolute East End (*Fires Were Started*, 1943). But viewers in every locality of the country saw with remarkable frequency one particular cinematic setting—a tidy village in the Home Counties, comprising picturesque inn, old stone church, shops, bridge over a stream, manor house, and adjacent somnolent countryside. They saw Chillingbourne, in other words, or "Bramley End" in *Went the Day Well?* (1942), or "Claverly" in the cavalcade-of-history film *This England* (1941), or the most extravagantly mounted and artificial village of them all, "Belham" in MGM's hugely successful *Mrs. Miniver* (1942). The inhabitants of these villages constitute a repertory company of familiar types, including squire and family, vicar, doctor, postmistress, ARP warden, stationmaster, soldiers home on leave or about to depart, farmers and farmwives, land girls, blacksmith or harness-maker, shopkeeper, country bus conductor, drinkers in the pub, servants, children. About and around the people and houses of the setting is the sense, rarely put in words but always clearly communicated, that in them reposes all that is most essential, timeless, and valuable in the national identity, that the village represents England itself. The village is "what we're fighting for."

Viewed in one light, of course, Englishness defined by thatched cottages is an all too timebound ideological construction, an object lesson in the fictionality of national representation[28]—or as skeptics in the 1940s would have put it themselves, a distortion, a smug and patronizing unreality. There were many critics of *Mrs. Miniver* and its picture-postcard setting ("a smooth Hollywood fairytale," "I . . . feel like swearing when an English family is presented as the Minivers. Wealth—to me fabulous—wealth every time"),[29] but English films too came in for their share of abuse. In his review of *This England,* George Orwell scorned its attempt to read the story of an industrial nation in the experiences of a rural hamlet: "the implication all along is that England is an agricultural country and that its inhabitants, millions of whom would not know the difference between a turnip and a broccoli if they saw them growing in a field, derive their patriotism from a passionate love of the English soil."[30]

Though *A Canterbury Tale* differs sharply in purpose from *This England,* a place like Chillingbourne unquestionably originates in a similar myth of the countryside and belongs to the same era of public-spirited fabulation (Orwell actually approved of *This England,* grudgingly, on grounds that it was good for morale). Nevertheless, Chillingbourne is not simply a Hollywood (or Denham) fairytale setting. Nor is it a Tory version of the Potemkin village, a hastily thrown-together assemblage of striking vistas and painted facades past which naïve visitors—filmgoers—are conducted to prevent their seeing the reality of wartime Britain. There is nothing deliberately deceptive or artificial about the village in *A Canterbury Tale*. Michael Powell would have argued that the setting was created equally out of memory, the East Kent of his childhood, and accurate observation of Chilham and Canterbury in 1943, and he would no doubt have affirmed his own passionately held belief in its representative Englishness, or at least in his country's need, in wartime, to establish *some* unifying notion of itself, some locality to which everyone could imagine belonging.

During a war which saw personal dislocations on a massive scale, sixty million changes of address in a civilian population of thirty-eight million,[31] such a belief would not have been eccentric or necessarily Tory. Even Orwell, with his regard for the full and exact truth, his personal knowledge of contemporary industrial and urban Britain, had his moments of mythologizing the village and its traditions, and he was far from alone. H. V. Morton meditated on one English village and what it meant in his 1942 book of reportage *I Saw Two Englands:*

> I can see the little hamlet lying below among haystacks and fields, the lime-washed cottages with front gardens bright with canterbury bells, geraniums and poppies . . . My own point of view—and, indeed, it is that of all the farmers, the farm labourers and the cowmen who compose our Home Guard—is that should the rest of England fall, our own parish would hold out to the last man. The responsibility of defending our own village has given to that village a gigantic significance in our eyes.[32]

Vera Brittain, a sharp-eyed journalist like Orwell, and a committed Londoner, had no Home Guard experience to shape her belief in the gigantic significance of rural villages, but believe in it she did. Her *England's Hour* (1941), a first-person account of the ordeal of London during the Blitz, somewhat oddly reaches its climax in a chapter called "Berkshire Village." Brittain acknowledges signs of war in this peaceful place (barbed-wire barricades, for instance, and the sound of German bombers flying overhead) but does much more with, lingers affectionately over, the same icons which Powell and Pressburger would put into *A Canterbury Tale:* "the square-towered, ivied church with its twirling weather-vane . . . the somnolent Horse and Groom Inn carrying the appropriate trade mark of a scarlet hop leaf," her hostess's red-brick house backing on to a large tangled garden, "dewdrops sparkling on the English gorse, the birds twittering in the rhododendrons, the faint autumn smell of far-off bonfires, the lacy pattern of ash-leaves across the grass." For her, she concludes, "and I suspect for most of us—it is this that the word 'England' represents."[33] Whatever their distrust of cliché and their political sophistication, their awareness of the savage economic inequalities and the terrible isolation of rural life, all three of these writers took village Englishness seriously, thought it a powerful and useful idea around which a beleaguered country might rally.

In *A Canterbury Tale* the village of Chillingbourne manages to be cinematically believable as well as mythically representative, largely because Powell and Pressburger's villagers are so wholly unaware that they might be representing something. The minor personages of the film—stationmaster, wheelwright, landlady of the "Hand in Glory," female bus conductors, land girls, and so on—go about their business and pay attention to their private agendas, in this sense exactly paralleling the major characters Alison, Peter, Bob, and Colpeper. Every idiosyncrasy revealed in the action or dialogue prevents the villagers' conforming too much to type and works against any temptation the Archers might have felt to set them to delivering patriotic speeches. On her farm Prudence Honeywood greets Alison with a humorously prolonged list of chores but says nothing about the dignity of manual labor or the splendid contribution women like Alison are making to the war effort. Prudence's only flight of rhetoric is addressed to country life—her devotion to it, her inability to find a husband willing to share it with her—and the flight is a characteristically modest and short-lived one. The wheelwright limits his talk to woodworking, the stationmaster to stations and trains. The villagers of Chillingbourne may be pulling together for the duration but they conspicuously fail to glamorize this effort; no one seems particularly conscious of wartime camaraderie or alliances (told by her excited son "Mother, this is an American soldier," a farmwoman driving a haycart responds "Don't point, dear, it's rude") or even of the war itself. No one ever looks around Chillingbourne and says anything like "this is what we're fighting for." Above all, no one delivers a ringing affirmation of purpose of the sort heard in *Mrs. Miniver,* when from his pulpit in the bombed Belham church Wilcoxen the vicar hurls Churchillian defiance at the enemy. The one aspect of Englishness Powell and Pressburger's villagers represent better than any other is reserve.

The whole film might arguably be called reserved, not only in the way it rejects a declamatory title along the lines of *This England,* but in its relatively undemonstrative or casual manner of establishing cinematic meaning. Colpeper's lecturing and a few key speeches aside, *A Canterbury Tale* "says" nothing explicitly. It renders all its themes, the importance of sustaining a tradition, the benefits of Anglo-American cooperation, the tug of private memory, the Englishness of Chillingbourne, in an accumulation of unobtrusive images (elm logs seasoning) and undramatic happenings (two sergeants eating blackberries together). Viewers of the film, like its sleuthing characters, must be on the alert for these accumulations, must pursue apparently insignificant clues to their true significance. They must also be prepared for a great deal that has nothing to do with significance. The film is peculiarly welcoming of random events, such as the casual movements of tourists and schoolchildren through the aisles of Canterbury Cathedral at the very moment Bob Johnson is undergoing his epiphany there, or, earlier in the plot, the sudden irruption, out of the blackout, of the village idiot. This gibbering, grotesque figure is briefly quizzed by Alison and the two sergeants, then passes abruptly out of the picture, as meaninglessly as he entered it. Immediately afterwards comes a morning scene in which local boys similarly appear out of nowhere, playing at soldiers. Eventually they assist Bob Johnson's detective work, but they are really brought into the film because Powell wanted them there, to have fun with in production, to round out the picture of village life, and no doubt to pay homage to yet another book, Arthur Ransome's children's classic *Swallows and Amazons.*[34] On screen, in a remarkable tracking shot which allows us to follow them at their own level and pace, without condescension, they stalk each other through the trees, and then they act out an amphibious assault—a genial parody of the real combat which *A Canterbury Tale* could not show, but which had somehow to be kept in mind. At the very end of the film, under the credits, two brief sequences appear: soldiers and girls walking arm-in-arm around the village, boys playing football. With a minimal effort each can be connected to the plot (Colpeper's segregation of the sexes has come to nothing, Bob's reward to the boys for their help has been a new football), but connecting hardly seems to be the point. The sequences suggest rather that more is contained in a village's life than can possibly be shown in any single film, including the film just ending.[35]

As for the visual appearance of Chillingbourne in the film, that too is a mixture of the significant and the haphazard. Early establishing shots of the village show a horse-drawn cart moving sedately down the street and a red telephone box, thus settling the Englishness of the place beyond a doubt (an oast house is added to the scene to specify the Kentish setting), but thereafter much more is photographed than is needed for thematic purposes. We see the village hall, a church exterior, the boys' secret hideout, the forge (around which village idlers gather in a rustics' chorus), the manure-yard of a farm, the interior of Bob's bedroom in the "Hand of Glory," and, in a montage sequence following Alison as she gathers information from previous victims of the Glueman, a bus stop, a railway embankment, and a shop with its show window. Adding image to prosaic image, Powell and his designer Alfred Junge build up a reasonably complete picture of the village, by far the most convincingly untidy picture of any tidy village of wartime films. This is a method of cumulative working markedly different from that of other Archers films of the 1940s, in which one overscale image tends to predominate and hold everything together by sheer pictorial force. The ruined and cursed castle in *I Know Where I'm Going* would be one example, the moving staircase stretching between the monochrome heaven and the Technicolor earth in *A Matter of Life and Death* another.

The design of *A Canterbury Tale* provides nothing comparable, and invites a different sort of attentiveness, for example to mundane elements of the countryside or the village falling into visual patterns of unexpected beauty. Some of these patterns were supplied by Kent and merely captured by the camera. Reviewers of the film commented with pleasure on its "lovely outdoors scenes" or "sense of pictorial values," and one of the most perceptive, William Whitebait, noted that amid the general run of English films ("reticent about landscape as about everything else") *A Canterbury Tale* was distinctive in giving viewers both visual beauty and a chance to savor it.[36] For a wartime audience, seeing the film must have been roughly analogous to hearing one of Dame Myra Hess's famous lunchtime concerts in the National Gallery. That is, it would have been an aesthetic experience which in the circumstances became a moral, even a patriotic, demonstration of values: "what we're fighting for" was the privilege not to have to fight for a moment, but rather to savor the Englishness of a landscape.[37]

Meanwhile, running parallel to and enhancing the shots of hillside or meadow or clouds in *A Canterbury Tale* are those lighting effects or visual patterns which had to be created by Erwin Hillier's craft. These include light reflected from the surface of the stream and moving decoratively over the bough of a tree, dappled light falling through leaves onto characters' faces, and Alison's dark figure silhouetted against a dimly lit map in the train station at the very start of the film. The extreme dark of the blackout (in itself, a realistic touch: *A Canterbury Tale* is the rare wartime film to suggest convincingly how infuriating and disorienting the blackout was) sometimes allows Hillier to work melodramatically, in ways that recall the Expressionism of the UFA studio or that prefigure noir films of the later 1940s: faces shot in a sudden stab of light from a torch or match, backlit tendrils of cigarette smoke curling into the air. John Seabourne's editing imposes patterns of its own, as in Alison's montage sequence mentioned above, which begins with dissolves, uses wipes to connect the three following episodes (first right to left, to match the movement of a train in the background, then left to right), and finally closes with another dissolve. Here, symmetry emerges from ordinary contingencies, not exactly drawing attention to itself, but giving a pleasure nonetheless. It is a sophisticated cinematic art which puts Chillingbourne and Canterbury on screen. As if to underline the sophistication by hinting at its opposite, Powell includes in the film a few amateurish frames from the home movie which Sergeant Roczinsky, Bob Johnson's friend, takes with his Kodak.

Powell once suggested in an interview that filmmakers of his generation needed to find purely visual means of expression, "create an old-new pattern of entertainment that does not lean on language,"[38] but in a curious way the one thing most clearly emphasized in the visual repertory of *A Canterbury Tale* is language itself. Instead of concentrating on a single grandiose castle or staircase, the film concentrates on an astonishing number of written texts. In Canterbury, for example, a long tracking shot gives Alison's view of blitzed businesses which she passes on her way to the garage. Stuck prominently on the rubble-strewn sites are placards telling customers where to find the temporary premises of the Sun Insurance Company, James Walker, Ltd., and so on. In effect, this is a tableau of British indefatigability, a message about defiance written directly on the bombed-out cityscape.

In Chillingbourne, texts tend to be on a smaller scale. During Alison's early encounter with Colpeper the camera gives glimpses of a gothic-lettered "Love and Honour the Truth" inscribed on a long wooden bar in the courtroom of the village hall—the bar of justice, in fact, behind which malefactors must stand to receive sentences from the magistrate. Later, when the land girl is chatting with the elderly barman of the "Hand in Glory," a second inscription appears, in Latin this time, scratched on a stone dug up on the Pilgrim's Way and now preserved in the inn as a curiosity. Originally, Pressburger had planned for Alison to examine in the inn a set of carvings of scenes from the *Canterbury Tales,* with titles and lettering interwoven on scrolls, but he must have been wary of obtruding too much Chaucer into the film and cut the examination. He similarly cut a moment in which Bob Johnson was to pass a bookshelf holding a complete set of "The Canterbury Poets" and the *Ingoldsby Legends,* the latter open to "The Hand of Glory."[39] Many more texts remained in the film as made. When Alison and the soldiers enter Colpeper's lecture room, they pass close by a medallion (identifying the "Colpeper Institute") with yet another printed motto, this time photographed in close-up, kept a long time on the screen, and read aloud by the characters, in other words forced on our attention: "Not heaven itself upon the past has power, / But what has been, has been, and I have had my hour," a Dryden rendering of Horace.[40] Each of these texts makes its modest contribution to the film's themes, or to its ironies: in his secret role as the Glueman, Colpeper scarcely loves and honors the truth. Taken as a group, however, as a little flourishing of words in the midst of an ostensibly non-verbal medium, they hint at *A Canterbury Tale*'s general engagement with things written, its literariness; they suggest just how little Powell and Pressburger could ever stop leaning on language.

Not just brief texts but books feature prominently in a late scene set in the study of Colpeper's handsome Georgian house. While engaged in conversation with the magistrate, Peter Gibbs happens to pick up *Climbing in the British Isles*—a confirmation of mountaineering interests already revealed in Colpeper's approving comment about the kind of man "who learns to walk step by step, so that one day he might climb Mt. Everest." Just before, Peter has casually perused a work pulled out of the bookcase, and the photograph of the island of Foula amidst its pages reveals that it is Michael Powell's own book, *200,000 Feet on Foula*,[41] about the making of his documentary *Edge of the World*. Peter's taking notice of these volumes is warrant for viewers to do the same with others. These the camera obligingly reveals to us in a slow pan across Colpeper's cluttered desktop. We see there an array that must have called on all of Alfred Junge's or some unnamed prop man's ingenuity to devise: a thin volume titled *Rough Stuff for Home Guards and Members of H. M. Forces*, another one labeled *Soil and Sense*, and for a third F. Fraser Darling's *Island Years*. All of these are perfectly real publications of the period,[42] and all of them belong plausibly to a man like Colpeper. The latter two books identify him as a gentleman farmer as definitively as an early shot in the film showing him scything grass. Darling's *Island Years* in particular expresses something essential about him. Together with its companion volume *Island Farm* (1944), this volume gives a comprehensive first-person account of the natural life, history, and geography of the Hebridean isles which the author's family explored and farmed. Fraser Darling was famous in his day for his advocacy of a non-materialistic way of life and the fostering of local traditions.

In the study scene, Peter notes a hunting rifle and fishing boots as well as books, so everything visible works together to create a coherent picture of Colpeper the landed gentleman, and all seems well with the film's exposition of his character—until we recall that other scenes and other props give us radically different versions of the man. Besides being a back-to-the-land visionary, Colpeper is an occasional and low-key terrorist; a philanthropist (he has arranged for the council to fund renewed excavations on the Pilgrim's Way); a misogynist who speaks approvingly of the ducking stool; a kindly paternal figure for Alison; a master of ceremonies; and a victim of events. The film can barely contain his variant identities, or clearly suggest how the audience should take him. As a sage to be admired? Yes, when his thoughtful face is shown in close-up and soundtrack music accompanies his exhortation to Peter Gibbs about climbing Mt. Everest. No, when we recognize just how shabbily egotistical is his method of increasing attendance at his lectures (about the glue Dilys Powell could manage only a tart "Well, really" in her review on BBC radio), or if we believe in the "dark sexual gratification" which more recent critics have diagnosed in the nighttime activities of this misogynist bachelor dwelling with his mother.[43] And this is to say nothing about the inherent ludicrousness of glue-throwing as Colpeper's chosen method of *attentat*. The glue was a compromise, Pressburger initially calling for the character to slash the dresses of his victims with a knife, but this was judged, presumably by Powell, "too sadistic," and like many compromises the glue plainly does not work. "A Continental idea that did not fit into an English film," the director commented, much later.[44]

The inconsistency in the magistrate-Glueman's handling does relatively little damage in a film otherwise so thematically and stylistically unified, but it does call for an explanation. Colpeper is overburdened with significance because he is less a character created by the free-ranging imagination than an assemblage of types drawn from different registers of the Archers' cultural memory, all of which, to use Powell's phrase, crowded in on them, "insisting to be used." As a suavely deceptive villain, he is developed from characters like Oliver Wiltsford, the impostor squire of Bramley End in *Went the Day Well?*, or from the Nazi U-Boat commander Hirth in the Archers' *49th Parallel*, a role also taken by Eric Portman. As a commanding presence in the plot, especially toward the end of the film when he stage-manages the bringing of good news to Alison and stands broodingly by in the cathedral, Colpeper represents a different archetype—the controlling, manipulating *magus*, always male, always something of a showman. This larger-than-life figure perhaps originates in Prospero from Shakespeare's *Tempest*, a work Powell had long dreamed of filming,[45] but has cinematic sources too. The Archers would have seen him in films like Harold Young's *The Scarlet Pimpernel* (1935), Leslie Howard's *Pimpernel Smith* (1941), or Carol Reed's *Night Train to Munich* (1940), and later they reproduced him repeatedly. The *magus* is not just Colpeper, but also Dr. Reeves in *A Matter of Life and Death*, the ballet impresario Boris Lermontov in *The Red Shoes* (1948), and Sir Percy Blakeney in the Archers' own version of the Pimpernel fable (*The Elusive Pimpernel*, 1950). Sometimes the magus must accept suffering or death as the price of his power. Lermontov renounces love, while Dr. Reeves perishes in a motorcycle crash, the surrogate for the RAF officer who should have died, and then acts as defense attorney in the officer's celestial trial. Colpeper, though alive and not even in danger of being turned over to the police at the end of *A Canterbury Tale,* suffers modestly in the here-and-now ("Far away, down the Nave, COLPEPER is standing. His penance is a lonely one"[46]) and will perhaps suffer more in the life to come. As he says to his accusers in the railway carriage: "If harm has been done, I shall have to pay for it . . . there are higher courts than the local bench of magistrates." Hearing these lines, and noting the onscreen solemnity with which they are accompanied (Colpeper looks meaningfully at the cathedral), we may feel we are not very far removed from that mood of exalted martyrdom which another drama about Canterbury, T. S. Eliot's verse play *Murder in the Cathedral,* had presented to audiences in the chapter house of the cathedral less than a decade before the film was released.

As for the quality of playfulness or trickiness in Colpeper, the frequent ironies of his speech and the near-anarchy of his pranks with the glue-pot, this seems to have literary rather than cinematic sources. It has been suggested, for example, that his exploits were inspired by the doings of the wildly eccentric characters in *The Club of Queer Trades,* by G. K. Chesterton, a writer apparently congenial to Pressburger as well as Powell. A more certain antecedent for Colpeper in this role—more certain because it accounts for the character's didacticism as well as his trickiness—is yet another creation of Powell's favorite author, Kipling.[47] In the series of stories collected in the volumes *Puck of Pook's Hill* (1906) and *Rewards and Fairies* (1910), the mischief-making Puck is conjured up by Dan and Una, two English children putting on their own outdoors performance of *A Midsummer Night's Dream.* Afterwards, in various settings of field or wood, the sprite teaches the children their heritage, summoning for them representative figures to act out dramatized historical vignettes, just as Colpeper attempts to teach Chillingbourne history in his lectures, substituting his magic lantern for Puck's magic.

Or perhaps the magic remains there after all. When Alison climbs to the top of Chillingbourne Hill, in the panorama scene already discussed (shot partly in the studio, partly on location), the camera closes in tightly on her entranced but also disbelieving features: she and the audience are hearing not far away the laughter and music of a medieval pilgrimage. Immediately thereafter Colpeper's voice breaks in on her reverie and the man himself starts up out of the long grass, his tie askew, his hair tousled in the wind. With their camera photographing blowing hair through blowing grass blades, Powell and Pressburger ingeniously connect the landed gentleman with the land. They transform him into a nature spirit, a 1944 Puck who like the 1906 version plays his best trick when he makes the past immediately present to a willing pupil. Again the lines from Kipling's "The Recall" seem pertinent: "Under their feet in the grasses My clinging magic runs."

Acting the double role of impresario and trickster, manager of complex events and disrupter of order, means in fact that Colpeper, as if he did not already have identities enough, has to shoulder yet one more: that of Michael Powell. That is, he exhibits qualities well marked in the director himself—qualities which the highly self-conscious Powell would have been well aware of. Powell commanded extensive resources and supervised the complex movements of dozens of workers so that Archers productions could be as well planned and efficiently executed as possible. But he was also a connoisseur of playfulness, someone for whom filmmaking in general, not just performing on miniature fiberglass bells, was a "lark." Powell rarely hesitated to bring the unexpected into his work: "To liven things up, I recruited a band of local boys . . . we had some fun with them."[48] No doubt Powell had equal fun when he put himself in his pictures—like Hitchcock, another directorial trickster, but more obliquely and interestingly. Powell's self-examination was prolonged, extending past the Colpeper surrogacy to the *camera obscura* sequences of *A Matter of Life and Death*—in which, as we have seen, Dr. Reeves surveys his town through a lens, very much like a film director—and culminating, notoriously, in *Peeping Tom*, in the complex and disturbing identifications which that film makes between Powell and Mark Lewis, the murderous voyeur-cameraman.

If in *A Canterbury Tale* the Glueman-magistrate is in some sense a version of the director, why would he be represented as a Tory traditionalist, indeed a despiser of the movies? To savor the irony of a character in a film attacking the very medium by which he exists, would be one answer. To differentiate "the movies" from *A Canterbury Tale,* would be another. In any case Powell is less intrigued by moral judgments about cinema-going than by validations of the power of his art, and it is just in this aspect that the figure of Colpeper can be of most use to him.

Consider the scene of Colpeper's lecture. Here the hall is darkened for slide-showing, and through the cigarette smoke a shaft of light is thrown from the magic lantern to form a brilliant circle on the screen. Against this Colpeper's head appears in silhouette. He responds to a question with the incantatory speech which has already been quoted in part:

> There are more ways than one of getting close to your ancestors. Follow the old road, and as you walk, think of them and of the old England. They climbed Chillingbourne Hill just as you did. They sweated and paused for breath just as you did today. And when you see the bluebells in the spring and the wild thyme and the broom and the heather, you're only seeing what their eyes saw. You ford the same rivers, the same birds are singing. When you lie flat on your back and rest and watch the clouds sailing, as I often do, you're so close to those other people that you can hear the thrumming of the hooves of their horses and the sound of the wheels on the road, and their laughter, and talk, and the musical instruments they carried. And when I turn the bend in the road, where they too saw the towers of Canterbury, I feel I've only to turn my head to see them on the road behind me.

At "the wild thyme and the broom" a restless musical theme begins on the soundtrack, an audible rendering of the lecturer's growing excitement. This theme is firmly associated with Colpeper; all of the major characters have their musical themes, in fact. Powell cuts away from Colpeper to Alison, who with her private memories of the Pilgrim's Way is the most susceptible of the listeners. Key lighting gives her a mask of light—the same mask which we saw when she talked about her fiancé Geoffrey for the first time, in a casual conversation at the "Hand of Glory." There the mask was naturalistic, an effect of light and shadows cast by the grillwork over the bar, but here it is contrived, a magical bit of theatrics, as it will be also when it appears a third time as Alison looks over her caravan in Canterbury. With such repetitions Erwin Hillier gives the film a purely photographic unity that parallels and complements its unity of theme. Practically, his using the mask in the lecture scene allows us to see the rapt expression in Alison's eyes. Colpeper's line, "when you lie flat on your back and rest," seems to hypnotize her, and she settles more comfortably into her seat. Powell then cuts back and forth, always in rhythm with the spoken lines, first showing Colpeper's face, which is now given exactly the same lighting as Alison's as he is drawn further into his own memories, then returning to the girl. The camera closes in until her face fills the screen. At "when I turn the bend" she shuts her eyes, and just as the music reaches its cadence and the narrative concludes, the light on her face goes out. Colpeper has worked his magic on her, and the magic will have lingering power to bring the pilgrims to her hearing when later she walks up Chillingbourne Hill. Here in the lecture hall, once Colpeper stops talking, the mood is dissipated in casual talk. One soldier, asked how he likes the lecture, comments "it makes a nice change," and even Alison can manage only a noncommittal "Mn" when the same question is put to her.

At the end of the sequence Peter facetiously says, "hey, Bob, *movies,*" but by this point we scarcely need the hint. What has just been shown is nothing less than a little allegory of the cinema, in which lecturer corresponds to director, darkened lecture hall to theatre, magic lantern to projector, the mesmerized Alison to the real audience of *A Canterbury Tale,* held in its seats—so the Archers would wish—by the power of moving images and of language recorded on a soundtrack. Every technique in the sequence, from the soundtrack music to the melodramatic lighting, the assertive camera work to the editing, draws attention to itself and thus declares that a filmmaker works his kind of magic too, that the spell which a place in the road casts on Colpeper and which Colpeper's narrative casts on Alison has in fact been cast on us by Michael Powell. "Those who know the effect of the cinema . . . will realize to what lengths it is possible to carry the principle that seeing even the most improbable events is believing."[49] None other than the snobbish Esmé Wingfield-Stratford was willing to concede this much to film, in *The History of British Civilization,* and Powell's accomplishment here is precisely to demonstrate the truth of the claim. In the lecture scene the persuasiveness of cinema is put on triumphant show and the past is re-created—temporarily, it may be—but re-created. The antiquarian Colpeper's England (and by extension Puck's England, and Chaucer's) turns out to be the film director Powell's England. There could be no clearer demonstration of the Archers' aims for the film than this ingenious merging of traditionalism and contemporaneity.

SCREEN PROCESSIONS AND VILLAGE PAGEANTS

Before viewers of *A Canterbury Tale* behold Chillingbourne, they are treated to a prologue so distinct from the film proper that it might be considered the cinematic equivalent of an epigraph—a quotation from some classic work affixed to a Victorian novel, or to the opening of a story by Kipling, who was very fond of the device. The Archers "quote" Chaucer, and the four imaginative minutes in which they do so suggest with particular clarity their film's motives and affiliations. To begin with, the quoting is literal: the screen opens on a manuscript page, the General Prologue to the *Canterbury Tales*. At the same moment the soundtrack supplies the ethereal music which will shortly be associated with miraculous blessings. After this comes a voiceover reading of Chaucer's verse, lightly modernized. England appears in the form of a map. This is not, as has been claimed, "the aerial perspective of fear in the 1940s: prone, vulnerable England . . . studied from the viewpoint of the bombardier,"[50] but a patently medieval map with quaint lettering and picturesque illuminations—a graphic *avoidance* of the war and all its anxieties.

Tracing the pilgrims' route on this map, the camera zooms in on Salisbury (where Bob Johnson will start his own pilgrimage with the seeing of a movie), then tracks eastward, not omitting a prominently labeled Chilham just outside Canterbury. Dissolve to a horseback procession of pilgrims in medieval costume, among them a clearly identifiable Wife of Bath merrily disporting with her companions. Meanwhile, the music has changed to the "pilgrimage" theme which Alison will hear on Chillingbourne Hill. Cut, with yet another change in music, to a bird flying across the sky and to a hunter launching his falcon at the prey. The camera follows the falcon until, in an ingenious graphic match across a nearly imperceptible cut, it is instantly transformed into a looping and diving Spitfire: the Archers' acknowledgment that the war and its anxieties are not going to be completely avoided. The falcon-becomes-Spitfire conceit was not the Archers' invention, having been employed

as early as 1940 in an A. P. Herbert newspaper poem extolling the young
pilots of the RAF, who may seem not what their fathers were, yet "like
falcons live and die,"

> And while we heave a single sigh
> They shoot a brace of bombers down.[51]

Yet the conceit is so brilliantly visualized by the Archers as to become
the most powerful single effect of the film, as well as the most influen-
tial, if the several critics are right who have suggested that it led in due
course to the metamorphosis of revolving bone into space station in
Stanley Kubrick's *2001*.

When in *A Canterbury Tale* we return to the falconer, he has become
a contemporary English soldier with tin hat and vigilant expression;
other soldiers and tanks appear on the landscape. In an accompaniment
to these modernizations, the same narrator who intoned Chaucer for us
now speaks Pressburger's own General Prologue:

> Six hundred years have passed.
> What would they see, Dan Chaucer and his goodly company today?
> The hills and valleys are the same;
> Gone are the forests since the enclosures came. . . .
> The Pilgrim's Way still winds above the Weald
> Through wood and brake and many a fertile field.
> But though so little's changed since Chaucer's day
> Another kind of pilgrim walks the way. . . .
> Gone are the ring of hooves, the creak of wheel;
> Down in the valley runs our road of steel.

In short order a train appears ("our road of steel"), the screen darkens,
and the plot proper gets under way.

What exactly does this prologue accomplish? It anthologizes Chaucer, so to speak, presenting (in the manner of *The Shelter Book* or *For
Ever England*) a famous heritage text to English viewers. It also re-
hearses images and themes to be elaborated later in the film. The page
of Chaucer's poetry is the first of the written texts which the Archers'
camera will render in close-up. The prospect offered to the medieval
travelers in Pressburger's verse ("What would they see . . . ?") is a survey
of the realm, an imagined version of the panoramic view which will be
awarded to characters atop Chillingbourne Hill. Time is also surveyed.

As the lines move from detail to detail, they succinctly establish the remoteness of the past, then convey us to the twentieth century of the main narrative. In visual corroboration of our arrival there, an aggressively clanking Army vehicle appears onscreen at "Another kind of pilgrim walks the way." But the preceding verses have even more emphatically declared ("the same," "still," "so little's changed") that the past, far from being superseded by modernity, is somehow persistent and accessible, while the camera gives shot after shot of the abiding landscape. Thus the Archers introduce the idea of continuity later to be associated with Colpeper. The poetry is of a sort Colpeper might have written himself, on a quiet Fire Guard night with no glue-throwing in prospect. Even verse form contributes to the theme: the meter and rhyme of the spoken lines makes them *audibly* continuous with Chaucer's.

The opening sequences of the Archers' films did not generally appear in the screenplays, but were improvised by Pressburger while Powell filmed the main story,[52] a method of working which perhaps explains why the prologue anticipates so much of *A Canterbury Tale*; the prologue would be a kind of précis of what was developing in the daily rushes. But the need to have a prologue in the first place has to be accounted for by something else. This is the Archers' patriotic yearning for history, a set wish to portray their country in the longest possible perspective. In the prologue of their film Powell and Pressburger most openly emulate the history books of the wartime period, the dramatized vignettes of *Puck of Pook's Hill* (when we watch the pilgrims on their way to Canterbury, we are in effect taking the role of Dan and Una in Kipling's tales), and the historical gestures of other filmmakers of the 1940s, who felt comparable attractions to the past. *The Way to the Stars,* for example, opens with a prologue like the Archers', but on a smaller scale. In June, 1945, when Asquith's air force film was released, the great allied bombing raids over Germany had ceased, and with admirable honesty the camera first shows the scene as a derelict, deserted airbase. The film then begins a flashback with "1940" inscribed over a shot of a stone tablet, which in turn declares that the base ("the Half-Penny Field") was recorded in Domesday Book. In other words the film goes far back in history, much further back than is necessary for its immediate purposes. Here and in *A Canterbury Tale* it is as though the accelerated pace of wartime happenings ("too much urgency," the old organist in Canterbury Cathedral mutters disapprovingly at Peter Gibbs) has produced, by reaction, a will to slow things down and get back to origins.

The prologue to *A Canterbury Tale* begins in the past, then flashes forward, and because it was created by the imaginatively self-indulgent Archers takes up much more screen time, looms much larger, than the opening sequences of other films, particularly in its elaborate depiction of Chaucerian figures riding along the Pilgrim's Way. Meticulously arranged and photographed, like everything else in the film, this procession is apparently offered to us as a "fact," and yet there is something inescapably stagey about it. The pilgrims' hilarity seems forced and overacted, their costumes more point-device than can be believed, the music on the soundtrack too insistently medieval; peasants stand about watching the pilgrims like spectators at a play. Or rather, as the reviewer Richard Winnington suggested perceptively in his notice of the film, at a village pageant.[53] The procession resembles nothing so much as an episode from this familiar and much beloved form of amateur drama, with its costumed vignettes of local history, its elaborate choreography and musical accompaniments, its acting on a scale to reach the back rows of a large unsophisticated audience. As a part of the national culture which the Archers inherited, and indeed which they set out particularly to celebrate in this picture, the village pageant plays a part even in the later, non-stagey sequences of *A Canterbury Tale*. For all its apparent fustiness, its closeness to the magic-lantern-illuminated methods of an antiquarian like Colpeper, the village pageant turns out to be surprisingly adaptable and surprisingly cinematic. Understanding the ways in which this is so will, however, require an excursus into theatrical history.

Twentieth-century novels and films such as *A Canterbury Tale* take village pageants for granted. They are simply there in the plots, needing no explanation and having no origin, an apparent fixture of rural culture. In fact, though, they had a quite specific origin in the ingenuity of Louis Napoleon Parker. This colorful late nineteenth-century figure was the child of expatriate Americans who led a nomadic life all through Europe, like characters out of Henry James. He eventually took musical training in London and settled, this time like one of Kipling's homecoming travelers, into life as a music master at Sherborne School. In midlife he became a successful playwright and theatrical producer, and in 1905 devised the Sherborne Pageant, a folk play for a few hundred local performers, on local themes, with music and dancing, given outdoors in Sherborne for an audience of all those in the local populace not in the cast themselves. Having made this "town pageant" a huge success, Parker went on to similar productions in Warwick, Bury St. Edmunds, Dover, Colchester, and York. In his autobiography of 1928 Parker summed up the principles of his invention:

> A Pageant is a Festival of Thanksgiving, in which a great city or a little hamlet celebrates its glorious past, its prosperous present, and its hopes and aspirations for the future. It is a Commemoration of Local Worthies. It is also a great Festival of Brotherhood; in which all distinctions of whatever kind are sunk in a common effort. . . . It calls together all the scattered kindred from all parts of the world. It reminds the old of the history of their home, and shows the young what treasures are in their keeping. It is the great incentive to the right kind of patriotism: love of hearth; love of town; love of county; love of England. . . . A Pageant is the History of a Town from its remotest origins down to a date not too near the present; expressed in dramatic form; that is to say, in spoken dialogue: in action: in song and in dance . . . It includes every form of drama: tragedy, comedy, even farce. It is based on authentic history, but it welcomes folk-lore and picturesque tradition.

More specific rules of dramaturgy follow, for example that a pageant performance is continuous, without interval, and that its impressiveness largely depends on the place in which it is performed (the more imposing and authentic the site, the better). A pageant audience should expect a beginning procession with music, including a Narrative Chorus, "commenting on what is past and foretelling what is to come," and thereafter a succession of familiar episodes:

> King Arthur, surrounded by his knights, hurls defiance at Rome . . . Danes and Saxons swarm over the land with ruin and slaughter . . . stout Abbot Samson rules with a strong hand . . . Sometimes the arena is crowded with thousands, battling, rioting, or feasting and rejoicing; and sometimes the vast space is a green background for two performers; as when Sir Walter Raleigh is discovered smoking, and is drenched by his panic-stricken servant . . . Queen Elizabeth, who seems to have pervaded every inch of England, drifts down the Avon in her gorgeous barge and kisses

a bright-faced boy whose name is Will Shakespeare . . . the "Invicta," a great battleship, is built and manned and launched before our eyes at Dover . . . and—and—and—

When the last episode has been acted, Parker concludes,

the Narrative Chorus joins forces with the Dramatic Chorus and together they thunder the Triumph Song: a poem in praise of the town whose history has been displayed. And while this is being sung, the performers of each episode, horse and foot, issue from every point of the compass and form a gigantic circle with all their banners and trophies and insignia; and when they are in place to them enters a shining and glittering procession . . . the entire body of performers, together with the audience, sing the first verse of the Old Hundredth and lastly the whole of the National Anthem, accompanied by all the bells of all the churches in the town . . .[54]

By the time Parker went on to the next stage of his variegated career, which suitably enough was filmmaking (in 1911 he produced *Henry VIII*, "the first British film adaptation of an important stage production" and "the first really important British film"[55]), his ideas had been widely copied. Edith Craig, for example, the daughter of the great actress Ellen Terry, produced pageants on suffragette themes, including *A Pageant of Great Women* in 1909, wherein Woman, longing to be free, pleads with Justice for social and political liberty, while Prejudice in the form of a man argues against her and against the famous heroines—Rosa Bonheur, Florence Nightingale—whom Woman calls to testify. Craig put pageants on in the Albert Hall and ultimately, like other producers, adjusted them to a scale suitable for villages, where they soon became a favored fund-raising device. (Parker himself had shown the way here, scripting a village pageant called "St. Benet's Abbey" for Potter Heigham in Norfolk and earning £300 for the church restoration fund.)[56] Craig's last production, in July 1946, a pageant based on classics of literature beginning with Julius Caesar and ending with a garden party for Jane Austen, actually took place in Chilham, Powell's home village and the source for his Chillingbourne.[57]

In 1934 no less prominent a literary figure than E. M. Forster wrote the narrative speeches and program notes for a pageant held in his home village of Abinger, also in aid of the local church. The production (music by Ralph Vaughan Williams, patronage by the local squire Lord Farrer) was orthodox in depicting "ancient Britons in skins gathering fuel in the Abinger woods; a cry of 'Romans, the Romans!'; arrival of the Saxons and of the Normans; the news of the Spanish Armada brought to Abinger," but unorthodox in stressing the role of trees, of woodland, in Abinger history. The *Times* thought the pageant worth a long approving review, probably because Forster had a hand in it, and noted among other things the appearance of Canterbury pilgrims singing a Latin hymn. At its conclusion the review quotes a question from the script which perfectly captures Forster's (and Emeric Pressburger's) dread of 1930s materialism: "Houses and bungalows, hotels, restaurants and flats, arterial roads, by-passes, petrol pumps and pylons—are these going to be England?"[58]

Pageants could also be adapted for the even smaller scale of school plays. In her 1941 book *The Oaken Heart,* a study of a Home Counties village adjusting to war, the detective story writer Margery Allingham recalls her daughter's appearing on a school stage "dressed up as a cross between Britannia and the Fairy Queen" and reciting Kipling's "Big Steamers,"[59] Kipling often being poet of choice for these patriotic occasions. Alternatively, the pageant could be expanded to fit a London venue—Olympia, for example, where the narrator of one of the late volumes of Anthony Powell's *A Dance to the Music of Time* remembers being taken before the war:

> Here, how often as a child had one watched the Royal Tournament, horse and rider deftly clearing the posts-and-rails, sweating ratings dragging screw-guns over dummy fortifications, marines and airmen executing inconceivably elaborate configurations of drill. Here, in the tan, these shows had ended in a grand finale of historical conflict, Ancient Britons and Romans, Saxons and Normans, the Spanish Armada, Malplaquet, Minden, Waterloo, the Light Brigade.

Nick Jenkins concludes his reverie with a wry reintroduction to the demobbing process of 1945, also held at Olympia:

> Now all memory of such stirring moments had been swept away. Rank on rank, as far as the eye could scan, hung flannel trousers and tweed coats, drab macintoshes and grey suits with a white line running through the material. If this were not a shop, what was it? Perhaps the last scene of the play in which one had been performing, set in an outfitter's, where you "acted" buying the clothes, put them on, left the theatre to give up the Stage and find something else to do.[60]

To be nostalgically recalled or gently mocked in this way was the usual fate of pageants in serious fiction, though Virginia Woolf's *Between the Acts,* her posthumous novel of 1941, obviously does more with and to the form. It thoroughly explodes and reinvents it. Admittedly, the village pageant performed in the grounds of Woolf's Pointz Hall looks deeply conventional at first. The formidable producer is Miss La Trobe, a fictionalized version of Edith Craig, whom Woolf had met through Vita Sackville-West.[61] As Miss La Trobe hovers fretfully at the back, a small girl comes out to say "England am I," a gramophone plays appropriate tunes, and one by one the vignettes unfold familiar history. Primitive British tribes dig themselves into the hilltop; armed warriors appear to the accompaniment of a braying and blaring popular melody; Canterbury pilgrims come on the scene:

> All the time the villagers were passing in and out between the trees. They were singing; but only a word or two was audible "... *wore ruts in the grass* ... *built the house in the lane* ..." The wind blew away the connecting words of their chant, and then, as they reached the tree at the end they sang:
>
> "*To the shrine of the Saint* ... *to the tomb* ... *lovers* ... *believers* ... *we come* ...*"*

Queen Elizabeth follows, then Albert the village idiot impersonating himself, as abruptly and meaninglessly as the figure in *A Canterbury Tale.* There is a play within the play, succeeded by an interval for tea (a violation of Parker's rules) as the music chants "Dispersed are we ..." When the pageant begins again, it has reached the Restoration ("reason holds sway") and a pastiche comedy is played. Cows in the fields suddenly start bellowing and become part of the action, exactly as happened in real life at Abinger ("animals were prominent entertainers also," reported the *Times*). More intervals succeed, a scene of Victorian London, another play within the play, until eventually the pageant reaches its climax. Perhaps it is to be a "Grand Finale," a lady in the audience speculates: "Army; Navy; Union Jack; and behind them ... the Church." Louis Napoleon Parker would have done it this way, satisfying the audience's longing for reassurance and continuity, but not the more ambitious and disquieting Miss La Trobe (and behind her, of course, Virginia Woolf). Miss La Trobe's scheme emphasizes discontinuity. At the finale, her actors, abandoning history, and with it any sense of progress, simply hold mirrors up to the audience. The present is "Ourselves," "not whole by any means" but individualistic and chaotic, caught in "orts, scraps and fragments," as a hectoring voice announces through a megaphone. A clergyman gives thanks afterwards and tries to rescue the occasion for conventional understandings ("We act different parts; but are the same") while the audience sings "God Save the King" in the best orthodox style; but the gramophone keeps on playing "Dispersed are we." Overhead, warplanes in formation, not dispersed at all, fly off to what we know will be the Second World War.[62]

By the outbreak of that war filmmakers had long succeeded in getting the pageant off the local stage and away from amateur actors, adapting its historical playlets for the screen. The American picture *Cavalcade* (1933), directed by the expatriate Briton Frank Lloyd, dramatizes a succession of private and public episodes from the Boer War to 1933,[63] while the Archers' *The Life and Death of Colonel Blimp* is in effect an expensively mounted national pageant concentrating on military history and reusing actors in the key roles—Deborah Kerr is like the village beauty who gets to appear in more than one historical vignette of the play. But the film most indebted to the pageant form, and most historically comprehensive, is one already touched on briefly, David MacDonald's *This England*. This picture, exactly contemporaneous with *Between the Acts,* is the diametric opposite of the novel, both in its conservative ideology and in its heartfelt acceptance of the style of Parker's shows.

The first shot of *This England* fills the screen with an image of the country. This is no map with illuminations or lettering, as in *A Canterbury Tale,* but simply the island itself, surveyed as a whole under a scrolling set of verses echoing the patriotic evocations of a Vera Brittain or an H. V. Morton:

> This earth of England is an old, old earth!
> Her autumn mists, her bramble-berry flames,
> Her tangled, rain-soaked grass were still the same
> Time out of mind before the Romans came . . .
> Though from the skies men hurl their slaughter down
> Still there will be bracken though brown.

The portrayal undeniably makes England seem vulnerable to aerial attack. As if in fulfillment of a prophecy, the local setting to which the film introduces us—Rookeby's Farm and the village of Claverley, with Beacon Hill looming above—suffers an immediate air raid, but the villagers show a visiting American journalist the stout fighting spirit of England when they move cheerfully from pub to shelter and then laugh off the damage the raid has caused. To these locals, war in defense of their village is nothing new, and nine minutes into the narrative, we are whisked off by a flashback to the first pageant-style vignette, a struggle between tyrannical Norman overlord and rebellious Saxon peasants in the year 1086. In the actors of this highly familiar period drama, *Ivanhoe* compressed into a quarter-hour of screen time, we recognize modern Claverley inhabitants already presented in the pub scene; the vicar, for example, has been metamorphosed into a gentle priest trying to talk some sense into his Norman master. Alternating melodrama with farce just as Parker had prescribed, calling "together all the scattered kindred from all parts of the world" (the visiting American turns out to be the daughter of a Claverley woman; like Bob Johnson, she is coming home), *This England* adds three more historical episodes to its program: in 1588, the Armada approaches; at the turn of the nineteenth century, Napoleon threatens; in 1918, Claverley celebrates the Armistice. It would be otiose to summarize these episodes since they tell essentially the same story of courage in adversity, the need for sacrifice ("we're in the middle of a war," says the Elizabethan Farmer Rookeby, felling his oaks to provide timber for sailing ships), and above all fidelity to the land. Again and again the stubborn peasant Appleyard (played by Emlyn Williams, who also wrote the script) reminds his betters that Claverley is what matters, not their own happiness. He is willing thrall to "the long, strong pull on its sons of a plot of English soil, the stubborn tradition of an earth that changes full cycle in a year, and no more in a dozen centuries," as Caroline Lejeune put it in a not very admiring review of *This England*.[64] It must be said that the plot of English soil is more an idea than a visual subject of the film, which lacks both *A Canterbury Tale*'s interest in showing people actually at work on the land and the Archers' success in capturing the beauty of landscape; *This England* is mostly interiors. Continuity from era to era is the MacDonald film's somewhat abstract theme, continuity from form to form—village pageant to modern film—its simple *modus operandi*.

For much of the time *This England* is less determinedly propagandistic, less a whitewash, than might be expected in a film of 1941. It admits village ignorance and superstition to its narrative, along with gambling and drunkenness (in the gentry), abject poverty (in the peasants), and even a measure of general disillusion at the Armistice. Yet the conclusion unhesitatingly lifts viewers up over poverty and disillusion and class antagonism ("distinctions of whatever kind are sunk in a common effort," Parker had said of pageants) into patriotism, into shots of fogs and clouds and landscape. Meanwhile, the 1914 version of Farmer Rookeby solemnly begins to intone the only possible text for the occasion, John of Gaunt's "This royal throne of kings" speech from *Richard II*, the source of the film's title and its equivalent of a final Triumph Song. The 1944 Rookeby finishes the speech, looking soulfully out of a window with Appleyard and the journalist toward Beacon Hill. Possibly it was this conclusion which Orwell thought good for national morale in the early days of the war, however much he disapproved of *This England*'s unbelievably agricultural reading of national history.

The only English film actually to depict a village pageant being performed, Anthony Asquith's *The Demi-Paradise,* was released two years later, in 1943, by which time questions of morale seemed less pressing and filmmakers were thinking more about alliances than a narrowly English patriotism. Significantly, Asquith's title, taken though it is from the same *Richard II* speech as *This England,* strikes a mildly ironic note, and the village pageant in the film is regarded, at least initially, as an antiquated relic. The plot centers on Ivan Kuznetsov (played by Laurence Olivier immediately before he essayed Henry V), a Soviet naval engineer sent to help with a ship being built in an English yard. A good Stakhanovite, Ivan would like to be working full time but is reluctantly pressed into watching the local pageant along with his equally unenthusiastic host ("I'm not happy." "None of us are, my dear fellow— this is a pageant"). One by one the standard episodes are trotted out, and by the time the Roman occupation of Britain has given way to Chastity welcoming Apollo in a masque for the Queen and then the breathlessly awaited news of Waterloo ("Who won?" "We did!"), Ivan declares it all laughable, testimony to the English preoccupation with the past. It is impossible not to agree with him, given the low comedy with which Asquith has surrounded proceedings, such as the heraldic trumpeter with his instrument wrong way round, the muffed lines, the grotesquely overplayed pageant director of Margaret Rutherford. Risible, silly, her production recalls the element of patronization often built into the depiction of pageants in more sophisticated works of art—the sense of superior people watching inferiors play at being important—which is perceptible as far back as the much-laughed-at Pageant of the Nine Worthies in Shakespeare's *Love's Labor's Lost* and still present in Woolf's amusement at the play-acting of history in the pageant at Pointz Hall.

Later in *The Demi-Paradise,* however, things change. At the point in the plot when Britain and the Soviet Union have become official allies, the pageant is rescued for wartime purposes by becoming internationalized. A new final tableau unveils Victory with her sword as contingents of flag-bearing Poles, Norwegians, Belgians, and Free French march past on parade. To the accompaniment of the "Song of the Volga Boatmen" (the local band cannot manage the "Internationale"), Ivan is brought on to the outdoor stage to receive the pageant proceeds, a thousand pounds destined for the relief of his home town of Nizhny Novgorod. Even this is not quite enough for Asquith or his screenwriter Anatole de Grunwald, who further modernize the pageant by industrializing it. They devise a completely non-comic tableau in the ship-launching sequence at the very end of the film. Here, with the Union Jack and the Red Flag unfurled side by side, the party of main characters on the platform above and the shipyard workers below, patriotic speeches demand applause "for the brave Russian people" or proclaim "today, we are allies, friends." The yard owner's daughter christens the new vessel "Druzhba"—"Friendship"—as the workers sing "For he's a jolly good fellow" while gazing up in rapturous solidarity.

Scenes almost exactly like this were enacted on real stages often enough in 1942 and 1943 to make Asquith seem more a theatrical documentarian than the director of a fictional film. These were the years when the village pageant became fully up-to-date and aggrandized, when in the Albert Hall or similar sites its broad dramatic gestures were put to political use. "The Pageant of the Four Freedoms," for example, was staged at Oxford in the summer of 1942, with production help from Pressburger and with a reenacted scene from the Archers' *The 49th Parallel* on the program. Later, at New Year's in both 1942 and 1943, "Pageants of Empire" took place before high-ranking representatives of all the allied nations. Here, the Imperial flags on parade and the contingents marching past—first Chelsea pensioners, then veterans of the First

World War, then representatives of twenty-nine fighting nations—were a variant of the unrolling historical episodes of old-fashioned pageants, a procession in space and ceremony rather than in time and playacting. In the 1943 Pageant the "mightiest cheers . . . were given for the three naval officers from the Soviet Union who bore the flag which has been defended so valiantly at Leningrad, Moscow, Voronezh, and Stalingrad," as the *Times* reported[65]—a link to the final scene of *The Demi-Paradise*, but also a reminder of the overwhelming importance of Anglo-Soviet friendship at this period. Whole pageants were devoted to this cause alone, and perhaps because these drew on the techniques of agitprop theater or the well-established tradition of leftist pageants in the 1930s,[66] they tended to be particularly spectacular. In June 1942, "An Agreement of the Peoples" (script by Montagu Slater) emphasized the union between the ordinary people of Britain and the USSR by including demonstrations of the work of industrial laborers and fire fighters. Even more elaborate was "Salute to the Red Army" of February 1943 (script by Louis MacNeice), a combination of marching military detachments, flags, choral singing, and a stylized enactment of highlights of Russian history, from the heroism of Alexander Nevsky (Laurence Olivier) to the voice of Moscow Radio (John Gielgud), with everything designed to symbolize "the resistance of a people and its army to"—here a touch which would have pleased E. M. Forster or the Archers—"a destructive materialism." The set for "Salute to the Red Army" conjured up a Russian city in a great curve behind the tiered seats at one end of the Albert Hall, with pulpits on high for the Spokesman and Spokeswoman, and with a space below for "the Nazi" to gesticulate and crouch "in his own shadow."[67] Photographs and descriptions suggest that in its general stylization, and in the combination of an amphitheater for the populace and set-apart elevated spaces for the main actors, this set must have strongly influenced the one Alfred Junge designed for the celestial trial scenes of the Archers' *A Matter of Life and Death*.

The producer of "Salute to the Red Army" was the well-known theatrical manager Basil Dean, who in the previous year had begun his wartime producing work by putting on "Cathedral Steps" at the west entrance to St. Paul's Cathedral. "Cathedral Steps" was national rather than international in scope, cultural rather than military in emphasis, and in several ways the culmination of the tradition, the most interesting and original of all the wartime pageants. It was certainly the most imposingly produced, with massed choirs, the bands of the Brigade of Guards performing music by eight different English composers, and a volunteer cast of such prominent stage and screen actors as Lewis Casson, Edith Evans, Sybil Thorndike, and Leslie Howard in his last public appearance (as Lord Nelson). Dignitaries including the Lord Mayor were in the audience, as were radio listeners in America, thanks to a simultaneous broadcast by the BBC. A few days after the first performance on September 25, 1942, the entire show was repeated in front of the ruined cathedral in Coventry.

"Cathedral Steps" in effect invited an audience to make a pilgrimage to the most important shrine in their city, and treated them, once there, to an exposition of English values, a demonstration of "our glorious heritage of freedom." In the familiar pageant manner, Dean's production staged episodes of history—"We have a story to tell you. It took two thousand years to write, but we will tell it to you in a lunch hour"— though the history took the unusual form of an anthology of readings compiled by Clemence Dane, editor of *The Shelter Book*. Boadicea's struggle against the Romans was conveyed in lines from Tennyson, for instance, with added comments or questions from allegorical figures named Patience, wearing royal blue, and Valour, wearing scarlet. Also present were Any Man and Any Woman, representatives of ordinary Englishness like the "Mr. A" and Mrs. A" of Auden's pre-war play *The Ascent of F6;* they sat modestly in the middle of the playing space and wore ordinary 1940s clothing. After Boadicea, "Cathedral Steps" carried on with twelve more episodes, including Agincourt, Country Peace, the Napoleonic struggle, and the 1914 War (Any Man put on a service cap and began taking a more active role), always to the accompaniment of recited verse. "Spenser, Hardy, Rupert Brooke, and Julian Grenfell touched hands as they moved toward their separate destinies," as the *Times* commented. The cathedral setting was of great importance throughout, as the *Times* also said, predicting that the pageant would "restore an ancient link to the many that already keep the cathedrals in touch with the general life."[68] The finale of the pageant was a singing of "Jerusalem" by all assembled. Louis Napoleon Parker would have been proud.

In "Cathedral Steps" the role of Valour was taken by Eric Portman. Anyone who saw both the pageant and *A Canterbury Tale* less than two years later would have interpreted Colpeper as a reprise of or development from Portman's pageant part. After all, as Alan Bennett once observed, film actors inevitably come "trailing remnants of their former roles, memories of . . . the inclinations of the characters they usually played."[69] Valour and Colpeper are both commanding figures in the war against materialism, both gatekeepers to the cathedral and its cultural blessings. But it is not just a coincidence of personnel or setting which links *A Canterbury Tale* to "Cathedral Steps"—and behind "Cathedral Steps" to a whole long twentieth-century tradition of pageantry. *A Canterbury Tale* is nothing less than a village performance put on celluloid and given national ambitions, a celebration of locality which calls the scattered kindred (Sergeant Bob Johnson) home from afar and shows all in the audience what treasures are in their keeping. It shares "the right kind of patriotism" with Parker's "love of hearth; love of town; love of county; love of England," and preaches that patriotism with a dramaturgy sometimes taken straight from pageantry, mixing music and choral performance with spoken dialogue, high solemnity with the farce of Colpeper's glue-throwing. At the start, the voiceover mimicking Chaucer's verse substitutes for the Narrative Chorus ("commenting on what is past and foretelling what is to come"). At the end, the parade of troops into Canterbury Cathedral serves as a grand recessional, "Onward Christian Soldiers" as the film's Triumph Song. Even the Archers' valedictory bell-ringing has an antecedent in Parker's ideas for a finale.

Still, if *A Canterbury Tale* is a pageant, it is an odd one, since after the prologue it disdains period costuming and omits the standard succession of vignettes. What are we to make of a film in which modern-day characters seem generally to escape from history and in which the mode of presentation is realistic rather than emblematic? In which, as a 1944 article in *Picture Post* observed, the poetry is taken out of Chaucer and what remains is dressed "in a lounge suit and a summer frock"?[70] In which the camera shows an ordinary empty hillside, even if the soundtrack, momentarily under the sway of Colpeper's magic, plays pilgrimage music? "The History of a Town from its remotest origins down to a date not too near the present," Parker had stipulated in his definition, as if he thought pageants could be damaged by too much contemporaneity; can Powell and Pressburger's work really belong to the genre if it gets all the way to the summer of 1944 and stays there for the duration?

Such questions lead, as questions about apparent inconsistencies in the Archers' films often do, to a recognition of the audacity that is their most valuable contribution to the English cinema. In *A Canterbury Tale* Powell and Pressburger appropriate the pageant to their purposes—far more originally than they had done in *The Life and Death of Colonel Blimp*—by reducing it to a single "vignette" and making that vignette depict *both* present and past. Their way of seeing is simultaneous, not sequential. In Chillingbourne, Alison is genuinely a pilgrim on her way to a shrine, and thus a figure out of the distant past, but a pilgrim entirely without medieval trappings—unlike, say, the figure in "The Land Girl," a 1944 poem in *Punch*:

> A gentil girl ther was with us al-so
> That from hir wonyng hadde longe y-go
> To swinken on a ferme, soth to seyn . . .[71]

There is none of this pseudo-Chaucerian mummery about Alison, and nothing of the pastiche. She does not act a part, as the characters of *This England* do as they proceed in their artificial and relentless way from episode to episode, but embodies it in her normal twentieth-century actions, checking on a caravan stored in a garage, letting sunlight into the caravan's dusty interior. In other words, this pilgrim never ceases to be a contemporary Englishwoman, any more than her fellow travelers Bob Johnson and Peter Gibbs cease to be contemporary sergeants, even when a sudden glare of light in the railway carriage puts a brief magical halo around the latter's head. Keeping entirely to the mise-en-scène of the present day, the Archers yet find an old pattern there, the pattern of seeking and finding a blessing. Gibbs is innocent of his light-induced sanctification ("I'll believe that when I see a halo around my head," he comments skeptically, having his back turned to the halo), but by the end of the film he and the other characters are granted some partial awareness of the whole process which has brought them to the blessing, so that they become spectators of the pageant in which they have acted. They and the audience in the cinema arrive together at what was always the main goal of historical pageantry, an understanding of the *meaning* of the past in its relation to the present.

To make these claims about Powell and Pressburger is to put them in a select literary company—with Virginia Woolf in *Between the Acts,* for instance, who brought the past directly into contact with the present and who via her trick with mirrors blurred the distinction between performers and audience; or with James Joyce, who fashioned a Ulyssean pageant out of the ordinary life of 1904 Dublin; or with T. S. Eliot, who in the last section of the *Four Quartets,* published two years before *A Canterbury Tale,* contemplated at length historical continuities of his own. This section, "Little Gidding," does not merely share a conservative ideology with the Archers, Nicholas Farrer's Anglican retreat being substituted for Canterbury Cathedral,

> A people without history
> Is not redeemed from time, for history is a pattern
> Of timeless moments. So, while the light fails
> On a winter's afternoon, in a secluded chapel
> History is now and England,

it also imagines the same metamorphosis as the film, a bird transformed into a warplane,

> The dove descending breaks the air
> With flame of incandescent terror,

and above all it sounds the Archers' pilgrimage themes in verse:

> If you came this way,
> Taking the route you would be likely to take
> From the place you would be likely to come from . . .
> If you came by day not knowing what you came for,
> It would be the same . . .[72]

Joyce and Eliot both subscribed to a method which the poet famously called "mythological," the manipulating of "a continuous parallel between contemporaneity and antiquity," a "way of controlling, of ordering, of giving a shape and a significance to the immense panorama of futility and anarchy which is contemporary history."[73] Powell and Pressburger are no less Modernist and mythological in *A Canterbury Tale,* no less dependent on old ideas to give significance to the actions of their contemporary narrative. Pilgrimage is their Chaucerian way of ordering lives otherwise random and unhappy. Chillingbourne is their mythic response to the threatening materialist landscape (to return to

Abinger Pageant once again) of "houses and bungalows, hotels, restaurants and flats, arterial roads, by-passes, petrol pumps and pylons."

If the Archers' overall approach seems less erudite or cosmopolitan than the High Modernists', the filmmakers' view of contemporary history less melodramatically despairing than theirs, then perhaps a better analogue to them would be J. B. Priestley, who when not authoring novels and editing anthologies like *Our Nation's Heritage* was in the 1930s writing plays. Stage works like *I Have Been Here Before* or *Time and the Conways* reveal in their musings on time and recurrence the influence of P. D. Ouspensky and particularly J. W. Dunne (*An Experiment with Time*, 1927), and the plays seem in turn, as Ian Christie has convincingly suggested, to have influenced *A Canterbury Tale*, or at least to belong to its world, where the things that happened then are the things that happen now (and also the things that will happen in the future); where reality needs to be adjusted by the insights of psychology, dream, and magic. The Visitors of Priestley's plays are like the Archers' *magus* figures, numinous and unexplained, but commanding.[74]

Even more analogous to the Archers, because more visual in method, is the homegrown visionary painter Stanley Spencer. In a long series of religious canvases and frescoes executed between the wars, Spencer brought Christ into a modern-dress world, usually the familiar world of his home village of Cookham, Berkshire, a place as small as Chilham or Chillingbourne. "Christ Preaching at Cookham Regatta" or "The Resurrection, Cookham,"[75] with their affectionate portrayal of the ordinary even amidst supernatural happenings, supply the closest parallel imaginable to the Archers' film, with its realistic presentation of country life, its willingness to portray the innkeeper scrubbing floors and the village idiot gesticulating in the street, while it also offers Colpeper conjuring up the past and Alison, Bob, and Peter journeying toward their cultural salvation. "The Pilgrimage, Chillingbourne" could be an alternate title for the film. Possibly the down-to-earth Powell and Pressburger would have found pretentious even a comparison to Spencer, and been willing to acknowledge as influences only the constant figures of their moral imagination, Chesterton or Kipling, but *A Canterbury Tale* really does belong to a wider intellectual world than that. For all the film's devotion to a small place and its history, there is nothing parochial about the eclectic and adventurous cinematic technique—one happy to begin with conventional pageantry, but not content to remain there—which succeeded in recording the small place permanently.

Lumber, Cargo from Jamaica, Cable Ship, Weather Forecast, Enough to Eat?, Shipyard, The Zoo and You, Welfare for the Workers, Aero Engine, Hospital Nurse, Land Girl, Telephone Workers, Housing Problems, The Smoke Menace, Children at School . . .

Much of the documentary work produced in Britain in the 1930s and 1940s, most famously by John Grierson and his disciples in the Empire Marketing Board or the G.P.O. Film Unit or the Crown Film Unit, is now lost or impossible to see outside of the viewing cubicles of film archives. The mere titles of the films, however, hint clearly enough at their earnestness and their simplicity. These are efforts to inform public opinion, often also to shape it or to cajole admiration for some under-valued sector of British labor or some underpublicized government service, and with the forthrightness of a Nonconformist sermon or a *Tribune* leader the documentaries march onward toward these purposes. Their ultimate subject and goal is a well-informed populace working collaboratively, purposefully together. Like some of George Orwell's re-portage of the period, which is equally devoted to forthright titling ("A Hanging," "Hop-Picking," "Clink," "Shooting an Elephant," "How the Poor Die"), the films seem to insist on a certain flatness of approach, as if this were a guarantee of their probity. When so basic a social issue as getting enough to eat or finding decent housing is involved, better to proceed by the most direct cinematic means possible: the plain title, the informative narration, the straightforward assembling of images. This is the essential Griersonian dogma, and there are moments in the documentaries which seem to justify it fully. London slum-dwellers, their abashed voices caught with a maximum of naturalness on the sound-track of *Housing Problems* (directed by Edgar Anstey, 1937), after seven decades still make an eloquent case for themselves.

Sometimes, especially with semi-heroic or romantic themes, Grierson gave a little liberty to the camera. His own silent documentary about the herring fishery, *Drifters* (1929), includes impressionistic sequences of the North Sea, edited rhythmically on Eisensteinian lines, just as its title implies something other than "The Herring Fishery" or "Drift Nets at Work." And throughout his career Grierson was a relatively tolerant sponsor of figures whose approach to documentary was more round-about and openly aesthetic than his own. Len Lye experimented with color and abstraction in shorts like *A Colour Box* (1935) and *Trade Tattoo* (1937). *Song of Ceylon,* written and directed by Basil Wright (1934), not only captures various musical sounds of the island nation but, as its title implies, itself takes the form of a lyrical celebration—a performance with images and sounds that comments only obliquely on economics or Imperial policy. In *Coal Face* (1935) the Brazilian-born, French-trained director Alberto Cavalcanti brings low-angle framing and dramatic lighting to bear on the seemingly prosaic topic of work in the pits, thus heroicizing the miners, just as Orwell does with the prose rhetoric—the incantatory rhythms, the admiring metaphors—of his almost exactly contemporaneous book of reportage *The Road to Wigan Pier.* Caval-canti finishes *Coal Face* with W. H. Auden's verse and Benjamin Brit-ten's avant-garde music on the soundtrack, as do also Wright and Harry Watt in the best known of the 1930s documentaries, *Night Mail* (1936).

Of all the documentarists, however, the one least simply informa-tional and most advanced in method was Humphrey Jennings. Jen-nings's most characteristic work—the three wartime films *Listen to Brit-ain* (1942), *Fires Were Started* (1943), and *A Diary for Timothy* (1946), followed by *Family Portrait* in 1951—came a few crucial years after *Night Mail, Song of Ceylon,* and other films of the mid-1930s. Unquestion-ably Jennings benefited from a knowledge of their innovations, but he went further, stretched the boundaries of the documentary idea, substi-tuted personal quirkiness for collaborative purposefulness, and in gen-eral reinvigorated a cinematic form which, under the pressure of war and post-war austerities, might easily have fallen into a routine dreari-ness. Jennings was the poet of the documentary film movement, as was admiringly said in the critical tributes paid to him at the time of his pre-mature death in 1950 (he was killed in a fall, while scouting a location on the Greek island of Poros). Admiringly—but also somewhat ruefully by those who worked with or under him, since Jennings's technique was highly improvisatory, time-consuming, even amateurish. The poetry of his films was less dreamed up in advance than stumbled upon in the camera viewfinder, the sound recordist's headphones, the editing suite.

Listen to Britain in particular shows Jennings's idiosyncrasies, the full extent of his remarkable achievement, and the even fuller extent of his literariness—all reasons why I shall be examining it closely here. A nineteen-minute depiction of scenes from the home front, *Listen to Britain* does without a narration and without the sort of manageable topic which can be summed up in a phrase like *Cable Ship* or *The Smoke Menace*. Seemingly accidental in arrangement, *Listen to Britain* is in fact ingeniously organized, as we shall see, and in its consistencies of tone and approach marks a startling advance on documentaries like *Night Mail*. Seemingly uninstructive, Jennings's film actually instructs the nation about something important. It offers a kind of argument, or insinuates a potent myth, about English solidarity, about the connectedness of wheat fields and factories, of popular music and high art. As for idiosyncrasy, the title of the film expresses that, being a polite request or invitation, as it were to a sonic performance or perhaps an overheard conversation. In no way is it a wartime command along the lines of, say, Frank Capra's 1945 documentary *Know Your Enemy: Japan,* nor the flat aggressive declaration which Jennings used for the slightly earlier documentary *London Can Take It!* (1940). Exactly what the audience of *Listen to Britain* are to learn if they accept the invitation to keep their ears (and eyes) open is not divulged, but it is in fact as much a lesson in putting documentary meaning together as a depiction of essential national character at a time of crisis. It is thus a close counterpart, in a different cinematic genre, to *A Canterbury Tale,* being bound up with the national culture (and with pageant-style celebrations of that culture) and yet set on rendering it in determinedly twentieth-century ways.

Brilliantly educated, first at the Perse School under W. H. D. Rouse, then in the Cambridge circle dominated by I. A. Richards and William Empson, Jennings might easily have followed a career in literary criticism or scholarship.[76] Soon after taking a Double First in 1929 he began a postgraduate thesis on Thomas Gray, and also edited Shakespeare's "Venus and Adonis." But Jennings was equally drawn to visual art, especially painting and the designing of sets for plays and operas. In 1936, with Herbert Read, André Breton, and others, he helped organize the important International Surrealist Exhibition which ran for a month in

London. Always devoted to the art of the present moment—he would criticize others' pictures by saying they lacked "1931ness"[77]—he worked on designs for modern fabrics, traveled to the south of France to paint, translated Paul Eluard, and published prose "reports" and poems, some of which have a superfine artist's sensibility ("As the sun declined the snow at our feet reflected the most delicate peach-blossom"[78]) and some of which look forward to the surreal postwar neo-romanticism of Dylan Thomas or Jennings's friend David Gascoyne.

As if all this aesthetic activity were not enough, Jennings also did a little acting and a little teaching, and in 1937, in conjunction with the anthropologist Tom Harrisson and the journalist Charles Madge, he founded Mass Observation, the most curious and English of twentieth-century documentary projects. Mass Observation was a scheme to enlist volunteer observers—the founders dreamed of eventually having 5,000 under their direction—to watch and listen closely to their fellow countrymen and to take detailed field notes, all in aid of studying such disparate phenomena as the behavior of people at war memorials, the aspidistra cult, anti-Semitism, and passers-by during the Coronation Day of George VI, among whom were, just outside Victoria Station at 7 PM,

> Man with a trumpet playing *It's a sin to tell a lie.* Man with small concertina playing the same tune, accompanied by a dog and a dwarf wearing huge boots back to front, who held the hat. . . . A party of foreign boy scouts. Some men all in black velvet, cocked hats with a baton and sheaf of papers in their hands. One in white gaiters, waterproof and monocle. I overheard the words "he darted into a cinema."[79]

In short, Jennings was an indefatigable collector: of quotidian activities for Mass Observation reports, of urban or country images, and from some point in the mid-1930s on, of extracts from English historical or literary texts. These documents, which he also called "images," were intended to make up a vast compilation, *Pandaemonium,* a kind of idiosyncratic history or museum of attitudes to the coming of the machine—the industrial revolution anthologized.[80]

Clearly, in the 1930s Jennings was working in a way which threatened to scatter his talents and issue in either minor accomplishments or vast unfinishable schemes. Documentary film-making never really changed or disciplined him—he continued writing and painting and collecting interesting images to the end of his life—but it at least gave him a way of concentrating his talents on works which could be completed (indeed, *had* to be completed, more or less on schedule and within budget) and which were intended for a broad, not a coterie audience. Documentary filmmaking simultaneously engaged him in watching his fellow countrymen and in arranging patterns of light and dark within a frame, as a painter would do. It depended on personal gifts which Jennings happened to have in abundance, such as a liking for ordinary people (he "was happy conveying the feel of a human being: the way a man walks, shouts to his friends, the way a girl sings at her work"[81]). Filmmaking also, in its fluidity and speed, seemed to respond, as Basil Wright noted, to his restless and fast-moving intellect.[82] Filmmaking in wartime Britain even catered to his surrealist predilections. As has often been remarked, any London street during the Blitz could produce incongruous juxtapositions, real life as accidental avant-garde bricolage. In *London Can Take It!* Jennings's camera captures a well-dressed woman stepping into a modiste's shop through the shards of its blast-shattered front window. In *Listen to Britain,* an armored troop carrier rumbles past half-timbered village houses and a sign reading "Guests – Teas." With perverse gratitude for what wartime events were handing him, Jennings noted that "coincidences," by which he meant unexpected juxtapositions of image with image or sound with sound, "have the infinite freedom of appearing anywhere, anytime, to anyone. . . ."[83]

At some point in 1934 Jennings began work for the G.P.O. Film Unit, in the same improvisatory and fast-learning spirit that would later shape his documentaries.[84] He designed sets, for example for Cavalcanti's experimental sound film *Pett and Pott,* and acted small parts, for example as a maniacally helpful grocer in *Pett and Pott.* He discovered how to edit on the short *Post Haste,* and by the end of the year began directing, with the twenty-one-minute film *Locomotives.* Though always an individualist, someone never close to or particularly admired by John Grierson, he benefited greatly from the collaborative ethos of Grierson's unit, learning over the years particularly from Len Lye, the director Stuart Legg, the producer Ian Dalrymple, and above all the gifted editor Stewart McAllister, who would eventually work side-by-side with Jennings in the key years 1941–1943 (McAllister is credited as co-director and co-editor of *Listen to Britain*).

In sixteen years Jennings worked on almost three dozen films, many very short, a few merely educational (*The Story of the Wheel*, 1934), some closely linked to his mania for collecting things (*Spare Time*, 1939, which dispassionately gathers up a range of British amusements), one or two on topics which apparently bored him (the revitalization of a coal mine in *The Cumberland Story*, 1948). Even in the most routine of Jennings films, however, a moment or two tends to draw on his idiosyncrasies and come unexpectedly to life on the screen. Toward the end of his not very impressive *The True Story of Lili Marlene* (1944), a history of the popular World War II song, a final tracking shot goes through a peaceful London market. The camera here sees shoppers, news vendors, and children at play, and sees them with the "quick affection and precision," the absence of "patronage and caricature," he brought to his more accomplished documentaries.[85] Tracking shots always seem distinctive in Jennings. They help to define his visual style, and his auditory style, since they are so often coordinated with music on the soundtrack, and were imitated by other filmmakers at moments which seemed to call for quasi-documentary treatment. In *A Canterbury Tale*, for example, Alison being tracked as she walks through the bombed streets of Canterbury resembles many urban figures photographed by Jennings's cameraman.[86]

The war enlisted Jennings in the national cause, just as it enlisted Powell and Pressburger. First for the Crown Film Unit, then the Ministry of Information, he directed *Spring Offensive* in 1940, and after that in rapid succession *London Can Take It!* (with Harry Watt), *Heart of Britain*, and *Words for Battle*. In *London Can Take It!*, stirring words from Milton's *Areopagitica*—

> Methinks I see in my mind a noble and puissant nation rousing herself like a strong man after sleep, and shaking her invincible locks. Methinks I see her as an eagle mewing her mighty youth, and kindling her undazzled eyes at the full midday beam—

are simplified and modernized for delivery by the narrator, the American newsman Quentin Reynolds:

> London raises her head, shakes the debris of the night from her hair, and takes stock of the damage done . . . London looks upwards towards the dawn and faces the new day with calmness and confidence.

Meanwhile a panorama of the awakening city and a shot of a bomb-damaged street fill the screen. *Words for Battle,* which in the style of *A Canterbury Tale* opens with a national map, this one taken from Camden's *Description of Britain,* then quotes the *Areopagitica* passage directly, following it with other stirring patriotic texts read by Laurence Olivier in a kind of cinematic and up-to-the-minute *Pandaemonium,* with images matched carefully to words. Similarly, in *Heart of Britain,* shots of factories at work and warplanes flying are matched carefully to the strains of the Hallelujah Chorus sung by the Huddersfield Choral Society.

Listen to Britain had a less obvious origin in English writing and a more prolonged gestation. Jennings began work on the film in the spring of 1941, but he had been thinking about images of homely English life for a long time, first attempting to record them in a prose work written the previous summer. This, "Picture: the 'Midi Symphony,'" is a kind of genre painting in words:

> Picture an English interior in the remotest village of Oxfordshire: a mother, a married daughter, the mother of an evacuee, reading and knitting quietly after dinner—the bombers going out from the neighbouring airfield while the radio plays the pathetic music of Haydn. On the walls are portraits, photographs, watercolours, of men—predominantly men—engineers and soldiers, going back to the days of Robert Stephenson and the Crimea—little framed fragments of regimental colours—photographs of railway bridges—men in uniform and men as children.
>
> How beautiful Haydn—what measure—what warmth of brass—what tears of strings—what march of ensemble—what forgiveness. Children of the grown-ups here listening and reading—children upstairs asleep. What a nostalgia the penultimate movement of the "Midi" symphony. Outside in the dark the corn ripens: it is the last day in July. The trumpets of Haydn call us. The bombers are all gone. The sky is clear. The flutes in the last movement thrill us. The ears of corn move for a moment. The knitting-needles click. The trumpets return. The bombers are already over the white coast-line.[87]

Here, home-front Britain is presented quite unconventionally, without any claims for valor and only the whisper of a suggestion about a national heritage worth fighting for. If Jennings's reserved domestic scene seems significant, it is so purely for its own sake. His prose puts oddly assorted elements together, backtracking from current miseries into safety and coziness ("the remotest village"), while still including signs of past wars on the walls, and even tokens of the present conflict in the noisy aircraft overhead. The passage is fast-paced in the way a documentary film would be, "cutting" rapidly from image to image, from inside to outside and from items seen in close-up (photographs of railway bridges) to items seen in extreme long shot (bombers crossing the coast-line); the ears of grain which Jennings imagines as being in momentary movement would in fact furnish the second image we see onscreen in *Listen to Britain*. More important, the passage anticipates what would eventually become the film's innovative emphasis on sound, all sound, classical music mixed with ambient noise. In "Picture: the 'Midi Symphony'" it is a filmmaker's (or a sound recordist's) sensibility which goes past the flutes and trumpets to capture the detail of the clicking knitting-needles—as it would turn out one of the few domestic sounds *not* preserved in *Listen to Britain*.

The progression of *Listen to Britain* from conception to completion was, as usual with Jennings, haphazard, involving improvised ideas and other short films begun but not finished, and at this remove of time it cannot be followed with any exactness. But certainly one early stage, perhaps developed from a suggestion by the actor and director Bernard Miles, would have entailed a shift from Haydn to Mozart and from Oxfordshire to London. This version would have concentrated solely on Dame Myra Hess's lunchtime piano concerts. A typed treatment dated April 28, 1941, explains how the film would begin with shots of Dame Myra playing the first movement of a Mozart piano concerto, proceed to establish the character of the audience, then widen out to show other rooms in the war-damaged National Gallery:

> We should go up on the roof, where the Office of Works men are mending the blitzed dome and from their point of view we should see, not only the orchestra and audience below, but London itself, sprawling out down river and across country from this which is, in fact, its centre.

Balloons rise, anti-aircraft gunners stand to, and a fighter patrol takes off:

> The Spitfires and the Hurricanes in the sun above the clouds and smoke, are beautiful shining things, flying in a world very like the lyrical world of Mozart.[88]

A detailed shooting script for this version specifies what "establish the character of the audience" means. Close-ups were to show a young music student, a woman air-raid warden, an old man, an artilleryman and his girl, two tough looking Canadian soldiers, a parson, a wounded soldier with head bandaged. The script also makes it clear that the film would have spent more time outside than inside the Gallery, would have given ample scope to Jennings the collector of scattered images, a few of these merely odd, "surrealist" (one of the lions at the Nelson Monument with sandbags for fire bombs between its paws), but most conveying a clear sense of national solidarity and high purpose. After its tour of a London battered and under siege but feisty (Jennings planned to show the boarded-up Eros statue in Piccadilly Circus with its painted slogan HIT BACK), the film was to dissolve from fighter squadron vapor trails to the National Gallery and the concert audience, "but now more settled down and happier," the artilleryman and his girl holding hands, before finishing with a long shot of the dome of St. Paul's.[89]

Photographing of the lunchtime concerts took place in the spring and summer of 1941, but in short order Jennings had expanded his notion of "the National Gallery film." The work now was to be called "The Music of War." "Do you think that modern war has no music?" asks a treatment of May 23 describing this version. "That mechanisation has banished harmony, and that because life is for the moment so grim Britain no longer thinks of singing?" The sequences of this film would have recorded not just Dame Myra Hess but soldiers singing as they marched, shots of the beloved concert site the Queen's Hall in ruins, bagpipers, a "jazzed-up" rendition of "Loch Lomond" played at a dance, birdsong at dawn, a Free French sergeant singing and whistling "En passant par la Lorraine," and the like. In other words, the film would have been *Song of Ceylon* shifted back to Britain and given more ideological purpose: "For music in Britain to-day is far from being just another escape: it probes into the emotions of the war itself—love of country, love of liberty, love of living, and the exhilaration of fighting for them."[90]

It is possible that both of these preliminary treatments were written chiefly as proposals for the filmmakers' masters at the Ministry of Information, not as real working documents, and hence were deliberately made propagandistic. Notes from Stewart McAllister on both say that they were intended to persuade civil servants to furnish the needed funds. In any case, Jennings and McAllister went on holiday to Scotland in the summer of 1941, discussed plans, and produced in August still another treatment, this time titled "The Tin Hat Concerto."[91] In the same month they resumed production, but of a markedly different film, more ambitious and more miscellaneous, more composed of the kind of oddly assorted elements that had made up "Picture: the 'Midi Symphony'." The work now got out of London (an important dance sequence was shot at the Tower Ballroom, Blackpool, for instance) and, thanks to the influence of Jennings's producer Ian Dalrymple, took a greater interest in ordinary Britons: "Dal has been a tremendous help in a quiet way about tackling people and not straying off into landscapes and trick ideas."[92] The film was also sufficiently loosened in conception to include a number of used and unused scenes from other documentaries, such as factory shots from *Heart of Britain* and dark images of coal miners from *Spare Time.*[93] By the time it was finished some twenty-five percent of its footage consisted of outtakes from previous filming: Jennings's compiling obsession at work again, perhaps, but now allied with McAllister's editing skills and a joint overall idea of what the film should do, and so resulting in a coherent work, not a farrago, still less a pandemonium.

Listen to Britain was completed in October 1941 and shown to theater audiences the following spring. It is a vastly more interesting work than either the National Gallery film or "The Music of War" would have been, partly because it has shifted from the idea of music to the more complex idea of *sounds*—something amounting, perhaps, to an avant-garde *musique concrète*, as Kevin Jackson has suggested, but a *musique concrète* composed of ordinariness.[94] Still another reason for the film's greater interest is that Jennings decided to fill it with wartime actualities not equated in a "poetical" and unconvincing way, as they are in the early treatments (Spitfires and Hurricanes as "beautiful shining things, flying in a world very like the lyrical world of Mozart"), but presented separately, in all their distinctness and peculiarity. Letters to his wife Cicely in America and journal entries attest that during the planning and shooting of the film what particularly struck Jennings about daily life was exactly its richness in specificity, in discordances. He gathered discordances greedily. For example, while securing the music for a different film, about a raid on the Lofoten Islands, Jennings and his crew recorded the London Philharmonic Orchestra playing "Rule, Britannia" and the Norwegian National Anthem. On coming out to their truck to listen to the tape, they "realized for the first time that there was a blitz going on. A full moon and the guns going hard and a plane overhead. Finally we recorded the Leonora Trumpet Call with a bomber on the end of the take." Several moments later they came upon severe damage and casualties in the street and retreated to a Lyons Corner House, but found that the war had preceded them there:

> inside on the unused tables there are wounded lying with their heads tied up and rescue squad men in white tin hats getting them food and drink. Then we go downstairs—there are people all down the stairway sheltering from the raid—but at the bottom the orchestra is playing a rumba and we eat bacon and eggs and the raid is forgotten.[95]

All this, Beethoven and the Blitz, casualties and the rumba, was wartime surrealism indeed, surrealism in the eye of the sensitive beholder.

Even away from London in a country cottage Jennings could hear the oddly mingled sounds of Britain at war. He wrote about them in a letter to his wife, in a passage which might serve as a summary of his filmmaking style and that of *A Canterbury Tale* too:

> This late afternoon I sit & think of you & hear for you the sounds of English summer: the buzz of the fly against the window pane—the bees in the sun—the curious whine of the Spitfire high up in the blue—the children shouting away down the valley.

"Now a big bird passes the French windows," he adds, "& the Spitfire returns and goes up towards London": not the avian image transformed by magic into the military icon, as in *A Canterbury Tale,* but rather two images preserved in all their incongruity. "Curious what war teaches one!"[96] he concludes. Much of what he found curious, what the war was teaching him, would go straight into the visual and auditory style of *Listen to Britain.*

As if recalling his summertime moment in the cottage, Jennings begins the film with items which might have been seen through the window there, a tree and a wheat field, then cuts to a shot of Spitfires. The first part of the opening sequence continues to alternate between two Englands, pastoral and military, land girls at their harvest work and sky-watchers with binoculars. (Sometimes the warplanes are shown high overhead; Jennings shared his fellow East Anglian John Constable's love for a pictorial sky, and filled *Listen to Britain* with images of billowing clouds, including the image which closes the film.) Day turns to night as a housewife puts a lamp in the window while a scrap of the BBC evening news is heard on the soundtrack. Sentries prepare to stand watch for the nightly raids, and orchestra music leads us from the Irish Sea past a poster and into the Tower Ballroom, filled with dancers. All through the film the soundtrack does this sort of thing, the aural equivalent of a dissolve in editing: it bridges gaps between disparate images. This is perhaps the most inventive technique in that careful coordination of sound and picture which distinguishes all of Jennings's work and which the *Times* singled out for praise in its review of *Listen to Britain:* "the sound-recording apparatus is used like a camera to pick out light and shade, to heighten contrast and suggest relief. . . ."[97] On the dance floor of the ballroom, men and women are box-stepping in a circle around the floor, gracefully or clumsily, putting abundantly on display what Orwell called the "mild knobby faces" of the English, "with their bad teeth and gentle manners,"[98] a few of the faces self-consciously aware of the camera trained on them, others fixed on singing "Roll out the barrel, we'll have a barrel of fun" with dutiful British mirth: a scene which in its utter plausibility and its ordinary pathos Graham Greene might have invented. There follows a cut to the outside and we see again the sentries on watch, silhouetted against the sunset sky. Fade to black.

The opening is the first of five sequences in the film, all of them set apart by fades, the last sequence much longer than the others. Together, as McAllister's biographer Dai Vaughan has observed, they bring us from one late afternoon to the next, a full twenty-four-hour day.[99] They thus structure *Listen to Britain* after the method of the Mass Observation documentary report *May the 12th,* which Jennings had helped edit in 1937, and, more to the point, after the method of the "City Symphony" films of the 1920s, most notably Walther Ruttmann's *Berlin: die Sinfonie der Großstadt* (1927), Cavalcanti's *Rien que les heures* (1926), and Dziga Vertov's *The Man with a Movie Camera* (1929), all of them day-long exposures of street life in European capitals—Paris in the case of Cavalcanti's film, Petersburg in the case of Vertov's. We know from his comments that Jennings saw these silent avant-garde productions, these "vivid, symphonic or generalized studies,"[100] that he worked closely with one of their directors, Cavalcanti, and that he was greatly interested in analogies between the cinema and music. The result of these influences is that *Listen for Britain* combines, like *Rien que les heures* in particular, a random-seeming surface with an ideology at depth. It nevertheless differs from the City Symphonies in geographic coverage, in its brevity—its disciplining of the whimsicality, the sheer expansiveness, of between-the-wars Modernism—and of course by Jennings's having recorded sound as an expressive device at his command.

The second sequence of Jennings's city-symphony-style documentary, then, introduces night-time industrial work, with the sounds of miners clumping along passageways to the pit, locomotives steaming, and aircraft being assembled, then flown across the dark sky. The third, turning away from male activity, shows an ambulance station with an audience of uniformed women passing the time by listening to the folk song "The Ash Grove"—an informal performance to match the one we have heard in the previous sequence, the singing of "Home on the Range" by some Canadian soldiers in their railway carriage (both episodes were sketched in Jennings's treatment "The Music of War"). If *Listen to Britain* were literally a symphony, the rendition of "The Ash Grove" would be its *moderato cantabile,* its lyrical short movement. The fourth sequence is about radio, from the familiar chimes of Big Ben and the equally familiar wartime announcement "This is London calling" to the actual mechanisms involved: broadcasting towers, glowing radio tubes.

With the final sequence we reach the new day, as suggested by a shot of sunlit trees and the sound of birdsong. After this, Jennings and McAllister gather a collection of images miscellaneous even by the standard previous sequences have set. We are shown an industrial town coming awake, a commuter striding to work (a calisthenics broadcast is on the soundtrack), a housewife looking out her window at children doing a folk dance, and an Army convoy moving through a village. The industrial town is itself miscellaneous, being constituted visually of smoking factory chimneys in the background and a slow-stepping dray horse in the foreground—a composite image of the type Jennings sought so assiduously for *Pandaemonium.*[101] Moments later, an important vignette starts by taking viewers to a lunchtime singalong held in a factory canteen—the setting which Frank Launder and Sidney Gilliat would use for the we're-all-in-this-together climax of their film *Millions Like Us.*

Listen to Britain's version of the canteen show features two stars of the Crazy Gang comedies, Bud Flanagan and Chesney Allen, in Jennings's opinion "the profoundest clowns in the country,"[102] performing the duet "Round the Back of the Arches." In the single most adroit transition of the film, their back-up band concludes on a chord blending imperceptibly with a chord from the Mozart piano concerto Dame Myra is playing at the National Gallery.

To this hallowed site the film now dissolves. It presents the musicians, characterizes the audience in the hall, and then opens out into London, just as Jennings's early treatment had specified. Mozart's music follows the camera to the porch of the Gallery as if it were still being heard by the casual lunch-eaters gathered there, but then is gradually lost as Jennings and McAllister move on to a tank factory full of effort and heavy clanking. After that, a military parade and a forge, the two being connected by the pounding rhythm which carries over from bass drum to iron hammer, and finally a conclusion with sky-borne clouds.[103]

What meaning did audiences find in this extraordinary gathering of images and noise? Apparently doubting the film's capacity to mean much of anything, especially to overseas audiences, the authorities insisted that it be shown to the Allies with a cautious spoken foreword. In this, Leonard Brockington, K.C. ("I am a Canadian . . . I have been listening to Britain") admits the miscellaneous quality of the sounds and images in the film, but finishes with a translation of them into reassuringly martial metaphors: "the trumpet call of freedom, the march of victory, the war song of a great people." Some of the same doubts were felt by viewers at home, including the documentary filmmaker Edgar Anstey, who was severe about what he saw as self-indulgent pointlessness:

> Much more elaborate in style and treatment is an expensive Crown Film Unit production called *Listen to Britain,* which will not encourage anyone to do anything at all. It sets out to assemble a varied collection of characteristic British sounds ranging from a piano recital at a National Gallery lunchtime concert to the clatter of a falling railway signal, and to illustrate the skilfully constructed jigsaw with an appropriate (and beautifully photographed) set of visual images. This is an aesthetic enough conception in all conscience, but by the time Humphrey Jennings has

done with it it has become the rarest piece of fiddling since the days of Nero. It will be a disaster if this film is sent overseas. One shudders to imagine the effect upon our Allies should they learn that an official British film-making unit can find time these days to contemplate the current sights and sounds of Britain as if the country were some curious kind of museum exhibit, or a figment of the romantic imagination of Mass Observation.[104]

Jennings might have countered Anstey's Blimpishness by proposing that even at a moment of national crisis a documentary could conceivably do many things besides urge viewers on to the fight; John Grierson did in effect answer Anstey when he said that Jennings's films *were* carrying on the fight, but by fighting for "the right to contemplate."[105] *Listen to Britain* is contemplative rather than hortatory, and contemplative of national activities which might be purposeful enough for any Ally's approval, as when factory hands assemble tank treads or BBC voices go out in many languages to occupied Europe—or which might not, as when members of the Orchestra of the Central Band of the RAF literally fiddle behind Dame Myra at the keyboard. During the National Gallery concert Jennings's camera captures for a few seconds a merchant seaman bending over to examine thoughtfully a painting of a merchant ship. It is a modest but exemplary action, in that the seaman does what Jennings arranged for all viewers of *Listen to Britain* to do as they bent forward in thoughtful examination of the film: pause, regard the representation of something utterly familiar and valuable, contemplate.

In the first years of the war these were not trivial activities. It is important to remember that while for us the film may be (in Anstey's formulation) a sort of museum, a repertoire of visual clichés which collectively spell out "the Blitz" (barrage balloons over London, pedestrians with tin hats hanging by their sides, the Houses of Parliament swathed in scaffolding), its first audiences saw fresh and current images before them on the screen, images which might have belonged to a newsreel; and that such contemplating as they did might have been of the pain of losing everything they were shown. When *Listen to Britain* appeared in theaters in the spring of 1942, the worst of the night-time bombing raids were over, and the country would not be under serious siege again until the V-1 and V-2 attacks toward the end of the war, but no one could then know that. Jennings could not know that he would not need to repeat his improvisation of 1940, when during a sudden raid in Oxford Street he and McAllister were forced to lie down on the sidewalk and cover the newly edited reels of *London Can Take It!* with their bodies.[106] While Britain's vulnerability is never emphasized in *Listen to Britain,* it is acknowledged. The ordinariness depicted in the film seems both indomitable and threadbare (in the film historian Gilbert Adair's phrase),[107] both a matter of pride and a stimulus to the particular kind of nostalgia attaching to things which may not survive. Each familiar feature photographed or recorded represents what Britons still had every right to think they were fighting for, and in this sense *Listen to Britain* is a full-fledged companion work to *A Canterbury Tale,* a reconfirmation of national emotions, and part of the large-scale project of cultural and moral stocktaking which went on in many genres during the first years of the war.

The film is close in mode to another important effort in the project, Orwell's *The Lion and the Unicorn.* Jennings read this extended essay at its publication in the month he began work on *Listen to Britain* and strongly agreed with its analysis of current events.[108] Like the documentary and unlike the Archers' past-haunted fictional film, *The Lion and the Unicorn* insists on being up-to-the-minute: its opening sentence is "As I write, highly civilized human beings are flying overhead, trying to kill me." Orwell's beginning premise is that "One cannot see the modern world as it is unless one recognizes the overwhelming strength of patriotism, national loyalty," and from this he moves on to a characterization of the particular nation in which he lives and to which he is loyally if also crankily devoted. England is defined in *The Lion and the Unicorn,* and defined initially by lists of sense impressions:

> The clatter of clogs in the Lancashire mill towns, the to-and-fro of the lorries on the Great North Road, the queues outside the Labour Exchanges, the rattle of pin-tables in the Soho pubs, the old maids biking to Holy Communion through the mists of the autumn mornings . . . solid breakfasts and gloomy Sundays, smoky towns and winding roads, green fields and red pillar-boxes.[109]

These items are the verbal equivalents of Jennings's photographed images and recorded sounds (Orwell is unusual among writers in *listening* to his subject), and are cinematic in their depiction of movement, their quick hitting off of locales, and their feeling for effects of light or color. As in the film, the images are seemingly listed at random, put together in a "muddle" from which the essayist momentarily despairs of drawing a pattern. Could there really be any common ground among them or between the two contrasted heraldic beasts, the lion and the unicorn? (The main title of *Listen to Britain* is superimposed over a similarly discordant blazon: a violin crossed with an anti-aircraft gun.) But of course Orwell does find a pattern; his discursive medium leads him to generalize. For him, the English are typically unartistic, unsystematic in thought, politically hypocritical but deeply moral in their attitude to life, old-fashioned in tastes, and conspicuously gentle:

> The gentleness of the English civilisation is perhaps its most marked characteristic. You notice it the instant you set foot on English soil. It is a land where the bus conductors are good-tempered and the policemen carry no revolvers.[110]

This claim *Listen to Britain* fully affirms. While literally omitting bus conductors or policemen, the film over and over again demonstrates the good temper of ordinary Britons as they eat their lunches or wait patiently for their trains ("Britons" rather than "English people" because Jennings's title makes the claim for the larger nation, though in fact his scenes seem to be recognizably English, rather than Scottish or Welsh). Young women smile at each other as they work at their machine tools and sing "Yes, My Darling Daughter" along with the radio. The Canadian soldiers shown in the second sequence wield a guitar rather than weapons, and even when on parade the British ranks move sedately enough past the camera, in that swaggerless British Army march which Orwell's essay, contrasting it with the Nazi goose-step, describes as a "formalised walk." Jennings's film must be the least belligerent depiction of a country at war ever made.

The most important claim made in *The Lion and the Unicorn* is about national unity. The essay acknowledges as it must the class disparities of the country (economically, "England is certainly two nations, if not three or four"), the unfair electoral system, the selfishness of the rich and the standoffishness of the intelligentsia, but repeatedly insists that national unity is a fact. The "vast majority of the people *feel* themselves to be a single nation . . . Patriotism is usually stronger than class-hatred." Orwell progresses from metaphor to metaphor—patriotism "runs like a connecting thread" through nearly all the social classes, the nation "is bound together by an invisible chain"—until he reaches the famous summarizing metaphor which concludes the first part of the essay:

> England . . . resembles a family, a rather stuffy Victorian family, with not many black sheep in it but with all its cupboards bursting with skeletons. It has rich relations who have to be kow-towed to and poor relations who are horribly sat upon, and there is a deep conspiracy of silence about the source of the family income. It is a family in which the young are generally thwarted and most of the power is in the hands of irresponsible uncles and bedridden aunts. Still, it is a family. It has its private language and its common memories, and at the approach of an enemy it closes its ranks.[111]

Listen to Britain lacks the political bite of this passage, and the sense so frequent in Orwell of angry leftist thinking at odds with a profound natural love of country. By comparison with the writer, Jennings is a naive, perhaps a casual or haphazard analyst, someone with instincts rather than a confirmed ideology, but he is very close to Orwell in his artistic standpoint, which is both apart from and in the midst of what he describes, and above all in his conception of Britain.

Jennings's film unquestionably defines *one* nation. Everyone from coal-miners to ambulance drivers is shown to be essentially engaged in the same effort, looking alike (uniforms and helmets abound), hearing the same radio voices on the BBC (that is one reason why *Listen to Britain* puts them on the soundtrack), classlessly cooperating.[112] Jennings gives the impression of looking over the whole country with genuine curiosity, impartially and eagerly. He never privileges the activities of a particular group over those of another, never even attempts to encompass the nation in any single essential or epitomizing image, as he might well have done (the "National Gallery film" would have ended with a shot of the dome of St. Paul's rising triumphantly over the rubble), or with any single sound ("The Music of War" would have worked through its various performances to a culmination at the National Gallery with Mozart, "the purest of all music"). The film as actually made refuses such judgments, judgments about which music is purest or which contemporary scene most heroically British. It looks around in many directions and keeps adding scene to scene, insisting on their comparable contribution to our understanding of a beleaguered nationhood. The National Gallery concert receives Jennings's full attention, but so does the crooning of "Round the Back of the Arches" at the factory canteen. During the Mozart, the camera glances at the Queen seated next to Sir Kenneth Clark, the director of the National Gallery and the just-resigned director of the films division of the Ministry of Information; during the canteen musicale, the camera observes no less diligently an old gaffer leaning over to spit meditatively on the floor; two audiences, Britons all. (The shot of the old man spitting was recycled from Jennings's earlier film *Welfare for the Workers:*[113] perhaps this is an indication that the image was deliberately chosen to counterbalance the image of sedate Royalty in the National Gallery.) Beyond this evenhandedness in presenting his vignettes, Jennings conveys national unity in shot after shot of people doing things *together:* workmen cooperate to put a piece of steel through the forge, Flanagan and Allen get the audience to whistle along with their song (they are employing the "private language" which Orwell's essay mentions), men and women circle about the ballroom. This is solidarity enacted, captured as it might be by a Mass Observer moving with avid eye and notebook among the crowds.

It is a relatively simple matter to record single images of common tasks, a more complex undertaking (one which required all of McAllister's talents) to emphasize the interdependence of Britons who are going about apparently separate activities. In the opening, for instance, we see a flight of Spitfires skimming by, then stalks of grain blowing in a gust of wind which clever editing makes it seem the aircraft have produced; the impression given by this two or three seconds of the film is that the RAF above and the harvesting below are *causally* connected, that the latter could not happen without the former to protect it. A moment or two later, after the film has dissolved to waves lapping on a beach, the filmmakers show in rapid sequence two gentlemen seated on a bench watching the sunset, a sentry putting on his coat, and the poster announcing the dance in the ballroom. We observe the circling couples for a minute or so, then return to the seashore as two sentries begin their duty. The clear implication is that the dancers can have their fun because others are prepared to stand watch. But meanwhile the filmmakers have put the music from the ballroom on their soundtrack throughout this little episode, over all the cuts from image to image, and thus *joined* the two groups, those off- and those on-duty. In the most natural way possible "Roll Out the Barrel" leaks outdoors, becomes common property, even includes the sentries in the merriment; the line from the song which we hear at the exact moment of the cut to their going on watch is "The gang's all here." Far from being set apart in virtuous self-sacrifice, the sentries are allowed to blend into the egalitarian scene, as is emphasized visually when Jennings and McAllister show them watching the sunset in exactly the pose taken by the gentlemen at the start of the episode. What this brief part of *Listen to Britain* portrays is the nation-family at the seaside.

A number of sequences in *Listen to Britain* connect action causally with action, often bringing civilian together with soldier—miners dig coal which powers a locomotive which carries troops—but the syntax of the film is not invariably so clear. The most remarkable and enigmatic of its vignettes begins with a woman fussing over crockery on her kitchen table. When she looks out her window McAllister cuts to a long shot of school children paired off in the playground across the street from her. They are doing their daily exercises by going through dance steps while a piano, presumably played by a teacher, sounds out the "Clapping Polka" from some nearby schoolroom. We may hear the single word "mummy!" on the soundtrack at this moment; it is hard to tell. Back to the woman, now in closer view, smiling and continuing to gaze out the window, and back in turn to the children, seen in a medium long shot. (All these cuts are made not quite in rhythm with the heavy downbeats of the piano music, perhaps because McAllister is carefully avoiding too contrived an effect. By contrast, during the National Gallery concert he edits in exact synchronization with the pulses of the Mozart concerto.) The girls and boys skip around in a circle, holding hands, miniature versions of those servicemen and their partners we glimpsed dancing in the opening sequence. When we see the woman again she turns her head, and the immediately following point-of-view shot displays the framed photograph of a soldier in kilts. Cut away to the dancing children, a few of them only, in close-up: one little girl moves around her partner a second too soon and has to restart. Jennings or McAllister might have edited this mistake out, but were wise not to: the mistakes or occasional moments of camera-consciousness in the film not only remind us that we are, after all, watching documentary, but as Malcolm Smith has observed, help keep the relationship between viewer and film informal; the "wrong" shots are like snap-shots in a family album.[114] Mistake and all, the close-up of dancing children concludes the vignette, a scant forty-five seconds after it started.

The origin of this vignette in Jennings's imagination is patently "Picture: the 'Midi Symphony'," with its English interior, women at domestic tasks, photographs of men in uniform, children close by, and ambient music. In the film he has radically simplified the furnishings and actions, thus turning what was an avant-garde fantasia on the sense impressions of war into a spare little narrative, and he has replaced Haydn with a thumping folk tune. In the process he has foregone aesthetic pleasure ("How beautiful Haydn—what measure—what warmth of brass . . .") but gained authenticity. Piano music from a school playground seems exactly what Britain, as opposed to Humphrey Jennings, might be overhearing at this place and time. He has also eliminated the sense of refuge or retreat, of smug aesthetic enclosure, conveyed by the prose piece. In the filmed vignette, the threat of war seems closer, the children more exposed to it, part of an ordinariness which at this moment appears particularly threadbare and vulnerable.

The specific story which Jennings dramatizes here is hard to read with any exactness. We surmise that the woman is a mother, perhaps the mother of one of the dancing children, while the soldier in kilts is her husband, fighting somewhere out of the country, or for that matter already fallen in battle or held in a prison camp. Or he could be an older child, or conceivably her own father in the costume of the previous war, in which case the scene would be a depiction of three generations. As for her pensive turn of the head from children to picture: is she thinking that the children are able to exercise in safety only because someone else is keeping the enemy at bay? That her husband would be happy to see the children dancing now? That the sight of happy children is worth the sacrifice of a loved one? Simply that she misses her man?[115] Whichever interpretation we may choose, the scene is in some sense about intimate dependencies among British people, and so relevant to Jennings's larger purposes. All the figures photographed are native speakers of a private family language, as were those British people in the 1942 theater

audience watching them, and the language is not the less communica-
tive for being entirely wordless, a matter of understood conventions and
expressive glances: British understatement, caught in a few minutes of
narration-less film. The measure of this vignette's (and *Listen to Britain*'s) curious power is that it can at once be so restrained, so moving,
and so ambiguous.

What the woman in this vignette does—turn thoughtfully from
one image to another—is an analogue to what the viewers of *Listen to
Britain* in 1942 did and we do now. It is a better analogue than the simple
gazing at one picture which Jennings provided in the National Gallery
with the merchant seaman and his painted ship. After all, we see in the
film a *succession* of images, familiar sights perhaps, and are required
to think about their relation in ways that might be wholly unfamiliar.
We hear a similarly ambiguous succession of sounds. Then we must assemble these elements into larger scenes or sequences. What is the relation between the woman-schoolchildren vignette and the episode preceding it (mixed brief shots of factories, then of a tree) or following it (an
Army convoy moving through a village street)? Beyond that, what is the
relation between the whole last sequence, of which the vignette is one
small part, and the rest of *Listen to Britain*? The challenge this film constantly presents is to put all its visible and audible material into an intelligible pattern. The challenge can be met, one must add; here at least,
Jennings is no obscurantist. We may feel confident in speculating, for
example, that the Army convoy on its way through the village amplifies
the picture of protectiveness already given in the framed photograph,
and that a little girl caught on film smiling and watching the convoy
supplies a clever reversal of the events just dramatized. That is, succeeding a contemplation of the innocent by their guardians, we have now
an innocent contemplating those who are guarding her. Similar modes
of organization, some so casual that they barely register on a viewer,
some contrived enough to be unmistakable, are at work all through the
film, and they give it its quality of subtle coherence, of combining (to
quote words of Michael Faraday which Jennings approvingly recorded
in *Pandaemonium*) "many effects, each utterly insensible alone, into one
sum of fine effect."[116] At the same time, of course, this artistic unity of
the film is perfectly complementary to its subject, the political and cultural unity of a nation, the "fine effect" of 1940s Britain. Both versions

of unity, the cinematic and the political, are improvised, unemphatic, plausible, as real as cultural artifacts ever can be.

After *Listen to Britain* Jennings and McAllister collaborated on *Fires Were Started,* about the work of the Auxiliary Fire Service, and then Jennings alone directed *A Diary for Timothy,* a meditation on Britain's post-war future cast in the form of an address to a newborn infant; its script is by E. M. Forster. In effect, the director's wartime work was concluded with his last film, a final effort in national definition, *Family Portrait* (made in 1949, again with McAllister as editor, and shown as part of the Festival of Britain after Jennings's death). All these are more conventional films than *Listen to Britain,* more plotted or predictably organized and in two cases employing spoken narrations. *Fires Were Started* and *A Diary for Timothy* are also much longer films. In their various ways these works pick up again the technique of direct-translation-of-literature-to-the-screen used in earlier Jennings documentaries like *Words for Battle* or *London Can Take It!* For example, *Family Portrait* quotes Kipling, Forster, and Shakespeare, and though it does not quote Orwell it seems bent on developing themes from him, putting his metaphor about England as a family into straightforward cinematic form. While snapshots of British life are turned over for us in a national photographic album, the narrator remarks: "Perhaps because we in Britain live on a group of small islands, we like to think of ourselves as a family, and of course with the unspoken affection and outspoken words that all families have." In *Fires Were Started,* a powerful narrative drive and superbly original images, of fire ladders and streams of water crossing the screen with baroque obliquity, are combined with more literary quoting, of Sir Walter Raleigh's famous peroration, "O eloquent, just, and mighty Death" from *A History of the World.* In other words, that film applies a sophisticated visual and literary perspective to a story of simple men at work, and in this resembles a notable subgenre of 1940s texts, fictions drawn from the active wartime service of intellectuals. Examples in this subgenre include John Strachey's *Post D* (about an air raid warden's routines, 1941), Henry Green's fire-service novel *Caught* (1943), and William Sansom's *Fireman Flower and Other Stories,* 1944 (by coincidence, Sansom acted the part of the rookie fireman Barrett in *Fires Were Started*).[117]

A Diary for Timothy, meanwhile, ponders at length the sort of question the main characters in *Millions Like Us* ask themselves during a hilltop contemplation of the sleepy village below: "What's going to happen when it's over?" "Are we going to slide back?" Jennings's film perfectly captures the attitude of its scriptwriter Forster, a gentle and tolerant man sure of the rightness of the war but unsure of its political consequences, a man much given to fretful questionings and deferred judgments. It is thoroughly Forsterian that *A Diary of Timothy* should once again use as an icon of the war Dame Myra Hess's concerts, but this time discoursing on the provoking aesthetic issues they raise. "Did you like the music that lady was playing?" the narrator asks baby Timothy. "Some of us think it is the greatest music in the world, yet it's German music, and we are fighting the Germans. That's something you'll have to think over later on."[118] Accompanying these ruminations on the soundtrack are strains of the Beethoven sonata Dame Myra is playing and phrases from a radio news report about the weather-plagued Allied retreat from Arnhem, while the screen fills with images of the piano keyboard, London houses under repair, and October rain in the streets—a montage explained and connected by the kindly tones of the narrator, Michael Redgrave, who throughout gives voice to Forster's liberal humanism. Jennings, like Forster, was an artist alert to all the forms of separateness in the world, and dedicated to finding modes of relation among them. Forster's famous phrase from *Howards End,* "the rainbow bridge that should connect the prose in us with the passion," is actually quoted in *Family Portrait,* while "Only connect," the epigraph of the novel, could equally well be an epigraph for all Jennings's films.[119]

The tone of condescension, of making things simple for an audience, is obvious in the question asked of Timothy and detectable elsewhere in Forster's script, as occasionally in the scripts of the other late documentaries. *Family Portrait* in particular can seem like a lecture accompanied by lantern slides; it is the sort of documentary which Thomas Colpeper from *A Canterbury Tale* would have produced for his captive audience, had he been a filmmaker. An important aspect of *Listen to Britain*'s distinctiveness is that it avoids this condescension, partly because it does without any sort of spoken commentary and the attendant risk of not setting the right tone, partly because it omits familiar quotations, with their flavor of the sermon or the textbook; but chiefly because it sets out to challenge its audiences' skills in putting together what they see and hear. It is genuinely exceptional among Jennings's works in this regard, an excursion into the making of cinematic implication. If it has a literary antecedent, that work is not some heritage text of the type recorded in *Words for Battle* or even, the film's closeness to *The Lion and the Unicorn* notwithstanding, Orwell's reportage. Rather, it is something remembered from study at Cambridge and the formative years of Jennings's intellectual life, namely the Modernist writing of the early twentieth century, with its repeated attempts to defeat expectations, reorder perceptions, make it new—the same writing which parallels the innovations of *A Canterbury Tale,* but in the case of Jennings, more engagingly rethought for the needs of a different sort of film.

In other words, if the Archers' work is the "Little Gidding" of the fictional cinema, *Listen to Britain* is *The Waste Land* of the documentary cinema. It stems, like Eliot's poem, from a surrealist taste, and just as *My Beautiful Laundrette* would do fifty years into the future, it sets its viewers the task of finding coherence among lovingly gathered cultural juxtapositions—"The Ash Grove" sung in the crypt of the Old Bailey, next to a marble statue and among hung-up ambulance drivers' helmets. *Listen to Britain* employs a rapidly metamorphosing style— "in Humphrey's mind, anyhow, the horse would rapidly dissolve into the steam engine and this would dissolve into something out of *Paradise Lost* and so on. Everything was always dissolving into something else"[120]—with Jennings's literal dissolves being the equivalent of Eliot's shape-shifting metaphors and half-buried allusions. The vignettes which suddenly take form in the midst of the miscellaneous sequences of *Listen to Britain* are like the short dramas emerging unpredictably from Eliot's poetic bric-a-brac—the pub-closing scene, the ascent to the Chapel Perilous. The film and poem both move with facility from monuments of high art to snippets of popular culture, and from the past to the present, as when in the National Gallery scene *Listen to Britain* cuts directly from the statue of Nelson on his pillar to the upright figure of a sailor looking out over Trafalgar Square. Jennings—or Jennings with McAllister—makes these images look much alike on the screen, two dark verticals centered on a bright field. In cinematographic terms, they form a graphic match, and accordingly "declare" that the sailor is as vital to the nation now as Nelson was in the nineteenth century. This is the mythological method of Modernism at work once more, the manipulating of a parallel between antiquity and contemporaneity. We see the sailor *becoming* Nelson before our eyes, just as in Eliot's poem we see Londoners of 1922 becoming the Fisher King or an Old Testament prophet, or as in *A Canterbury Tale* we see Bob, Alison, and Peter becoming pilgrims.

The Waste Land contains vestigial traces of the earlier, simpler genres from which it derives and which it is determined to supersede. Alone among Jennings's documentaries, *Listen to Britain* does something similar. When the film puts a series of discrete scenes before viewers, scenes made to be of equal importance and all on the same overall subject, it is hinting at its debt to an older dramatic genre, the same one which *A Canterbury Tale* rewrites—the village pageant, with the distinction that in Jennings's handling the pageant serves not the telling of a familiar story but the presenting of familiar actuality, and of an idea. After all, at the heart of Louis Napoleon Parker's old form is the notion of an audience seeing *itself,* joining collaboratively in the production of meaning (village inhabitants are the actors, recognizable locales are the set), and this notion lies at the heart of *Listen to Britain* too. To be sure, instead of sitting still while history is marched past them, the film's audience are carried about with Jennings's roving camera and microphone, but nevertheless they view scenes in a meaningful sequence, and those scenes accumulate until they define and celebrate Britain just as the pageants once defined and celebrated their small part of the country.

By the 1940s the old-fashioned pageant had dwindled into something precious and antique, or worse, into the pathetic form in which we glimpse it in Jennings's *Spare Time,* a tableau of Britannia with shield and trident being trundled past shabby crowds as the Manchester Victorians Jazz Band plays a slow-time version of "Rule, Britannia" on their kazoos. As we have seen, pageants had to be reinvented, theatrically and cinematically, for the mid-twentieth century—and Jennings undertakes this task at least as thoroughly as the Archers with their reworking of the genre, and far more imaginatively than Clemence Dane with "Cathedral Steps" or David MacDonald with *This England.* Jennings compresses his show as if under time pressure (nineteen minutes seems to be all that the war effort will allow) but expands its ideological scope by taking it out of the realm of significant great events. In such events, he is simply not interested, except as they briefly become visible in a statue or building. Contemporary Britain is his and his audience's concern— *Listen to Britain* has all the 1941ness that could be wished—and the vignettes of the film show episodes of daily life rather than the Victory of Waterloo or the Queen's Jubilee. This is to say that Jennings democratizes the pageant as well as dehistoricizes it. He casts his drama with ordinary men and women, in effect plucking Any Man and Any Woman from "Cathedral Steps" and giving them starring roles, and in the process he rescues pageantry from patronizing laughter. The audience here cannot laugh at the actors set before them; they *are* the actors. What is the true "pageant of history"?, Leonard Woolf, Virginia Woolf's husband, had asked in an essay. It is not the "mere cavalcade of kings and queens and great men and 'historical' events," but rather the "pageant of the ordinary man going about his ordinary work . . ."[121] It is this kind of pageant which *Listen to Britain* provides.

Moreover, Jennings's film sets the pageant in a new venue: not the country-house lawn or village green but the movie palace, or even more demotic sites. During the war documentary films were routinely shown in shelters, military bases, schools, and workplaces, and it is entirely possible that an audience for *Listen to Britain* could have watched Flanagan and Allen singing in the factory canteen while seated in a factory canteen themselves. Whatever the locale of the showings, there is abundant evidence that working-class people greatly enjoyed seeing their own work and their own pastimes brought back to them in this pageant about ordinariness:

> One of the non-theatrical films under the heading of "general" in our jargon which was liked and applauded was Humphrey Jennings's magical *Listen to Britain*. All sorts of audiences felt it to be a distillation and also a magnification of their own experience on the home front. Especially factory audiences. I remember one show at a factory in the Midlands where about 800 workers clapped and stamped approval. Films got very short shrift if they touched any area of people's experience and did not ring true.[122]

The most notable accomplishment of *Listen to Britain* is its bringing together ("Only connect" again seems the pertinent motto) of many disparate elements: working-class viewers with a filmmaker's avant-garde sensibility, Flanagan and Allen with T. S. Eliot, sounds with images, documentary authenticity with cinematic contrivance, an old-fashioned dramatic form with current happenings, audience with performers. Unity matters to Jennings. Like Woolf's Miss La Trobe, he holds mirrors up to ordinary Britons, reflecting their lives back to them, but he shares nothing of the melancholy of her close ("Dispersed are we . . ."), and he ends his pageant with a choral—rather than kazoo—performance of "Rule, Britannia."

TWO

AMERICAN GANGSTERS, ENGLISH CRIME FILMS, AND DENNIS POTTER

Still, maybe the boy friend Willie was getting all worked up about her, kidding himself that somebody was going to frame her for a murder. What damned rot! That sort of thing just didn't happen in England, it only happened in America and on the pictures—or did it?

PETER CHEYNEY, *URGENT HANGMAN* (1938)

In 1944, as if the bloodletting of the war were not enough, England was shaken by a violent crime at home, the Cleft Chin Murder. In this notorious affair, which judging by contemporary accounts provoked titillation and moral censure in equal measure, an American army deserter, Karl Hulten, and an aspirant English strip-tease artiste and nightclub hostess, Betty Jones, joined forces in a haphazard love affair and crime spree. Their *folie-à-deux* featured the killing of a London taxi driver—at first unidentified, the victim had a cleft chin which supplied the newspapers with a lurid headline—for pickings of £8, some of which Hulten and Jones spent in a cinema the next day, seeing Deanna Durbin in *Christmas Holiday*. Their spree also featured appallingly reckless and stupid attempts to get away, quick apprehension by the police, mutual recriminations in court, and finally the noose for him, long imprisonment for her.[1]

A half century later, in 1990, the Working Title film *Chicago Joe and the Showgirl* presented a fictionalized account of the Cleft Chin Murder, the second feature, as we will shortly see, to do so. As directed by Bernard Rose and written by David Yallop, *Chicago Joe and the Showgirl* stays relatively close to the facts of the case and unhesitatingly brings its violent sexuality out of the shadowy past. It is frank in depicting GIs copulating with tarts in the ruins of a bombed-out building, or revealing Betty Jones's arousal as she stares with a dreamy smile at a fight between soldiers in a London dance hall; frank also in its depiction of Jones and Hulten as pathetic inadequates, amateur actors lost in a rapidly developing drama which they never make meaningful, still less turn into a tragedy. For all its frankness, however, *Chicago Joe and the Showgirl* fails to provide much cinematic interest, as reviewers of the film were not slow to point out. What Rose does best is put on the screen Jones's and Hulten's movie-fascinated imaginations. The most interesting sequence of the film shows these two (separately) in a Hammersmith movie palace, transfixed by the sight of Fred MacMurray and Barbara Stanwyck onscreen in *Double Indemnity,* a scene from which is intercut with shots of the cinema audience, so that we go back and forth between two darkened, glamorously smoke-filled spaces, and two sets of characters with predatory gazes. Jones leans forward eagerly to mouth Stanwyck's lines, lighting her cigarette just as the star lights hers, and finally imagining (a clever special effect here) her boyfriend Hulten as wearing MacMurray's suit, speaking MacMurray's world-weary farewell, and finally firing a gun at his trampy lover.

This is a melodramatic moment, Betty Jones in the process of being simultaneously thrilled and ruined by Hollywood, but scarcely an unbelievable one, given what we know about the influence of American crime films on English audiences. Betty Jones was hardly alone in fancying herself an American *femme fatale* and trying hard to dress the part; other young women wore their hair in an on-the-shoulders mode copied from Veronica Lake. Nor were young women the only fans. We know of at least one razorman for the Kings Cross mob in London who donned black suits and white ties in imitation of George Raft.[2] The real issue of influence, however, involves something more than mass-audience clothes and hairstyles. It involves the two countries' film industries; it involves the question of how the English *cinema* has had to negotiate with and around an all-pervading transatlantic influence—the extent to which it too might be thought thrilled and ruined by Hollywood. And few would disagree that the problem of negotiating has been most acute with the very genre *Chicago Joe and the Showgirl* represents, the crime film—by which I mean not country-house mystery stories or courtroom dramas or police procedurals (all genres in which English filmmaking has had indigenous traditions to guide it), but rather films focusing on criminals themselves, their lawbreaking, their alluring violence, their distinctive language and dress, the gangland milieus which spawn them.

Starting with the 1930s (at least), American crime films have moved ceaselessly and provocatively across English screens, drawing audiences together in spite of generational or class divisions. "James Cagney was the one up both our streets," the poet Tony Harrison has written in an elegy for his working-class Leeds father; Cagney's "was the only art we ever shared."[3] No less has the American crime cinema fascinated English filmmakers, creating narrative conventions so compelling as to seem classical, inevitable. Behind every English gangster biopic has been the pattern established early on by *Little Caesar* and *Scarface* and *The Public Enemy,* just as behind each potential homegrown film noir have loomed the dark shadows, listless tempos, and betraying dames of American pictures like *Criss Cross* and *Out of the Past.* Behind a film like *Chicago Joe and the Showgirl,* determining its themes and techniques no less insistently than the historical Cleft Chin Murder, stands a long line of American sex-and-crime-spree thrillers: *Double Indemnity* itself, Joseph H. Lewis's B-picture *Gun Crazy,* Arthur Penn's *Bonnie and Clyde.* No one could miss these influences; no one could evaluate *Chicago Joe and the Showgirl* without taking them into account. "Awkward gangster pastiche," "as dangerously hooked on fantasy worlds as Chicago Joe and the Showgirl themselves," "it quotes feverishly," "a major larceny from *Sunset Boulevard,*" critics wrote of the Rose film, lamenting its derivativeness, its inability to cope with the burden of everything American preceding it.[4]

Coping with the burden is precisely the subject of this chapter: how English filmmaking has felt the threat of derivativeness and responded to it, how in a wide range of screen works—some determinedly local like *Hell Is a City* or *The Long Good Friday,* some assertively Americanized like *Stormy Monday* or *Empire State*—the contest between the home-produced article and the glamorous import has been played out. This subject is obviously part of a much larger issue, the defining of postwar Englishness, the nation's contested, fractious, enlightening, ongoing conversation about what its cultural identity is and how that identity might be maintained in the face of a powerful American influence. The subject also involves social and cultural understandings of crime itself, the admission that violent lawbreaking can be luridly thrilling, countered by the acknowledgement of how much, in terms of human suffering and pain, it finally costs. Among the twentieth-century intellectuals writing on the subject, George Orwell was the first to understand and articulate its larger ramifications, which is why I will begin with essays of his which direly contemplate the Cleft Chin Murder and attack what he saw as the popular-culture products of a newly depraved English taste, above all James Hadley Chase's novel *No Orchids for Miss Blandish*. Orwell's essays will in turn furnish terms for defining a particularly domestic and English kind of crime film, exemplified by David MacDonald's film *Good Time Girl,* the first screen work based on Hulten and Jones's spree, then by 1940s features—*It Always Rains on Sunday, Brighton Rock, They Made Me a Fugitive* (all three works deriving from domestic crime novels)—followed by Mike Hodges's masterpiece from 1970, *Get Carter,* taken in concert with its fictional source; and finally by Dennis Potter's television miniseries *The Singing Detective.* If the film versions of *No Orchids for Miss Blandish* and *Good Time Girl,* in their timid imitativeness, their copying of the superficies and shying away from the essentials of American-style gangland violence, represent one sort of encounter with Hollywood, the engagement with criminal narratives fantasticated in *The Singing Detective* represents another, an altogether more complex and impressive engagement, as will become clear. Potter's television drama goes in all sorts of directions—musical, parodistic, autobiographical, political—without ever losing sight of its main themes: the causes of violence, the crime of betrayal, and the bringing of both American thuggery and an American private-eye's toughness to bear redemptively on English family history.

GEORGE ORWELL VERSUS JAMES HADLEY CHASE

In *A Canterbury Tale,* as we have seen, a Yank debates national values with two Brits and then joins them to hunt down the Glueman, thus adumbrating the cultural alliance between homelands which the war made strategically desirable, and which a great many wartime films held up for admiration. But even the most celebratory of these blood-is-thicker-than-water productions, say for example the Archers' *A Matter of Life and Death,* could and did express doubts. At the center of *A Matter* is the celestial dispute between English and American civilization, a *Kulturkampf* ending awkwardly in a legal stand-off, with the raucous voices of the competing advocates still sounding and with the national animosities left in place, unrebutted and mildly disquieting. For all the coziness of the Anglo-American romance at film's end, questions linger. Is the gap between the two nations truly unbridgeable? Is there (to take the English perspective) something not just unintelligible but inherently corrupting about American civilization, and the more corrupting because of its glamour?

Questions like these have of course been habitually raised by English writers, from Matthew Arnold onward, but beginning with the 1930s they were raised with a new intensity, raised in order to be answered in variation after variation upon that most English of twentieth-century critical themes, the inferiority of American demotic culture, especially as exported in the most American of all forms, the cinema. F. R. Leavis's *Mass Civilisation and Minority Culture* (1930) is a representative document in the indictment. This pamphlet, published in and very much addressed to Cambridge, sweepingly denounces the Americanization of the Press and the disastrous potency of Hollywood films. The latter, Leavis says, "involve surrender, under conditions of hypnotic receptivity, to the cheapest emotional appeals, appeals the more insidious because they are associated with a compellingly vivid illusion of actual life."[5] Graham Greene wrote for a much wider audience and in a more generous spirit, and his film reviewing of the 1930s praises this Hollywood production or that, *These Three* or *Barbary Coast,* this American performer or that, W. C. Fields or Bette Davis, but nevertheless, time and time again, scorns the vulgarity of "the great New World," its "sentimental idealism," its "hollow optimism about human nature." At his most captious Greene could scarcely restrain his old-world loathing for the "unformed unlined faces" of youths in American films: "clean-limbed prize cattle mooing into the microphone. . . . What use in pretending that with these allies [Greene is now looking back at

World War I] it was ever possible to fight for civilization?"[6] For the novelist and journalist J. B. Priestley, not vulgarity and naiveté but American materialism was the target—indeed, the threat— in that the materialism seemed importable, as Emeric Pressburger and E. M. Forster had also feared. Priestley's 1934 travel book *English Journey* is dismayed at the prospect of England being littered by such American cultural bric-a-brac as "arterial and by-pass roads . . . filling stations and factories that look like exhibition buildings . . . giant cinemas and dance-halls and cafés, bungalows with tiny garages, cocktail bars, Woolworths, motor-coaches, wireless, hiking, factory girls looking like actresses, greyhound racing and dirt tracks, swimming pools, and everything given away for cigarette coupons."[7] By far the most interesting of these writerly attacks, however, most interesting because it brought the most considered and specific complaint against American civilization, came during the war, when within three months of the release of *A Canterbury Tale* George Orwell wrote a short critical essay, "Raffles and Miss Blandish," publishing it in *Horizon* in the autumn of 1944.

Far from celebrating an Archers-style alliance between nations, "Raffles and Miss Blandish" argues that a violent American importation is threatening a stable and time-honored aspect of Englishness— namely, the country's perspective on crime and criminals. From the start, Orwell takes a frankly Manichaean view: "a time when people had standards . . . Now for a header into the cesspool."[8] He locates old-fashioned, home-grown standards in the turn-of-the-century *Raffles* stories of E. W. Hornung, the cesspool in James Hadley Chase's sensational 1939 bestseller *No Orchids for Miss Blandish*. Chase was an Englishman but, luckily for Orwell's argument, an Englishman profoundly and obviously influenced by American pulp fiction writers, and by William Faulkner, the plot of whose *Sanctuary,* as Orwell observes, Chase "impudently" copies in *No Orchids.*

The essay argues that while Raffles, gentleman cracksman, cricketer, and man about town, may survive by burgling the country houses of his society friends, he at least lives according to a well understood code of behavior, or set of chivalric-sporting instincts, and moreover commits his thefts almost entirely without violence. He finally expiates such wrongdoing he has been guilty of by dying gallantly in the Boer War. In stark contrast, the hero-villain Slim Grisson of *No Orchids,* thug and rapist, lives entirely in a world of betrayal, kidnapping (of the Miss Blandish of the title, a millionaire's daughter), torture, and sexual perversion—"eight full-dress murders, an unassessable number of casual killings and woundings, an exhumation (with a careful reminder of the stench), the flogging of Miss Blandish, the torture of another woman with redhot cigarette ends, a strip-tease act, a third-degree scene of unheard-of cruelty . . ."[9] Thus Orwell adds all the degradations up, as reportorially precise as in the 1930s he had documented scenes of poverty in London or Wigan. The police of *No Orchids* are no less brutal than the gangsters, he notes, and the novel ends not with acts of justice or expiation but with Slim's meaningless death, followed immediately by the ruined Miss Blandish's suicide. In Chase's novel, it is as if the kindly Anglophilia of Sergeant Bob Johnson, with his readiness to share woodlore and his longings for connection to the old country, has been supplanted by America at its sleazy worst, the gangsters' underworld depicted in the "American crook film" or in "Yank Mags"—pulp novelettes imported to Britain as ballast in ships, then sold cheaply to people starved for reading matter.

Is all this violence owing to the mingled "boredom and brutality" of the war? Orwell traces it further back than that, to the "power-worship" of the early twentieth century:

> Chase is presenting, as it were, a distilled version of the modern political scene, in which such things as mass bombings of civilians, the use of hostages, torture to obtain confessions, secret prisons, execution without trial, floggings with rubber truncheons, drownings in cesspools, systematic falsification of records and statistics, treachery, bribery and quislingism are normal and morally neutral, even admirable when done in a large and bold way.

The hypothesis is distressing enough to the future author of *1984*, but not the most distressing thing to him, which is that power politics have made their debut in England and that the English view of crime may in fact be less morally superior than it seems. After all, even before the arrival of those corrupting Yang Mags and crook films, the thrillers of the *English* novelist Edgar Wallace showed themselves to be suffused with bully-worship of the police and a "fearful intellectual sadism," and now

Orwell's homeland has taken transatlantic amorality and brutality yet closer to heart:

> the career of Mr. Chase shows how deep the American influence has already gone. Not only is he himself living a continuous fantasy-life in the Chicago underworld, but he can count on hundreds of thousands of readers who know what is meant by "clipshop" or the "hotsquat," do not have to do mental arithmetic when confronted by "fifty grand," and understand at sight a sentence like "Johnnie was a rummy and only two jumps ahead of the nut-factory." Evidently there are great numbers of English people who are partly Americanised in language and, one ought to add, in moral outlook. For there was no popular protest against *No Orchids*.[10]

Given Orwell's faith in the defining gentleness of English civilization, as described in *The Lion and the Unicorn* and portrayed there in affectionately gathered images of national life ("the bus conductors are good-tempered and the policemen carry no revolvers"), it is easy to see why *No Orchids* alarmed him. The Chase novel concocts a world in which the police carry revolvers freely, use them at will, and are apparently admired by English readers for doing so.

Two years after "Raffles and Miss Blandish" Orwell produced a companion piece in "Decline of the English Murder," which again juxtaposes the English and the American conceptions of crime. This time the contrast is made on aesthetic rather than ethical grounds, and deals with actual rather than fictional cases. In the recent past, Orwell says, we find the classical English murder as committed by intensely middle-class figures like Dr. Crippen[11] or Joseph Smith, with its atmosphere of stifling respectability, its careful advance planning, its struggles within the murderer's conscience. Such a background permits a crime to have "dramatic and even tragic qualities which make it memorable and excite pity for both victim and murderer." These "old domestic poisoning dramas," Orwell claims, were products "of a stable society where the all-prevailing hypocrisy did at least ensure that crimes as serious as murder should have strong emotions behind them." Now, however, we have a different paradigm, the Cleft Chin Murder, in which there was "no depth of feeling . . . The background was not domesticity, but the anonymous life of the dance-halls and the false values of the American film . . . movie-palaces, cheap perfume, false names and stolen cars."[12] When he reviewed films for *Time and Tide* in the early years of the war, Orwell had frequently expressed a Graham Greene-like disdain for Hollywood productions—insisting on "the intellectual contempt which American film producers seem to feel for their audience," their "utter lack of any decent, intelligent vision of life"[13]—but now, in the pages of "Decline of the English Murder," critical scorn has been sharpened into large-scale cultural diagnosis.

Needless to say, Orwell's essays scarcely impeded the career of James Hadley Chase, who published more than ninety crime novels after *No Orchids,* most set in America, a number of them made into French or Italian films. Nor did it prevent the development, in time, of an English imagination of crime, both in fiction and films, fully as violent as anything imported from America: the early twenty-first century world of, for example, Terry Winsor's *Essex Boys* and Paul McGuigan's *Gangster No. 1* and Julian Simpson's *The Criminal.* The significance of "Raffles and Miss Blandish" and "Decline of the English Murder" lies elsewhere than in the realm of practical morality. It lies in the exceptional clarity and the sense of urgency (this still comes off the page, half a century after the essays were written) with which they connect the ideas of crime and national identity and thus initiate a debate. This debate has been an informal and intermittent one, conducted largely without Orwell's moralizing terms, and not even in his mode of the discursive essay. Rather, as Orwell himself foresaw would happen more clearly than anyone, it has been conducted in the operations of popular culture: the crafting of scripts and fictional plots, the composition of key images, the reporting on and reviewing of the media; the day-to-day business of taste-making, of producing, diffusing, and responding to cultural ideas—which is to say the slow formation, on the widest possible scale, of national attitudes and assumptions.

What he foresaw with even more clarity was how pertinent to such a debate the nation's attitude to crime and criminals would be, crime being a nexus in which themes of violence and rebellion, isolation and community, order and morality, suffering and excitement, indeed civilization and all its discontents, would be revealingly gathered. About all this Orwell was no narrow-minded puritan, nor even a narrow-minded patriot. He well understood the seductive glamour, especially in the grey and still-rationed life of England immediately after 1945, of American modes of criminality, tacitly acknowledging that glamour even for himself in the way the prose of his essays curls so attentively around this or that detail of transatlantic brutality, a rape here, a precisely described bludgeoning there. And he realized that for others—for countless Betty Joneses, dreaming their blood-spattered dreams to the beat of American pop music, the roar of big American cars, the rat-a-tat-tat of American guns—the glamour might be most seductively communicated on-screen. Hence his essays' perturbed fascination with the "false values of the American film" coming out of movie palaces into English life.

No Orchids for Miss Blandish was made into a highly successful West End play, as "Raffles and Miss Blandish" notes in passing, but Orwell's disquiet about the novel would surely have deepened had he known that its glamorization of criminal brutality would be further disseminated in a *film*—worse yet, an English film, one made by Renown Pictures in 1948, with the Englishman George Minter as its producer (in his first studio assignment), and with script and direction by the Englishman St. John Legh Clowes (in his last studio assignment). While Orwell apparently never saw the *No Orchids* film, other reviewers stood in for him in attacking it, though in cruder terms than he would have used:

> the most sickening exhibition of brutality, perversion, sex and sadism ever to be shown on the cinema screen . . . a script laden with suggestive dialogue. All the women are sluts and most of the men vicious murderers. One after another come scenes of unpleasant bedroom interludes and revolting orgies of beating-up and murder almost on the scale of massacre.

On and on the censorious judgments go ("sordid and unedifying," "unbridled viciousness"); in the opinion of one editorialist, arguing desperately against widespread local attempts to ban screenings of *No Orchids,* no film in the history of British show business had ever had such a "ruthlessly condemnatory Press."[14]

There are indeed beatings in *No Orchids,* as well as passionate kisses exchanged between the film's Miss Blandish (the English actress Linden Travers, who had starred in the stage production) and its Slim Grisson (the American B-movie star Jack La Rue). And beatings and kisses are not the only features faithfully copied from American gangster films. We are given also the slangy dialogue, the big-city nightclub and the seedy roadhouse, the car stick-up, the police radio calls setting up a dragnet. One or two moments imitate perfectly the style, melodramatic but with sparing means, by which Hollywood was crafting film noir in the late 1940s, as when Miss Blandish emerges from a locked room to meet her captor for the first time, and into the silence breaks the expressive nasty rattle of Slim's dice thrown on a plate. The film is saturated with this sort of B-movie aesthetic, even with an awareness of B-movies: "She's got class!" exclaims one character, and gets the response back: "Sure, they all got it now. It's the movies." Meanwhile the stand-up comic in the nightclub floorshow does impersonations of Sidney Greenstreet and Peter Lorre.

But is this *No Orchids* really "a sickening exhibition of brutality"? The stridency of English reviewers' attacks on it must seem astonishing to anyone who has actually watched the film, for the ironic truth is that, even by the standards of the period, Legh Clowes's work is relatively restrained in depicting violence and perversion, reluctant or unable to match American films in moral nihilism. Many of its beatings are kept well off-camera, for instance. Moreover, Slim Grisson, far from sharing any sort of perverse or degraded relation with Miss Blandish, actually grows to be devoted to her, acting, as Robert Murphy has observed, "the perfect gentleman—like a shy, polite Humphrey Bogart . . . [he] risks, and loses, everything in a bid to save their doomed romance."[15] Indeed, the romance is as much domestic as doomed. Toward the film's close, Slim and Miss Blandish, together in an isolated cabin, breakfast cozily on trout cooked by the gangster himself. In this respect, *No Orchids* is the approximate cinematic analogue to the crime thrillers produced before and after the war by the English novelist Peter Cheyney. Books like *Urgent Hangman* or *Uneasy Terms,* the latter another artifact of 1947, center on a private eye named Slim Callaghan. He may be good with his fists and may grin as sardonically as Dashiell Hammett's Sam Spade, his obvious prototype, but Callaghan is courtly, occasionally even sentimental, around women, whether they are his clients, the seductive suspects of his cases, or young damsels in distress, like the seventeen-year-old in *Uneasy Terms* who adopts the same Veronica Lake coiffure as

Betty Jones.[16] In Callaghan, hardboiled ruthlessness is tempered by old-fashioned chivalry, just as (more ludicrously) his speech is an amalgam of private-eye slang and upper-class English.

The same year which saw *No Orchids* and *Uneasy Terms* also brought an English film version of the Cleft Chin Murder. This was *Good Time Girl*, directed by David MacDonald for Rank, with a script by Muriel and Sydney Box after Arthur La Bern's engagingly noir-titled novel *Night Darkens the Street*. La Bern was a crime novelist of considerable ambition and interest—one of his later thrillers became (in 1972) the source of Hitchcock's next-to-last film, *Frenzy*—and for *Night Darkens the Street* he freely adapted the incidents of Hulten and Jones's escapade, shaping from them a clinical study of delinquency and violence. His anti-heroine, Gwen Rawlings, runs away from home, becomes a hat-check girl in a Soho nightclub, and being unjustly convicted of theft, is sent to a reform school. From this she escapes, only to fall in first with flash Brighton gamblers, then with AWOL American GIs, and in a drunken accident behind the wheel of a car she kills a bicyclist.

It is not just hard luck and poverty which push Gwen toward her crime. She is as much a media victim as Cheyney's seventeen-year-old or as the real-life Betty Jones, who had worked as a cinema usherette and who kept a scrapbook with details of film stars' lives. In terms which might have been borrowed from Orwell, La Bern attributes Gwen's downfall to Hollywood:

> In her jejune mind screen plays were not something to be measured against the warp and woof of reality. To Gwen Rawlings life itself was measured against the technicolor pattern of romance as viewed from the cinema stalls, and in this comparison it was not surprising that life itself was found wanting. . . . She regarded herself as a heavenly blending of all the sweetest physical attributes of Veronica Lake, Ginger Rogers, and Gene Tierney—but without their opportunities in life. Her father she regarded as a shaggy-moustached Wallace Beery but not so lovable. Her brothers and sisters were Dead End Kids, but not so amusing. Her mother was Louise Rainer in a depressing role.[17]

In MacDonald's film all this movie consciousness is reduced to a few pin-ups of Hollywood stars above Gwen's bed, but the more significant change from La Bern's book is a noticeable softening of violence and a muting of sex. Exactly as with *No Orchids,* the virulence of the reviewers' diatribes against *Good Time Girl* ("as unedifying a specimen of the gentle sex as the screen has given us"; "it made me vomit")[18] seems bizarrely at odds with the actual work—which surrounds Gwen's story with a moralizing frame and which carefully sets those few beatings and stabbings it does depict in shadowy obscurity. When the sleazy owner of the Blue Angel Club refuses to take Gwen on as a hat-check girl without assessing the shapeliness of her legs, she reluctantly hikes up her skirt for him, but not for the camera, which retreats bashfully behind a desk. The fact is that *Good Time Girl*, far from being a header into the cesspool, is a celluloid sermon against adolescent rebellion, as *No Orchids* is a noir love story, *Brief Encounter* with gunplay. No doubt the cautiousness of both films testifies to the power of English cinema censorship,[19] but whether they are merely timorous, or bespeak a lingering English habit of decency, the end result is that they play with a made-in-the-USA amorality only to reject, soften, or (in their occasional ineptitudes) mismanage it. They might finally have reassured Orwell.

CONTENDING WITH AMERICA

To survey the English crime film in the second half of the twentieth century is to see variety, of course, in technique, settings, ranges of ambitiousness, degrees of accomplishment; but variety above all in the ways films have responded to the American crime cinema. There has been resistance to Hollywood and frank copying of Hollywood, assertions of independence, postmodern denials that "independence" is meaningful, adaptations, exercises in quotation or pastiche. English films have joined *Chicago Joe and the Showgirl* in featuring characters besotted with American crime movies, as with *Gumshoe* (1971), Stephen Frears's second directorial assignment, featuring a trenchcoat-wearing nightclub comedian who dreams private-eye dreams. English films have portrayed villains talking like Americans, or trying to; the legal issue on which Peter Medak's meticulous real-life drama of 1991, *Let Him Have It,* turns, involves the four fateful words of the title. Spoken on a rooftop from one cornered burglar to another, do they mean "give the policeman your gun"—their English meaning, one might say—or rather what they convey in a hundred Hollywood B-pictures, "shoot the cop"? There have been odd shiftings of locale, as in Michael Winner's 1978 remake of *The Big Sleep*, its action transferred from Southern California to London, and there have been depictions of internationalized crime, as in Danny Cannon's 1993 *The Young Americans*, in which the London drug turf is disputed between transatlantic invaders and old-fashioned East End villains. An American film about an English crook in America, Steven Soderbergh's *The Limey* (1999), is matched by an English film about an American crook in England, Jules Dassin's *Night and the City* (1950). In the latter, Americanness is imported to the old country not only in the crook's hustling success ethic but in the "popularised Freudianism that underpins the scenario."[20]

Within highly conventionalized subcategories of the crime film, there have been varieties of response to Hollywood too. Consider the heist movie. Here, American works from the 1950s like John Huston's *The Asphalt Jungle,* Stanley Kubrick's *The Killing,* and Robert Wise's *Odds against Tomorrow,* established a repertoire of themes and images— the reluctant villain drawn into one last foolproof caper, plan-making around a scarred kitchen table, suspicions of treachery or squealing to the cops, the explosive confrontation with safe or bank vault or armored car, getaway vehicles careening through city streets—seemingly not to be avoided. Certainly English heist films from the succeeding decade, like *The Italian Job* (Peter Collinson, 1969) and *A Prize of Arms* (Cliff Owen, 1962), do not avoid them. Nor do the more recent works, *Sexy Beast* (Jonathan Glazer, 2001) and *Face* (Antonia Bird, 1997), for all their insistence on clever variations, as with the former's ironic ending and underwater vault break-in, the latter's political outspokenness, its laying of criminal recidivism at the door of Thatcherite policies (Bird makes sure we notice politics by prominently including in the mise-en-scène a poster for Ken Loach's film *Hidden Agenda*). Nor are Hollywood conventions entirely avoided in humorous versions of the heist film, like Charles Crichton's *The Lavender Hill Mob* of 1951 or Alexander Mackendrick's *The Ladykillers* of 1955. In both these Ealing productions, the humor lies precisely in a clash of differing cinematic conventions, the clichés of Ealing cosiness opposed by the clichés of criminal enterprise. In both, too, violence is mostly sublimated into verbal contests, the traditional mode of English high comedy, though a whisper of violence remains to remind viewers of the dark worlds from which their plots derive. There is more than a whisper of violence, meanwhile, in a late 1990s version of the comic heist film like Guy Ritchie's *Lock, Stock and Two Smoking Barrels* (1998). For that reason, Ritchie's work seems yet more American-influenced than the Ealing films, even as it continues to trade in verbal comedy, for example in its playful subtitling of a dialogue sequence spoken in Cockney rhyming slang.

In seeming contrast to all these works, Basil Dearden's *The League of Gentlemen* (1960) works hard to establish its idiosyncrasy and its Englishness. This film's criminal mastermind, an ex-Colonel resentful at being shelved by the Army, nevertheless follows Army methods in logistics and recruiting, gathering about him a group of similarly cashiered or compromised officers to form a commando, keeping them all to a militarily precise schedule, insisting on discipline, as if to assert the superiority of home-grown criminal tactics, to prove that breeding matters. Englishness is a still more prominent theme in *Hell Is a City* (1960), written and directed by Val Guest. In this, strictly speaking a murder-and-robbery rather than a heist film, the emphasis falls as much on the dogged police as on the ruthless criminals. The ends of justice are fully served (in the conclusion, the chief crook Don Starling is hanged), and violence is kept within certain decent limits. For example, when an errant wife (an early role for Billie Whitelaw) sees her unloved husband struck down by her boyfriend Starling, she reacts with horror, not pleasure; in moral outlook, she has not yet been Americanized, as Orwell would say. Moreover, the Manchester setting of *Hell Is a City* is painstakingly conveyed, insisted on, in location shooting of the city's random traffic and in careful recording of Mancunian voices. In what the director later deemed a "documentary" style, the film takes the trouble to depict such a curious local custom as "tossing schools"—cloth-capped men gathering in deserted sites outside the city to bet on coins being tossed in the air—as if anthropology, not crime, were on the agenda. Even the film's title, which sounds like something dreamed up by Warner Brothers for a B-picture, is home-grown, being taken from a poem by Shelley, as is disclosed in a scrap of dialogue in the Maurice Procter novel which Guest adapted for his screenplay.[21]

Significantly, though, and despite their assertive Englishness, both Dearden's film and Guest's seem constrained to hint at something American in their distant backgrounds, in the very nature of the violent genre to which they belong. The Don Starling of *Hell Is a City*, a Man-

chester boy in Procter's novel, in the film is played by the American actor John Crawford, speaking throughout in a frank American accent.
Whatever the motive for this bit of casting,[22] its effect is to link snarling
Americanness with the character's exceptional brutality; as he is being
taken into custody, Starling kicks the police detective who lies shot and
bleeding at his feet. As for *The League of Gentlemen,* when the Colonel
in that film forms his gang he sends prospective members a copy of a
paperback book, *The Golden Fleece,* described as being by the American
writer "John Seaton," which supplies, he says, the perfect plan. America,
in other words, is made out as the home of criminal ingenuity. (In fact,
the source of Bryan Forbes's screenplay for the film is a 1958 novel by the
English writer John Boland.)

Onscreen in the crime cinema, books like *The Golden Fleece* are no
less convenient and telling props than they are in *A Canterbury Tale,*
economically suggesting an American affiliation or theme or debt. *Look
Swell in a Shroud* is the fictitious American thriller being savored by
Mrs. Chalk and Henry Holland in *The Lavender Hill Mob.* A real American thriller, Dashiell Hammett's *The Thin Man,* is being read in Penguin paperback by the would-be detective in *Gumshoe,* while a second
American work in the genre, Raymond Chandler's *Farewell, My Lovely,*
appears at the start of Mike Hodges's *Get Carter,* where it is read by
Jack Carter as he travels to Newcastle on his mission of vengeance. A
bus passenger in Hodges's later (1972) *Pulp* leafs through the American
magazine *True Detective.* Clearly, the books and the magazine are not
casual features of the mise-en-scène but deliberate allusions. They are
specific tributes from filmmakers (not from authors: in the Ted Lewis
novel which was the source of *Get Carter,* Jack's train reading is *Pent-
house*) to the world from which they have taken their inspiration. In
Get Carter, Hodges may have meant the allusion to be sharply limited
in meaning; he has claimed that the point was merely the valedictory
title *Farewell, My Lovely*—a way of bidding a proleptic farewell to the
hero, since the man who will eventually shoot Carter is seated opposite
him in the train as he reads.[23] Still, the allusion is there, just as it is in
a film which probably influenced Hodges, Godard's *Alphaville* (1965),
with its early shot of the hero Lemmy Caution reading *Le Grand Som-
meil,* the French translation of Chandler's *The Big Sleep.* (Lemmy Caution himself, played by the American actor Eddie Constantine, is yet

another hardboiled character invented after American prototypes by Peter Cheyney.) With aesthetic gestures of this sort Hodges and Godard prepare for the way for the even more sophisticated *hommages* of late twentieth-century filmmaking, for the kinds of cinematic relatedness playfully insisted on by *Chicago Joe and the Showgirl* or by Richard Loncraine and Ian McKellen's 1995 film version of *Richard III*. The latter is a gangster biopic of sorts, though one based on Shakespeare's history play rather than sagas of Al Capone or Legs Diamond. At the climax of the film, the villainous king, cornered by the soon-to-be-victorious Richmond, throws himself into flames exactly in the manner of Cody Jarrett, the James Cagney character in *White Heat* (1949), throwing himself off the burning chemical-plant tower into perdition. At the moment of royal immolation we hear on the *Richard III* soundtrack the song "I'm Sitting on Top of the World," a reference to Jarrett's famous dying cry "top of the world, Ma."[24] It is only fitting that a flamboyantly cinematic work like this version of *Richard III* should by these means declare its debt to a film. That it should be an American film complements the concept of McKellen's production, with its depiction of an easy commerce between nations (Queen Elizabeth and her relatives are American; we see Rivers arrive in a transatlantic airliner).

Commerce between England and America is notably more complicated in English crime films of the 1980s, which, as John Hill has argued, were produced with an ambitiousness new to the genre. Not only do they fuse "thriller formats with the stylistic and thematic preoccupations of traditional art cinema," they make a point of combining "gangster story-lines with a degree of social and political commentary."[25] That is, they have something explicit or implicit to say about the condition of urban Englishness in the late twentieth century, and confirm that Englishness can hardly be contemplated without an assessment of American-English relations. Three films in particular focus on the theme of national rivalry and for that reason call for closer examination: *Empire State, Stormy Monday,* and *The Long Good Friday.*

Ron Peck's *Empire State* (1987) is a survey of male prostitutes, petty gangsters, drunken club-goers, and legitimate though greedy businessmen and women, viewed in grimly Hogarthian caricature, though this cinematic analogue to *Gin Lane* or *The Rake's Progress* entirely lacks Hogarth's encompassing moral sensibility. All of Peck's characters are on the make, all striving for imported dollars in an East End itself in the process of becoming crassly Americanized. A mural of the Manhattan skyline decorates the "Empire State" dance club.[26] A 1950 Pontiac convertible appears conspicuously in the ravaged docklands, emblem of the moneyed world and the quasi-Imperial power for which these English hustlers yearn. (American cars turn up in the English crime cinema with astonishing frequency: in *Let Him Have It,* in John Guillermin's *Never Let Go,* in *Get Carter* in the form of a massive Cadillac sedan.) A newspaper editor in *Empire State,* sending his reporter out to get a lurid story, can find no better model for what he's after than a transatlantic one: "bring me back . . . an American detective novel, Dashiell Hammett." In the end, the ruthless American investor goes home with his millions intact, and the English characters fall into graphically depicted bare-knuckle fighting and gunplay, as if to insist that if London cannot have overseas funding, it can at least have overseas violence. The film's title hints that the nation now enjoys a merely colonial status, but beyond this *Empire State* hardly cares to go. The meaning it is contented with conveying is the meaninglessness of life as suffered or enjoyed by these particular contemporary Londoners.

Stormy Monday (1988), Mike Figgis's debut feature as writer and director, is a more accomplished work, to begin with because it has a noticeable style. This appears to derive entirely from Hollywood. As commentators noted, *Stormy Monday* is a film "in love with the look and the sound of the US," a film so noir-influenced that it is *about* "the way light falls on wet pavement stones, and about how a neon sign glows in a darkened doorway . . . about lonely furnished rooms . . ."[27] Car headlights probe down nighttime streets; the camera peeps in on lovers through a windscreen sheeted with rain. Visual touches like these obviously belong to an art-cinema aesthetic, a movie-fascinated consciousness, and yet they also seem requisite for the depiction of a provincial city, Newcastle, which even more completely than the East End of *Empire State* has been enthralled by American popular culture. In the course of the film we are treated to the Muzak and glitter of a Newcastle shopping mall, to the city's chromium-plated bars, to its restaurants (one of them named "Weegee" in homage to the famous American tabloid photographer), and to its clubs, in front of which bouncers stand wearing New York City cop uniforms. That in Newcastle a commercial promotion happens to be going on—"America Week," with a giant Pepsi balloon and red-white-and-blue bunting everywhere—merely exaggerates the normal state of things, the facts of late twentieth-century commercial and pop-cultural life. To be sure, not every aspect of America is successfully copied. At one point, a marching band parades down the street, just as it does in the same Newcastle setting in *Get Carter:* Mike Figgis's homage to Mike Hodges, it may be. But the effect in *Stormy Monday* is closer to the pathos of the marching kazoo band photographed in Humphrey Jennings's pre-war documentary *Spare Time,* that is, the pathos of the English trying hard but failing to catch the right tone of razzmatazz. Brendan, a jazz fan and drifter at the center of Figgis's plot, is trying pathetically hard himself, wishing he had the money to revisit the States, keeping posters of Manhattan on his bedroom walls, a copy of Hemingway next to the bed. As the critic Charlotte Brunsdon has observed, the only intrusion of "British naturalist space" into Brendan's world is the rotting windowsill of his room.[28] Out of this window he stares blankly at the gray townscape, a version of Jimmy Porter in Richardson's film of *Look Back in Anger,* but consumed with blues-tinged longing rather than trumpet-blared anger.

Brendan's antagonist is Cosmo, a suave thug of an American businessman, topcoated, smoking cigars, gladhanding the locals, bent on redeveloping the Tyneside quays even if a few businesses have to be forced out of the way and a few city councilors bribed. He is the embodiment of attractive ruthlessness, like the old-fashioned cinematic gangsters (Paul Muni's Scarface, Jimmy Cagney's Tom Powers) who are clearly his ancestors. A Minnesota girl, Kate, is vaguely attached to Cosmo but breaks from him to start an affair with Brendan. This is a *folie-à-deux* of innocents, a partnership reversing the nationalities of the Cleft Chin Murder pair and also reversing their fate, since Brendan and Kate are more hurt (Cosmo's thugs beat them up) than they hurt others. In the end, they escape the bomb Cosmo has planted in their car, but the real triumph of the film is an ethical one, a temporary victory for English decency and local independence. Brendan is tempted to shoot Cosmo when he has the chance, administering street justice, but finally drops his gun and walks away, while the Newcastle jazz club owner who has been negotiating a sell-out to the American refuses the deal and decides to stay on. *Stormy Monday* is thus a story about denying transatlantic violence and rapacity even while there is no chance—in cinematic style, especially— of refusing transatlantic culture; it is a parable of resistance and acquiescence.

By far the most considerable of this trio of films is *The Long Good Friday*, John Mackenzie's study of the sudden downfall of the racketeer Harold Shand. Widely and rightly praised on its release in 1981, *The Long Good Friday* benefited from shooting on several well-chosen London locations (a stock-car racing track, docks on the Isle of Dogs, a Brixton street, a tarted-up riverside pub); it is as deliberately localized a work as *Hell Is a City*. *The Long Good Friday* also benefited from a fine cast including Bob Hoskins as Shand, and from a brilliant screenplay by the East End playwright Barrie Keeffe, whose only film work this is, and who in creating it drew on personal memories of the twin Kray brothers, gangsters and folk-lore heroes.[29] The plot, complicated enough to be challenging for first-time viewers to follow, nevertheless holds together with perfect logic—in part, it may be, because the logic eventually seems familiar, that of classic Hollywood gangster biopics: the violent hero, commander of a criminal empire, overreaches himself and is finally brought down by successors even more violent than he. Harold Shand's overreaching is an attempt to redevelop the derelict Thames docklands into an Olympic stadium site, a project for which he hopes to secure Mafia funding. (In a nicely allusive bit of casting, Charlie, the Mafioso who flies to London to meet Harold and hear about the scheme, is played by Eddie Constantine, Godard's favorite American tough guy.) While Charlie is being wooed, a sudden killing and mysterious bombings put Shand's empire at risk. He desperately searches for those responsible, then works his revenge on some of his betrayers, including a trusted young lieutenant, whose throat he bloodily cuts in a paroxysm of rage—we are a long way now from the reticences of the 1940s crime films. Charlie and his tame lawyer refuse to invest ("This country's a worse risk than Cuba was. It's a banana republic") and return to New York, while Shand learns that the bombers belong to the IRA, in whose enterprises he has become accidentally entangled. In the last sequence we see him held captive in an IRA car, being driven off to his own execution.

In the introduction to his published screenplay, Keeffe reveals that early preparations for the film included extensive viewing, with his producer Barry Hanson, of gangster films, French and Italian as well as English and American.[30] Plainly, the dialogue and visual conventions of these movies were absorbed. Plainly also, they were not just imitated. It is originality which chiefly differentiates *The Long Good Friday* from sophisticated pastiches like *Stormy Monday,* a willingness to violate convention, sometimes in the direction of a convincing realism, sometimes in other ways. When Shand has the local villains brought in for an interrogation, he puts them in a startlingly odd place, the meat locker of an abattoir, where like so many carcasses they depend from meat-hooks for his bullying; the cinematographer Phil Meheux matches the camera work to the strangeness of the setting, employing an upside-down shot from the point of view of the trussed victims. Down the line of them Shand struts, "a Roman emperor" as one critic said,[31] though in the course of the scene imperial power seems visibly to be slipping from his grasp, and in the end he simply lets all the villains go, as if belatedly aware that old-fashioned despotism is not going to work any more. Or take the character of Shand's mistress Victoria, played by Helen Mirren. She never quite ceases to be the blonde trophy moll, as seen in dozens of films (including Peter Greenaway's *The Cook, the Thief, his Wife and her Lover* from 1989, where Mirren herself reprises the role, less interestingly). But Victoria also acts as Shand's essential diplomatic partner, the smoother of his way into yachting receptions and critical negotiations ("Harold, your trouble is, you just don't understand their psychology"). Her name, her regal bearing, and at least once the way she is photographed, in a framing against the floodlit façade of St. Paul's Cathedral, turn her into the emblem of a new sort of nation, savvy and successful. No sooner have we been led to interpret her this way, however, than she dissolves into helpless and shaking fear, when the bombings come closer and closer to the brittle world, full of glitter and expensive bad taste, which she and Shand have fashioned for themselves. In an early poem, Dylan Thomas—a great aficionado of films, and the author of many screenplays—wrote

In this our age the gunman and his moll,
Two one-dimensioned ghosts, love on a reel,
Strange to our solid eye . . .[32]

Mackenzie and Keeffe succeed in bestowing a three-dimensionality on the flat old stereotypes, making this gunman and his moll seem no less solid and substantiated than the viewer's eye perceiving them. The "new Victoria style of dialogue" may have taken its departure, as Keeffe acknowledges, from the Bogart-Bacall dialogue in *To Have and To Have Not,* but it has moved a fair distance from its source.

The gunman himself has moved even farther from his sources. Shand is funnier than the racketeers of the old American biopics, more vulnerable, as quick as they to lash out in rage but more likely to regret what he has done, more aware of social class, more interested in respectability, a believer in certain kinds of decency (he's disgusted by the sight of a drug syringe), someone who sees the larger picture. Intermittently, he displays a political awareness entirely missing from the Hollywood movies. Commenting on the sudden violence in his patch of London, for example, Shand says it's like "fucking Belfast on a bad night." Stung by Charlie's refusal to fund his scheme, he angrily confesses a kind of geo-political faith in his native land, using terms (Jim Leach has observed) of which Margaret Thatcher would have been proud.[33] In other words, Shand fully articulates that rivalry between nations which films like *Empire State* and *Stormy Monday* treat merely as subtext:

> No wonder you've got an energy crisis your side of the water. Us British . . . we're used to a bit more vitality . . . imagination . . . touch of the Dunkirk spirit—know what I mean? . . . The days when Yanks could come over here and buy up Nelson's Column and a Harley Street surgeon and a couple of Windmill girls are definitely over!
> . . . What I'm looking for is someone who can contribute to what England has given to the world . . . Culture . . . sophistication . . . genius . . . A little bit more than a hot dog—know what I mean?

It may be that Mackenzie and Keeffe, confident that the cinematic overreaching of *The Long Good Friday* has been successful, are describing themselves in this rhetoric. After all, they are the ones with more "vitality" and "imagination" than their Hollywood rivals; by making their film they have added to the store of what England has given to the world.

But in the speech they unquestionably deny any triumph to their character. Shand's is the hollow defiance of a man without bodyguards at his back, as his exit into the IRA trap will immediately confirm. In the end Mackenzie grants Shand, though not in words, some of that final self-awareness which tragic heroes are supposed to have, and which hardly seems out of place by the time we have finished watching this ambitious film. The last thing screened is a close-up of the gangster's face as he stares into the barrel of the silencer-equipped automatic pointed at him. For an extraordinary minute and twenty seconds of screen time, with only one brief cut to his smiling assassin, we watch Shand as he comes to understand his hollowness. His eyes lose their frustration and slowly fill with resigned knowledge, his bluster about energy and the Dunkirk spirit trails off into the silence—and seems to leave more open than ever the question of an English place in the world, a distinctive English contribution to criminal enterprise.

IN SEARCH OF AN ENGLISH CRIME FILM

Could there be such a thing as a purely English crime film? To use Harold Shand's desperately patriotic terms, could the nation's "culture, sophistication, genius" have shaped the genre in a distinctive way?

Historians of the crime film in England, chief among them Robert Murphy and Peter Wollen, have in effect answered this inquiry by identifying an especially English subcategory of the genre, the spiv cycle of pictures.[34] Spivs were gaudy denizens of the late-war and postwar urban underworld, low-level crooks and con men, blackmarketeers, wide boys with a distinctive style of dress and a flashy glamour. In films like *Waterloo Road* or *They Made Me a Fugitive, Noose* or *It Always Rains on Sunday, Dancing with Crime* or *Black Memory, Brighton Rock* or *The Third Man* (the two culminating masterworks of the cycle), a mass cinema audience was made familiar with the spivs' sharp knowingness, their trilby hats worn at the right rakish angle, their propensity for violence and their lurid final deaths. As Wollen points out, Harry Lime's dying attempt to force his way through that famous Viennese sewer grating in *The Third Man* "recapitulates a whole series of set-piece finales in which the spiv dies melodramatically and often semi-suicidally . . ." All the spiv films are working-class dramas, generally realistic and localized in setting, often expressionist or even surreal in style, combining "the lived experience of the street" with "the darker, more sinister side of Britishness." They had remarkable box-office (rarely critical) success in the late 1940s until the public grew "as sick of racketeering and the black market as they were of rationing and austerity," began admiring the forces of law and order, and made successful a new genre of police-procedural films, inaugurated, according to Robert Murphy, by *The Blue Lamp* in 1950.[35]

Responding as they do to a bit of English socio-criminal actuality, depicting it with a black-and-white, low-budget authenticity that seems utterly characteristic of the work of English production companies (Alliance, Ealing Studios, Gainsborough) at the time, the spiv films are incontestably English. There is nothing very much like them in Hollywood;[36] they belong to their place and moment. But by taking a closer look at one of them—Robert Hamer's melodrama for Ealing, *It Always Rains on Sunday* (1947)—we can find enacted there a different aspect of Englishness, one that has little enough to do with the historical phenomenon of 1940s spivvery, or with any specific subgenre of crime film. It involves instead a cinematic way of conceiving crime, of putting it into an intelligible context—social, political, familial, psychological, and finally, indeed, moral. It is a characteristic attitude, a typical approach, and hence something which helps to shape a wide variety of home-produced films, from a heyday immediately after the war on through to the 1980s, and then to a falling off in the relentless internationalization of the cinema in the last twenty years—though as we shall see it has had a few notable recent expressions. This distinctively English mode of putting crime onscreen may be hard to define with precision, glimpsed sometimes only in brief moments of a work, perhaps a mere matter of emphasis or shading, but it has nevertheless had a real and continuing existence, a significant effect in generating plots and sounds and images and in shaping an audience's understanding of those plots and sounds and images.

In writing the script of *It Always Rains on Sunday*, Hamer and his collaborators Angus MacPhail and Henry Cornelius adapted a play which was itself adapted from still another novel of Arthur La Bern, his first, published in 1945. In the novel version of *It Always Rains on Sunday* there are a few telltale signs—a one-day plot, a focus on street life, recurrent colorful minor characters including a blind man who goes tapping his way down the pavement—that its author has read and admired Joyce's *Ulysses,* but on the whole the work is much less avant-garde than naturalistic, a cold-eyed study of life in the East End, as represented by the Sandigate family.[37] The two Sandigate daughters have become involved with shady characters, one a spivvish Jewish arcade-proprietor who drives the requisite American car, "a streamlined terra-plane affair, all blue and silver." Meanwhile their mother Rose is compelled by circumstances to give shelter to her former lover, the escaped convict Tommy Swann. In due course La Bern dispatches his characters to their predetermined fates, the daughters to bitter disillusion, Rose to attempted suicide, the recaptured Tommy to the gallows for the one crime he did not commit. Nevertheless, he sends them in no particular hurry, not without creating, in the best pages of the book, a well-detailed portrait of street life: cries of peddlers, popular songs leaking out of crowded shops, small-time burglars trying ineptly to get their swag fenced, police detectives constantly nosing around, half menaces and half chums. One of the detectives is described as reading a "Yank mag" of the sort Orwell described, *Ace Detective Yarns.*[38]

As for Hamer's film, it refines, like other works of its period, some of the coarseness of its source, injecting a little regard for justice here, a little sympathy for a character there, making in general "an effort to soften down the all-pervading degradation" of La Bern's East End.[39] The film also concentrates, predictably, on the convict-on-the-lam part of the tale, giving us in rapid succession the desperate search for hiding spaces in Rose's tiny house, Swann's callousness, Rose's slow surrendering to old feelings for him and then the revulsion that leads her to the gas oven in the kitchen, and the final chase through a railway goods yard—which, visually, with its looming black shadows and belching clouds of steam, is as thrillingly melodramatic as anything in *The Third Man.* Crime films *must* convey exactly this sort of thrill; that is their reason for being, the key to their success in indulging the audience's craving for temporary danger. Crime films counterfeit an infinitely seductive world of outlaw morals and transgressive excitement. But not only that world: the significant thing about an English crime film like *It Always Rains on Sunday* is that it counterfeits the ordinary world as well, with its familiar codes of behavior and its day-to-day life going on as unexcitedly as always. Within certain limits (of budget, of available screen time, perhaps of cautious regard for the censor), Hamer and his collaborators were able, no less than La Bern in his novel, to put the ordinary Bethnal Green on the screen, not omitting the

> little low street where on Sunday (apparently) it can't help raining; sawn-off steeple in the distance; trains passing roof-high; Petticoat Lane; dance-band leader with a gramophone shop and a lure for girls; the Hyde Park marchers, with banner, setting off; boozer and coffee-stall, dance-hall and youth club . . .

These items are some of those which William Whitebait catalogued in a sort of reviewer's prose-poem, as he set out to pay tribute to the film, a "fresh little lyric about a neighbourhood," a throwing of "everyday surroundings" into "vivid relief." Similarly, Virginia Graham, while finding fault with the film as a thriller ("so many people demanding attention and so many subsidiary interests"), commended it highly as a documentary.[40]

The ordinariness of *It Always Rains on Sunday* is not the sort of routine background glimpsed in Hollywood B-pictures—innocent passers-by going about their business, a criminal's family briefly depicted, a wife weeping or wringing her hands or stoically waiting, children vaguely around—nor a bit of local color noted in passing on our way to what really counts, the violent satisfactions of the crime itself. What the critics praised in *It Always Rains on Sunday* is the demonstration, managed with considerable subtlety, of how inextricably urban proletarian life is bound up with petty lawbreaking, and then, perhaps, serious crime. The violence and betrayals and petty corruption in *It Always Rains on Sunday* come from somewhere, and are furthermore shown to have consequences, a train of human complications all set in motion by the convict's unlooked-for appearance in his old haunts ("lives are altered" by Tommy Swann, the *Punch* reviewer blandly summed it up).[41] Crime in this and other English pictures, of this period and indeed later, is contextualized. It is comprehended, not just presented, and furthermore comprehended with an English collectivist, as opposed to an American individualist, mentality. That in turn means that it comes regularly attended with melancholy, as opposed to gangsterish exhilaration. David Thomson has written eloquently of the distinction:

American noir is all very well; I love it as much as the next depressive. But it's a kind of rhetorical poetic gesture in a land and a culture in which "happiness" is so unstoppable, it'll drive you mad long before you can get properly sad. In American noir, the cornered guys have such panache—they have shrugged off ordinariness; they know no shame. They shoot at the darkness and utter amazingly melodramatic lines, and the films love them for it. But English noir is much more an extension of social realism—it's there in the knowledge that the cities can be awful places, that the system is corrupt, and that people like us don't stand a chance. Whereas, in America, poor buggers, they all think they're going to win.[42]

When viewed in the English way, criminals never shrug off their ordinariness—which paradoxically invests them with larger significance, perhaps the "dramatic and even tragic qualities" Orwell wrote of in "Decline of the English Murder" in 1946, not knowing that in Hamer's film a year later Ealing would supply something to offset the decline.

The "old domestic poisoning dramas," a phrase Orwell's essay applies to the classic murders he valued, the ones "with strong emotions behind them," supplies a useful term. *It Always Rains on Sunday* and English crime films like it, whether from the 1940s or later, tend toward the *domestic,* in the sense that they habitually return crime from its most glamorized settings to the ordinary, small-scale, thickly peopled spaces where we can best witness both its origins and its ramifying effects; where wrongdoing can be regarded with a certain clarity, moral or otherwise, and with the complex emotions proper to it (Orwell: "pity for both victim and murderer"). Sometimes the domesticity is literal. Bypassing momentarily the darkened streets, prison yards, barren moorscapes, or other cliché locales of the genre, an English crime film will slow its pace and close up its characters in a house, flat, or single room, observing for a moment the within-walls life of a family or a couple—Slim Grisson and his Miss Blandish, for example, breakfasting on trout in that snug love nest.

A more contemporary example of domesticity can be found not in a feature film but a television miniseries, the 1989 English-German co-production *Traffik.* This quasi-documentary on the drug business, written by Simon Moore, directed by Alastair Reid, is global rather than domestic in scope, taking the widest and grimmest possible view of its subject. Nevertheless, nothing in it is as harrowing as a three-minute scene between two family members, a dying old man in hospital and his teenaged granddaughter, who has come to visit him. The child of Jack Lithgow, the crusading anti-drug politician at the center of the series, she is herself an addict, and has to deflect a few of her grandfather's dismayed questions about heroin. The moment between them is still peaceful, though, simply rendered in the camera work and script, full of the sense of the characters' relatedness, her love for him and his for her. He finally drifts off; she kisses him with great affection; and then on her way out she steals his wallet so she can buy more heroin, impugning all the feelings for him which the scene has just dramatized, but not quite making those feelings seem spurious. It is as though the makers of *Traffik* could not regard their story of international drug-dealing as complete until they showed its operations at this level, the level of family affection and betrayal, of the ordinariness of a hospital visit with its heart-felt banalities ("life's not so bad," the dying man whispers). Family relations show in a harrowing perspective some of the day-to-day consequences of drug addiction, generating those strong emotions which Orwell thought should be attendant on crime. If *Traffik* as a whole conveys the darkly glamorous excitements of the drug (and anti-drug) trades, this moment in the hospital conveys the "ordinary recognizable agony," as Graham Greene once wrote in praise of Fritz Lang's film *Fury,* "life as one knows it is lived."[43]

Significantly, there is nothing like the grandfather-granddaughter scene in *Traffic,* the 2000 American version of the miniseries. It is a contemporary *English* moment which *Traffik* depicts, one matched five decades previously by a scene in the English crime thriller *They Made Me a Fugitive.* Directed by Alberto Cavalcanti, released, like *It Always Rains on Sunday,* in that richest of years for crime melodrama, 1947, and like Hamer's picture a story of an escaped convict, this film is infinitely superior to its source, a 1941 potboiling novel by Jackson Budd, *A Convict Has Escaped.* *They Made Me a Fugitive* follows its ex-RAF hero Clem Morgan from his casual involvement with a gang of black-marketeering spivs to his being made the fall guy in the murder of a policeman. After breaking out of prison, and being wounded by a blast from a warder's shotgun, he seeks revenge on a sadistic crime boss, with the aid of a chorus girl, the boss's discarded mistress. Morgan erupts into the girl's cramped bed-sit in the noir style which is typical of the film and which, as the critic Tim Pulleine has noted ("the sets might have been designed at Ufa in the 1920s"),[44] seems more than a little indebted to German Expressionism. Morgan is haggard, ill-shaven, wearing a black leather jacket, his face melodramatically lit from below, and his first action is correspondingly gangsterish; he violently closes the girl's window curtains, to the accompaniment of cliché dialogue ("Get away from that door!"). Thereupon the scene takes a quite different turn. Morgan and girl begin to establish a relationship ("Stop haggling and get me a drink") and the lighting returns to normal. They banter with each other as he removes his jacket like a husband coming home from work; there are comfortable silences; suddenly they seem domestic; you feel that at any moment one of them might say "Life's not so bad . . ." The girl offers to remove the shotgun pellets in his back, and does so, one by one, with her eyebrow tweezers. As each lead pellet is dropped audibly into a bowl, Morgan comments (between clenched lips): "she loves me, she loves me not, she loves me . . ." The lines, nowhere to be found in *A Convict Has Escaped,* may be copied from a notorious moment in Greene's novel *Brighton Rock* (1938), where the teenaged gangster Pinkie captures a wasp, begins to pull off its legs and wings one by one, and grotesquely intones: "she loves me . . . she loves me not. I've been out with my girl, Spicer";[45] but the effect in *They Made Me a Fugitive* is completely different, the sign not of a psychopath's playfulness but of a developing relationship. Morgan's hard protective irony and the girl's fear of becoming involved are yielding, cautiously, to a growing ease with each other. Whatever these two establish between themselves will soon be lost, as the film around them returns to noir mode, but meanwhile the scene has moved them along a little from the exotic world of the thriller. It has set them—to use language from another Greene novel—on "the edge of the profound natural common experiences of men."[46]

It is important not to overstate this claim about English domesticity and crime, to imply that the nation's gangster biopics and heist thrillers are really only slice-of-life studies or variants of the kitchen-sink drama. When the crime films work, which of course they do not always do, they perform a balancing act, putting crime into some sort of intelligible context without making the criminality itself any less thrilling. *Traffik* performs this sort of balancing act (unlike a purely slice-of-life, drugs-destroying-the-family melodrama such as *Nil by Mouth,* for example). So does *They Made Me a Fugitive,* which features, besides the domestic moment between Morgan and the girl, a nighttime burglary, a desperate search for help in London, the torturing of a helpless woman by a sneering villain, a violent rooftop struggle, and a fall to the streets. The English crime cinema as a whole is "marked by an *interaction* between restraint and excess," between the realism of recognizable life and the tinsel of exciting melodrama, to adopt the terms of Robert Murphy's comprehensive study of the 1939–1948 British cinema, *Realism and Tinsel.*[47] Or we can say that it is typified by a counterpointing of worlds, the normal and the luridly abnormal, each commenting on and in a sense validating the other. The carefully observed Manchester of *Hell Is a City* comments on the violent robbery of the film, making it seem localized and plausible, not just an artifact of "the movies"; the violence brings interest and drama to the flat urban scene. The viewer of such a film is held at a certain distance from both worlds, contemplating both, absorbed into neither, engaged most of all by their interplay.

To take a few further examples: *Séance on a Wet Afternoon* (Bryan Forbes, 1964) establishes a dreary suburban locale and sketches a marriage, then provides the excitements of the kidnapping resulting from the sad complicities of that marriage. *The Krays* (Peter Medak, 1990) constantly modulates between the twin gangster brothers' viciousness and the question of how they got that way, of what sort of domestic life, East End clannishness, wartime conditions, or overwhelming female anger at the childishness of males, might have created them. In *Dance with a Stranger* (Mike Newell, 1985), about the real-life Ruth Ellis, the last woman to be hanged in Britain, the balancing act is between the lurid coloring of the nightclub world, where Ellis works as a hostess, and her drab but genuine devotion to her young son, her domesticity ("a class analysis of family life," one critic called the film).[48] *10 Rillington Place* (Richard Fleischer, 1970), a third film taken from real life, does admittedly come fairly close to kitchen-sink drama in its setting. Fleischer and his collaborators create an imprisoning monochrome house and impoverished streets where it seems fully believable that the ignorant young Welshman Timothy Evans might be framed into conviction and execution for a crime he did not commit. The abortion subplot of *10 Rillington Place* recalls *Look Back in Anger;* the helpless film-fascinated innocence of its characters (Evans's wife goes with him to the pictures, and in the pub afterwards says touchingly that he looks like Gregory Peck) comes close to what we see in *Good Time Girl* or *Chicago Joe and the Showgirl*. But another part of the film belongs to the monstrousness of the serial killer John Reginald Christie, whom the actor Richard Attenborough brings dangerously and attractively alive.

Many years earlier Attenborough had brought Greene's much younger Pinkie alive in the Boulting brothers' film of *Brighton Rock*. That 1947 work is balanced too. Pinkie supplies all that could be wanted in the way of transgressive excitement—with his fingering of the bottle of vitriol, his sudden outbursts of petulant brutality, his killing of the journalist Hale on the ghost train as that ride's grotesque cardboard images swim up from the seaside darkness like so many demons from a killer's subconscious. Meanwhile Pinkie's "girl," the teenaged waitress Rose, is someone imported from the ordinary world to share his life of crime, to envelop him in a little ragged domesticity, and so in due course to be made to feel the "ordinary recognizable agony." For that matter, Pinkie himself, though less fully in the film version than in Greene's novel, has his ordinariness, is depicted as having emerged from somewhere. Not just a psychopath who tears the wings off a wasp, he belongs to the slum back streets of Brighton where he grew up, and he becomes fully understandable only when interpreted in the streets' terms.

In other words, even the young man Pinkie is a ruined boy—the extreme example of a much favored figure in the English cinema and in English fiction, the child brought too young into contact with betrayal, cruelty, or criminal violence. Such children are either gravely threatened, as in the cases of the ambassador's little boy in Carol Reed's *The Fallen Idol* (1948), another Greene adaptation, and of the twelve-year-old girl Gillie in J. Lee Thompson's *Tiger Bay* (1959); or they are psychologically damaged, like Leo Colston in Losey's *The Go-Between* (1970), the script for which Harold Pinter adapted from the L. P. Hartley novel. In extreme cases, the children are killed, like Stevie Verloc in *Sabotage* (1936), Hitchcock's version of Conrad's thriller *The Secret Agent*. The closed-in, suffocating atmosphere of the Verloc household, tucked in their hideaway behind a shabby cinema and brilliantly caught by Hitchcock's camera, especially in the fugue-state scene where Stevie's sister

picks up the carving knife from the dinner table and uses it on her anarchist husband, contributes to making *Sabotage* among the darkest—
and least American-influenced—of English domestic crime films. Still,
the most terribly victimized child of all must be Mark Lewis in Michael
Powell's *Peeping Tom* (1960). In the Powell film, Lewis's killings of tarts
with a blade-equipped deadly camera are traced directly back to his father's maltreatment of him as a psychological research subject, in ex-
periments meant to photograph the naked emotion of fear. This particular case of father-son relations is of course perverse and horrible, but
that does not make it any less domestic. In all of these films domesticity
is something more than a bland background to criminality. It is a world
in its own right, an alternative, a causative factor, a measure of victimi-
zation, a source of feeling; part of the story.

Mike Hodges's *Get Carter,* by general consent the best English crime
film between *The Third Man* and *The Long Good Friday,* would seem initially to have little to do with domesticity or ordinary life. True, its main
figure Jack Carter, played by Michael Caine, travels from London to
Newcastle to investigate something familial, his brother Frank's death,
and then takes bloody revenge on the local villains who have contrived
it. But Frank enters the picture only as a waxen figure reposing in a coffin, in a drastically foreshortened framing, a nightmare image hastily
cancelled as the coffin lid is screwed down. He is then replaced, so to
speak, by his shotgun, which Carter finds, takes from his house, and
smilingly adds to his arsenal of weapons. It would be reasonable to think
of the brother's death merely as the spring of action, and of that action
as remaining from start to finish entirely in the world of the revenge
cinema—of works, say, like John Boorman's *Point Blank* (1967), with
which *Get Carter* has obvious similarities in plot and tone. Hodges's
film is full of the conventions of the genre, some of which, as Jonathan
Coe has observed, date back as far as the Hollywood Western, with its
entry of the revenging gunman into the frontier town to purge it of vil-
lainy.[49] Other qualities of *Get Carter,* like the warnings from higher-
ups not to become involved, or Jack Carter's menacing hard stare, come
straight from the noir world. Throughout the film Carter shows the "bitter serenity"—a brilliant phrase from an Antonia Quirke retrospective

notice of the film[50]—which we associate with both Old West gunslingers and hardboiled private eyes, the serenity coming from a belief in absolutely nothing except the stoic code of their violent lines of work (the French title of the film, *La loi du milieu*, neatly captures this). Having few connections to other people, unpolitical (in contrast to the Harold Shand of *The Long Good Friday*), wrapped up in an apparently impenetrable stylization (his "emotions are as carefully controlled as the stiff upper lips of the naval officers in fifties British war films"),[51] Carter is able to proceed expeditiously to his acts of revenge. These include a knifing outside the backyard privy of a betting shop; the throwing of a petty racketeer off a car-park balcony; a point-blank shooting; a clubbing with the butt end of the shotgun and a disposal of the corpse in a bucket for dumping coal slag; the deliberate administration of a heroin overdose followed by a drowning; and the impassive standing-by as a car goes into the Tyne with a woman locked up in its boot. (So Orwell might, in painstaking dismay, have enumerated the brutalities of this very brutal work.) The falling racketeer lands on a car with women and children in it, a detail important, according to Hodges, because it shows how viewers may come to be involved with violence. "It's not in some separate world apart from you . . . you lived in this world."[52]

From the start, *Get Carter*'s ambitiousness is on display. It is a film "not just about the villain," but about observing "social structures." That petty racketeer thrown off the balcony has a place in his world, even a role to play in his family. Hodges shows him coming home early one night to find his daughter in the midst of a rave with her friends, the normal teenaged wildness of which will contrast with adult depravities soon to be depicted. In other words, we see the racketeer as an exasperated father before we see him as a corpse, the next target in Carter's project of revenge. *Get Carter* expands its gaze from the family to Newcastle itself: workers' back-to-back cottages running steeply downhill toward factory chimneys, a race track, a bingo hall with a portentous sign ("The Game Is Final") on the wall, a betting parlor, a seedy lodging house (the "Las Vegas," as its neon sign announces) where Carter stays and seduces the landlady—all of this decayed authenticity meticulously recorded in a quasi-documentary style by the cameraman Wolf Suschitzky, and all of it, like the violence of his film, something required by Hodges's faith in realism:

The country at that time had a totally hypocritical view of itself. It wasn't what it was pretending to be. We thought that the police were wonderful, that corruption was only an American phenomenon and American gangsters were horrible and ours were nice. Once I'd decided to tell the truth, I had to do it with the same ruthlessness as a surgeon opening up a cancer patient . . .[53]

Ruthless too is Hodges's handling of the finale, in which Carter walks cheerfully down a North Sea beach, his mission complete, only to be picked off by an assassin with a high-powered rifle and telescopic sight—the delayed revenge of one of the crime bosses he's brought down, and the confirmation that there's no escaping the retributive world Carter and his like have created.

Initial reviewers of the film had mixed feelings about its realism. James Fenton in the *New Statesman* found it "repulsive but thrilling," John Russell Taylor in the *Times* "unpleasant and powerfully effective." A number of reviewers were united in thinking that the Raymond Chandler allusion in the opening sequence—that perusing of *Farewell, My Lovely* on the train—misleading, or unearned. Carter's thuggishness seemed to them too far removed from Philip Marlowe's chivalry and depth of feeling. As Taylor put it, Carter is "no soft-centred crusader beneath the familiar tough exterior," while Tom Milne in *Sight and Sound* looked in vain for a "whiff of the aura of legend that accompanied Bogart in his adventures down dark alleys and turned them into crusades no matter what he was up to."[54] The particular sort of dimensionality which they were seeking they might have found, had they looked for it there, in the novel which was the source of Hodges's screenplay, *Jack's Return Home* (1970), by Ted Lewis, a north-of-England writer whose favorite author was Raymond Chandler, and whose grittily realistic style and provincial authenticity link him with a figure like La Bern.[55] In *Jack's Return Home,* Carter, if not precisely a Chanderlesque or Bogartian crusader, is recognizably a man with antecedents and connections, a past, the capacity to recall an ordinary childhood. When the Carter of the novel leaves a casino, he recollects that the posh area around it, now full of "California-style houses," used to be "Back Hill," where he and his brother Frank played as kids:

We used to go up there on a Saturday morning and it seemed as though we'd wander for bloody miles. There were all kinds of secret places that were Frank's and my private property. When we were older, getting on for sixteen, we'd stroll about taking turns carrying the shotgun, placing it in the crook of the arm, just so, like cowboys, Wellingtons making that good slopping sound . . . You could walk to the top (and there was a top, a small flat plateau covered in grass that whipped about in the wind) and you wouldn't turn round until you got to this plateau, and then you'd look down and over the tops of the trees and you'd see the town lying there, just as though it had been chucked down in handfuls, with the ring of the steelworks, the wolds, ten miles away to the right, rising up from the river plain, the river itself eight miles away dead ahead, a gleaming broadness, and more wolds, even higher, receding beyond it. And above it all, the broad sky, wider than any other sky could be, soaring and sweeping, pushed along by the north winds.

This is a surprising passage to find in a thriller, with its willingness to pause and take the long view—yet again the panoramic-view-of-the-town-from-the-hill, as made familiar in English kitchen-sink dramas of the 1960s and in *A Canterbury Tale*. Even more surprising is the provision of a rapturous voice, a poetic descriptiveness ("a gleaming broadness"), for the hard man Carter. We learn here about the brothers' shared shotgun, which turns out to have its own part in family history and so is set up for the talismanic role it will play later in the plot. The passage as a whole, of course, reveals the depth of Carter's fraternal feelings and explains his vengefulness. There are several other memory passages in Lewis's book, for example about a beach in "spitting distance of the gasworks and smelling distance of the fish docks" but nevertheless of special emotional importance to the brothers, or about another site on the shore where they once played hide and seek and where years later Carter hunts down and kills a treacherous chauffeur, one of his brother's betrayers.

Meanwhile, the novel gives Frank a voice of his own and thus helps turn him into someone whose death *matters*. His remembered talk expresses, it turns out, the same sad longing for transatlantic glamour which we've seen in Brendan in *Stormy Monday* or Gwen Rawlings of *Good Time Girl*:

America. That'd be the place, though, wouldn't it? Imagine. Those cars with all those springs that rock back and forwards like a seesaw when you put the brakes on. You can drive one of them when you're sixteen over there. Just think, our kid. Driving one of those along one of them highways wearing a drape suit with no tie, like Richard Widmark, with the radio on real loud listening to Benny Goodman. Gor! I reckon when I leave school I'll go to America. . . . And you can go to pictures at two in the morning and see three pictures in one programme.[56]

All these passages in the novel amount to an invocation of ordinary life. They help to account for what Jack Carter has become while at the same time giving readers some perspective with which to judge what he has become.

Films are not novels, obviously. If Mike Hodges fails to supply cinematic versions of these ruminations on the past, and it is hard to see how he could possibly have done so, he at least contrives two photographable moments which put Carter in perspective, give viewers the opportunity to understand and assess him. In the first, on his way to a dockside shootout with three of the villains, Carter takes the ferry, and while on board idly watches the other passengers, among them a happy mother with two young daughters, an ordinary family. Michael Caine, as Carter, gives a wintry smile at this domestic sight, then a warier look through half-closed eyes—an essential moment of the film, according to Hodges, a look meant to convey that Carter "knows that he's really sick, that he's never been normal. These are normal people by his standards, and he'll never be like that . . . there's a sort of sadness in him."[57] The mother and her children go innocently on their way, exiting the ferry well before the gunplay starts; the intention has not been to make their normality seem vulnerable, only unobtainable.

In the second moment, Carter watches a cheap black-and-white pornographic film produced by a local racketeer. There is some irony in this, since Hodges, in the most sexually explicit episode of *his* film, has just depicted, in color, Carter making sweaty love to one of the skin-flick's actresses; it is from her bed that he watches the film. Nevertheless, the scene is designed to reveal something more important than an irony. As Carter gazes with sated boredom at the lesbian seduction and then heterosexual rape of a primly dressed schoolgirl, he suddenly realizes that she is being played by Frank's daughter Doreen, an innocent who has been treated in previous scenes to Carter's money and avuncular counsel (or paternal counsel: he once had an affair with Frank's wife, and Doreen may in fact be his own child). Now, as Carter watches her degradation onscreen, we watch *him* in an ingenious framing with a mirror that also shows us what he is seeing. The whirr of the projector goes on and on while tears track down Carter's cheek in close-up, as he hangs his head in something resembling shame. From this point on, his familial motive for revenge is of course greatly strengthened, the plot accelerates, the killings pile up, but the real point of the episode has been those tears. They connect him with another human being, connect him in more than one way, in fact, since in a pub scene after Frank's funeral we have already been shown (also in close-up, and in a similar framing) a tear running down Doreen's cheek. A few tears, a guarded look at a normal family on a ferry: these may seem minimalist crackings of the gunman's professional impassivity, in Hodges's genre-respecting style all that is permitted by way of emotional expression. And yet they have an effect. They broaden; they suggest a world outside the borders of criminality; they gesture at the contextualizing effort so often made by English crime films. They render Carter himself not domestic, exactly, nothing could do that, but ordinarily human.

THE SINGING DETECTIVE AS SUMMA CRIMINOLOGICA

Nicholas Shakespeare in the *Times,* reviewing the third episode of *The Singing Detective* in November, 1986, said that the miniseries was developing into "the most compelling television drama I have ever seen." After the last broadcast, he said simply that it was "the best thing I have ever watched on television."[58] What called forth such superlatives from him and from many other reviewers of Dennis Potter's miniseries was an obvious seriousness of intention and a brilliance of production: the performances of Michael Gambon as Potter's hospital-bound, remembering, hallucinating alter ego, and (for instance) of Patrick Malahide as the metamorphosing villain of those hallucinations and memories. The reviewers were thinking as well of the imaginative cutting from plot to plot; the dazzling writerly cleverness of many passages of dialogue; the no-expense-spared musical numbers arising unpredictably from the action, as when white-tuxedo-clad crooners and frilly-dressed chorines abruptly commandeer Marlow's hospital ward for two lip-synched minutes of Fred Waring's "Dry Bones." "Vacuous American pop of the 1940s," one sniffy British academic critic later called "Dry Bones," sounding like the anti-American advocate of *A Matter of Life and Death,*[59] but it is precisely Potter's achievement that in context the song seems the opposite of vacuous. It is brilliantly entertaining; it provides a momentary escape from the burden of having to watch Marlow's skin disease close up; it also showcases the doctors' relentless anatomizing of the helpless patient (xylophone riffs are played on skeletons) and mocks their medical mumbo-jumbo.

All these qualities of *The Singing Detective* are still visible two decades after its initial broadcast, but what can be seen more clearly about it now is the way it culminates a whole tradition of English filming. It is an encyclopedia of themes and images from a half-century of screen work. The "Dry Bones" production number, for example, extends and hugely improves on the sour performance of the same song, complete with horsewhips cracking against top-boots, in Peter Medak's *The Ruling Class,* the 1972 filming of Peter Barnes's play. More especially *The Singing Detective* recapitulates motifs of the crime cinema. Like *Gumshoe,* it dramatizes characters' own self-dramatizations, their obsessive dreaming of themselves into stereotyped roles learned from Hollywood, but it does so on much larger scale and with far greater psychological acuity, and far more effectively than *Chicago Joe and the Showgirl* would be able to do four years after *The Singing Detective.* Picking up on that consciousness of American crime stories so often hinted or winked or protested at in English films, Potter's drama constructs a fantasia on intertextual relations between an LA private eye named Philip Marlowe and a Forest-of-Dean-bred, has-been novelist named Philip E. Marlow: "What else could I have done except write detective stories?," the latter laments to his nurse in the first episode. Above all, *The Singing Detective* locates its crimes—these are in the plural, and some of them barely resemble the simple violent acts we are used to in gangster pictures—in personal history. Betrayal and violence are shown to come with a fully worked-out biography, of the sort more usually associated with crime novels (e.g., *Jack's Return Home*) than with the films made from them. Potter's Philip Marlow is a more completely realized Jack Carter, an exile from childhood paradise; also, a more completely realized Pinkie Brown or Mark Lewis, a child damaged by those close to him who then damages others when he grows up. That Marlow's adult acts of violence are largely imagined on the pages of his lurid pulp fiction or in the bouts of his feverish paranoia, and invariably imagined in stylish and entertaining ways, a richly noir scene on a staircase, the best final shoot-out between shamus and thugs ever to take place in a hospital ward, does not make them any less disturbing or susceptible to understanding, to tracing back to their sources in ordinary life and private pain. That Potter should insist, by the whole design of *The Singing Detective,* that these acts *be* traced back, is why his miniseries belongs to the tradition of *It Always Rains on Sunday* or *They Made Me a Fugitive,* works in which the pathos of ordinariness and the glamour of crime are held in fine balance. *The Singing Detective* is in fact the most ambitious and fully achieved of English domestic crime films.

As a young man, Potter regarded working for television as an act of cultural politics, a declaration of his Labour beliefs and the substitute for the parliamentary career which he did not manage to attain. The broadcast medium was a part of his working-class origins, his English ordinariness, and by reviewing programs for the *Daily Herald* and by writing teleplays for the BBC he could demonstrate that he had not, despite Oxford and his early journalistic successes, dispensed with that ordinariness. For him, television was

> a medium of great power, of potentially wondrous delights, that could slice through all the tedious hierarchies of the printed word and help to emancipate us from many of the stifling tyrannies of class and status and gutter-press ignorance.[60]

"Switch on, tune in and *grow,*" he added. On the (several) occasions when he attacked the drab naturalism of so much television drama, he did so because that style seemed to him quiescent, and acquiescent: "one of the troubles of supposedly showing things-as-they-really-are . . . is how difficult it then becomes . . . not to make people feel deep in their souls that this is also more or less the way things have to be."[61] Drab realism from the BBC or ITV would not help people *grow.*

Some of this idealistic fervor about a very cynicism-provoking industry persisted to the end of Potter's life—the quotations above are from the MacTaggart Lecture which Potter delivered in Edinburgh in 1993, the year before his death—but by that point his experience had suggested many more reasons, non-political ones, to stay with television as his medium. He benefited enormously from the skilled collaborative help which the BBC gave him, his early career coinciding, by a stroke of great good fortune, with the period when the Corporation most generously supported and encouraged original television drama; Potter's willful genius often needed (though it did not always accept) the skepticism or practicality of others. At this period the BBC was effectively a movie studio, as Potter's regular producer Kenith Trodd has said. It was willing to charter a plane to research the right oak trees to stand in for the Forest of Dean (Trodd: "it felt like real movie-making"), willing to pay for studio production values more associated with the cinema than with teleplays, willing to budget for extensive rehearsals, willing to photograph *The Singing Detective* on 16mm film, not on videotape. The overall result is that the miniseries "feels and looks like a movie."[62] Potter benefited most of all, of course, from the BBC's generosity in funding his writing at miniseries length. "I wanted to do a portrait . . . that accumulated," he had written of his first six-part series, *Casanova*, in 1971, a portrait

> that sifted through layers of various incidents, and how they changed perspective, like the things we think about. We're walking compendiums (in a way) of memory, and previous instincts embalmed by present states of mind, and we know that we change perspective as we mature or decay . . . And to do one's own thing over six hours suddenly seemed to be a valid and rather exciting thing to attempt . . .[63]

Potter required the big television canvas for his best and most characteristic work, a fact which began to be clear with *Pennies from Heaven* in 1978 and which was fully confirmed eight years later with the success of *The Singing Detective*. (It was confirmed in a different way by the marked inferiority of the two American feature-length versions of these series, directed by Herbert Ross in 1981 and by Keith Gordon in 2003, Potter's sanctioning of these movie projects, and his authorship of both screenplays, notwithstanding.)

The Singing Detective required its full six-part, 420-minute length partly to accommodate Potter's expansiveness about genres. "I'm playing with the conventions," he said in an interview, "the musical convention, the situation-comedy convention, the detective-story convention—in order to try to see what TV drama can do." He was contemptuous of the strict formulas which he had had to live with at MGM, when turning *Pennies from Heaven* into a movie ("Was it a detective story? Was it a musical? Was it a romance?" people kept asking him)[64] and now wished to compound all the genres, even at the risk of initially unsettling the audience. More pressingly, *The Singing Detective* required time to do justice to complex mental states, as explored first with *Casanova* and its changing perspectives on memory and instinct, the past's being inescapably "embalmed" in the present. For their part, viewers also needed time to follow the complexities of *The Singing Detective* as they made their steady way through the six Sunday evenings of the original broadcast. So, in an earlier era, they would have been able to take their time with the monthly part-issues of novels by Dickens or Thackeray. The drama which viewers watched in 1986, unlike *Casanova*, was autobiographical—Potter's *David Copperfield*, and his *Oliver Twist* too, his nightmare tale of childhood betrayal—and its painful reworking of the various events of Potter's life brought with it still further complications. Potter was an expert not only on what had actually happened in the Forest of Dean and in wartime London, but on how he had disguised what had happened, and how the effects of what had happened nevertheless came to the surface, forcing him (so he thought) into the angers and excesses of an unruly life. All this would take time to hide and reveal in a television drama.

Of the three major plot-lines in *The Singing Detective*, the most directly autobiographical, and the earliest which Potter conceived, is the hospital story. P. E. Marlow suffers terribly from psoriatic arthropathy—head-to-toe rash, skin in flakes and tatters, crippled hands and useless legs, fevers and hallucinations—all of which pathology faithfully replicates Potter's state in 1972. "I went through everything Marlow does," he said in a newspaper interview when *The Singing Detective* was being broadcast.[65] Twenty years' experience of being a patient also went directly into the series, which economically captures the self-pity, petty humiliations, and boredom of life on the hospital ward, its depression and drama (two of Marlow's ward-mates die in the course of the series) variegated with moments of nervous comedy. The funny moments belong chiefly to two fellow-patients of Marlow's, Mr. Hall and Reginald, a bickering pair as inseparable as any music-hall or sitcom duo. Mr. Hall complains querulously, and the barely literate Reginald undertakes a word-by-word reading of Marlow's old pulp novel, the one which lends its title to the drama. Reginald's thick-headed curiosity about how the plot of *The Singing Detective* book is going to turn out ("'Oo killed her, then?") seems to warn viewers against worrying too much about such things. Incidental humor arrives by way of other old and variously gaga men on the ward, including one constantly shaking sufferer from Parkinson's disease—old Noddy, a bystander who in an early conception of the screenplay was to have been revealed as the master-dreamer of all the plots, in other words the stand-in for Potter the creator.[66] This was a baroque complication, a detour to the echo-chamber of self-referentiality, of the sort Potter was sometimes susceptible to (his novel *Ticket to Ride,* published two months before *The Singing Detective*'s premiere, is much prey to it) and which *The Singing Detective*'s director Jon Amiel rightly insisted be cut out.

The medical staff in the hospital includes Nurse Mills and Doctor Gibbon. The nurse is there to be solicitous and to be admired by Marlow. "You are the girl in all those songs," he eventually finds himself declaring to her, the "songs you hear coming up the stair . . . When you're a child. When you are supposed to be asleep . . . ."[67] Earlier, her casual remark about the hospital ward being a cabaret, old chum, sets up some of the musical numbers performed there, whether in Marlow's imagination, as with "Dry Bones," or in reality, as with the sudden irruption into a peaceful Sunday morning of a band of self-appointed evangelizing medicos banging a tambourine and singing "Be in time!" The latter is a good example of the way Potter's pet antagonisms, here against organized, pushy religion, insinuate themselves into the roomy structure of *The Singing Detective.* For the most part, Marlow keeps Nurse Mills a *princesse lointaine* safely apart from the imaginary degradations visited on his other women, but once or twice she features in the hallucinatory cabaret herself, down in the cavern of the wartime nightclub Skinskapes, a sexy torcher singing "The Blues in the Night," or legging it with the other chorines in the "Dry Bones" number, her skimpy white costume nevertheless recognizably a version of her nurse's uniform.[68] (Key contributors to the success of the miniseries were the brilliant BBC costume designers Hazel Pethig and John Peacock, and the overall designer Jim Clay, who in an interview commented interestingly on his efforts to transform nightclub into hospital, hospital into nightclub.[69]) In all its features "Dry Bones" exemplifies a truly filmic comedy, an incongruous juxtaposition of contrasting worlds which could only be accomplished on a screen and with a soundtrack.

As for Gibbon, a psychiatrist brought in to help the depressed dermatological patient, his role at the start is essentially comic too, that of the straight man, feeder of cues to the wise-cracking Marlow:

> DR. GIBBON ... Why did you agree to be wheeled here?
> MARLOW Gets me out of the ward.
> DR. GIBBON What's that?
> MARLOW I said it makes a change from the bedpan and sick old farts talking in their sleep. Lets me see The Warp and Woof of Life In All Its Rich Texture. You know—crap like that ...
> DR. GIBBON This is an act. This is desperate pastiche.
> MARLOW No. I don't like Italian food.
> DR. GIBBON You can't keep it up.
> MARLOW Oh, little do you know!

Here and elsewhere Marlow is a performer with language, a Stoppardian monologist, even a sort of Joycean free-associator, as in his frenzied attempt, when Nurse Mills applies ointment to his private parts, to damp down his excitement by thinking of boring things:

> John and Yoko. Ethiopian Aid for pop stars. Mark Thatcher in the desert. Dust to dust. Pyramids. Christ, no. Not pyram—*Gardener's Question Time,* chaired by Peter Hall. Plastic pitch at Queen's Park Rangers. Fog Philips on a horse. An evening's viewing from the National Film School. ...

The same hypercleverness appears in the word game he plays with Gibbon:

> DR. GIBBON ... I say a word, any word, and—
> MARLOW And I throw up the word *I* associate with it.
> DR. GIBBON Instantly.
> MARLOW (*Rapid fire*) Nescafé.
> DR. GIBBON (*Laugh.*) We haven't started yet.

Soon enough, however, the game turns serious, that is to say therapeutic, touching on the dark associations of sex and dirt and death which have made Marlow the scabby imaginer he is. Via words, Gibbon gets the patient back to his past, and though the full elucidation of the traumas suffered there awaits the working out of the other plots, the psychiatric sessions produce a visible recovery in Marlow. In the slow course of the six episodes we watch his skin get clearer, his hands unclench enough to hold a pen or light a cigarette, his legs begin to carry him.

In the pulp-mystery plot of *The Singing Detective,* some things do happen according to the book. For example, the client-to-be, Mark Binney, approaches Skinskapes via a deserted, full-of-menace London street, passing an old busker, apparently a disguised confederate. Binney drinks with one of the nightclub hostesses, finds the murdered "busker" hidden in a closet, and, seeing two mysteriously threatening, trench-coated thugs, leaves. In his sepia-toned flat—no bright colors in the photography of this plot; everything is period, everything is nocturnal, everything is being remembered—he pays another hostess, a Russian girl, Sonia, for sex, and then accuses her of working for the NKVD. Meanwhile we first glimpse the singing detective himself, also named Marlow, on Hammersmith Bridge, where the naked body of the drowned Sonia, pulled up from the sullen waters of the river, will soon be unceremoniously dumped.

A little later Binney finds Marlow in rehearsal, crooning with his band in the Laguna palais-de-danse. (The role of singing in *The Singing Detective,* and the effect of the particular popular tunes sung, will have to be discussed at length in a later chapter. Here, I will observe merely that Potter has made the detective's odd musical sideline at least plausible: the young Marlow's father sang for an admiring audience in the working men's club of the Forest of Dean, and once grown up, Marlow the novelist has arranged for his hero to do more or less the same thing, in a sort of filial tribute, or a recovery of happy moments. In *The Singing Detective* people are always trying to get away from present pain to mellow remembrance of some such tune as "Cruising down the river on a Sunday afternoon.") Binney hires Marlow to find out what he can about the two thugs and the missing Sonia, explaining that the police have been on to him. Later, after Marlow accuses his client of helping to whisk Nazi rocket scientists away from the Soviets, a tart-under-the-lamppost named Lili Marlene is shot by one of the thugs and dies in the detective's arms, but not before she can confirm his suspicions by whispering the message "Skinskapes . . . a front for . . . rockets." Now it is the detective who represents a threat to the consipracy, and at the Laguna the two thugs send bullets his way, as up on the bandstand he croons "The old umbrella man." This is a brilliant opportunity for the cinematographer Ken Westbury and the designer Jim Clay to re-create one of the master cinematic images of the 1940s, something at the heart of *Listen to Britain* and film after other film: women in flowered dresses, men in uniform, couples circling under the benevolent gaze of a white-tuxedoed bandleader. More precisely, Westbury and Clay create here a pastiche of the dance-floor-and-violence scenes in crime films from Hitchcock's *Young and Innocent* in 1937 to Paddy Carstairs's *Dancing with Crime* and Cavalcanti's *They Made Me a Fugitive* in 1947. At the moment when the gunfire breaks out, missing Marlow but killing his drummer (a streak of blood runs decoratively down his trap set), or when the thugs make their getaway from the Laguna in the rain, *The Singing Detective* encloses viewers in an almost purely cinematic, a noir world. It seems Potter's intention that we be made temporarily as movie-besotted as Betty Jones, while also standing back from and recognizing our besottedness.

After the violence, according to the rules of the genre, we might expect some fuller explanation, at least of the rocket scientists business, but in this drama Potter turns such a conventional thing into a joke ("Marlow: I think I know this dame. Her name is—Her name is E. Lucy Dation"), or into a hopeless prospect ("irreducibly beyond elucidation"). Dr Gibbon intones the latter, Joycean, gnomic phrase to his patient at the start of one of their sessions, as if to foreclose any possibility of unraveling Marlow's mysteries. "Postmodern" this frustrating of expectations may be, as has been claimed. Or, more persuasively, Modernist, in the sense that it signals the "figure of the creative artist who tries *and fails* to use art to sublimate pain and order disordered reality."[70]

In any case, the refusal of explanations is creatively liberating. It permits the replacing of conventional exposition with the more filmable possibilities of collage. The two mysterious thugs wander seemingly at will through Marlow's mind, in and out of the action, portentously threatening Binney, firing at the detective, trading shoptalk or wrangling with each other like their ultimate sources, Al and Max, the gunsels in Robert Siodmak's American noir *The Killers* (1946). They "sound like strays from a bad film," Binney comments, speaking for anyone who has ever seen the parade of tough guys following Al and Max into Hollywood clichédom. Other influences on Potter's thugs seem detectible. In casting actors for the parts, the small Ron Cook and the large George Rossi, Amiel was thinking of Laurel and Hardy, whom when they are funny the thugs do superficially resemble, while in the atmosphere of menace that still hangs about the thugs, they recall Gus and Ben, the banal, wrangling hitmen of Harold Pinter's 1960 play *The Dumb Waiter*. Eventually, when the thugs grow aware of themselves as scriptless bit-part players and begin to wonder in bewilderment what exactly they should do, they seem Pirandellian, or Stoppardian—pop-culture versions of the main figures of Stoppard's 1966 *Rosencrantz and Guildenstern Are Dead*. So multiple an ancestry and so complicated an allusiveness is nothing unusual for Potter and his collaborators.

As the collage-making of *The Singing Detective* goes on, taking us deeper into the psoriatic Marlow's dreamy fixations, the thugs' bewilderment becomes the viewer's. Images are repeated, seemingly at random: close-ups of trouser-clad walking legs, Venetian blinds drawn apart for a stealthy glimpse outside a room, the silent watchers on Hammersmith Bridge, the woman's naked body drawn from the river—different women's bodies, in fact, as Marlow remembers or misremembers the old novel. Or as he reshapes it cinematically: one interpretation of what is going on, never quite confirmed, is that Marlow is planning a screenplay of the novel. Or is he remembering and misremembering an already written screenplay? Deliberately revising a screenplay? Marlow as the obsessed recycler of his previous work, the constant reinterpreter of old scripts, would be yet another version of Potter himself, who for a number of scenes in *The Singing Detective* recycled features of his earlier television dramas, especially *Vote, Vote, Vote for Nigel Barton* (1965) and *Emergency Ward 9* (1966), as John R. Cook has shown.[71]

Whatever Marlow's mental exercise may be, exactly, it results in the replaying of scenes in different ways. In Skinskapes, for example, Mark Binney is introduced to Sonia in two quite distinct takes, with changed dialogue. What matters in all this is obviously not the furtherance of a narrative. It is the maintenance of a certain style, by means of the old-movie music on the soundtrack, the melodramatic handling of the camera (Amiel's is in places as canted as Carol Reed's in *The Third*

Man), and above all the hardbitten cleverness of the singing detective as he backchats with his client or talks directly to the camera, and to us ("Am I right or am I right?"). From his fedora and trenchcoat to his handiness with a gun, Marlow belongs to a 1940s, hardboiled, American world, and clearly we are meant to think of his creator P. E. Marlow as a novelist along the lines of James Hadley Chase, the taker of that header into the American cesspool. Equally clearly, we are meant to think of the detective himself as a version of Philip Marlowe, the most famous invention of Raymond Chandler.

Chandler had been a writer of obvious significance in the 1940s, when his four major novels, and the Hollywood films adapting them, were acclaimed in England as well as the States. Indeed, Chandler could be welcomed by the English as one of their own; though born in America, he had been raised in England and educated at Dulwich College—an American Anglicized, rather than James Hadley Chase's Englishman Americanized. After the War, Chandler never stopped being of interest in England. His first-person, hard-boiled style was copied, for instance, by Kevin O'Hara in *It Leaves Them Cold* (1954), a farrago of wisecracks, nightclubs, gunplay, heads being sapped, and blondes; and as we have seen, Chandler's novel *Farewell, My Lovely* plays a role in *Get Carter* in 1970. Three months before the broadcast of *The Singing Detective*, the *Times* writer Douglas Thompson declared 1986 "The year of the fedora" and listed such manifestations of the Chandler style as reprints of all his novels, stage adaptations, some proposed new Chandler films, and the hour-long Chandler adaptations produced by London Weekend Television and broadcast in Britain just two years previously, to considerable critical approval.[72] Perhaps it is all this retrospective currency which accounts, in *The Singing Detective,* for Dr. Gibbon's familiarity with the American writer. Sparring with his patient Marlow, Gibbon alludes casually to the "not raining in the foothills sort of stuff," the "Down these mean streets sort of stuff," establishing that by now *The Big Sleep* is simply a part of everyone's culture. Dr. Gibbon also mimics the tough-guy talk ("So you won't play ball") which Chandler and Humphrey Bogart between them had made famous. In the same spirit Marlow himself imitates the famous opening of *The Big Sleep* ("I was wearing my powder-blue suit . . . I was calling on four million dollars") in a voice-over before a visit from Nurse Mills ("I had on my best py-jamas, the ones with red stripes and blue forget-me-nots . . . A million dollars was about to call"). Later, he whispers a sardonic "Farewell, my lovely" to his estranged wife Nicola, as, abruptly truncating her visit to the hospital, she runs away from his disease and his foul-mouthed resentment of her. All this knowledge is ironic, it is knowingness surrounded by quotation marks, in a way we might take to be characteristic of cultivated England at the end of the twentieth century: a wry acknowledgment that hardboiled America has crossed the Atlantic to stay, that the moral issues of crime and violence exercising Orwell in the 1940s have long since been superseded by a fascination with style—with "Chandleresquerie," to use the term of Potter's published screenplay. "Paperback-soiled" is Marlow's own nicely evocative phrase for the style.

Chandler was not a part of the original conception of the miniseries. Interestingly enough, as the BBC's commissioning note for *The Singing Detective* suggests ("Set in London at the end of the Second World War, the story of a private investigator tracing a missing girl who is believed to have disappeared with a deserter from the American Services"[73]), the original conception seems to derive yet again from the Cleft Chin Murder. But Chandler soon entered the picture, having always been a writer for whom Potter felt a strong affinity. Humphrey Carpenter notes that as early as 1976 Potter had included a passage from *The Big Sleep* in the BBC Radio 4 anthology program *With Great Pleasure,* explaining on the broadcast that it was "one of [his] riper fantasies" to imagine himself as Marlowe. Perhaps Carpenter is also right in thinking that writing the screenplay for the mystery thriller *Gorky Park* (1983) had helped Potter rediscover a predilection for detectives, and for Philip Marlowe in particular.[74] Beyond this, it would be interesting to discover evidence (none has come to light) that Potter had seen and been influenced by the *film* versions of Chandler, especially, perhaps, by *Lady in the Lake* (1947), in which Philip Marlowe moonlights as a writer of pulp fiction; one of his stories is "I wake up bleeding," which would be an appropriate title for Potter's own drama. A second film which seems to lurk tantalizingly in the background of *The Singing Detective* is *Hammett,* from 1982, since Wim Wenders's film also fantasizes on the relations between private-eyes and hardboiled novelists (here, Chandler's predecessor Dashiell Hammett), and on the reciprocities of violent action and writing about violent action.

In general, it is frustrating to know so little about Potter's movie-going. That he was fascinated by films when young is on record. He reminisced about sitting in the palatial Hammersmith Gaumont, watching the curtains part, the organ rise "like a demigod out of the pit"—formative images to be elaborately recalled in Potter's six-part series for Channel 4 in 1993, *Lipstick on Your Collar*, with its cinema usherette heroine. At the Gaumont he saw certain works, *Tarzan*, *State Fair*, the latter eventually furnishing one of the songs lip-synched in *The Singing Detective*, "It Might as Well Be Spring." At the Scala in Oxford, according to his friend the American writer Willie Morris, Potter watched *The Third Man* and *The Thirty-Nine Steps*, plus many B-pictures.[75] Of the crime films by which his imagination must have been nourished, however, Potter said nothing. Did he watch George Marshall's *The Blue Dahlia* (1946), with its screenplay by Chandler, its plot about a conniving, faithless, murdered wife? Did he know Dassin's *Night and the City*, in which Harry Fabian is killed on Hammersmith Bridge? Had he seen *Get Carter*, and watched the manhandling of Margaret's naked corpse—an image remarkably similar to that of the women hauled out of Potter's Thames? Beyond the noir genre, did Potter see John Schlesinger's *Billy Liar*, and did the fantasy sequences of that 1963 film influence his own way of picturing Marlow's inventions?

In any case, what attracted Potter to Chandler is clear enough. Philip Marlowe is the narrator of his own deeds, a man adroit with words—a capacity which Potter admired and enjoyed himself, even to the point of imitating bravura Chandleresque similes: a writer's scattering clues in his plot is like "throwing grit to the hens." Chandler's Marlowe was even more valuable to Potter because, alone among the hardboiled private eyes, he is "a man of honor," "the best man in his world," to quote the peroration of "The Simple Art of Murder," an essay which brings an Orwellian moral seriousness to the business of crime-writing ("In everything that can be called art there is a quality of redemption"). Down those famous mean streets of which Chandler's essay speaks Philip Marlowe goes, not himself mean, and chiefly not mean in his conspicuous chivalry about women. The bad girls encountered in

Marlowe's cases (Chandler: "I think he might seduce a duchess") never shake his belief in good girls ("I am quite sure he would not spoil a virgin"), in feminine innocence as something to be protected, as Marlowe protects it in Merle Davis, for instance, in *The High Window*.[76] This was a quality absolutely necessary to Potter, something which had to be imitated. In *The Singing Detective,* by the time Marlowe's English avatar takes on his client Binney's case, we have already witnessed Binney's crude lovemaking with the nightclub hostess Sonia, his degradation of (and by) her, and so we have some basis for understanding Marlow's oddly puritanical disapproval:

> BINNEY   What I want is someone to find that girl, or the men who
> were outside the house, or to prove that nothing nasty happened to
> her from *my* hands when she was with *me*—
> MARLOW   But it did.
> BINNEY   What?
> MARLOW   Something nasty *did* happen to her at your hands.
> BINNEY   (*Hotly*) I'm telling the truth, Mr. Marlow!
> MARLOW   I didn't say you weren't, Binney.
> BINNEY   Then I don't—
> MARLOW   All I said was something nasty did happen to her when she
> was with you. Wouldn't that be the way her mother would see it?
> BINNEY   (*Snort*) Her *mother*—for God's sake—

If Marlowe the perfect gentleman stands behind Marlow the singing detective, there still remains the question of why he should have to be shaped this way, of the ultimate source of that obsession with the something nasty and with all the ways of indulging or punishing or protecting girls from it. This question is not, as it turns out, a matter irreducibly beyond elucidation, but rather the chief concern of the latter episodes of *The Singing Detective,* the tracing of Marlow and all his qualities back to the childhood of the detective's creator.

We are conducted to the Forest of Dean via a panoramic shot of green forest trees. It is a startling shift away from the mean-streets or London-hospital setting of everything previously seen, and well exemplifies Potter's aesthetic of deliberate strangeness. It is an important goal of the miniseries to unsettle viewers, to lead them to think that anything at all might suddenly appear on the screen. But demonstrating conti-

nuity is equally a goal of the miniseries. Perched in one of the trees is a
ten-year-old boy, the young P. E. Marlow, and when in a little while he
speaks he does so straight at the camera, in a manner which irresistibly
recalls the singing detective's speaking straight at the camera, cracking
wise. Later, we understand that the little boy scratching at the rash on
his forearm grows up into the bedridden psoriasis patient. The bright
pupil in the rural school, always with his hand up, eventually becomes
the know-it-all wordsmith. The bright pupil who cracks under the strain
of being the teacher's pet, puts a turd on her desk, is fearsomely inter-
rogated, blames another boy for the deed, and finds himself not just believed by the teacher but by his classmates, who hasten to corroborate
the tale, eventually becomes a *novelist,* a professional crafter of plausible narratives, a shifter of nastiness away from himself onto imagined
others.

What happens with his schoolmates is nasty enough. The adult
Marlow is able to confess his guilt from the episode only in the last of
his sessions with Dr. Gibbon—"I sat in my desk, perjurer, charlatan,
and watched and listened and watched and listened as one after another they nailed that backward lad hands and feet to my story. . . . Oh,
she beat him. Oh, she beat that poor boy, the vicious old bitch!" At this
point, catharsis complete, the patient stands and walks. But it is young
Marlow's family, as opposed to the school, who really make him what
he is. In the miserably cramped miner's cottage of his grandparents he
has forced on his attention his mother's anger at the fecklessness of his
father, and he thinks: "*My fault. Me. It's me. Me. It's all my doing.*" Later,
in the Edenic Forest, he witnesses the primal betrayal: his father's friend
Raymond making love in the ferns with his nervous, transported, and
weeping mother—the scene which on broadcast infuriated prim viewers and self-appointed campaigners for television decency, less because
of its sexual explicitness, perhaps, than because of Potter's insistence
that we be placed right in the ferns with the only partly comprehending
young Philip, watching him watch, guessing the effects on him to follow (highly provocative too was Potter's intercutting the sex scene with
the death of old George Adams in the hospital ward). After her adultery, Mrs. Marlow runs away to London, taking her son with her. In the
cramped house of his grandfather, Philip hears the word "tart" and the

song "Lili Marlene"; in an Underground station with a train entering he abandons her to her misery; and (off screen) she drowns herself in the Thames at Hammersmith Bridge.

The settings of this history are the claustrophobic domestic spaces of 1940s films like *It Always Rains on Sunday*. There, such settings would have sociological ramifications. Theft or violence or fraud would be revealed as the consequence of working-class penury, stifled hopes, slum dwellings. In Potter's no less deterministic but rigorously psychosexual drama, crime is first of all to be understood in broader terms than theft, violence, or fraud. It begins as betrayal or cruelty or the infliction of pain, a desperate woman's adultery in the forest or the teacher's pet's crude revenge on the teacher, and then, in a key step, it is displaced from the actual to the imaginary. Crime is what the grown-up Marlow cannot get out of his head and so puts into his book or his nightmare. That innocent schoolmate blamed for Marlow's own nastiness—"Mark Binney, Miss. It was *Mark Binney!*"—gives his name to the nasty client of the pulp novel, while the boy's father, the adulterous Raymond, furnishes the client's appearance; the actor Patrick Malahide plays both Binney and Raymond, of course, carefully differentiating the two in accent, clothes, and manner, yet making sure the viewer sees them for what they are, a composite Enemy. Similarly, Alison Steadman plays both Mrs. Marlow and Lili Marlene, the sacrificial victim of the pulp-mystery plot, sacrificed there so that Marlow will be able to kill the maternal sexuality he witnessed years before, and simultaneously be able to weep over the necessity of the killing. You always hurt the one you love, as the Ink Spots sing in one of the numbers compulsively performed in *The Singing Detective*. The guilt and the disgust at sexuality which Marlow caught as a child, like a disease, go on and on through his adulthood, mental complements to the psoriatic rash on his skin, disfiguring every encounter which he can put into his plot. The client Mark Binney's sweaty congress with the Russian girl Sonia is one example; the basis of this is Marlow's own copulation with an English prostitute. (She is played—the alert viewer of *The Singing Detective* will have come by this point to anticipate the device—by the actress who took the part of Sonia; the encounter takes place in a flat we are meant to recognize as the original of Mark Binney's.) Afterwards Marlow apologizes to the

English girl, for his language chiefly ("It wasn't really *me* calling you those names. I don't mean them"). His defenses are down; he is himself, not his alter ego the singing detective, whom he has created precisely for the sake of the impenetrable, invulnerable stylization which comes with the character. "You won't catch me feeling the feeling," says the private eye out of the side of his hard-bitten mouth.

Eventually even the pulp-mystery plot becomes insufficient to dramatize Marlow's guilt and disgust, and so instead of continuing with the mental rewriting, he constructs a new misogynist fantasy, that his wife Nicola is betraying him by scheming to sell the screenplay of the old book to Hollywood. Her co-conspirator is the last of the incarnations of Raymond, "Mark Finney" this time, a brilliant translation of duplicity into contemporary terms: short modish haircut; casual movie-producer's clothes; a transatlantic accent as he says "fabulous . . . fantastic" on the telephone to the American studio boss.[77] Potter treats this new development a little more elliptically, teasing viewers, allowing them briefly to think that Marlow might possibly be right. That is, the Nicola who loves her husband mixes seamlessly with the imagined, conniving Nicola who in classic film noir style kisses him seductively in order to get his signature on the crucial optioning document. In a scene of considerable complexity, we watch the hospital patient hiding incongruously in the staircase of Finney's flat (Mark Binney's flat, in fact, redecorated) and then improvising dialogue for Nicola and her lover to speak, complete with punctuation marks. At this moment, finally, Marlow's paranoia is frankly revealed, along with its etiology. His need to punish sexual degradation has invented the "conspiracy," not to mention its finale in treachery and murder, Nicola's knife in Finney's throat, a copy of the stolen *The Singing Detective* splashed with blood, a blue police light pulsating just outside. It is a B-movie ending, impeccably recreated by Potter and Amiel, but like many such endings in the British cinema it succeeds admirably, and it does so by balancing cheap thrills with hard-won understanding, the luridness of violence with some sense of what violence comes from. While believing the outrageous events dramatized on the screen, we also stand disbelievingly back from them, noting their origins in Marlow's diseased imagination.

Much the same could be said of the yet more B-movie sequence which closes the whole miniseries, a cleansing-via-gunpowder to match the cleansing-via-analysis Marlow has already received from Dr. Gibbon. Amiel photographs this shootout in the hospital ward in a monochrome closely approximating black-and-white and fills it with lovingly rendered visual clichés (curtains to hide behind, glass broken by gunshots, the detective grimacing as he sees—here a quick point-of-view shot to the revolver—that there are only two bullets left). Pastiche, movie fantasy, is wittily blended with the routine of medical personnel going blandly about their tasks until they are cut down by gunfire. The private eye's opponents are, inevitably, the two mysterious gunmen, who by this stage have wandered from a 1940s gangster picture to the Forest of Dean, and from the Forest of Dean to contemporary London. The private eye's big revolver does the killing work expected of it, but the last bullet is reserved—one final surprise from Potter—for the psoriatic Marlow in his bed. That version of Marlow needs to die and be replaced by a healthier, clearer-skinned persona, namely the healed patient who walks out of the ward the next morning, on Nicola's arm, wearing a trenchcoat and hat that looks like the singing detective's. On the sound track Vera Lynn sings "We'll meet again," perhaps hinting ironically at future recurrences of skin trouble and paranoia,[78] perhaps merely taking us back to a historical period more tolerant of happy endings. Birds also sing: a last (and benign) intermixing of the pulp novel and the hospital and the Forest.

Any analysis of *The Singing Detective,* including the one just given, will make it seem a little simple and schematic—"dollar-book Freud," as Orson Welles said dismissively of the Rosebud business in *Citizen Kane*—rather than the continuously challenging thing that it is. On screen, Potter's miniseries proceeds by indirection. It is full of repetitions, relentless circlings back to the same powerful images; also full of flash-forwards to images that cannot be understood until later in the series. It veers unpredictably from tense drama to ludicrous comedy. It preserves certain inconsistencies: "Noddy did it," Marlow says at one point, mystifyingly; this is a relic of Noddy's one-time role as conceiver of the entire drama. The series also leaves curiously unshown the exact circumstances of Marlow's mother's suicide. At least to some extent, then, Potter prefers clues to solutions, as his character Marlow does. The patient says grimly that solution-less puzzles are simply "the way things are," or, more eloquently, in an important speech to Dr. Gibbon, that he believes in no systems,

> no ideologies, no religion, nothing like that. . . . I just think that from time to time, and at random, you are visited by what you cannot know cannot predict cannot control cannot change cannot understand . . .

If Potter believed this himself, he might be expected to indulge an aesthetic of the odd, the startling, the random, the playfully unexplained. And he does. Illogically, Potter arranges for the flesh-and-blood Nurse Mills to encounter the two mysterious men, complete figments of the imagination. (In fact, this visit by the two gunmen to the hospital resulted from a late story conference between Potter and Amiel; it was Amiel's idea. He was the right director for *The Singing Detective* partly because he shared Potter's liking for the inexplicable.) Potter also contrives a scene in which little Philip runs away from his mother in the Underground only to appear, still running, in the grown-up Marlow's deserted hospital ward. This is the kind of thing that the published screenplay calls "weird," admiringly. As for the plots of *The Singing Detective,* if these readily become distinguishable in analysis, the truth is that the miniseries, when actually seen, moves so fluidly among them that it makes the very concept of discrete plots seem inapplicable and crude. According to Potter, it was the process of editing that constituted "the last rewrite"; the cutting-room rewrite of *The Singing Detective* put all the plots inextricably into one design.

For the invention of this fluidity, the daringness of the whole design, Potter is of course chiefly responsible, but it was the director Jon Amiel who shared the editing with Potter, and who sometimes had to rein in his author's excessive daringness, Potter's liking for the weirdly and endlessly exfoliating. (The two mysterious men, for instance, were originally going to sing a Flanagan and Allen duet: could it have been "Round the Back of the Arches"?) More generally, Amiel's task was to translate Potter's grand design into actual images and sounds. He did so with remarkable success. *The Singing Detective* amounts to an anthology of cinematic devices, some flashy and attention-getting, some not necessarily meant to be noticed, but all put into service of the story. A slowly panning camera sweeps over Gloucestershire faces in the working men's club (all local people, recruited for the miniseries) until it stops at the grown-up Marlow, in pyjamas, covered with his rash, smiling across the years at his crooning dad; extreme close-ups on faces convey how threatened by adults little Philip feels while a canted camera hints at irreality or hallucination. In other demonstrations of camera work, the neon sign over the Laguna palais is so tightly framed that all the viewer sees on the screen is the talismanic word "gun"; Amiel employs a closely following shot on Mark Binney (the director's first-ever use of a Steadicam, in fact) as that character moves through the dark passages of Skinskapes on his way to finding a corpse. Or consider arrangements of mise-en-scène: the scarlet woman Nicola's costumes always have a splash of crimson about them; to locate the key scene between Marlow and the prostitute in its time, the 1960s, a poster of *Blowup* (1967) is stuck prominently on the wall of Marlow's flat; to get the right authentic look, the outdoor noir scenes are shot with old carbon-arc lighting, such as would have been used in the 1940s. On the soundtrack, gently falling rain is heard during Marlow and Gibbon's crucial word game, to make the momentary silences between them more perceptible, while sound bridges—a beeping heart monitor, for example, or B-movie tremolo strings—effortlessly shift the drama from one locale to another. Constant graphic matches have the same smoothly transitional or even metaphorical effect, as when the blue curtains around Marlow's bed dissolve into the waters of the Thames. This is the equivalent in images of Potter's verbal matching, sometimes Joycean in its ingenuity, as when Nicola's line "Who's a good boy?" to her husband in hospital precedes a cut to the Forest of Dean schoolroom and its good little boy Philip; or when Nurse Mills, bringing a drink of water to the feverish Marlow, hears him say "Spring" through his delirium, responds prosaically "No. Tap water," then gets back in return "Rustle of Spring"—the display piano piece his mother played on the upright in the working men's club.[79] Amiel often had to find filmic expressions for the ideas of a very book-soaked author. Potter sets Marlow to quoting Dame Julian of Norwich, as T. S. Eliot had ("All manner of thing shall be well"). Similarly, playing with the suggestive name "Marlow," Potter makes his character comment bitterly that his mother should have called him "Christopher," and then follows up (in the published screenplay) with seven quoted lines from *The Tragical History of Doctor Faustus*. Amiel let Dame Julian stay but took Christopher Marlowe out, preferring cinematic to literary allusiveness when possible. "Was I quoting *The Third Man*?," the director said about the way he filmed Binney's approach to Skinskapes through a melodramatically shadowed London street. "Yes, of course I was."[80]

A catalogue of visual and auditory techniques in *The Singing Detective* might be indefinitely prolonged, but after all what counts, and what needs some final commentary, is how techniques are combined in the individual sequences which make up the whole. Take the important sequence which follows Philip and his mother as they leave the Forest of Dean for London. We see first the father bidding their train farewell with a long-held gesture, a stiff uplifting of his arm. For all of Potter's disdain of television naturalism, this is a naturalistic depiction, the observant rendering of the sort of pose, formal and embarrassed at the formality, which such a man would adopt at such a moment. Next, in an assertion of continuity from past to present, or memory to imagination, the gesture is exactly replicated by the singing detective, who is glimpsed in a brief cutaway to the Laguna as he performs "Paper Doll." The lyrics of the Mills Brothers' song—"I'm going to buy a paper doll that I can call my own/ A doll that other fellows cannot steal"—carry over to a reminder shot of Philip's father, still stuck on the platform, still mourning the departure of the wife Raymond has stolen. Then the camera enters the train, and when Philip shuts the compartment window, his action stops the song.

Inside, mother, son, and some traveling soldiers are all crammed into the small space. Extreme close-ups of the soldiers' faces show how large they loom to Philip in his confused disquiet. He notices them looking hungrily at his mother's stocking-clad legs, and when he says to his mother, "Mam, Dad was wavin', he was wavin' all the time," the line transparently attempts to reassert his father's rightful place in the family. In fact, the whole scene is built out of point-of-view shots, the next of which is Philip's, looking at the headline of the newspaper his mother is reading. "War Rushing to an End!" it exclaims, prompting an interior monologue from Philip in which he tries to buck himself up. His thoughts quote the headline, exclamation point included—an even more important gesture toward continuity, since we will shortly hear the adult Philip thinking in identical monologue, even to the point of including punctuation marks:

> The rooks gather in the lost trees comma like premonitions of the night full stop Why do they cry question mark . . .

What happens next in the train sequence may derive from an old film. The wartime (1941) thriller *Pimpernel Smith* starred Leslie Howard (who also directed) as a British secret agent who disguises himself as a scarecrow placed close to a railway line, therefore close to a Nazi work party making repairs. One of the Nazi guards, out of pure sadism, and to show the prisoners what might happen to them if they don't work, fires at the scarecrow, wounding the agent. It is an unimportant moment in a forgettable film, but if Potter (or Amiel) remembered it, he found in it a powerfully suggestive conception. A scarecrow appears to Philip's view in the train of *The Singing Detective*. Out in a barren field, dressed in trenchcoat and fedora, making the by now familiar uplifted arm gesture, greeted by old-movie music on the soundtrack, the scarecrow gathers familiar motifs together; understandably, Philip is fascinated by it. Its clothes anticipate the style of the fictional private-eye whom he will later create; at this present moment it replaces his missing father. The scarecrow is "weird," as Potter would say, but also obscurely meaningful; it will take on other appearances and develop other meanings later.

Meanwhile, we are returned to the grown-up Marlow in hospital, by a dissolve. This is a standard enough device, but one so frequently and ingeniously employed in the editing of *The Singing Detective* that it might be thought of as the series' master technique. The dissolve's dislimning of one appearance into another, of actuality into recollection or recollection into actuality, is a synecdoche for the complex multilayering of the whole. "The only way to dissolve these walls around us is to use the magic of our minds . . . Pictures. Sounds," Potter had his imprisoned Casanova say in the earlier series, but in *The Singing Detective* it is the walls of conventional narrative and fixed time-frames, of ordinary televised drama, that Potter's pictures and sounds do away with. As one critic has melodramatically written, Potter's drama abolishes the present tense;[81] it would be truer to say that it abolishes the *tyranny* of the present by constantly dissolving back and forth between now and then. It could not establish its chains of causality, reveal the sources and expressions of character, without that dissolving back and forth.

In the train sequence, the return to the present-day, bedridden Marlow of course reminds viewers that the whole episode has come out of his dreaming mind; everything seen is a prolonged point-of-view shot, or point-of-memory shot. Memory includes a reprise of "Paper Doll," lip-synched now by Philip's lonely father. When the Tommies in the train compartment take up the lip-synching, shyly smiling, they are strongly reminiscent of the Canadian soldiers singing "Home, home on the range" in a cramped train compartment in Jennings's documentary *Listen to Britain;* or perhaps they simply go back to a common store of remembered World War II images. Certainly Amiel's cutaway shots of the train exterior, provided occasionally throughout the sequence, recall the photogenic trains and tracks of 1930s and 1940s filmmaking: locomotive smoke streaking across the frame, shiny rails stretching into the wet distance.

After one more cut-in interruption, to the hospital ward at night, with Marlow pensive, the episode closes with an elaborate fantasy. To the tune "Lili Marlene" (shortly to be heard again in the pulp-mystery plot), Philip reimagines the scarecrow as Hitler, whose suicide the paper has announced ("That's bloody old Hitler done for, then," Philip declares to himself), and whose Nazi salute the scarecrow's arm gesture now seems to copy.[82] Out of his boyish ordinariness, Philip wants Hitler dead. Out of his particular emotional needs, too: Philip has witnessed his father's betrayal, and must respond violently to it, being a ten-year-old Hamlet driven into his own sort of madness. In his tree in the Forest, hearing his mother and Raymond below, he reached over to a ladybug and crushed it; much later in life, he will fantasize onto paper the violent revenges of the singing detective. Now, his war-influenced fancy puts the soldiers in the compartment into the field with their rifles, ready for an ambush, to do the deed for him. They fire, and the scarecrow goes up in flames like an Old Guy on November Fifth, consuming bloody old Hitler, consuming Raymond Binney.

What the whole sequence conveys, technique by technique, is "the possibility of simultaneous communication on several different channels ... a rich synaesthesia." The words are those of David Lodge, novelist and television screenwriter, theorist of both arts, writing in his essay,

"Novel, Screenplay, Stage Play," about the expressive potentials of filming. As Lodge reminds us, literature issues its meanings sequentially, one word at a time, whereas screen works operate in several dimensions at the same time. They can "fuse the description of the hero *and* the sunset into which he rides into a single instantaneous image," and add to the effect the strains of appropriate music.[83] This claim about simultaneity in filming would seem to refute, convincingly, the attack on filming made by a novelist who died in the infancy of the art, without seeing any of its real accomplishments, Proust:

> An image presented to us by life brings with it, in a single moment, sensations which are in fact multiple and heterogeneous ... What we call reality is a certain connection between these immediate sensations and the memories which envelop us simultaneously with them—a connection that is suppressed in a simple cinematographic vision, which just because it professes to confine itself to the truth in fact departs widely from it.[84]

Simultaneity, the display of multiple and heterogeneous sensations, is precisely what *The Singing Detective* provides, repeatedly, with more imagination and less literalism than the generic Western movie Lodge is describing—indeed, with the profound sense of connectedness Proust is describing as an aspect of life itself. Potter's drama fuses a description of its hero with a revelation of the past into which, Marcel-like, he falls, and from which he seems initially unable to recover; and to all these psychological complications it adds the effect of music, plentifully.

For a summary of *The Singing Detective*'s accomplishment even more perceptive than Lodge's, we might go, paradoxically, to a critic who never saw it, George Orwell. There is a real affinity between Potter and Orwell, in their radical politics, their self-assurance as writers, their love of England. In 1968 the former wrote a cautiously admiring essay on the latter. Potter praises Orwell's courage in facing ugliness, which he of course shared:

> He was able to locate a distant whiff of gangrene in the dustily genteel parlours of the "aspirin chewing outer suburbs" and to bury a face contorted with disgust deep into the foul armpits of malodorous ideology: moods, emotions, premonitions, obscure prejudices and even the lightest of random speculations could be mutated into a lingering smell on the landing or the grubby sheets on the bed in the attic.

In the essay Potter sometimes seems to be not so much describing the older writer as looking in a mirror:

> he felt the slime sticking to his skin in a sort of disfiguring or even disabling anguish . . . His nausea was perpetually at war with his antique nostalgia, his real pity for the oppressed tangling always with his guilty identification with the oppressors. It is this tension, in his life and in his prose, that made Orwell such a disturbing and influential writer: we draw out of him our own guilts and nightmares and hypocrisies.[85]

As for what Orwell contributes to our understanding of Potter, that is given in the essay "New Words," probably written in 1940, where the essayist speculates on "the extraordinary powers that are latent in the film," "the powers of distortion, of fantasy, in general of escaping the restrictions of the physical world":

> Properly used, the film is the one possible medium for conveying mental processes. A dream, for instance . . . is totally indescribable in words, but it can quite well be represented on the screen. . . . If one thinks of it, there is very little in the mind that could not *somehow* be represented by the strange distorting powers of the film. A millionaire with a private cinematograph, all the necessary props and a troup of intelligent actors could, if he wished, make practically all of his inner life known. He could explain the real reasons of his actions instead of telling rationalised lies, point out the things that seemed to him beautiful, pathetic, funny etc—things that an ordinary man has to keep locked up because there are no words to express them. In general, he could make other people understand him.[86]

For an old-fashioned moralist like Orwell, the castigator of *No Orchids for Miss Blandish,* this is a surprisingly tolerant, freely speculative statement. And a prescient one: it is right about all the things *The Singing Detective* would eventually be able to do, the conveying of mental processes, the giving of real reasons for actions, the expression of things ordinarily locked up. It is wrong merely in postulating that eccentric millionaire. In the event, it took only the BBC, and Dennis Potter.

THREE

TWO TEXTS TO SCREEN

An adaptation . . . must be an act of loving criticism as well as vandalizing bravado.

DENNIS POTTER

One of the ways that English screen works might arguably be considered quasi-literary, script-centered enterprises, has been their eagerness to ransack published fiction for usable stories. As early as 1898 a tiny part of Dickens's *Oliver Twist* was seized on for the screen sketch *Mr. Bumble the Beadle.* More than a century later, in 2005, the BBC was adapting (for the third time) the entirety of Dickens's *Bleak House* for a multipart television series. In between these two dates come many dozens of screen versions of Dickens's works (including two silent adaptations of *Bleak House* from the 1920s, one with Dame Sybil Thorndyke as Lady Dedlock) and of works by similarly classic authors, Eliot, Scott, Austen, Forster, Thackeray, Lawrence, Greene; and many hundreds of screen versions of middle-brow or pulp fiction. If "ransack" seems too violent a metaphor for the English film industry's habit of deriving plots from novels, consider the metaphor that Virginia Woolf uses in her 1926 essay "The Cinema": "The cinema fell upon its prey with immense rapacity, and to the moment largely subsists upon the body of its unfortunate victim."[1]

To take only one director as an example of this rapacity, Alfred Hitchcock in his English period, between 1927 and 1939, adapted scenarios from novels in both categories, high and low. He filmed classic spy thrillers by John Buchan and Somerset Maugham, and Conrad's domestic crime tragedy *The Secret Agent* (under the title *Sabotage*), but also novels by figures merely of their time like Marie Belloc Lowndes, Walter Mycroft, and Clemence Dane, and novels which now would be entirely forgotten, such as Ethel Lina White's *The Wheel Spins*, had not Hitchcock transformed them into something more ingenious and impressive, as he transformed White's potboiler into *The Lady Vanishes*. Of the nearly two dozen films directed by Hitchcock in England, half derive from novels, another eight or nine from stage plays. His film *Secret Agent* belongs to both categories, being adapted from Maugham's *Ashenden* by way of an intermediate stage play by Campbell Dixon— a derivation much repeated in English film history, as with *Brighton Rock* and *No Orchids for Miss Blandish, The Prime of Miss Jean Brodie* and *The Good Companions,* all novels which became considerable stage successes before becoming films. To the end of his career Hitchcock was text-dependent, his last two films, *Frenzy* and *Family Plot,* both being based on English novels, Arthur La Bern's *Goodbye Piccadilly, Hello Leicester Square* and Victor Canning's *The Rainbird Pattern.* Hitchcock was perhaps more text-dependent than most of his English contemporaries, but not by any great measure. A documentary short titled *Reflections,* directed by Paul Bernard for a 1994 UK/LA Festival and celebrating the achievements of British filmmaking over the decades, consists of seconds-long snippets of almost two hundred famous films, from *The Titfield Thunderbolt* to *Tom Jones.* Of these, fully two-fifths adapt works of fiction. The proportion would be higher if the documentary excerpted more run-of-the-mill films, not to mention television adaptations of fiction, the products of a booming (and to some extent export-oriented) late twentieth-century industry. It is in fact the small screen's devotion to adaptable texts which is unparalleled in other countries, distinctive to England.

For some film historians and critics, the English reliance on texts has become a matter for disapproval, the clear expression of a logocentric timidity, perhaps a cultural conservatism, which has compromised the English cinema and made it less independent—less assertively a medium in its own right, distinct from writing—than is desirable. Whether desirable or not, the industry's willingness to help itself to works of fiction is a fact, and a fact which has had its due share of critical attention: there have been theoretical inquiries into the possibilities (or impossibilities) of adaptation; author-based studies of literary-minded filmmakers or film-minded novelists, among whom Graham Greene is the favorite example; categorizations of the different kinds of adaptation, from the most slavishly literal to the most freely transformative; and of course academics' or reviewers' comparisons of particular adaptations with their originals. Even now, these comparisons often amount to examinations of *fidelity*—how much of a written work's plot and characterization has been translated into the new medium, how comprehensive and intelligent an understanding of the original (its strengths, its weaknesses) underlies the translation. Perhaps, as Imelda Whelehan has suggested in the introduction to a gathering of essays on the subject, such comparisons have generally been made by critics with a literary perspective and with a conscious or unconscious tendency to privilege text over film. In any case, it is only recently that the issue of fidelity has been considered with greater rigor and nuance, as Thomas Leitch does for instance in his book *Adaptation and Its Discontents*, taking it as "a problem variously conceived and defined by the filmmakers at hand, not as an unquestioned desideratum of all adaptations."[2]

As we have seen already, with *Get Carter* in its relation to Ted Lewis's novel *Jack's Return Home,* or *It Always Rains on Sunday* in its relation to the Arthur La Bern novel which is its source, questions of fidelity can conduct us a long way into the operations of a film, as long as the approach is not too narrowly construed as an issue of preservation, of keeping fully intact what was there on the page to begin with. Achieving faithfulness to a text has everything to do with finding cinematic replacements for what *cannot* be translated. As we will see, finding replacements is the quite remarkable achievement of the two screen adaptations to be examined in this chapter.

The two works are the second of the television versions of *Bleak House,* a 1985 BBC miniseries directed by Ross Devenish; and the 1993 film version of Kazuo Ishiguro's novel *The Remains of the Day,* produced by Ismail Merchant, directed by James Ivory, and written by Ruth Prawer Jhabvala, who if not nominally part of the "Merchant-Ivory" brand has always been an indispensable partner in the filmmakers' work.

There are obvious differences between the two source texts here, of length, of period, of tone, of standing in English literary history. Ishiguro is a scrupulous realist, Dickens both a realist and the sort of visionary symbolist capable of imagining a character—Krook, the old legal-waste-scavenger in *Bleak House*—who out of the greasiness of his person and the wickedness of his character breaks spontaneously into all-consuming flames. Nevertheless, *Bleak House* and *The Remains of the Day* have important things in common. Both are intimate narratives, love stories, which against the characters' wishes (they would like to keep private matters private) open out into and eventually become inseparable from vaster stories of national corruption. In Dickens's case, the corruption is of a fog-shrouded English legal establishment, together with its police apparatus, its retinue of moneyed supporters, its rag-tag army of victims, and its complicity in poverty, crime, and disease. In Ishiguro's case, the corruption is of the aristocratic owner of Darlington Hall, the great house which by rights ought to be a moral center for the nation at a time of political crisis in the 1930s, but instead is a site of appeasement and political stupidity. Both novelists insist on the inseparability of private and public happenings. It is the key mechanism of their plots and the most pressing of their themes. Both novels, then, present to their adaptors similar problems of having to scale up and scale down, move flexibly between character study and history, intimation and rhetoric, the close-up scrutiny and the long-shot perspective.

Both novels also are narrated subjectively, either in part, with the portions of *Bleak House* related in first person by the heroine Esther Summerson, or wholly, as in Ishiguro's book, where the telling of the tale is ceded to the imperfect understanding of his main character, Stevens the butler. Subjectivity of this sort presents an obvious challenge to filmmakers who decide to preserve it, or present a simulacrum of it. To some extent they can fall back on the standard cinematic devices for conveying the perspective of a single character, such as the voiceover or the point-of-view shot. Or they can contrive new devices.

Hitchcock's genius in doing this was displayed early on, when in *Blackmail* (1929), portraying his guilty heroine's visual imagination, he puts the illusion of a slashing knife into a neon advertising sign at Piccadilly Circus, or when he dramatizes her equally lurid auditory imagination, by turning ordinary breakfast-table chatter into a mumble from which only the word "knife" emerges, intolerably to her. In deploying these Expressionist, derived-from-UFA techniques, Hitchcock was aided by a melodramatic story and a driven-to-extremes character, a woman who kills in self defense and suffers thereafter from a fugue state. Merchant-Ivory and the BBC makers of *Bleak House,* having saner characters and more ordinary situations to deal with, needed to find subtler and more sustained means of conveying their characters' inner states.

It is important to say something about what both these versions accomplish as adaptations, and to take the time to substantiate the accomplishments in detail, since success in adaptation—not quite the same thing as faithfulness to an original—is not so common as to be taken for granted. But it is not the only thing to say about the works. The production histories of *Bleak House* and *The Remains of the Day,* like their plots, reach outward, suggesting larger contexts and general lessons, hinting at a variety of relations between film and literature. After all, page-to-screen adaptation is only one of the processes at work in the national culture to which texts and screen works both belong. There are also understandings and misunderstandings about each medium, complementarities, rivalries and antagonisms, easy transferences of artists from one performing mode to another (Richard Attenborough starred as Pinkie in both the stage and film versions of *Brighton Rock*)—and on several of these matters our two adaptations touch. In the way it works, *Bleak House* refutes the claim made by a contemporary English novel that film versions of Dickens are unworkable, doomed to fail; *The Remains of the Day* derives from a novel which itself derives from screen works, namely, episodes of the television series *Upstairs, Downstairs.* Based as they are on exchanges that ultimately can be shown to be more reciprocal than one-directional, *Bleak House* and *The Remains of the Day* demonstrate a rather more complicated and interesting interrelatedness between two arts than is usually comprehended in the idea of adaptation.

HOW TO ADAPT DICKENS, AND HOW NOT TO DO IT

In 1982 Peter Ackroyd published *The Great Fire of London,* the first of his novels and the beginning of his distinguished career as mediator between England's bookish past and its shabby (and anxious, and violent) present. Its title notwithstanding, *The Great Fire* does not go back to the seventeenth century, like Ackroyd's later thriller *Hawksmoor,* but only as far as the nineteenth, presenting a complicated encounter between Charles Dickens's late masterpiece *Little Dorrit* and contemporary London. Ackroyd's characters—an on-again, off-again young couple, a psychopathic dwarf running an amusement arcade, a leftist polytechnic lecturer (he carries about with him a copy of Henry Mayhew's *London Labour and the London Poor*), a gay Canadian academic, a filmmaker and his troubled wife—create in their various interactions something resembling a plot, and this touches at numerous points on the happenings of *Little Dorrit.* The young couple, Tim and Audrey, lives close to the site of the Marshalsea, the debtor's prison which is the central setting and controlling image of the Dickens novel. Audrey has a feckless, hopeless-with-money father, like Little Dorrit's father William. Spenser Spender, the filmmaker, seeks funding from a government agency not unlike Dickens's Circumlocution Office. A Cambridge don at high table gabbles on about Derrida in the ludicrously logorrheic style of Dickens's Flora Finching: "Goodness me how extraordinary I was examining the text could you pass me a little more bread please how kind only the other day but it seems to me that the verbal associations without wishing to sound too pretentious are locked in as it were to a mode of discourse . . ." (90).[3] The psychopathic dwarf is called Little Arthur, in ironic allusion to Dickens's hero Arthur Clennam.

Spender intends to bring *Little Dorrit* to the screen. His motivation is double: previous experience in making a documentary film on a prison—"about an inmate, and how his freedom had destroyed him" (11), a good shorthand description of William Dorrit—and the inspiring if vague memory of a single extraordinary passage which he has read in the Dickens novel. As Little Dorrit and her feeble-minded companion Maggy walk the dark streets, waiting for the gate of the Marshalsea to be opened to them, a prostitute suddenly appears, calling out in angry distress that Little Dorrit, whom she thinks a child, should be out so late. Having sardonically identified who she is and what she is doing ("Killing myself"), the prostitute realizes that Little Dorrit is actually a grown woman, and half apologizes to her: "I never should have touched you, but I thought you were a child." She then goes away with a "strange, wild cry."[4] A certain taste for luridness and a radical social sympathy, then, draw Spender toward Dickens, not to mention a bleakness of vision; he decides to conclude his film with Arthur Clennam carrying Little Dorrit out of prison "after she had fallen into a dead faint at the thought of the weary vacancy, the purposelessness, of her new freedom" (35). He also decides to update the story by shooting the Marshalsea sequences in a modern prison. Work on the film begins, and after a meeting in a clichéd Wardour Street office with a clichéd movie producer ("No stars means problems for our publicity boys," 30), we seem well launched into a predictable kind of English fiction, in which the fineness of an individual's cinematic vision is poised against the crassness of the picture industry—the sort of thing Christopher Isherwood produced in 1945, with *Prater Violet,* or John Mortimer in 1947, with *Charade.*

Ackroyd, however, soon goes in another direction. The issue of his novel turns out to be not how to do *Little Dorrit* right, but how to do it at all. London with its random outbreaks of violence, its constant petty betrayals and temporary sexual alliances, its politico-cultural complexities, impinges disastrously on the film project. Just when Spender is shooting Little Dorrit's encounter with the prostitute, for example, the siren of a fire engine or police car sounds nearby, ruining the audio track. An arc-light falls, and its snapped cable cuts a technician's face; the crew subsequently go on strike, alleging unsafe working conditions. In the end, the now-crazed Audrey, crazed among other things by the terror of being possessed by the spirit of Little Dorrit, torches the set. Spenser is trapped inside and killed, while the fire becomes the Great Fire: "popularly believed to have been a visitation, a prophecy of yet more terrible things to come" (165). Little Arthur escapes from his prison ward, connects the damaged arc-light, and triumphantly shorts out the electricity for the whole prison; the inmates escape.

The Great Fire of London is not, of course, simply about a series of catastrophes. It is about a film project doomed from the start by the incapacities and confusions of its participants. These include the scriptwriter's doubts ("I can't really see any proper way of bringing Dickens to life—he is not our contemporary," 158) and by the director's inability to choose from among the conflicting interpretations of Dickens thrust upon him. The weary vacancy and purposelessness Spenser has planned for his Little Dorrit seem in the end to belong rather to him, and to the rest of the film's creative team. Beyond that, the novel is about a contemporary culture's failure to understand, to respond adequately to, its history. In Ackroyd's London the past consists of contextless or fragmented sound bites, such as a pub's mock-Victorian music-hall program, a ballad from which ("Who passes by this road so late?" Blandois's song in Little Dorrit) feebly contends with the blaring of a television set. Visually, history has dwindled into the décor of a mock-Edwardian restaurant, where "old English agricultural implements had been stuck haphazardly upon the walls, and behind the cash register there was a large blown-up photograph of 'Derby Day 1911.' Next to that was an even larger photograph of two children, shoeless, in ragged clothes, begging in the East End" (15). In these phantasmagoric surroundings Spenser's Little Dorrit film seems only another corrupting pseudo-work, another assemblage of disparate images and competing sounds.

That Ackroyd should espouse this skeptical view of the cinema is scarcely surprising. He was in 1982 and has remained throughout his career not just a bookish writer, but a believer in the preeminence of words. For him, written texts are the key to the imagination, the imagination the doorway to the past. Why bother to produce screened images of Little Dorrit when Dickens's text is there and available, as stimulating as ever? Why bother to cast actors when Ackroyd's own imagined characters can undertake, at his bidding, the leading Dickensian roles? (Audrey becomes a bedraggled Little Dorrit when at a séance, in a "clear, small voice," she declares "I am so little but I was born here . . . I am the child of the Marshalsea," 40). There is a direct line between such magical reincarnations and the odd fictional interludes to be found in a non-fictional Ackroyd book, his 1991 biography of Dickens. In the first and most engaging of these interludes, Dickens himself is made to encounter Little Dorrit and Maggy in the midst of their memorable walk through night-time London. Dickens quizzes them, expresses sympathy, confesses his own family's lamentable history of debt and impris-

onment, and accompanies them to the Marshalsea. He hears the prostitute's wild apology to Little Dorrit for thinking her a child, then watches
her brush against the sleeve of his coat as she goes off, once more to
hide "within the dark margins of the novel."[5] The interlude recreates
Dickens, in other words, and it does so precisely at the point where
Spenser Spender's filmed re-creation of Dickens failed. It exemplifies
the only and best way (as Ackroyd would have it) of making the past accessible to the present, through the agency of words on a page.

If the teaching of *The Great Fire of London* is that Dickens cannot now be adapted to film—How Not to Do It, in the Circumlocution Office sense of the phrase—it was a lesson lost on the film director
Christine Edzard, who a mere five years after the novel's appearance released her screen adaptation of *Little Dorrit*. This was a much-heralded
production. It was many years in the preparation, a triumph of individual dedication over industry doubts (the film's funding was unsure
until the last moment), and a work of undoubted seriousness and ambition (six and a half hours long, it was nevertheless shown theatrically,
not serialized on television: it was a *film*).[6] Edzard wrote the script and
directed; her husband Richard Goodwin produced; their joint company,
Sands Films, employed working methods as closely collaborative as the
Archers.' Their *Little Dorrit* promised a singleness of vision, an auteur-
ist approach, not seen in Dickens adaptations since David Lean's famous
Great Expectations and *Oliver Twist* of the 1940s. Edzard's *Little Dorrit*
seemed of further, feminist interest because it made so much of Little
Dorrit's own perspective on happenings. Following up on a line from
Dickens himself, "This history must sometimes see with Little Dorrit's
eyes," Edzard divided her film into two parts, the first from Clennam's
point of view, the second from Little Dorrit's. In this schema, identical
scenes are sometimes given to the viewer twice, in different framings,
with different lighting, the mises-en-scène and dialogue subtly adjusted:
a dank Clennamesque view of Dorrit's Marshalsea room, and then a
brighter, cheerier, Little-Dorrit-influenced view of the same chamber.
"The mere lighting of a candle, which sheds a gaunt and sickly pallor
in Arthur's half of the film, is a joyous outburst in [Little Dorrit's]. Her
eye brings colour and warmth to dingy and depressed surroundings";

so John Carey commented in a commendatory pamphlet accompanying the film's release.[7]

In 1987, then, Dickens's *Little Dorrit* turned out to be filmable after all, and filmable in a way many reviewers could praise, for such things as Alec Guinness's performance as a monstrously egotistic William Dorrit, or for the authenticity of the Victorian costuming; Edzard had worked previously chiefly as a designer, and took enormous care with such things as fabrics, shoes, and men's tall hats. No critic then or now could deny the thoughtfulness or the thoroughness, within fairly severe budgetary limits, of her film.[8] But critics then and now have also drawn attention to the obvious shortcomings of the adaptation—its omission of key characters of the original (the villainous Blandois, Little Dorrit's antitype; the servant Tattycoram; the perverse Miss Wade), the uniformly flat and unimaginative camera work and utterly conventional editing technique; the bright-hued cheerfulness imposed on what is after all among the darkest of Dickens's fictions, and therefore the systematic exclusion of the novelist's powerful sense of evil.[9] To this might be added her exclusion of Dickens's sense of strangeness, his liking for the grotesque and the conspicuously unthematic. The film's Mr. F's Aunt is toned down, a shadow of that figure of malevolent lunacy, unexplained and unexplainable, given to us by the novel. It is significant also that Edzard omits Little Dorrit's chance meeting with the prostitute and her *strange* wild cry.

By far the most considered and persuasive of the critiques the film received is an essay by Grahame Smith, published three years after the film's release—persuasive partly because Smith moves with such skill between this one version of Dickens and the more general, much argued about, highly theorized issue of film adaptation. Smith is not like Ackroyd, or like the ideologues who (more rigorously if less entertainingly than Ackroyd) argue for the radical incommensurability of film and literature, of image and word. On the contrary, and following the film scholar Dudley Andrew's lead, Smith acknowledges in a commonsense way the elements that film and literature have in common, such as dialogue, character, setting, and imagery with a connotative as opposed to merely denotative force. The problem according to Smith is just that, in this filmed *Little Dorrit*, these elements are haphazardly and unconvincingly handled.[10]

Arguably, it is Edzard's failure to provide imagery of the connotative sort that matters most. Her minimalist mise-en-scène may be
accounted for by limited funds, may even seem gallantly achieved in
the face of difficulties, but it is still meager in implication, and it still
amounts to a disservice to Dickens. At a key moment of the plot, Little
Dorrit meets Clennam on the Iron Bridge over the Thames. In the film,
the bridge is a cramped studio construction, set against a wholly unper-
suasive matte background of ships; it conveys nothing. In the novel, the
bridge is a place of escape from the claustrophobia of the Marshalsea,
an opening to the sky, the site where Little Dorrit's heart begins to open,
the perfect emblem of Dickens's management of space throughout the
novel, of his modulation between the tight little prison cells where his
characters lock themselves up and that vast, indifferent, unmanageable
city ("They went quietly down into the roaring streets . . .") receiving
them in the end. As another acute critic, Graham Petrie, has observed,
Dickens creates "a world . . . that exists effortlessly and simultaneously
on many levels and fuses the experience of the individual with the social universe in which he moves." This Dickensian world is formed by
images—which might indeed be moving images on a screen, in a film
adaptation of sufficient ingenuity—that seem to be the "inevitable reali-
zation" of a pattern, and that appear both literal and dream-like. Indeed,
in Dickens, the normal and abnormal, the individual and the social,
the visualized and the hallucinated, the denotative and the connotative, tend to merge into each other, obscuring the categorical distinctions between them.[11]

It follows that capturing multivalent images, putting mise-en-scène
at the disposal of larger meanings, must be one essential task of Dickens
adaptations. A no less important task is the aspect of film work so obsessed over in ordinary reviewing and so oddly neglected in academic
film scholarship, acting. Performance is, obviously, the means of putting an author's text into dramatized form. It furnishes an interpretation of that text (Dennis Potter's "act of loving criticism" in the lines
quoted at the head of this chapter), sets a mood, and establishes a pace.
On a small scale, individual character is acted. On the largest scale, an
overall stylization is acted. In the Royal Shakespeare Company's brilliantly successful 1980 staging of *Nicholas Nickleby*, a production which
a number of reviewers of *Little Dorrit* praised at Edzard's expense, the

performances were not just individually commendable, Roger Rees's earnest Nicholas, David Threlfall's compelling Smike, and so on. The performances were of a piece: consistently declamatory and theatrical, anti-naturalistic, surrounded as it were by a circle of Dickensian stage fire. All this befitted a novel so full of grotesque and comic turns, of melodrama, and of theatrical characters, namely, Vincent Crummles and his tattered but game troupe of players, from whom the RSC directors John Caird and Trevor Nunn seemed to take their artistic cues.[12]

When Edzard filmed *Little Dorrit,* she had a very different fiction to adapt, a novel of restrained gestures and imprisoned feelings, and in the best moments of her work she and her actors seem to find together a performance style commensurate with the original. Derek Jacobi, as Clennam, on his way out of the Marshalsea on the occasion of Dorrit's triumphant release, touches a banister with delicate lingering affection. This is his farewell to the place (and to his incipient love for Little Dorrit), the substitute for the gesture which William Dorrit himself, newly at liberty and swollen with pride, would not deign to make. Alec Guinness, meanwhile, as Dorrit, conveys everything it is possible to convey about that character's tatty lordliness in the inflection he gives to the word "money." But in too many other instances the acting in Edzard's film falls flat. Her Little Dorrit (Sarah Pickering, a previously unknown drama student), for instance, is merely neutral, blank in reaction shots, unvarying in voice and posture. She shows no sign of the repressed yearning in the character, a yearning signaled by many textual passages and carefully depicted in some of Phiz's original illustrations to the novel, above all "The Story of the Princess."

The real problem, however, may lie less with actors' skills or Edzard's experience directing actors than with cinematic technique. In a film, a performance is what *appears.* It originates in acting and directing but manifests itself fully in photography and editing as well, the attention given to a face in a close-up, a certain camera angle, a dissolve from one action to another. These are conventional enough cinematic devices. They constitute a language which filmmakers and viewers have all learned—but which Edzard's *Little Dorrit,* in its predictable framings and flat presentations (the camera fails to isolate and draw attention to that delicate gesture of Jacobi's), awkwardly misspeaks. For a Dickens adaptation more fluent in this language, and thus for a more convincing rejoinder to Ackroyd's skepticism, we will have to look elsewhere.

In 1985 the BBC broadcast an eight-part television serialization of *Bleak House,* with a script by Arthur Hopcraft, art design by Tim Harvey, and direction by Ross Devenish. The BBC producers were John Harris and Betty Willingale, the first of whom would go on to have a hand in producing Dennis Potter's *The Singing Detective,* while the second, a veteran of a BBC *Mansfield Park* miniseries in 1983 and a longtime script editor, would produce Potter's adaptation of *Tender Is the Night* in 1986. Supervising the project as executive producer was Jonathan Powell, the then head of BBC drama, who by the mid-1980s had produced many television versions of classic English fiction, including Hardy's *Mayor of Casterbridge* as adapted by Potter, and who had worked with Arthur Hopcraft on a brilliant serialization of John Le Carré's *Tinker, Tailor, Soldier, Spy* in 1979.

When broadcast in Britain and a few months later on PBS in the United States, this *Bleak House* was enthusiastically received, with much of the reviewers' approval going to the performances of its stars, Diana Rigg as Lady Dedlock and Denholm Elliott as Mr. Jarndyce. Even Peter Ackroyd praised the first episode, though temperately, and he foresaw accurately that the series would be more serious than the original ("closer to Dostoevsky than to Dickens"). As could have been predicted, he also lamented the fact that television adaptation had become a substitute for reading texts—"a problem for those who like their fiction 'straight.'"[13] In later years, the series has gotten its share of academic commendation—"modestly faithful to the novel's labyrinthine gloom"; the "casting could not have been faulted"; "a series of brilliant transitions"—though scarcely in such terms as to keep it current, while a recent, highly theorized study of Dickensian adaptation brought the series up only to misremember ("the Diana Rigg-Trevor Howard *Bleak House*") who was in it.[14] Plainly, without a famous creative name attached to it, without the intensely personal vision a figure like Potter brought to his multipart dramas, without the innovativeness of Edzard's *Little Dorrit* or the cachet of being a film, the BBC *Bleak House* has fallen into the obscurity suffered by many television miniseries after broadcast. On video, it was long out-of-print and only achieved DVD publication in 2005, the year when the BBC serialized *Bleak House* yet again, in a longer but less accomplished version directed by Justin Chadwick and Susanna White.

Obscurity, to be sure, is routinely the fate of Dickens miniseries. Any one version of the novelist's work is now difficult to notice against the background of the relentless serialization which has gone on in the last thirty years. Since 1975, there have been a dozen or more television adaptations of major Dickens novels, some of them (*A Tale of Two Cities, Our Mutual Friend*) done twice. In 1985 alone *Bleak House* was preceded by a twelve-part BBC *Pickwick Papers* and followed by a twelve-part BBC *Oliver Twist*. All these adaptations, whether produced at the BBC or elsewhere (Granada made a notable *Martin Chuzzlewit* in 1994, with a script by David Lodge), have their various strengths. What the 1985 *Bleak House* does, however, in demonstrating the possibilities of screened Dickens, is distinctive; distinctive in a way that involves a governing conception, a considered response to the original, but even more a steady inventiveness with small details of design, acting, and camera work. In other words, it benefits from close reading, as if it were a written fiction, as if it were *Bleak House* itself. It rewards attention beyond that which it received on the eight Wednesday evenings of its transmittal twenty-five years ago.

Every adaptation of Dickens faces the problem of coping with a long book's miscellaneousness, the jumbled Krook's-warehouse quality of the author's imagination. *Bleak House* the novel, though markedly less miscellaneous than, say, *Nicholas Nickleby*, has its oddities, often comic ones. When the main characters go in search of Neckett's orphaned children they run into a street boy who grotesquely suckles and fondles the iron spikes of a wicket gate; or there is a figure like Guster, maid to the law-stationer Mr. Snagsby, who thinks there is treasure buried in Snagsby's cellar, money "guarded by an old man with a white beard, who cannot get out for seven thousand years, because he said the Lord's Prayer backwards."[15] Meanwhile that figure of probity and compassion, John Jarndyce, the moral center of the entire fiction, comes attended by eccentric whimsicalities—his obsessive fancy about the bitter east wind, his Growlery, his mussing of his hair in embarrassment. Early adaptations of Dickens, for example George Cukor's famous MGM version of

David Copperfield (1935), tended to revel in this sort of thing: "I just had to go with the vitality of the thing," Cukor commented.[16] Confronted by the same sort of thing, Arthur Hopcraft determined on a different proceeding, a monumental task of pruning and compression.

The script Hopcraft wrote cuts back sharply on whimsy and keeps, in the main, to the essential plot lines of the original. These are the marriage of Ada and Richard, the two wards in Chancery, and Richard's disastrous involvement in the disputed-will lawsuit Jarndyce versus Jarndyce; the lawyer Tulkinghorn's power-play against Lady Dedlock, based on what she accidentally reveals of her feelings for her long-ago lover Captain Hawdon; the eventual murder of Tulkinghorn by Lady Dedlock's resentful French maid; the secret of Esther Summerson's parentage; Esther's alliance with her mother Lady Dedlock, and the pursuit of the desperate Lady Dedlock by Esther and Inspector Bucket; the contention between Esther's gratitude to John Jarndyce (a more serious figure, in Hopcraft's script, than in the original) and her love for the young physician Allan Woodcourt; the disfiguring fever Esther catches from Jo the crossing-sweeper, and Jo's own pathetic death. That all these developments are managed as fully as they are is due to the expansiveness of the eight-part television form, but also to the genius of Hopcraft, who seems to have well understood what is central in Dickens's novel—the fog of Chancery, spreading out through all classes of society like a miasma, a disease of obfuscation and delay—and what is peripheral to it. When he cuts characters, he does so with minimal loss. Mrs. Jellyby, the African philanthropist who grievously neglects her own children, might go, because the point about shortsighted social reform is sufficiently made in the figure of Mrs. Pardiggle, the Tractarian bully accompanying Ada and Esther to the working-class families in the brickyards. (Hopcraft may have found it particularly easy to delete Mrs. Jellyby's vaporings about "Borrioboola-Gha, on the left bank of the Niger" because before becoming a television dramatist, he had been a reporter with a social conscience, and had published a substantial book of African reportage, *Born to Hunger,* in 1968.)

If Hopcraft decided to keep neither the spike-fondling boy nor Guster's interesting theory of the treasure (Guster herself appears for a minute or two in the series), he did preserve a measure of Dickensian grotesquerie, for example in the paralytic bill-broker Grandfather

Smallweed and his retinue, whose comedy could be conveyed visually, or in Krook's famous death by Spontaneous Combustion (filmed with a shadowy vagueness, as if allowing Dickens's conception to register without necessarily endorsing a belief in it). In his script Hopcraft found room also for the demented Miss Flite and her collection of captive birds, for the unctuous preacher Chadband, and for the lawyer's Cockney clerk Mr. Guppy, a young, florid-waistcoat-wearing would-be gent of the type Dickens repeatedly portrayed, partly because he had once been that type himself. Above all, Hopcraft gave prominence to Harold Skimpole, who in *Bleak House* fulfills the role of Mrs. Gamp in *Martin Chuzzlewit* or Flora Finching in *Little Dorrit*—the role of the performer with words, the monologuist, whose cascades of verbiage allow Dickens to laugh at, to exaggerate and render harmless, an effusiveness which he shared, and knew he shared. Skimpole, equally in the novel and the television drama, is a splendid talker, so splendid that we come to know he is dangerous, and in conveying this sense of Skimpole's nature Hopcraft later had the expert help of the BBC director of photography Kenneth MacMillan. MacMillan shot Skimpole almost always in the same medium close-up, at a performer's distance from his fascinated audience, whose faces we see in repeated reaction shots. It is as though the very force of Skimpole's theatrical personality keeps the camera well back. The acting of T. P. McKenna as Skimpole, markedly better than Nathaniel Parker's rendering of the part in the 2005 *Bleak House,* is full of studied gestures and well-timed glances, of phrasing which the character is in love with the moment it leaves his mouth, and of course it collaborates in the effect.[17] Altogether, this presentation of Skimpole demonstrates what Edzard's *Little Dorrit* so signally lacks, the close coordination of writing, acting, and photographing.

The performer with language whom we do not see in the BBC *Bleak House* is the heroine herself. Dickens's Esther Summerson shares in the telling of the story. She does so in past-tense, first-person chapters alternating with present-tense chapters from an omniscient, or at least more knowledgeable and sardonic, point of view. This double narrative, unique in Dickens, allows the novelist to cover much ground—scenes which Esther could not possibly witness, perspectives she could not entertain—while he simultaneously is able to characterize Esther in her own voice. As much as she becomes present to the reader in her actions, the cosseting of Ada or the jingling of her household keys, she becomes present in her words, her constant self-deprecation ("I know I am not clever" is the first thing she says), her dreadful coyness about her love for Allan and his for her, her inability to stop talking about her disfigurement by the fever, even while she lectures herself about the need to stop talking. On television, *Bleak House* puts "I am not clever" into a line of Esther's dialogue but does little to convey her interpretations of events. It could scarcely do so. Graham Greene, who might have been expected to know about such things, once flatly observed that you "cannot tell a story from the single point of view of one character in a film. You cannot look through the eyes of one character . . ."[18] Such film techniques for first-person presentation as there are—the voice-over, the point-of-view shot—are limited in effect, and only the second is employed in *Bleak House,* sparingly. In fact point-of-view shots are reserved chiefly for Jo, as when he enters the crowded inquest and sees a room full of hostile adults looming ahead.

What the series does do, in time-honored fashion, is use acting as a simulacrum for the subjective voice. Over and over again the series captures Esther in the act of looking at something—or, often enough, looking away from it. The Esther Summerson here (Suzanne Burden) glances compulsively down whenever she receives attention: when the Lord Chancellor names her, when she remembers Miss Barbary's cruel words to her as a child ("It would have been better, Little Esther, if you'd never been born"), when a seedy gentleman stares at her on Krook's staircase (her father Captain Hawdon or "Nemo," though she knows nothing of him as yet), or indeed when she sees Krook fingering Ada's beautiful blonde hair, since a momentary glimpse of sexuality or vulnerability, even in other people, is enough to shame her. This bit of actor's business is closely analogous to Phiz's illustrations of Esther in the original, with her head turned away or bowed down or obscured by her bonnet in an extraordinary number of plates ("Light" in Chapter 51 is a particularly good example). If Phiz's illustrations are meant chiefly to portray Esther's sensitivity about her scarred face, they also diagnose, like the head-bowings of the television series or the self-deprecating phrasing Dickens gives Esther to speak, the pathology of female shame.

It is not solely a business of downcast eyes and averted glances. When Mr. Guppy makes his avowal of love to Esther, she sharply refuses him. She then falls back, in the novel, to forced cheerfulness and busy-bee activity ("I sat there . . . finishing my books and payments, and getting through plenty of business") followed by an emotional reaction which even the relentlessly analytical Esther cannot quite understand:

> I surprised myself by beginning to laugh about it, and then surprised myself still more by beginning to cry about it. In short, I was in a flutter for a little while; and felt as if an old chord had been more coarsely touched than it ever had been since the days of the dear old doll, long buried in the garden. (141–142)

In the television version, by contrast, Esther closes the door on the rejected Guppy and retreats to the hall in considerable agitation. As we watch from the side, she examines herself in a mirror, ineffectually tidies her hair, and then moves in dismay back from the wall, as if pushed physically away by the sight of her own face—which we are never shown, since the point of the shot is not the image but the strangeness of the way she watches the image. This Esther seems both fascinated and appalled by the attractiveness which has conquered Guppy. It is an ingenious and convincing movement, more efficient than Dickens's text in communicating complex feelings. And it is filmed without words.

Perhaps all screen versions of Dickens novels must seem non-verbal in comparison with the originals' talkativeness, their "crowded, many-voiced, anonymous world of jokes, stories, rumours, songs, shouts, banners, greetings, idioms, addresses,"[19] their foreign or class-based or regional accents, their reachings for eloquence and delight in malapropism. But the BBC *Bleak House* is especially non-verbal. Esther's explanation for why she has not revealed her engagement to Jarndyce, "We have respected each other's reticence," might be the motto of the whole enterprise. In its opening scene, we are given a bleak silence broken only by the ticking of a clock, and leading into Miss Barbary's catechizing of the child Esther about guilt. In this case, the cue comes from Dickens ("The clock ticked, the fire clicked; not another sound had been heard in the room," 25–26). Other subdued scenes were invented by Hopcraft. At a fatigued moment in their pursuit of Lady Dedlock, Esther and Inspector Bucket examine, wordlessly, the body of a woman who has apparently hanged herself; nothing is heard but the dripping rain and a barking dog. Later, after Richard's death, a stricken grief falls on Bleak

House. Esther sews with her maid Charley in silence while a clock ticks oppressively; this is a parallel, of course, to the opening scene of the serialization. Meanwhile, in an exterior shot, with no sound at all, not even music, John Jarndyce walks outside, looks at the grey day, pokes idly with his stick at a shrub, and goes back in, communicating his aphasic sorrow by little more than slow movement and a meaningless gesture.

In a sense, such photographed moments are true to the novelist Dickens was becoming as he wrote *Bleak House,* discovering that he could get by with less of the verbal boisterousness of works like *Nicholas Nickleby* or *David Copperfield,* attempting more of the restraint and melancholy which are such marked features of *Little Dorrit* (serialized a little more than two years after *Bleak House*). Like the later novel, *Bleak House* includes moments important because of things left unsaid or actions not taken in them. One or two of these are admirably conveyed in the BBC *Bleak House,* as when Jarndyce sees Esther crying and reaches out to her, only to hesitate and pull his hand back from her shoulder, constrained by knowledge of his age and her youth. (The BBC film editor cuts away to this finely acted small gesture in close-up; he makes something of it, unlike Christine Edzard with Derek Jacobi's comparable gesture in her film of *Little Dorrit*).

Still, Dickens's *Bleak House* is not quite his *Little Dorrit.* It remains something of a "loose, baggy monster," to use Henry James's famous phrase for nineteenth-century novels, a mixture of facetiousness and earnest moralizing, of comedy and melodrama. It is emotionally and verbally indulgent, and for its nineteenth-century volubility the BBC apparently felt a need to substitute a more modern aesthetic, of controlled feelings and expressive simplicity. "O my child, my child, I am your wicked and unhappy mother! O try to forgive me!" Dickens's Lady Dedlock declaims to Esther at their climactic recognition scene in the summer house at Chesney Wold. Hopcraft has her say "I am your mother . . . [pause] . . . forgive me . . . [pause] . . . forgive." He brings a similar spareness to his version of Jo's death, in which the street-sweeping waif does not, as in the original, try to follow Woodcourt in saying the Lord's Prayer. For Hopcraft, the character's inarticulateness is precisely what makes him affecting.

Whatever the motive for these adjustments to Dickens, these simplications of language and excisions of humor, their effect is to give the film a consistent tone, which the novel lacks—or disdains to attempt. The BBC *Bleak House* is more monochrome than parti-colored, monochrome literally in several of the settings, like the dusty or smoky blue-gray of the brickmakers' hovel, or the black-and-white of the Court of Chancery. Structurally, too, the film aims at unity. It begins with Esther's blighted childhood and ends with the joyous birth of Richard and Ada's baby. And it makes extraordinary efforts to link its plots together by cinematic means.

These efforts depend on editing. At their simplest, they connect past with present. The face of Esther the little girl dissolves into the (equally sad, equally self-controlled) face of Esther the grown woman. Or simple action is paralleled with simple action: Miss Flite leads Esther, Richard, and Ada upstairs to her room, and on her line "Follow me, please!" the film cuts to a footman leading Tulkinghorn upstairs at the Dedlock mansion, in a blaze of candlelight; there follows a cut back to the dark staircase at Krook's. Not a great deal need be implied by this sort of graphic match and contrast of settings, or by thematic versions of the same technique, as when Lady Dedlock talks to Rosa, the pretty girl whom she keeps by her side as maid and pet. Does young Watt Rouncewell love Rosa? "He loves you . . . trust me," Lady Dedlock says decisively, and there follows a quick cut to an extreme close-up of Lady Dedlock's own love letters to Captain Hawdon, now being fingered by Tulkinghorn, the pink ribbon around them coming loose. More complex effects are, however, possible. Tulkinghorn's face dissolves into Guppy's face; these are two expressions of the Law, one threatening, one comic. In a light-hearted debate with Jarndyce, Skimpole airily speaks of a "child of the universe," whereupon Jarndyce, furrowing his brow, responds that "the universe" makes "rather an indifferent parent"—and in a quick cut we have displayed for us the actual victim of indifference, Jo at the inquest on Nemo, Jo being casually exhibited in all his appalling ignorance. Moments later Skimpole drops another remark about businessmen loving their children. There follows a quick ironic cut to the business-like Tulkinghorn menacing Jo, forcing him over a banister, trying to extract information about Nemo from him.

Dickens's text furnishes antecedents for these transitional devices, including the ironic ones:

Every body starts. For a gun is fired close by.

"Good gracious, what's that!" cries Volumnia with her little withered scream.

"A rat," says my Lady. "And they have shot him."

Enter Mr. Tulkinghorn. . . . (598)

Indeed, there are passages in *Bleak House* so cinematic in style that they seem to belong to a screenplay, with specified cuts, camera angles, tracking shots, and lighting effects:

> The day is closing in and the gas is lighted, but is not yet fully effective, for it is not quite dark. Mr. Snagsby standing at his shop-door looking up at the clouds, sees a crow, who is out late, skim westward over the leaden slice of sky belonging to Cook's Court. The crow flies straight across Chancery Lane and Lincoln's Inn Garden, into Lincoln's Inn Fields.
>
> Here, in a large house, formerly a house of state, lives Mr. Tulkinghorn. . . . (145)

Though a film would be able to accomplish almost instantaneously what must still be time-consuming on the page, for example the flight of that crow, followed linearly through Dickens's paragraph, the important point is that Dickens shares an essential technique with filmmakers. He devises parallel plots and contrives means of narrative connection or ironic disjuncture between them. This is of course the essential argument of the best-known twentieth-century essay on Dickens and film, Sergei Eisenstein's "Dickens, Griffith, and the Film Today" (1944), which traces ideological montage—the intercutting of parallel plot lines, their being placed in various modes of amplification or contention by juxtaposed images, the stimulation of the audience to thought by that juxtaposition—from Dickens to D. W. Griffith and onward to contemporary filmmaking.[20] It is in fact something like an Eisensteinian montage we see when the *Bleak House* series gives us first Esther's fever-ravaged face, then a slow dissolve to Rosa's insipidly pretty one, centered within the frame precisely as Esther's was, and reflected back to us by a boudoir mirror—that same item of furnishing kept scrupulously out of Esther's bedroom, lest she see what sickness has done to her. By this dissolve, the film drives home its point, or points: the unfairness of what has happened to the heroine, the pathos of Lady Dedlock trying to provide herself with a substitute for her lost daughter, the ignorance about their true relations from which all the characters suffer, the apparent distances separating Tom-All-Alone's and Bleak House and Chesney Wold, the real and disturbing connectedness of all these places; the artistically pleasing and thematically expressive coherence of the film itself.

Like *The Singing Detective, Bleak House* benefited greatly from the ambitiousness and resources of the BBC in the 1980s. The series was a full year in production; a substantial budget (about £2.8 million) permitted among other things the shooting of *Bleak House* entirely on film, as opposed to a mixture of film for exteriors and videotape for interiors; it was the first Dickens dramatization to receive this treatment.[21] What was photographed on that film was a mise-en-scène remarkable in its consistency and its suggestiveness. The executive producer commented that he wished his Victorian London to look like the streets of Calcutta,[22] and this he achieved. Darkness and mud are everywhere, some of the latter being swept up in hit-or-miss fashion by Jo; poverty and riches go on random display; sightlines are blocked by the sheer mass of Londoners moving through the streets. He also wanted fog, as any adaptor of *Bleak House* would, since fog is the central conception of Dickens's novel, an atmosphere "thickened by stagnancy and corruption" that can actually be seen, that hangs about the Lord Chancellor on his bench and gives him a "foggy glory" as he sits "mistily engaged" in one of the Court's hopeless causes.[23] Fogginess came at some cost to the BBC production. Smoke machines were too noisy to be run during takes, and so contrivances had to be found to keep the smoke confined within the set; Denholm Elliott remembered that the smoke gave everyone asthmatic coughs.[24] Still, it was essential, and in the finished series it is to be seen almost everywhere, in the streets, inside Krook's and the brickmakers' houses, in the arched passages outside Chancery, curling over Hawdon's wretched burial place. Many interior scenes, if not literally foggy, were photographed in soft focus or with a diffusing filter, so that they look in keeping with the exteriors. This is a *Bleak House* gauzily illuminated with flickering firelight, candles, daylight coming through dirty windows, gaslights flaring. The dining room of the Jarndyce house in the evening, in a scene just before Inspector Bucket secretly removes

Jo from his safe lodging there, is a magnificent composition of candles and lamps, all with their little halos of blurry light, and of faces moving in and out of the glow or the shadow. When Bucket marches Jo away, holding the sick boy at a safe arm's length, photographed by a long-focal-length lens that slows down their progress and makes it look emblematical of a cruel social policy getting nowhere, they move through a bluish fog not unlike the light we have just seen indoors. Naturalistic and symbolic, denotative and connotative, this is precisely the sort of multivalent image which adaptation of Dickens requires.

"Appropriately shrouded and bespattered," one reviewer wrote of the series, "the most visually authentic Dickens yet brought to television." "You could smell the mustiness," commented another and, adding his own superlative, "the most perfect use of lighting that there has ever been on television."[25] Amid all this deserved praise some room might have been spared for notice of the series' framings, which are often complex and interesting. When Jarndyce welcomes the young people to their new home for the first time, Bleak House is photographed in a long shot framed by the decorative hanging boughs of trees, giving a picture-perfect, indeed too picture-perfect effect. The impression conveyed is that all this happy domesticity is being smugly taken for granted, or may be at some unspecified risk from events to come. The pictorialist effect is reinforced seconds later when a shot through an arch inside the house gathers Ada and Esther protectively within its border, as if the BBC's director of photography were imitating one of Phiz's cosy compositions. In a later street scene, by contrast, all is chaos. Mr. Guppy in the foreground jealously watches Esther and Woodcourt in the background, but watches them through the out-of-focus items on a street-hawker's cart, then over a pair of horses drawing a carriage, and through busy traffic crossing and re-crossing the scene. In other words we have something more than a straightforward point-of-view shot. We have a point-of-view shot which is disordered by the viewer's, Guppy's, hectic emotions and which is simultaneously subject to indifferent London life. That life is going on whatever mini-dramas of love and jealousy are taking place in its midst. The world the camera shows is that essentially Dickensian one which (to quote Graham Petrie again) "exists effortlessly and simultaneously on many levels and fuses the experience of the individual with the social universe in which he moves."

In Dickens's world also, ordinary objects—his writerly mise-en-scène—are at certain moments imaginatively transformed under the pressure of the life around them, which is to say the pressure of Dickens's metaphorizing energy. In a scene of high tension when Tulkington enters Nemo's room on the prowl for incriminating evidence, we read, in quick succession, that in Nemo's fireplace sits a "rusty skeleton of a grate, pinched in the middle as if Poverty had gripped it"; that his desk is a wilderness with a "rain of ink" upon it; and that the sides of his shabby portmanteau have collapsed "like the cheeks of a starved man" (151). No adaptation could hope to realize figurations like these on film, or no adaptation in realist mode, like the BBC *Bleak House* (more symbolist versions, like Peter Barnes's extremely theatrical *Hard Times* of 1994, might have some chance).

What the director and designer of *Bleak House* between them do is work in a different way with mise-en-scène. They animate it with acting, or they embed acting within a setting that clarifies and supports it; the process is reciprocal, obviously. To take one example, Diana Rigg's performance as Lady Dedlock has much to do with reserve—aristocratic hauteur, the guardedness of a woman with a secret, an inexpressible unhappiness—and the reserve becomes visible not just in her fixed gazes or peremptory line-readings but in her relation to surroundings at Chesney Wold or in London, where she seems to take refuge within the pompous Dedlock furniture. Her costumes and fantastically elaborate (and no doubt historically accurate) hair-do contribute even more to the effect. She looks assembled by an act of will rather than alive, a masterwork of "enforced composure," as the novel puts it. When she faints at the sight of Hawdon's handwriting, dropping the fan which has been part of her armor, or later when she strips her fingers of her jewels (a melodramatically acted moment, as it should be, accompanied by melodramatic music) and leaves Sir Leicester, the sense of release is all the more powerful. Rigg is too good a performer, however, to overdo the changes in the character. When her Lady Dedlock lies prostrate and dying at the burial place of her lover and speaks to Esther (a major change from the novel, where the guilty mother dies before her daughter finds her), there is some reserve left yet in her farewell, a touch of aristocratic self-control at the moment of final abandonment.

Even more obviously, the villain Tulkinghorn belongs to his costume, the buttoned-up lawyer's black suit, the tight white cravat. Peter Vaughan, playing the part, modeled Tulkinghorn on that Lincoln's-Inn-Fields crow mentioned in Dickens's text: "he's like a huge bird walking about . . . I became a bird, like him."[26] But this is a noticeably silent crow, unwilling to give anything away. Vaughan's small pursed-up mouth only stingily lets out the character's declarations. Or the actor merely gestures. In the scene when Tulkinghorn has Jo brought to his London house to confront the French maid dressed as Lady Dedlock, and wishes to indicate that Jo should listen to the veiled figure's voice, he merely points to his open mouth. With Lady Dedlock herself, Tulkinghorn similarly holds himself firmly in, grudgingly issues his demands to her, as if aware that his power is best communicated by impassivity, especially if impassivity can force *her* to displays of passionate feeling. At the opening of the final meeting between them, when Tulkinghorn complains of Lady Dedlock's untrustworthiness, Vaughan uses the slightest of tics to convey Tulkinghorn's impatience or suppressed excitement; he rubs his hands back and forth over his knees. At the end of the scene, Lady Dedlock acknowledges her secret, and Tulkinghorn for once takes her up sharply. "*My* secret," he says, two words which Vaughan speaks with a miser's greedy pleasure and a wicked glint in his eye, confirming what Lady Dedlock has said about his motives. Far from wanting to protect Sir Leicester's reputation, Tulkinghorn is eager only to hoard up the passions of fear he inspires in others.

All this lawyerly guardedness has of course to be photographed in extreme close-up, so a viewer of the series grows remarkably familiar with the contours of Peter Vaughan's face, and of Diana Rigg's face. Andrew Davies, the scriptwriter for the later, 2005 BBC version of *Bleak House*, has said in an interview that it was difficult to rid his mind of images of these two actors in these two parts.[27] Indeed, Vaughan as Tulkinghorn is no less memorable when shown in long shot, solitary in the grand vertical spaces of Chesney Wold or his own London house. Against this background his stillness or considered movements register with particular clarity. Meanwhile the house interiors are photographed in ways to emphasize their hulking pretentiousness. An especially fine sequence begins with following Jo's point of view as he stares at Tulkinghorn's painted ceiling, then continues with a slow tilt downward past sconces and law books to Jo's bedraggled figure, still pathetically holding on to his broom, viewed at a distance and dwarfed by these surroundings. If we turn to a very different location, Krook's warehouse, we witness a correspondingly different camera technique. Any large-scale moving shot here would run into the bric-a-brac of Krook's obsessions, the piles of legal documents (which Krook cannot read), the bags of ladies' hair, the miscellaneous ironmongery. Accordingly, Kenneth MacMillan shoots at a claustrophobic nearness to the action, in and amongst the junk and the characters trying to negotiate it, holding the camera steady or moving it minimally.

The effect achieved at Krook's, by both photography and design, is far from static or boring. When Esther and the wards in Chancery, Richard and Ada, follow Miss Flite there, they enter a setting that looks (and is photographed to look) like a haunted house. It is very dark, with dust and fog crept in from the streets outside. Over the jumbled mess Krook presides, the "Lord Chancellor" of his realm. He lights a lantern, the better to scrutinize his visitors—or his potential prey. "All's fish that comes to my nets," he jests, in hoarse, congested tones that by the end of the scene come to seem an aural analogue to the murk within the house. The yellow lantern light isolates faces, and in a series of rapid cuts the camera comes closer and closer to them while Krook intones the talismanic names "Jarndyce," "Carstone," "Barbary," "Clare," and "Dedlock"; soundtrack music also begins here. Everyone holds still, human fixtures amid all the other jumble of the warehouse. Krook relates the story of Tom Jarndyce's suicide. The veteran character actor playing the part, Bernard Hepton, who had worked with a Hopcraft script before, the adaptation of Le Carré's *Tinker, Tailor, Soldier, Spy,* beautifully conveys Krook's mingled amusement and sadism, qualities which he shares not just with the Lord Chancellor but with Tulkinghorn, and which are conveyed here in the same sort of screen-filling close-up used with the lawyer. Meanwhile horror registers on the faces of his young listeners, also shown in close-up, and lighted now from below in a particularly Gothic way; Krook is holding the lantern low. Krook finishes the tale by blowing out the candle in the lantern on the last word of the line "I heard the shot go echoin' and rattlin' right down at Chancery itself . . .

Tom Jarndyce, gone!" (he has a taste for striking effects, obviously), and the only sound heard thereafter is his wheezy laughter and water dripping in the silence. Altogether, it is as though the filming has momentarily come under the influence of Krook's melodramatic aesthetic and produced a scene according to his tastes and specifications.

In a rigorously realist production, this scene with Krook might be an aesthetic mistake. But it is not a mistake here. It is like the several other moments of the BBC *Bleak House* which prefer stylization to naturalism and a powerful cinematic rhetoric to understatement. On the prowl for Jo, Inspector Bucket approaches Bleak House in the form of a film-noirish, looming shadow, a representation perfectly in keeping with the character's self-dramatizing tendencies, and with the mystery of his ethical standing in the plot: is he a repressive police agent? A force for good? Or consider Miss Flite. Upon hearing the news of Richard's death, close upon the revelation that his Jarndyce inheritance has all been eaten up in legal costs, she despairingly frees her birds from their cages. In a nearly two-minute-long montage sequence, they fly out through the blowing fog and toward the viewer in slow motion, with an eerie flute solo on the soundtrack and with their owner chanting their names ("Hope, Youth, Joy . . . Madness, Death . . . the Wards in Chancery . . .") in a bizarre threnody. The slow motion—the flamboyant sort of thing which Dennis Potter loved and wished television did more of—captures both Miss Flite's stunned grief and the continuing entrapment of her mind within its obsession. At an equally important moment, Jo's death, Jarndyce calls out sardonically to the England which has so cruelly neglected the boy, in the indictment Dickens himself spoke in the novel: "Dead, Your Majesty. Dead, my lords and gentlemen. . . . And dying thus around us every day!" The frame freezes on Jarndyce's face, distorted with indignation and looking straight at the viewer.

This is a nearly perfect translation to film of that quality which George Orwell identified in a famous claim about the novelist:

> When one reads any strongly individual piece of writing, one has the impression of seeing a face somewhere behind the page. . . . [I]n the case of Dickens, I see a face that is not quite the face of Dickens's photographs, though it resembles it. It is the face of a man about forty, with a small beard and a high colour. He is laughing, with a touch of anger in

his laughter, but no triumph, no malignity. It is the face of a man who is always fighting against something, but who fights in the open and is not frightened, the face of a man who is *generously angry* . . .[28]

In other words, the stylized scenes in the television *Bleak House* express an aesthetic that after all does not belong to Krook, but to Dickens, or Dickens in his most demonstrative mode: impatient, insistent, declarative. It is an aesthetic emblematized by that figure on Tulkinghorn's painted ceiling which Jo sees in uncomprehending wonder, the Roman soldier ("Allegory") pointing straight down at the cautionary sight of the murdered lawyer. To convey his generous anger at societal wrongs (or his despair at the workings of the law, or his admiration for feminine loyalty) Dickens never hesitated to do exactly that, point; he wanted to make sure his readers would understand. Adaptations of Dickens, whatever subtleties and complexities they attempt (and must attempt, since in another mode Dickens is subtle and complex) must similarly not hesitate to point. The BBC *Bleak House* does its pointing in Krook's story, in Jarndyce's speech, and in Miss Flite's montage with the birds. It also does so in a single image summing up everything necessary to communicate about Richard Carstone's suffocation in the blank indeterminacy of Chancery. The frustrated litigant leaves the Court with Miss Flite, who is chattering on as usual. They walk slowly out through a framing arch, as if into some sort of emblematic design, just as with that earlier framing under a cosy arch of Bleak House. But nothing protective is intended this time. A glaring white fog gathers around the two silhouetted figures—it is a little painful to look at, actually—and gradually they exit into it, vanishing into vagueness. It is an image nowhere to be found in the novel but which Dickens, had he worked in television, would have been proud to invent.

ISHIGURO AND MERCHANT-IVORY, UPSTAIRS AND DOWNSTAIRS

What makes a particular novel a candidate for adaptation? The question hardly arises with novels like *Bleak House*, so popular over so many years, so much a part of readers' understanding of themselves and their culture, so *English*. To film Dickens is to confirm a national tradition by contributing to it. To do so at the end of the twentieth century or the beginning of the twenty-first is to participate in a specifically screen tradition as well, with David Lean's or Cavalcanti's versions of the novels still being remembered and still furnishing some basis for comparison with later efforts, with television miniseries still being produced and offering their episode-by-episode interpretations to an enormous audience.[29] To film Dickens is also to benefit from the obvious practical advantages which his books offer, such as familiar plots, cherished lines of dialogue, sharply drawn characters (many of them household names), a winning mixture of comedy and pathos, the appeal of period settings and costumes—an appeal which, in the case of *Bleak House*, is complicated by being yoked with an anti-Establishment anger ("Dead, Your Majesty. Dead, my lords and gentlemen . . .") that cannot but appear contemporary in its dark unanswerability.

To film Kazuo Ishiguro's novel *The Remains of the Day*, by contrast, the work of a writer relatively unknown at the time of publication (1989), the story of a conspicuous English political failure and a love affair that never comes to anything, would seem a riskier undertaking, with a range of arguments both for and against adaptation. On the one hand, the book, Ishiguro's third to be published, was a considerable success, winning the Booker Prize and contributing (like Salman Rushdie's even more successful works) to a widespread feeling that at the end of the twentieth century English fiction was in the process of being invigorated by new, youthful, cosmopolitan voices: "the Empire striking back." A valuable box-office property, then, and of the cutting-edge sort, the novel yet featured such traditional and photographable aspects of Englishness as a great house, a lord, a butler, a journey across the pastoral landscape, a heartbreaking farewell in the rain. Throughout, it was a highly visual piece of writing, a fiction constructed largely out of characters' views. These might be literal views, of the great house in question, Darlington Hall, or of quintessentially Home Counties scenes:

> . . . I could see early daylight at the edges of the curtains.
>
> When I parted them just a moment ago, the light outside was still very pale and something of a mist was affecting my view of the baker's shop and the chemist's opposite. Indeed, following the street further along to where it runs over the little round-backed bridge, I could see the mist rising from the river, obscuring almost entirely one of the bridge-posts.

Equally, they might be characters' views of each other as meaningfully disposed in a landscape or as arrayed in a certain kind of photogenic domesticity:

> . . . I can recall distinctly climbing to the second landing and seeing before me a series of orange shafts from the sunset breaking the gloom of the corridor where each bedroom door stood ajar. And as I made my way past those bedrooms, I had seen through a doorway Miss Kenton's figure, silhouetted against a window, turn and call softly: "Mr. Stevens, if you have a moment." As I entered, Miss Kenton had turned back to the window. Down below, the shadows of the poplars were falling against the lawn. To the right of our view, the lawn sloped up a gentle embankment to where the summerhouse stood, and it was there my father's figure could be seen, pacing slowly with an air of preoccupation—indeed, as Miss Kenton puts it so well, "as though he hoped to find some precious jewel he had dropped there."[30]

In other words, *The Remains of the Day* could be seen as offering an invitation to perspectival framings and intelligent camera work.

With camera work and the other processes of filming, indeed, Ishiguro had some significant acquaintance. In the 1980s he had written screenplays for two television dramas for Channel 4, *A Profile of Arthur J. Mason* and *The Gourmet,* both produced by Ann Skinner and directed by Michael Whyte.[31] He was obviously at home in the film world, the sort of contemporary writer to whom film-language similes came easily ("I would search through history books in the way that a film director might search for locations for a script he has already written"[32]) and whose teachers were cinematic, not just literary. Repeatedly in interviews Ishiguro acknowledged being influenced equally by Chekhov and by the great Japanese filmmaker Yasujiro Ozu. On at least one occasion, he claimed to derive the same thing from the two of them, "the courage and conviction to have a very slow pace and not worry if there isn't a strong plot."[33]

On the other hand, as must have been obvious to all would-be adaptors, *The Remains of the Day* presented certain difficulties. It abjured the Dickensian, demonstrative, emphatically dramatic mode ("there isn't a strong plot"). Stylistically, it might be said to point at nothing, but rather proceed by indirection and irony: subtleties hard to convey onscreen. Even more obviously, Ishiguro's narrative, being couched in the first-person reminiscences of Stevens, butler to Lord Darlington, would present problems of subjective rendering. Stevens's narrative was the heart of the novel, a dazzling bit of ventriloquism on Ishiguro's part, an utterly convincing performance of "butlerspeak."[34] That is, it was a performance of decorous clichés (Salisbury Cathedral described as an "august building," 27) and ponderous impersonality ("it is just that one never knows when one might be obliged to give out that one is from Darlington Hall," 11). It mimed the sort of linguistic dignity that is copied, perhaps imperfectly, certainly unconsciously, from the butler's employer's speech, just as the butler might also be happy to wear, without thinking twice about it, his employer's cast-off suits. It was a voice without color, without stridency, and not meant to be noticed (giving the "illusion of absence," Stevens says, is necessary to a good butler's waiting at table).

In filming, this on-going first-person commentary could not be replicated, though dialogue could express much of its flavor. The real challenge for the filmmaker would be replicating Stevens's perspective on events, which, much more than Esther's perspective in the alternate chapters of *Bleak House,* is skewed. The point of *The Remains of the Day* is everything Stevens fails to understand—everything, to use Ishiguro's metaphor, hidden in the "mist" which obscures his view and muffles his responsiveness. Stevens's narration of events is unreliable; wrong, evasive, self-serving, having to be adjusted or corrected by afterthoughts. In the Darlington Hall of the 1950s, Stevens notes nagging little problems in his day-to-day work of butlering and hastens to attribute them to a "faulty staff plan"; the reader understands without having to be prompted that they are actually the errors of an aging man searching for his lost competence, and searching no less pathetically than Stevens's father searches for the cause of *his* failure, as in the summerhouse-seen-from-a-window passage quoted above. In the Darlington Hall of the 1930s Stevens misreads or deliberately fends off the housekeeper Miss Kenton's delicate advances to him, and then later, when it is too late, when she has married a man whom she does not love for lack of the man she does, he imagines that she might still feature in an improved staff plan, and return to him. And nearly throughout the novel Stevens serves, and admires, an English peer whose political stupidity, or sentimentalism about the class solidarity of Anglo-Saxon gentlemen, makes him a pawn of pre-war Nazi diplomacy. As much as

Lord Darlington himself, Stevens subscribes to a belief in gentlemanly amateurism: "debates are conducted, and crucial decisions arrived at, in the privacy and calm of the great houses of this country" (115). The hollow greatness of Darlington Hall, the limitations of old-fashioned gentlemanliness, together with Stevens's disposal of his devotion in exactly the wrong quarter, are the two essential themes of the novel, and indeed the interconnected themes, as Thomas Leitch has observed: "the tight-lipped success of Stevens and Miss Kenton . . . in repressing their attraction to each other" is "a figure for England's prewar success in repressing its resistance to Hitler."[35] Repression in the smaller and the greater worlds is what any film adaptor, winding his way through the butler's elaborate self-justifications, would have to find cinematic means to convey.

Ishiguro's book was optioned by Harold Pinter, who wrote a screenplay from it, planning on a film to be produced by John Calley and directed by Mike Nichols. In his long and distinguished career as scriptwriter, Pinter had had prior experience with master-servant relations in two important films by Joseph Losey: *The Servant,* 1963 (adapting Robin Maugham's novel), and *The Go-Between,* 1970 (adapting L. P. Hartley's novel). Both of these fictions, with their first-person narrations, gave Pinter valuable experience in translating private memory to the screen, in contriving (as he implied in a later interview) for the eye to take over from the voice the task of communicating understandings and misunderstandings. With a script made from a first-person original, Pinter said, "You're looking through a keyhole"[36]—meaning, presumably, that the camera guiding the eye, even in apparently constricted framings, is capable of opening up into all sorts of wider meanings, including ones kept secret by (or from) the characters.

In the event, Pinter's screenplay was not used, at least not in its original form. Nichols was too committed to other projects to direct the film. Besides, "Mike felt that it was so *very* English that he would be rather uncomfortable doing it."[37] Accordingly, *The Remains of the Day* was turned over to James Ivory, Ismail Merchant, and Ruth Prawer Jhabvala, the director, producer, and screenwriter respectively of a team which had begun collaboration with *Shakespeare-Wallah* in 1965 and had achieved world-wide fame and success with their literary adap-

tations of the 1980s and early 1990s, Forster's *A Room with a View,*
Howards End, and *Maurice* chief among them. Given their reputation
for meticulous production values and respect for literature, they were
the filmmakers who might have been considered most appropriate for
Ishiguro's novel from the start; even Pinter thought so at one stage ("I
expect to work with Merchant Ivory on this one"[38]). For an American
(Ivory), a Muslim Indian (Merchant), and a German Jew married to
an Indian (Jhabvala) to adapt the novel of a writer born in Japan, with
financing for the project coming from Japan and the United States,
would on the face of it be to make an international rather than an English film. And yet the locations would be English, not to mention the
cast—in the lead roles, Anthony Hopkins and Emma Thompson, who
had just starred in *Howards End*—and above all the story. The Ishiguro-
Merchant-Ivory *Remains of the Day* would in effect be a joint effort in
defining a certain kind of Englishness from the outside. It would come
afresh to the archetype of the gentleman's gentleman (that "mythical
figure in British culture," according to Ishiguro[39]) and to a significant
national emblem, the great house and its life, rather than taking such
things for granted. It would constitute a cultural reappropriation, or
willed act of artistic resettlement, analogous to that dramatized in the
Archers' *A Canterbury Tale,* with its travelers coming from afar to af-
firm values at a central and hallowed place. Darlington Hall would re-
place Canterbury Cathedral as the central place, and the American
director James Ivory would stand in for the American sergeant Bob
Johnson, with the odd pleasing coincidence that Ivory too was raised in
Oregon and had a father in the lumber business.[40]

In writing her script, Jhabvala apparently retained much of Pinter's
conception (he was offered co-writing credit for the film, but declined)
while omitting his most politicized readings. Whether on her own or
following Pinter, she unquestionably preserved what was essential in
the original novel, including its fascination with scenes of watching. The
passage about seeing Stevens's father through the window, for example,
is faithfully reproduced. In the film, Miss Kenton calls Stevens to the
window, and glances at him as he looks out in a fixed stare; there follows a cut to what they are both spying on, the old man's sad search for
the cause of his tripping and falling with the loaded tea tray, "his pacing
slowly with an air of preoccupation," exactly as Ishiguro describes him.

All this was easy enough to dramatize and to photograph. In parts of the novel not so rewardingly cinematic, Jhabvala made cuts. Consider a series of passages beginning with Ishiguro's description of an English panorama, a hilltop view reminiscent of the ones incorporated in Forster's *Howards End* or elaborately photographed in *A Canterbury Tale*. Sent on holiday by his new American employer, Stevens stops his car and climbs to the top of a hill. His literal and very Forsterian view from there, of "field upon field rolling off into the far distance," of land rising and falling gently, of hedges and trees and sheep, of a square church tower almost on the horizon (26), might indeed have been photographed, but not so Stevens's later rumination on the *meaning* of what he has viewed:

> The English landscape at its finest—such as I saw it this morning—possesses a quality that the landscapes of other nations, however more superficially dramatic, inevitably fail to possess . . . the feeling that one is in the presence of greatness. . . . I would say that it is the very *lack* of obvious drama or spectacle that sets the beauty of our land apart. What is pertinent is the calmness of that beauty, its sense of restraint. It is as though the land knows of its own beauty, of its own greatness, and feels no need to shout about it. (28–29)

What is most pathetically on display here, of course, is Stevens's own personal and professional commitment to restraint, his middle-aged man's resignation to dullness, and his butler's condescension to foreign, less well-mannered, shouting nations, which might well have to be put in their place or shown the door. The point is that *all* the qualities of the paragraph, the commitment to restraint, the patriotism, the incipient aesthetic sense, the revelation of Stevens's inadequacy, would have to be demonstrated by other means, such as dialogue and, as we will see, Anthony Hopkins's acting; the only hilltop view actually provided in the film is a brief sunset shot.

The two most significant alterations which the film makes to the novel involve the depiction of Miss Kenton and the ending. The Miss Kenton of the novel does things, of course, moves about, speaks her dialogue, but in a real sense exists primarily in Stevens's memory or hope. Stevens calls her "Miss Kenton" (for most of the book's timeframe, she should properly be "Mrs. Benn") because the butler likes to conceive of her that way, even if he prissily corrects himself from time to time. Narratively, she acts and speaks at his emotional behest, with the result that some things about her are left uncertain—is she really crying behind her closed door? Or does Stevens's need to be loved put those tears in her eyes? The film gestures toward this essential subjectivity with one or two virtuoso point-of-view shots. For example, after Stevens's argument with Miss Kenton about the misplacement of the porcelain figure of a Chinaman, and what that misplacement portends about old Mr. Stevens's failings, she walks angrily away, the butler closes the door on her, and then he leans down to peer at her rigid figure through a keyhole, as if Ivory were determined to put into screen action that metaphor invented by Harold Pinter. Much earlier, under the opening credits in fact, Ivory shows Stevens gazing at Miss Kenton through a circular window in a door. Along with the butler, we see her striding down the long corridor, coming closer to him, only to disappear in a slow, reluctant dissolve; an idea adapted from one of Satyajit Ray's films, according to the director. These are exceptional moments, it must be noted. On the whole, the film prefers less striking effects and keeps to an understated, realist aesthetic. It hides away its cinematic devices, exactly as in a brief scene Stevens hastily hides the tools of his trade: the broom and the dustpan go behind his back when Lord Darlington passes him on the stairs, lest the owner should glimpse the workaday mechanisms by which his domain is kept clean. The film—to adapt Ishiguro's phrasing—knows of its own beauty and feels no need to shout about it. Ivory seems to acknowledge as a virtue of directing what Stevens declares to be a virtue of butlering: giving the "illusion of absence" (72).

The Miss Kenton of the film, because she is for the most part straightforwardly, objectively presented, is a much more determinate figure.[41] We see her for ourselves, not just from Stevens's perspective; we can *tell* there are tears in her eyes. We hear her letter to Stevens for ourselves, as opposed to the situation in the novel, where the letter comes to us through the self-serving medium of Stevens's drab hopefulness. Throughout the film she is simply more *present* than in the novel; present in a more independent, purposive, and feisty form. Jhabvala's script gives her real anger to act in that dispute about the Chinaman, for instance. Throughout the film her independence, the prominence of her role in the house and in the drama, are even more tellingly conveyed by the energy of Emma Thompson's portrayal, and by the regular framing of Miss Kenton and Stevens in symmetrical two-shots, or by the some-times combative shot/reverse-shot editing of scenes between them.

As for the ending, the novel's consists of a complex layering of event and rumination. Stevens visits the seaside resort of Weymouth, and recollects while there meeting Miss Kenton two days earlier in Little Compton, where he heard her confession of regret ("I get to thinking about a life I might have had with you, Mr. Stevens," 239). They part in an excruciatingly painful exchange of conventionalities. The narra-tive then returns again to the pier at Weymouth, where Stevens breaks down in tears as he speaks to a chance-met stranger, who happens to be a manservant as well; and finally Stevens recovers himself, at least to the extent of resolving to adopt "a more positive outlook" and add to his butler's repertoire the technique of bantering with his employer.

All this is radically simplified and concentrated in the film, which locates everything in the seaside town and omits the stranger. In a clev-erly photographed scene recalling all the melancholy seaside moments of British cinema, from *Brighton Rock* and *A Taste of Honey,* to *Wish You Were Here* and *The Entertainer,* Stevens and Miss Kenton walk to-gether on a pier crowded with ordinary people having fun. Sedate En-glish fun under dripping skies this may be, but it is just what has al-ways eluded the butler and the housekeeper. Later, the two part forever in the pouring rain amid tears, at least from her: a remake of *Brief En-counter,* as Anthony Hopkins exclaimed while he and Emma Thompson were filming it,[42] with David Lean's departing train being replaced by a country bus with an open rear platform for a kerchiefed, weeping Miss Kenton to stand on and glance backward from. Stevens's recov-ery, meanwhile, is dramatized in his return to Darlington Hall and its owner—not Mr. Farraday, as in the original, but in another understand-able simplification the same Senator Lewis who featured in the 1930s history of the house. There is no particular banter between Stevens and Lewis, but a pigeon flies down a chimney and becomes trapped in a sunny room. Master and man working companionably together free it. "In no way symbolic," Ivory later commented. He settled on the busi-ness after scouting the location and seeing a bird actually trapped there, thinking it would merely be "an interesting way to end."[43] However un-symbolic the act of freeing is meant to be, it lightens the mood at the close of the film, and draws Stevens to the French door for one more shot of a character watching something or someone else. As he turns away, returning to his duties, Darlington Hall appears reflected in the glass, and then starts receding. This is the start of the film's final sequence, a prolonged aerial shot leading viewers further and further away from the house and its park. It is an image precisely matching the film's opening, where viewers are led into the narrative by a camera mounted on a car driving through the park *toward* Darlington Hall.

Is the Merchant-Ivory Stevens faithful to Ishiguro's Stevens? On the whole, yes. The character in the film has only dialogue, not narrative at his disposal (there is one brief voice-over passage), but he displays the same stubborn loyalty to Lord Darlington, followed eventually by the same grudging admission of Lord Darlington's failure. In him is the same imperturbable reluctance to reveal feelings about Miss Kenton, the same conception of a servant's place in the scheme of things, the same obsession with the dignity of his calling. In Anthony Hopkins's performance, the human being is absorbed into the butler with remarkable plausibility. The actor's stooped posture and rigid bearing contribute to the effect. So does his way of cautiously forming the shapes of words with his lips before he lets speech escape. So does his handling of props. His Stevens comes straight from waiting at the banquet to receive the news of his father's death, still awkwardly clutching a carafe of wine. Hopkins's gestures are expressive in being so little outwardly expressive. Speaking with his father after the latter first falls ill, the butler puts his spread-out left hand protectively over his heart, as if simultaneously to admit and to contain whatever filial sympathy he feels. Later, when the old man lies dead in his bed, Stevens feels his forehead with the back of his hand. It is a formal and caressing gesture, and is followed by Stevens's turning his hand over and staring curiously at it for a moment. Is he noticing the age spots on his skin for the first time? No doubt; but Stevens also seems puzzled by the nature of the gesture he has just made, as if taken aback by his own regret, his own sorrow.

The most expressive gestures, from both Hopkins and Thompson, are required for the single important intimate scene between them, one following Ishiguro's original, though with some significant changes. Miss Kenton enters Stevens's curtained room with flowers, finding him drowsing over a book. "You're reading . . . It's very dim in here, can you see?" she remarks, with something like a wife's nagging solicitude; one of the most touching aspects of the scene about to be played between these two characters never to be married to each other is that it is so marital. She arranges the flowers in a vase, carrying on with questions which are a little simplified from the version given in the novel ("Now I wonder what it could be you are reading there, Mr. Stevens." "Simply a book, Miss Kenton." "I can see that, Mr. Stevens," 165), but exactly as in the novel, the film's Stevens backs away from her curiosity, her flirtatiousness even, into a corner of the room. Trapped there, he spars with her about the book (Is it too racy to be shared with a woman? Would a racy book be found on his Lordship's shelves?) as the camera looks over her shoulder at him, then comes in for a close-up. She grows more playful, music starts up on the soundtrack, and she stretches out her hand to the book which Stevens is holding over his heart, exactly as he held his hand over his heart in the earlier moment with his father. Whether the volume is part of his protective armor or held dear because it secretly objectifies his longing for her, she gently pries his clutching fingers away from it as he helplessly resists. This desire-filled contention between them mirrors something seen earlier in the film, in extreme close-up, namely, Stevens prying his stricken father's fingers away from the latter's cleaning cart. The link between moments of high feeling was apparently specified in Pinter's original screenplay.[44]

The touching of fingers of course brings Stevens and Miss Kenton closer to each other than at any other moment in the film, before or after. The Stevens of Ishiguro's novel had cautiously backed off from intimacy and looked away from Miss Kenton ("I judged it best"), twisting his head at an unnatural angle to do so, but Stevens as played by Hopkins is far from being able to judge anything. He looks on Miss Kenton's face with a kind of stunned rapture. His right arm has been supporting his leaning head but now moves tentatively toward her hair, then hesitates and holds still. Then finally he recovers himself. Taking back the book, which she has meanwhile discovered is a sentimental old love story, he passes it off as something to further his education and, becoming more butlerish by the second, dismisses her with a plea not to disturb the few moments he has to himself. This line is not to be found in the novel, where Stevens the narrator—"I cannot recall precisely what I said" (167)—promptly covers up for the failure of Stevens the man. In the film, the camera, as if dismissed by Stevens too, backs off, Miss Kenton exits, grim-faced, and we are left with a medium shot of the butler clutching the book to his heart again. "At the end of each take I was very close to fainting," Thompson said of this scene, to her an "Incredibly sexy" one.[45] This it is, more so than in the original, certainly, while still being true to Ishiguro's technique of hiding intimacy away in the stubbornness of the characters' repression and in the punctiliousness of their language.

When *The Remains of the Day* was released in 1993, it made a good deal of money, was nominated for its share of awards, and apparently pleased Ishiguro, at least to the extent of encouraging him to work with Merchant-Ivory again (he furnished the script for their 2005 film *The White Countess*, an adaptation of his novel *When We Were Orphans*). Reviews of *The Remains of the Day*, however, in England especially, were carping. The issue critics tended to raise was not fidelity to the novel, that being taken for granted or perhaps condescendingly acknowledged; in *TLS*, Nicholas Lezard called the film "literature for people too busy or bored to read." The issue was rather Merchant-Ivory's handsomely photographed views of grand houses and tasteful costumes ("everything looks swell"). In judgments like these, an anti-formalist bias is plain to see. For Ivory to set up as beautiful a shot as he does of Miss Kenton telling Stevens of his father's death, two motionless half-length figures shown in silhouette against the astonishingly blue staircase of Powderham Castle (one of four stately homes drawn on to provide interiors and exteriors of Darlington Hall), would be for a certain kind of contemporary critic simply an evasion, of ugly realities, of raw feeling, of the analytical, socio-political responsibilities of the cinema, of popular culture. Or for a certain kind of contemporary filmmaker: the director Alan Parker called Merchant-Ivory productions, notoriously, "the Laura Ashley school of film-making."[46] Accompanying the anti-formalist bias in the reviews was an anti-historical leaning, a dislike of period details and of shooting on old-money locations. "We have baying hounds," Geoffrey Macnab began an indictment-via-scornful-catalogue in *Sight and Sound*, "cheery cooks in the pantry, elegant dinner parties, tea in the conservatory, soirées in the drawing room, rustic pubs, and lots of English autumnal scenes." In short, *The Remains of the Day* was savaged, like prior Merchant-Ivory productions, for dwelling pictorially and nostalgically in a lost or fantasized English past; for being a "heritage film."[47]

An academic critic considerably more rigorous than the reviewers, Andrew Higson, used this damning phrase in an essay published just at the time of the film's release. "Re-presenting the National Past: Nostalgia and Pastiche in the Heritage Film" was about films of the 1980s, not about *The Remains of the Day* as such (and some of its arguments were softened or qualified in a later Higson essay),[48] but it raised and still raises issues of importance in the evaluation of Merchant-Ivory's and similar filmmakers' work. In the essay, Higson calls films like *A Room with a View, Howards End, A Handful of Dust* (directed by Charles Sturridge), and *A Passage to India* (directed by David Lean) "heritage" films not simply because they draw on an important English literary heritage, but because they turn their grand settings into a *visual* heritage, a museum-like, self-enclosed, fetishized or commodified spectacle. Higson makes an elaborate socio-political phenomenon of heritage films, coupling them with Thatcherite ideologies, American cultural imperialism, and "heritage-industry" enterprises like the National Trust, but the heart of his analysis is a quite simple claim about cinematic style. The "visually spectacular pastiche" of the films, he says, invites a nostalgic gaze that works against the "ironies and social critiques so often suggested narratively" by them. Mise-en-scène, divorced from the point of view of the characters, is displayed seductively for the viewer; the emotional engagement we draw from drama is sacrificed for "beautifully conserved and respectfully observed spectacles of pastness."[49]

There is a certain justice in these remarks, as applied for instance to a work Higson mentions only in passing, the Granada television adaptation of Evelyn Waugh's *Brideshead Revisited.* Every viewer would agree that this 1981 series, directed by Michael Lindsay-Hogg and Charles Sturridge, puts "pastness" on self-indulgent display. The honey-warm stonework of Oxford architecture, the beautiful structure of Brideshead itself, seat of the equally beautiful Flyte family, the over-ripe plants in the Brideshead conservatory, the furnishings, the linen summer suits, the vintage automobiles, the gilded Roman Catholic chapel—all are equally celebrated, in the slowly circling camera work or in lingering dissolves from one aesthetic object to another, while the voice-over narration of Charles Ryder caresses the objects in words. The expansiveness of the television form gives scope for this sort of treatment, while the warrant for it, a sympathetic critic would say, is the nostalgia of the series' source, Waugh's novel, full of admiration for the lost past, full of handsomely expressed regret.

As for the Merchant-Ivory adaptations of the 1980s, they are visually seductive in their own way. The turn-of-the-century Florence of *A Room with a View*, the most touristy of their films (and the adaptation of the simplest of the Forster novels), seems put in the film simply to be beautiful, as much as to work its Italian witchery on the characters. In the film of *Howards End*, the country house of the title is in its ostentatious and meticulously photographed beauty a simpler, less carefully evaluated, more nostalgically regarded thing than the house—the *idea*, really—of Forster's original novel. Even in *Howards End*, though, camera work, however seductive, is scarcely divorced from the point of view of the characters. At the opening of the film, under the credits, we are treated to a tracking shot of Howards End in the evening, surrounded by flowering shrubs, looking its Edwardian best, but the camera is in the company of Mrs. Wilcox as she wanders around her beloved property, apparently reminding herself of what it means to her, then looking through its window at the boisterous family to which she barely seems to belong.

The Remains of the Day renders its views in an even more character-driven way. The porcelain Chinaman of Darlington Hall, undeniably handsome as an *objet d'art,* a bit of spectacular furnishing, is in the film in order to be seen out of its proper place by Miss Kenton and to provide an emotional rallying point in her argument with Stevens. To shift to something heard rather than seen, Schubert's "Sei mir gegrüßt," sung in the drawing-room after Lord Darlington's banquet for the conference delegates, registers as plot complication rather than entertainment. The seduction it accomplishes is not of us but of Lord Darlington, whom we see gazing with gentlemanly longing at the blonde Nazi singer. This episode, not in the novel, was invented by Jhabvala. Meanwhile, the long corridors of the house, tokens like its high ceilings and broad terraces of an aristocratic spaciousness, are there so that the heart-struck Stevens may see a mirage of Miss Kenton walking down them toward him. After she vanishes, the corridors provide a particularly bleak background for his loneliness.

Even the establishing shot which opens the film, that entry into Darlington via car-mounted camera, is less voyeuristic than Higson's analysis would make it ("Almost all of these films contain a recurrent image of an imposing country house seen in extreme long shot and set in a picturesque, verdant landscape"). In fact, the car delivers viewers to a tent where furnishings of a noticeably drab Darlington Hall are being auctioned off, while a voice-over of Miss Kenton's letter to Stevens informs us of the possible pulling down of the house itself. Far from being a cosy depiction of heritage, this is a look at heritage going under the hammer. Merchant, Ivory, and Jhabvala are not, in fact, commodifiers. They are cold-eyed depictors of the process of commodification—in the instance of the auction, the packaging of aristocratic Englishness for sale to a rich American. In another instance, during the German foreign minister's secret visit to the house, they note how his underlings remark the fineness of Darlington paintings, then how the foreign minister turns to them—he has been taking his own connoisseur's interest in the Chinaman—and says "note it down for later." All in all, the Merchant-Ivory perspective on rich trappings or Darlington itself, the way their film shows the house in depth and over time, in framings or with camera movements expressive of characters' angles and plot turns, insists on the house's connections to the outer world, and so keeps it from being "self-enclosed."

Of all the ways Merchant and Ivory keep Darlington from being merely spectacular—another Brideshead, as it were—none, surely, is as effective as their focus on the house's downstairs life. The filmmakers show in detail, considerably greater detail than Ishiguro, exactly how the house functions: the making of beds, the carrying of luggage, the blackleading of fireplace grates, the preparing of food, the setting of tables, the ironing flat of pages of the *Times;* everything the servants do. Portrayed in this way, Darlington becomes a machine or a social organism. Perhaps we are allowed to satisfy a museum-goer's curiosity about the way the old-fashioned machine runs, but our view is never allowed to be complacent or superficial. In montages of servants preparing the house for its foreign guests—the director here was Merchant rather than Ivory, as it happens—the dominant notes are of haste and effort. No sign of those "cheery cooks in the pantry" mentioned in the *Sight and Sound* review. The cooks we see in the kitchen are in fact harried and anxious, an impression reinforced by restless music on the soundtrack.

Earlier in the film, while Darlington Hall is merely carrying on with its regular routines, we witness the start of a fox-hunt. Here we have hounds and horses gathering at the front of the house, blue-velvet-coated riders, the doffing of helmets or top hats, the whole picturesque business, shot from an angle high enough to allow us to take it all in. (Throughout, the film emphasizes verticality—high angles, the camera tilting up or down—when dealing with the hierarchical Darlington world. With Stevens and Miss Kenton on their own, it favors horizontal views, wide angles.[50]) Lord Darlington, who according to Stevens neither enjoys nor approves of hunting himself, is nevertheless photographed moving affably among his hunting neighbors, always the gentlemanly host. When Stevens and his footmen offer stirrup-cups, the camera shifts down to their level. The butler lifts a silver goblet to a mounted gentleman who, in conversation with someone else, ignores him. For five long seconds Ivory keeps the camera on Stevens with his arm extended, polite and ridiculous, humiliated even, forcibly reminding us that the character, a great man in his own little world of the servants' hall, is in the upstairs world merely a servant. "It just tears your heart out," Emma Thompson later commented on the sequence.

To put it more academically, the sequence is a multivalent image, denotative and connotative at once, like images of fog in the television *Bleak House.* It invites a certain nostalgia for the grand life, then qualifies or ironizes the nostalgia by revealing its human cost. "Our English films are criticized by the British newspapers for being too nostalgic," Ivory once wrote. "They even call *The Remains of the Day* a piece of nostalgia. But nostalgic for whom? Are the tasks of swabbing parquet floors and polishing brass in the Old Manor so very wonderful to recall?" Or of holding up stirrup-cups? What Ivory said he and his collaborators were doing in the film is lifting "the bright glass on the shadow box," allowing their unnostalgic viewers "to peer more easily into its recesses."[51] If we accept the premise that film-making attitudes (and social convictions) are formed in early youth, then we might recall that Ivory's favorite movie image when a boy was from Irving Cummings's 1941 Civil War melodrama *Belle Starr:* a "Yankee officer, cigar at a rakish angle, holding a candelabra to the lace curtains of a plantation house, then dashing the torch contemptuously through a windowpane."[52] So much for Ivory's alleged reverence for stately homes and their owners.

Mark Steyn's review of *The Remains of the Day* in the *Spectator* said of the film that it was "content to look like an adaptation," as if contentment with that category would in itself be an artistic failing, reason enough to dismiss the work from serious consideration. To deny that film, *proper* film, has or should have anything to do with the wholly different mode of literature, is a familiar enough purist line, but one that can hardly be maintained in the face of the facts of film history— the thousands of film adaptations of novels or plays, the famous figures (Graham Greene, Humphrey Jennings) who both wrote and worked on films, never feeling any purist compunction about doing so. Memories of Kipling inspired Powell and Pressburger in the making of *A Canterbury Tale,* as we have seen, and perhaps an analogous distant influence—Galsworthy's *Forsyte Saga*?—was working in Ivory's or Ruth Prawer Jhabvala's mind when they addressed themselves to Ishiguro's book. The mise-en-scène of *A Canterbury Tale* conspicuously includes books, with that slow camera pan over the litter of country-squire literature on Colpeper's desk; and something similar may be intended in *The Remains of the Day,* with its dwelling on Lord Darlington's book-lined study and its close focus on his perusal of one book. Alas, it is a proto-Fascist one; with gentlemanly English precision Darlington intones an anti-Semitic passage from it, in voice-over.[53] Then there is that sentimental old love story, not quite in the frame clearly enough for its title to be read, which Stevens attempts to hide from Miss Kenton. All these photographed volumes, essential props for the characters, are emblems also of the pervasive influence literature has had on filmmakers. They are homages, or at least hints of what artists like Merchant-Ivory owe to artists like Ishiguro.

The truly remarkable thing about Ishiguro's *The Remains of the Day,* however, is that in its case the influence has worked in the other direction as well, from screen work to novel. The curious fact is that in order to shape crucial elements of his plot and characterization, Ishiguro drew for inspiration on episodes of the 1970s television series *Upstairs, Downstairs.* This is an influence nowhere discussed in the critical or biographical literature on the novelist, but which, on the evidence, seems incontestable. It also seems predictable, given the overwhelming popularity of *Upstairs, Downstairs* in its time, its early and complete staking out of the territory of master-servant relations in early twentieth-century England. It was the popularity of the series, its near-mythical status, which one reviewer of Ishiguro's novel was drawing on when he casually made "Upstairs Downstairs" his title.[54]

To summarize the well-known history of the television series: the actresses Eileen Atkins and Jean Marsh brought an idea for a comedy-drama about servants to Sagitta Productions; their conception was developed and significantly altered by the producers John Hawkesworth and John Whitey, who sold the series to London Weekend Television and soon brought into the project the veteran television and cinema screenwriter Alfred Shaughnessy, who eventually became script editor; the first episodes were filmed and broadcast starting in October, 1971.[55] A huge success followed, in fact television history was made. Hawkesworth and Shaughnessy had hit upon a cunning formula. Equal attention would be paid to upstairs and downstairs—the aristocratic Bellamy family, residing at 165 Eaton Place, Belgravia, and their servants, Hudson the butler, Mrs. Bridges the cook, Rose the parlor maid, and so on. The lives of all the characters would entwine with historical events from before World War I to the Slump of the 1930s—Lady Marjorie would die in the sinking of the *Titanic*, the Bellamy son James would serve as an officer in the trenches, then later as a temporary bus driver during the General Strike of 1926, and so on. Each episode of the series, relatively self-contained as a drama, would sustain the general lines of character development. Each episode also, typically, would be scripted by a different writer, though all the writers (fifteen of them, during the five-year run of the series) worked under Shaughnessy's close supervision.

Two episodes of *Upstairs, Downstairs* in particular furnished material to Ishiguro: "The Understudy," televised in November, 1975, during the series' last year, when the novelist was twenty-one, and "A Change of Scene," televised during the third season, November, 1973, when Ishiguro was nineteen. Both episodes are variants of the most famous of all early *Upstairs, Downstairs* dramas, "Guest of Honour," in which King Edward VII comes to dinner at Eaton Place just as a maid-servant's pregnancy creates a crisis downstairs; a social catastrophe is narrowly avoided. In "The Understudy," written by Jeremy Paul and directed by James Ormerod (one of eleven directors at work on the series), the Bellamy family entertains the French ambassador to dinner. Political issues are at stake. For example, Lord Bellamy warns his family to keep off the subject of Germany, which has just been admitted to the League of Nations, as the French are still rankled about it. Meanwhile the redoubtable butler Hudson has suffered a heart attack, throwing his fellow servants into anxiety and confusion. From this donnée, it seems clear, Ishiguro developed the episode of the conference at Darlington Hall, with its French-German contentiousness and the threat of its disruption by trouble belowstairs, namely Stevens's father's stroke. Ishiguro seems even to have borrowed a scrap of dialogue from "The Understudy." In the sparring among the servants over who is to deputize for Hudson, we witness a testy exchange in their basement quarters, with Daisy the under-parlormaid attacking the ambitious footman Frederick, who is trying to learn about wine. What is he reading? she asks. "It's a book," he replies. "I can see that," she retorts—an interchange exactly replicated in the Stevens-Miss Kenton book scene of *The Remains of the Day* fourteen years later.

"A Change of Scene," written by Rosemary Anne Sisson, directed by Bill Bain, made a more considerable contribution to Ishiguro's plot. Here, we have a country-house story—a rare instance of *Upstairs, Downstairs* getting out of its London setting (and its cost-saving studio sets). Exterior filming of the episode took place at a country place called Burley-on-the-Hill, which became "Somerby Park," the grand home of the aristocratic Newburys. James Bellamy, invited there for a weekend of shooting, brings with him Hudson as loader. In the drawing-room a certain amount of flirtatiousness and mischief-making takes place, but the main plot concerns the Newburys' elderly butler Makepeace, whose drinking and forgetfulness almost ruin the outdoors luncheon provided for the houseguests. Luckily Hudson assumes command, running everything so efficiently that he comes to Lady Newbury's attention as a potential replacement for Makepeace. Would he be willing to move from Eaton Place to Somerby Park? The offer is hinted at in a tête-à-tête with the Newbury housekeeper, who seems interested in Hudson on her own account; at least, she welcomes him into her private sitting-room and appraises his vitality with a gleam in her eye. Back in London, Hudson is tempted, but when his master compliments him ("I don't know what we'd do without you"), and when he recalls the dead Lady Marjorie—there is a soulful point-of-view shot here, at her framed photograph—he decides finally to stay with the Bellamy household. Loyalty trumps any possible employment elsewhere and any possible life with the Newburys' housekeeper.

It is transparently easy to map these plot elements onto what happens in *The Remains of the Day*. Somerby Park becomes Darlington Hall, the shooting of pheasants the hunting of foxes; the failing Makepeace becomes the failing old Mr. Stevens, unable to cope with his duties, pathetically demoted. Hudson becomes Stevens, of course, resolute in a crisis, determined that the guests upstairs should not be troubled by upsets among the staff. The liaison which never happens between Hudson and the Somerby housekeeper—her name, incidentally, is "Mrs. Kenton"—becomes the love affair which never happens between Ishiguro's Stevens and Miss Kenton. Hudson's loyalty to Lady Marjorie, the motive of his renunciation of wider possibilities, becomes Stevens's loyalty to Lord Darlington. "Am I to take it," Miss Kenton says to Stevens just after she has announced her prospective marriage to Mr. Benn, in a last desperate attempt to provoke Stevens's jealousy, "that after the many years of service I have given in this house, you have no more words to greet the news of my possible departure than those you have just uttered?" She has his warmest congratulations, Stevens replies, taking his leave, turning once again in Lord Darlington's direction, but "there are matters of global significance taking place upstairs and I must return to my post" (219).

What exactly was the connection between *Upstairs, Downstairs* and Ishiguro? Presumably the novelist saw the two episodes as a young man and then unconsciously recalled them when he began to plan *The Remains of the Day*. The writing of his television drama *A Profile of Arthur J. Mason*, which concerns a butler and his loyalty to the idea of service,[56] might have been an intermediate step. The process of remembering and recasting the television episodes must have been akin to what happened in the writing of Ishiguro's second novel *An Artist of the Floating World* (1986), in which a father's affection for his daughter-in-law is adapted from the central relationship of Ozu's great 1953 film

Tokyo Story.[57] Regardless of the exact circumstances of borrowing, it is important to note that in both these cases Ishiguro changed what he borrowed. Both novels make something different of, greatly develop, their sources. In *The Remains of the Day* Ishiguro deals in social history, not the period clichés of *Upstairs, Downstairs.* Somerby Park also is shown to be tainted, admittedly, inhabited by monied idiots and scheming parasites who fail to live up to its architectural grandeur, but it is in no sense criticized as a social institution. Somerby Park does not betray the nation, as Darlington Hall is shown to do. Moreover, Ishiguro turns the plot-driven melodrama of *Upstairs, Downstairs* into an investigation of knowing and not knowing; his characterizations are vastly more detailed and subtle than those of the series. "A Change of Scene" moves expeditiously from situation to dilemma to resolution, from characters' confusions to a secure knowledge of who they really are, and it concludes with the kind of crisp decisiveness appropriate to a fifty-minute television program: that sealing of the letter of acceptance to Mrs. Kenton, that earnest look at Lady Marjorie's photograph, that tearing up of the letter, that final wistful comment that Somerby provided a pleasant change, "for a while . . . ." By contrast, *The Remains of the Day* moves slowly through its time shifts and spatial displacements, with both artistic deliberation and butlerish decorum, and it culminates in partial self-knowledge at best. It is a study of indecisiveness, avoidances and failures, resignation and regret; not to be summed up in an easy phrase, not to be concluded in a look at a photo and a change of heart.

There are, in other words, unmistakable differences in artistic ambition and achievement between the television series and the novel. Still, they are linked in a common enterprise, as the Merchant-Ivory film is in turn linked to them. Screen works lie behind written works; written works lie behind screen works. (For background in making *Upstairs, Downstairs,* John Hawkesworth read Vita Sackville-West's *The Edwardians;* Jean Marsh acknowledged that the close, conspiratorial relationship between parlormaids in the series was inspired by two servants in Henry Green's novel *Loving,* set below stairs in a country house.)[58] That is the real lesson of a book like *The Remains of the Day* and a television drama like *Upstairs, Downstairs:* the need to consider such works in all aspects of their relatedness, the entanglement of filming with writing which has marked the histories of both arts from the beginning.

FOUR

THE STRANGE POTENCIES OF MUSIC

Play something light and sweet and gay
For we must have music
We must have music
To drive our fears away.
While our illusions swiftly fade for us,
Let's have an orchestra score.
In the confusions the years have made for us
Serenade for us, just once more.

NOËL COWARD, *SHADOW PLAY,* FROM *TONIGHT AT 8:30*

There comes a point in the film of *The Remains of the Day* when the butler Stevens takes a few minutes of ease, chatting to a fellow manservant and solacing his heart with a song played on the gramophone. As the soprano glissandos down from a high note, "Ah, listen," Stevens says, gesturing expansively (for him) with his cigar, "that's so touching, isn't it?" On the commentary track of the DVD edition of the film, Emma Thompson observes that what's being demonstrated at this moment— what even this emotionally stunted butler becomes temporarily subject to—is the "potency of cheap music." She tosses the phrase in casually, as a commonplace known to everyone, which in fact it is, a catchy formulation employed frequently in reviews of pop music, films ("but behind myth and over-the-top performances, one senses the pain of real events underlined with the potency of cheap music"), even political strategies

("A strummer himself, Blair should understand the potency of cheap music and its mood-altering effects on an era").[1]

Emma Thompson attributes the phrase, correctly, to Noël Coward. The source is the first act of Coward's play *Private Lives* (1930). Two English sophisticates, recently divorced from each other, both with new spouses, meet by coincidence on the veranda of a French hotel, bicker, then hear a melody in the distance. It apparently holds memories for them:

> ELYOT That orchestra has a remarkable small repertoire.
> AMANDA They don't seem to know anything but this, do they?
> *She sits down on the balustrade, and sings it, softly. Her eyes are looking out to sea, and her mind is far away.* ELYOT *watches her while she sings. When she turns to him at the end, there are tears in her eyes. He looks away awkwardly and lights a cigarette.*
> ELYOT You always had a sweet voice, Amanda.
> AMANDA (*a little huskily*) Thank you.
> ELYOT I'm awfully sorry about all this, really I am. I wouldn't have had it happen for the world.
> AMANDA I know. I'm sorry too. It's just rotten luck.
> ELYOT I'll go away to-morrow whatever happens, so don't you worry.
> AMANDA That's nice of you.
> ELYOT I hope everything turns out splendidly for you, and that you'll be very happy.
> AMANDA I hope the same for you, too.
> *The music, which has been playing continually through this little scene, returns persistently to the refrain. They both look at one another and laugh.*
> ELYOT Nasty insistent little tune.
> AMANDA Strange how potent cheap music is.[2]

Consider the implications of that word "cheap." At the very moment Amanda's heart is giving her access to old feelings, her head insists on noticing that the access is via shoddy goods.

Amanda represents that variety of twentieth-century sophistication which, drawn irresistibly to popular culture (Thomas Mann spoke of the Modern artist's "gnawing surreptitious hankering for the bliss of the commonplace"), still stands back in well-bred amazement from it. It is the sophistication, say, of Anthony Powell in his novel *Casanova's Chinese Restaurant*, writing into the cultural complexities of a post-

War, bombed-out London, and into the layered ironies of his narrator's memory, the simplicity of a song, "strong and marvelously sweet,"

> Pale hands I loved beside the Shalimar,
> Where are you now? Who lies beneath your spell?

Still more is it the sophistication of T. S. Eliot, who in *The Waste Land* repeatedly uses cheap music to perk up the etiolated world of his characters, as in

> "Are you alive, or not? Is there nothing in your head?"
>   But
> O O O O that Shakespeherian Rag—
> It's so elegant
> So intelligent . . .[3]

All the while Eliot does nothing to hide how déclassé these bits of song are or, to put it another way, how daring his poetic slumming in their neighborhood is. After her seduction by the pimply clerk, the typist of *The Waste Land* puts a record on the gramophone, like Stevens, but in a more evasive and automaton-like way: the poet makes her a shabby victim of the age of art mechanically reproduced.

As a dramatist Coward is less high-toned than these writers, or than Amanda. When he uses music in his plays, he does so without noticeable concern for its cheapness *or* its sophistication, but instead with regard for the power it exerts over human beings, or the clarity it is able to bring to their doings. He is willing to go so far as to trust the conclusions of dramas to music, for example ending his pageant-of-time play *Cavalcade* with one of the characters singing "Twentieth Century Blues" in a nightclub. The nightclub's decoration should be "angular and strange," Coward's stage direction stipulates, and the song itself "oddly discordant":

> Blues, Twentieth Century Blues, are getting me down.
> Who's escaped those weary Twentieth Century Blues?
> Why, if there's a God in the sky, why shouldn't he grin?
> High above this dreary Twentieth Century din,
> In this strange illusion,
> Chaos and confusion,
> People seem to lose their way. . . .[4]

For an allegory-of-the-nation play, this is the perfect ironic conclusion, the mordant disclosure that after years of strenuous effort and meaningful historical action, 1930s England has no idea of where it is. Perhaps in the end it is too ironic a conclusion: after the song and a montage-style recapitulation of scenes, Coward's script calls for lights out and then a rendition of "God Save the King" by the whole cast, with the Union Jack flying over their heads. In 1997, "Twentieth Century Blues," sung by Coward himself, became the brilliantly effective final-credits music for the television miniseries version of Anthony Powell's *A Dance to the Music of Time*. It is mordant there too.

Coward's *Shadow Play*, a one-acter from the 1936 collection *Tonight at 8:30*, uses songs more extensively, so much so as to be subtitled "A Musical Fantasy." Here the characters are another quarreling upper-class couple. The wife takes sleeping pills and under their influence dreams the earlier stages of their falling in love, most of them accompanied and indeed emotionally determined by songs: "Then," "Play, Orchestra, Play," "You Were There." In a striking bit of avant-garde dramaturgy, striking at least for the West End, Coward presents his characters as being simultaneously trapped in the past and standing dispassionately outside it. Always, however, wherever they happen to be psychologically, they are compelled by the songs to play over the plot of their love. "We must have music," they sing, in the lines quoted at the start of this chapter; "We must have music / To drive our fears away."

Shadow Play was never filmed, but Coward's *Private Lives* was, by MGM with an American cast in 1931. In the veranda scene, Norma Shearer as Amanda follows the play text, more or less (she says "Extraordinary . . ." rather than "Strange how potent cheap music is"), then does her singing of the song to a tune which, if still insistent, is not particularly nasty. Hearing her performance, we realize the force of two other key words in her famous line: "strange" and "potent." The Amanda of the film seems less a snob about music, more a wondering victim of music's emotional hold over her. Of course the Amanda of a stage performance might give the same impression, but she would have to give it without the sort of presentation which filming makes possible, the solo framing inviting viewers to share the character's feelings and memories, her *pianissimo* vocalizing of the melody, the close-ups of her teary eyes and half-amused, half-confused expression.

It is precisely the strange potency of music which has been essential to the cinema, and not just the cinema of MGM. In countless English screen works, played or sung music works on and through character, exposing feeling and forcing action, often in a way that seems extravagant, unpredictable, or mysterious to the ordinary consciousness. In the Boulting brothers' film of Graham Greene's *Brighton Rock*—to take one out of many possible examples—Pinkie explodes with rage on hearing Ida's singing in the Brighton pub. He could never account for the rage himself, and only later is the viewer able to do so, perceiving how antithetical Ida's big-hearted outgoingness is to Pinkie's tightly controlled gangster's persona, and to his dread of being weakened through feeling. As the plot of the film unfolds, Pinkie handles himself better, managing a sullen impassiveness when he sits with Rose at the dance palace and listens to the girl singer fronting the band:

> More than ever, you're in my mind and heart,
> We are never far apart.
> More than ever, I need you as my guide,
> Please be forever by my side.

Indeed, he manages to be more impassive than the Pinkie of Greene's novel, who on hearing the music—a completely different song, as it happens,

> Music talks, talks of our love.
> The starling on our walks, talks, talks of our love.
> The taxis tooting,
> The last owl hooting,
> The tube train rumbling,
> Busy bee bumbling,
>   Talk of our love—

says to Rose "it gets you," and feels the lyrics stirring in his brain "like poetry," like a "huge brazen suggestion" of the power of love.[5] If the filmed *Brighton Rock* can convey nothing so figuratively powerful as this, it does at least reveal Rose's fascination with what she's hearing. She looks with terrible longing in the band's direction, then turns to Pinkie with her face lighted up. Moreover, a long-held tracking shot in the film shows the dreamy absorption of the ballroom dancers into the song—emotional potency spread out through a whole room. Above all, of course, the film does what no novel can do: it puts Leslie Julian Jones's syrupy tune "More than ever" on the soundtrack. We *hear* the brazen suggestiveness which is such a threat to Pinkie.

We hear a similar suggestiveness—tinselly, perhaps, rather than brazen—four decades later, in Mike Newell's *Dance with a Stranger* (1985), when the doomed Ruth Ellis sings in the after-hours club where she works as manager and hostess. Her number is Mari Wilson's "Would you dance with a stranger?":

> Would you dance with a stranger, on a night made for love?
> Would you dance with a stranger, with the starlight above? . . .
>
> There's a thrill that comes stealing with the soft violins,
> What a wonderful feeling, here's where romance begins . . . [6]

What at this point ought to be a pleasing digression from a grim story into soft violins and wonderful feelings is nastily disturbing, partly because simultaneously with the singing Ellis notices her worthless boyfriend entering the club with his new fiancée, but mostly because as a performer she seems so disaffected. She's slightly drunk, holding a glass and a cigarette in her hands as she sings, slurring the words a little, professionally deadened to any considerations of romance. The music never "gets" her at all; it gets the viewer instead, or at least gets the viewer to understand what it is costing Ellis to have to do without romantic considerations. The point of the music, in other words, is to be painfully at odds with plot and character, the soundtrack commenting ironically on photographed action (and vice versa).

A similar effect is produced by the singing in a film from 1963, halfway between *Brighton Rock* and *Dance with a Stranger*. This is Joseph Losey's *The Servant*. Here, the song is the bluesy jazz number "All Gone," with lyrics by Harold Pinter and Losey perfectly capturing a certain kind of love-sick obsessiveness:

> Now while I love you alone
> Now while I love you alone
> Now while I love you
> can't love without you
> must love without you alone
> Leave it alone it's all gone
> Leave it alone it's all gone. . .

The upper-class weakling Tony plays "All Gone" on his stereo, like Stevens playing *his* song on the Victrola, for solace, for the pleasure of hearing Cleo Laine endlessly croon the refrain "Now while I love you alone . . ." As *The Servant* develops and Tony falls more and more into the power of his manservant Barrett and Barrett's tarty girlfriend Vera, the possibility of loving or being loved by someone alone recedes further and further into the distance. Cleo Laine's singing is potent, all right. It presides sardonically over most of the film, pointing up Tony's helpless ignorance of the situation into which he's been maneuvered. It is also strange, the exploitation of a weakness (like Tony's alcoholism) which is never accounted for, just presented as being disastrously there in his personality.

In all three of these films, the songs are diegetic, that is, belonging to the diegesis or story and thus heard by the characters. That "All Gone" belongs to the diegesis only via a Cleo Laine LP, not the sort of live performance we witness in *Brighton Rock* and *Dance with a Stranger,* does not matter. It still furnishes part of Tony's world and he still listens to it, even if he listens to it in a different way from the more clued-in cinema audience. Nondiegetic music, in contrast, is by definition outside the story, belonging only to the soundtrack and heard only by the cinema audience: Richard Robbins's fretful orchestral music for *The Remains of the Day,* for example, or the ballad "Mona Lisa" sung by Nat King Cole over the opening credits of Neil Jordan's *Mona Lisa* (1986). These elementary categories are useful for analysis but, as we will see, less fixed than they initially appear. In many films they blend into each other as seamlessly as image dissolving into image onscreen. Almost immediately after the credits of *Mona Lisa,* for example, the main character puts the tape of Nat King Cole's song into his car stereo and starts playing it, instantly transforming it from nondiegetic to diegetic (the music sounds exactly the same, though in the car it has to compete with dialogue and ambient noises). The process is reversed in *The Servant.* After several playings of Tony's record, the film's soundtrack picks up the melody of "Now while I love you alone" and gives it to an off-screen orchestra, making it nondiegetic. Even shorn of words, though, the music has the same acrid effect.

Fluid these categories may be, but in any case the categorization of film music will not be my main business in this chapter. Nor will it be a survey of all possible musical techniques and styles in the English cinema, from the earliest explorations to the fascination with pop music which has so marked contemporary screen work.[7] My concern here will rather be with a handful of films and the interpretation of the musical performances within them, distinctively English performances, exceptionally inventive ones. We will see how these film performances work, in detail; how they are linked with but also different from other musical contexts (the radio broadcast, the music hall program, the jazz club concert); how they participate in the back-and-forth between convention and innovativeness, the pleasure of recognizing old genres poised against the enticement of coming to terms with new ones, which has always characterized English filmmaking. Ultimately, these matters will involve a question about *awareness* of music, the extent to which filmmakers have let their works articulate its potency while they make use of it as a technique. Ultimately also, because vocal music has the most direct possible relation to individual character and is linked most intimately with words, the chapter will focus on singing onscreen—singing in Gracie Fields musicals from the 1930s, in the Beatles' *A Hard Day's Night* and late-twentieth-century films like *Little Voice,* and finally in the song-besotted and literary cinema of Terence Davies and the song-besotted television of Dennis Potter. There will be diversions, though, to instrumental playing, as with Jimmy Porter's jazz trumpet in *Look Back in Anger,* and my starting point will be orchestral film music, the most old-fashioned seeming of techniques, in some ways the most hidebound and constraining. But classical music on a soundtrack has its own powers to impose on film characters, its own satisfactions to offer ("While our illusions swiftly fade for us / Let's have an orchestra score," they sing in Coward's *Shadow Play*), and as we will see in the case of *Brief Encounter,* its own kinds of inventiveness to display.

RAWSTHORNE AND RACHMANINOFF

From the early 1930s at least through the late 1950s, the English cinema made routine use of orchestral film scores—like the cinema worldwide. If there was anything distinctive about the practice of English studios, it might simply have to do with richness of resources, since "quality" English filmmaking of this period had a remarkable classical musical establishment at its disposal.[8] Ensembles like the Philharmonia Orchestra or the London Symphony Orchestra, conducted often by the tireless Muir Mathieson, who began working for Alexander Korda in 1934 and thereafter directed the music for well over three hundred productions, might play scores by such English luminaries as Arthur Bliss (Menzies's *Things to Come*), Ralph Vaughan Williams (the Archers' *49th Parallel*), William Walton (Olivier's *Hamlet*), or Arnold Bax (Lean's *Oliver Twist*). In some of this music composers were responding to the magnificence of a photographed landscape, as for example in Vaughan Williams's score for *Scott of the Antarctic* (Charles Frend)—later to become the basis of the composer's *Sinfonia Antarctica*—and preeminently in David Lean's *Lawrence of Arabia*, with its lush (and by 1962, old-fashioned-sounding) score by Maurice Jarre, the replication in orchestral sound of desert grandeur and heroic maneuverings across the sands.

But such depictions of terrain in music characterized American films chiefly.[9] What audiences tended to hear in the English cinema was music directed toward character-driven and intimate film passages. Predictable moments these might be, the passionate embrace between long-separated lovers, the heart-broken farewell, but also, and more significantly, moments of regret, abnegation, or reticence—encounters governed by that most persistent of cliché character traits, the upper-class abstention from emotional display. In film after English film, the function of orchestral music is to "get close to people and things" and thus counter the pernicious national habit—Satyajit Ray thought it pernicious, in a famous critique of British filmmaking—of staying aloof, of cloaking "harsh truths with innuendoes."[10] Music reveals what is under the cloak, subverts controlled gestures and flatly spoken lines, "says" the unsayable. Music, to pick up again on one of the key words from Coward's line, seeks to "intensify and prolong that impression of *strangeness, of departure from photographic truth*, which the director is seeking."[11] This was the opinion of the French film composer Maurice Jaubert, the distinguished collaborator of René Clair and Jean Vigo, in his 1938 essay "Music on The Screen." Jaubert was not especially commenting on his English colleagues, but nevertheless captured something important and distinctive about their practice.

Take for example the 1946 Ealing film *The Captive Heart*—could there be a more emblematic title for an English work of its period?—a

prisoner-of-war melodrama directed by Basil Dearden. This was an un-
enthusiastically reviewed film,[12] unremarkable, therefore representative; one of several stories about the familial consequences of the war
(Dearden's *Frieda* is another) to come out in the later 1940s. *The Captive Heart* opens with shots of British prisoners being marched along
French roads toward Germany while a solemn voice-over speaks of
their dedication and sacrifice ("the men who held on until the German armor thundered past their lines"). Under this, we hear music by
Alan Rawsthorne, a classically trained composer (and ex-serviceman)
whose first feature-film score this is; he went on to write many others,
the best known of them for *The Cruel Sea* in 1953. Rawsthorne's music
for the prisoners in *The Captive Heart* is strongly rhythmical, to match
the tramping images on screen; it is also in a minor key, a kind of sour
Mahlerian march representing defeated soldierliness, and hinting at a
dismay which the British disdain to admit. They move stoically and un-
smilingly toward their unknown fate; "a pretty bad show all around,"
as their senior officer comments blimpishly a moment later, but "we
mustn't let the Jerries see we're down." Close-ups on marching soldiers'
faces dissolve to memories of their last moments at home, setting a pattern to be followed throughout the film, of alternation between prison-
camp and home-front scenes. In another Mahlerian touch Rawsthorne
accompanies one of the dissolves with fading melancholy trumpet calls.

In its domestic sequences, *The Captive Heart* is full of closed and
wary faces, of waiting wives and sweethearts. In the film's prison-camp
sequences—according to the film historian Jim Leach, these were photographed largely on location, in recently vacated German camps[13]—
the wariest face of all belongs to Michael Redgrave playing an inmate
named Hašek, a Czech partisan who earlier has taken the clothes and
assumed the identity of a British officer he found dead on the battlefield.
The Gestapo is suspicious of Hašek, and to preserve his incognito he
must continue to appear as English—that is, as stiff-upper-lip—as possible, and he must also write answers to the letters he receives from the
English officer's wife, who has no notion of her husband's death. Eventually, on his release and repatriation to England, Hašek and the wife
meet, and by the Armistice they have fallen in love, to predictably romantic strains from Rawsthorne.

All the orchestral music of the film is nondiegetic and thus the
property of the audience, yet it also belongs to the characters' world,

in the sense that it is the sort of thing they (the officers more than the Other Ranks, of course) like to hear, what they are used to; what we may assume to be sounding in their heads or even what they themselves once performed. In a pre-prison-camp scene one of the English officers plays a piano composition for friends, a spiky chromatic piece much in the Rawsthorne style. Later, during a montage of day-to-day camp activities accompanied by the usual nondiegetic orchestral music, the same officer starts playing the prison-camp piano, while simultaneously Hašek is writing one of his letters to "Celia." At this moment diegetic music merges with nondiegetic music in a way to make distinguishing between the categories more or less irrelevant. What matters, as Hašek says in his letter, and as we hear being spoken in Redgrave's voice-over—in the same tones the actor had employed for the commentary in Jennings's *A Diary for Timothy*, precise, gently cultivated, a little melancholy at having to bear the burden of its integrity—is that music "describes our life here better than I could ever do with words. It tells of men emerging from the twilight, turning their faces from the wire, creating in miniature a world of their own . . ." In such an articulation, music—that modest element of the filmmaker's art, that readily understood, taken-for-granted component of the language shared between filmmaker and audience—begins to enlarge its role a little. It offers itself as an idea, a theme; it asks to be noticed.

Whether pushed forward for attention or merely in the background, orchestral music is especially called upon to convey feelings unsuited for verbal expression ("better than I could ever do with words") in English films from the 1940s, a period much given to dramas of restraint and hard-won release from restraint. Allan Gray's orchestral score for *A Canterbury Tale* has this function, for example. So does William Alwyn's in *The Fallen Idol*, Carol Reed's exceptionally fine 1948 rendering of a Graham Greene short story. Alwyn's music first comes into play in various conventional, expressive, not very noticeable ways: over the opening credits; during haphazard wanderings of the lonely little boy Phile, an ambassador's son, who is at the center of the drama; in love passages between Phile's best friend the butler Baines and Baines's mistress (a love they take care to hide from the boy); in an extended sequence showing a game of hide-and-seek in the darkened embassy, with *agitato* music complementing both the rapid movements of the actors and Reed's quick editing. This sequence is an ingeniously consistent stylization, capped by canted camera angles, as effective here in showing emotional strain and moral uneasiness as they would be in Reed's *The Third Man* the following year. The music becomes much more noticeable toward the climax of *The Fallen Idol,* when Phile runs in panic away from the embassy, thinking that Baines has pushed his shrewish wife down the grand staircase to her death. All of Phile's frenzy, his confusion, his child's loyalty put to the test, his child's resentment at the impossible position in which the adults have placed him, everything he could not possibly put into words, comes out vicariously here, in Alwyn's music. Quick descending passages in the strings draw attention to the boy's dash down the fire escape, and then obsessively repeated phrases express his inarticulate anguish and his hopelessness. Everything is of a piece, the up-tempo and dissonant musical style, the quick cutting, the odd framings of Phile's legs splashing through puddles, the abrupt camera pans as he hurtles down the deserted streets toward the end of the sequence, when he runs into a policeman and a sudden silence falls.

In general, this nondiegetic music of *The Fallen Idol* seems perfectly suited for the diegesis of the film. Ambitious, classical, "high class," it consorts with the conventionally grand settings in which the film characters move, the embassy with its high ceilings, formal spaces, and superbly curving staircase—all features emphasized by Reed and his designer Vincent Korda (Greene's original story was titled "The Basement Room," and usually remains within that much more modest setting). This principle of coordinating music and mise-en-scène is taken a step further in the universally acknowledged masterpiece of 1940s English melodrama, *Brief Encounter* (1945), directed by David Lean, written largely by Noël Coward after his own *Still Life,* another playlet from the collection *Tonight at 8:30.* In *Brief Encounter* there is no nondiegetic music at all, except for what is played with the credits and a few moody scraps under the heroine Laura Jesson's early voice-overs. What we hear on the soundtrack throughout is the Rachmaninoff second piano concerto, performed by Eileen Joyce with the National Symphony Orchestra, Muir Mathieson conducting. The important point, however, is that the music emerges from the mise-en-scène and is heard by Laura herself. In the sitting room of her suburban home, with her husband Fred sitting staidly by, doing the *Times* crossword, she gets up restlessly and turns on the radio, presumably to the BBC. The radio plays the concerto, which thereafter accompanies the extended flashback recounting Laura's impassioned but unconsummated affair with Alec Harvey. In other words, the Rachmaninoff belongs both to the character in the present, conditioning her recollections and her wifely guilt, and to the audience, helping them interpret her feelings during the past affair. In this double role it draws considerably more attention to itself than Rawsthorne's score in *The Captive Heart* or Alwyn's in *The Fallen Idol.* Coward himself insisted on the music's indispensability for his purposes. He refused Muir Mathieson's request for a specially composed score in place of the Rachmaninoff, commenting flatly that Laura is the sort of woman who "listens to Rachmaninoff on the radio," just as "she borrows her books from Boot's library and she eats at the Kardomah."[14]

Aside from what it tells us of Laura's conventionality, the Rachmaninoff was a brilliant choice. It was already in filmgoers' ears, being performed by the pianist heroine of Muriel and Sidney Box's huge 1945 box-office hit *The Seventh Veil,*[15] and musically it offered exactly the right style, of high-minded perturbation, hectic romanticism, yearning phrase piled on yearning phrase. In *Brief Encounter,* the concerto provided plentiful opportunities for close coordination with dialogue, voice-over, or camera work, always with the purpose of communicating more than could be stated in words alone. Early on in Laura's flashback, for example, we see her with Alec in the station buffet, the two of them beginning to fall in love over the teas and the Bath buns. He speaks of his doctor's idealism, warming to his theme as he proceeds from preventative medicine to pneumoconiosis to coal mines. She abruptly responds to something in his face:

> LAURA   You suddenly look much younger.
> ALEC   Do I?
> LAURA   Almost like a little boy.
> ALEC   What made you say that?
> LAURA   I don't know . . . yes, I do.
> ALEC   Tell me.
> LAURA   No, I couldn't really. You were saying about the coal mines . . . ?

Rachmaninoff begins to be heard precisely on her line "I don't know," as if purposefully forcing Laura on to the confessional honesty of "yes, I do." When in the next instant honesty fails her ("I couldn't really") the music becomes louder, substituting for what she prefers not to spell out to him.

At later stages of the film, of course, Laura and Alec are less reticent. Their hearts come out of captivity, they acknowledge what they feel, they meet repeatedly, they eventually embrace and kiss in the passageway under the platforms of Milford station. Lean's originality at this point lies in *not* accompanying the kiss with a dramatic outburst of music, as standard practice—the practice of *The Captive Heart,* for example—would have him do. Instead, the Rachmaninoff becomes gradually audible, emerging from the rushing noise of a train passing overhead and accompanying the lovers' breaking hurriedly apart at the approach of other people, an approach signaled by looming film-noir-like shadows cast on the brick wall. The effect is of music manifesting Laura and Alec's guilt or uneasiness, not their abandonment to each other. It is guilt which they could not now admit, so the music has to admit it for them—the music, and the complex dissolve we immediately see onscreen, which merges the underground scene with a return to Laura's sitting room. For a few seconds we behold the double-exposed image of Laura in her armchair, listening to Rachmaninoff crescendo on the radio ("D'you think we might have that down a bit, darling?" her husband asks). She is the sad homebody seeming to sit in judgment on that other Laura scuttling along the dark passageway with the man, not her husband, she has just embraced.

Still later in the film, Alec's importunity makes her agree to meet him in a flat borrowed from a friend. Before they can make love there, the owner unexpectedly returns, Laura flees, Alec falls into tetchy argument with his friend and exits, closing the door. At this point, and on a *fortissimo* chord in the music, Lean cuts dramatically to Laura running down the street in the rain, the camera tracking along first behind her, then in front. Again, the music expresses emotional turmoil, relief at not having yielded herself to Alec, regret at not having yielded, embarrassment, dismay at having to think up some plausible excuse for her husband. Only after the music has expressed all this does she put part of it into words in a voice-over ("I felt utterly humiliated and defeated and so dreadfully dreadfully ashamed"), at which point the music, no longer needed, stops. The overall effect is so similar to little Phile's music-accompanied escape in *The Fallen Idol* that it is impossible not to conclude that Carol Reed was imitating in his film what he had seen in *Brief Encounter* three years before.

The most complex musical effect of all in *Brief Encounter* comes just after the kiss in the dark tunnel. The sad homebody reverts once again to the romantic fool: that is, Laura recalls traveling homeward on her train, happy, to the sound of the concerto in its most extravagantly romantic mode. Like that other dreamy train-traveler, the young Marlow in *The Singing Detective,* Laura looks through the train window into a series of fantasies; for her, fantasies of life with her lover. In fact she turns the window into a movie screen, the fantasies being not merely described in her voice but presented as *films,* framed, lighted, and photographed as film scenes would be. First there is dancing in his arms under crystal chandeliers, then the two of them in a box at the Paris opera . . . together in a gondola on the Grand Canal . . . windblown in a convertible traveling down the highway . . . in evening clothes at the railing of a cruise-ship . . . on a tropical beach in the moonlight. . . . Lean had the wit to silence Rachmaninoff during this montage and furnish each of the micro-movies with its own appropriate music, a waltz for the ballroom, a mandolin for Venice; these eventually yield to Rachmaninoff again and then to prosaic wheels-on-tracks sounds as Laura's train pulls into her station. All in all, it is a brilliantly contrived sequence, balanced between Laura's indulgence in feeling and her awareness that it is all silly and school-girlish (her reflected thoughtful face never quite disappears from the movie screen of her fantasies); balanced between the new discovery of love and the old clichéd scenes which are all this suburban housewife can imagine to express love in; balanced finally between a sympathetic focus on Laura's mood and an ironic demonstration of the techniques of movie-making, musical techniques included.

The literary source of *Brief Encounter,* Coward's *Still Life,* has no flashback structure and no shift of locale to Laura's home; all of its action keeps to the station buffet. Nor of course does it have Rachmaninoff on a sitting-room radio. The only counterpoint to Laura and Alec's upper-class voices is the working-class banter of Myrtle and Beryl and their male friend Albert at the tea counter—Coward's equivalents of the mechanicals in a Shakespeare play, ironic commentators on and cheery alternatives to the troubled principals. For something in literature analogous to the musical techniques of Lean's film, we would have to turn instead to fiction, as proposed by Maurice Jaubert in "Music on the Screen." At key dramatic junctures, he suggests, film music is the equivalent of a novelist's interrupting his story "with an expression of his feelings, argumentative or lyrical, or with the subjective reactions of his character . . ."[16]

One example of this sort of novelist's interruption, chosen from countless possibilities, would be a passage in the fifth chapter of Forster's *Howards End,* where the narration of plot is suspended for an elaborate description of the characters' reactions to music—Beethoven's Fifth Symphony, being performed in the Queen's Hall. The Schlegel sisters, habitués of the classical-music world like the British officers in *The Captive Heart,* are elaborately differentiated in their modes of listening, the down-to-earth Margaret attentive to the performance *per se,* the romantic, even rhapsodic Helen turning the Beethoven Scherzo into a cosmic drama. She visualizes goblins "walking quietly over the universe, from end to end." The goblins deny the possibility that "splendour or heroism" could exist in the world; then elephants dance; then finally the goblins are scattered in a mighty major-key Beethovenesque flourish: "Gusts of splendour, gods and demigods contending with vast swords, colour and fragrance broadcast on the field of battle, magnificent victory, magnificent death!"[17] This is thinking (or feeling), not speech. Helen could hardly say these extravagant things aloud, an Edwardian young lady as she is, obeying certain social codes as she unconsciously does (Forster observes that when she stretches out her hands exultingly toward Beethoven's triumph, they are *gloved* hands). The novelist must articulate rapture on Helen's behalf. In the same way, music on a film soundtrack articulates—if more vaguely, perhaps—a character's unspeakable emotion. Beethoven's music itself might express such emotion. Indeed, in the Merchant-Ivory film version of *Howards End* (1992), this is exactly what the Scherzo of the Fifth Symphony is made, very cleverly, to do. The music comes up late in the film, loudly and assertively, in a manner meant to dramatize and draw attention to its power. Technically nondiegetic, it nevertheless derives from the whole circumstance, of character, of personal history, of state of mind, which the scenarist has labored to create. It is not so much applied from the outside as elicited from the inside. The music accompanies the nightmare of Leonard Bast, the shabby-genteel clerk who aspires to the cultivated Queen's Hall world of the Schlegels. Bast has listened to a Beethoven lecture there along with Helen, has become entangled in their lives, has slept with Helen. Now, feeling a despairing guilt, he dreams of her looking questioningly at him from the other side of a locked iron gate, as those goblins of Beethoven do their nihilistic marching over the universe and through his sorrowing mind. They bear a private message of denial: no Helen for him; no heroism in Leonard Bast's world.

ROLLING OUT THE BARREL, LOOKING UP AND LAUGHING

Rawsthorne's score and the officer's piano are not the only music in *The Captive Heart*. Early on, when the prisoners are first mustered in the camp, something different enters the picture. On loudspeakers the Germans play a propaganda news broadcast followed by a recording of the soldiers' song "Wir fahren gegen Engeland." At this, the British begin singing themselves, like the night-club artistes putting "La Marseillaise" up against "Die Wacht am Rhein" in Warner Brothers' *Casablanca* of four years before (no doubt Dearden or his screenwriters borrowed their idea from the American film). What the prisoners' chorus sings is "Roll Out the Barrel"—not, strictly speaking, a British song,[18] but one very popular and thoroughly assimilated into the home culture, as its employment in Jennings's *Listen to Britain* indicates. In the camp, "Roll Out the Barrel" carries the day, out-bawling the loudspeakers. It is a minor triumph for the captives, and particularly for the cheerful broad-faced corporal who starts the singing—a role enacted, inevitably, by Jack Warner, who specialized in such types and became much beloved in the process of doing so.

The performance of "Roll Out the Barrel" exemplifies an alternative mode of English film music, popular rather than classical, drawn from working- or middle-class rather than cultivated traditions. It tends to be diegetic rather than nondiegetic, is sung more often than played (and usually sung chorally), and nearly always uplifts or at least sustains the spirit; its function is to proclaim exuberance or comfortable understanding, rather than reveal cloaked feeling. It has parallels in other national cinemas, of course, but expresses a certain Englishness in its consciousness of class identities and solidarities, and in its collectivist mentality. Singing together is fundamentally the same as working together, that action so often depicted and celebrated in English feature films and documentaries. And the popular mode is unquestionably derived from well-established English performing institutions, above all the music hall.

It is popular music which we hear at the conclusion of Gilliat and Launder's *Millions Like Us* (1943), when in the canteen of the aircraft factory the entertainers and the factory workers, not omitting the newly widowed heroine, join together in singing "Waiting at the Church," a favorite number in turn-of-the-century music halls. If the lyrics seem cruelly to mock the heroine's situation—

> Just think how disappointed I must feel,
> I'll be off me crumpet very soon.
> I've lost my husband—the one I never had!
> And I dreamed so about the honeymoon . . .

—the jaunty tune and the friends nearby nevertheless get her singing and smiling. Factories and canteens are a natural site for musical camaraderie: that is where the girl lathe-tenders in *Listen to Britain* sing "Yes, My Darling Daughter" along with the broadcast from the Tannoy—working collectively, singing collectively—and where Flanagan and Allen perform "Round the Back of the Arches" in the same film, just before Jennings cuts to the concerto at the National Gallery, counterposing and conjoining the two music traditions for his we're-all-in-it-together documentary. Even more conspicuously, the popular mode is heard in Jennings's 1943 quasi-documentary about the Blitz and the Auxiliary Fire Service, *Fires Were Started.* Amidst the conventional nondiegetic music of this film (composed by William Alwyn, conducted by Muir Mathieson) comes an informal diegetic performance. The firemen enter one by one into Watchroom 14-Y, reporting for the night's work. One of their number vamps at the upright piano, and another starts singing the children's song "One man went to mow, went to mow a meadow." Each new entrance of a fireman gets a verse ("Two men went to mow . . . Three men went to mow . . ."), the piano music or tempo slyly adjusted to the personalities of the entering team members. By the end, seven of the eight men of the squad have joined in, the song finishes, and the air-raid-warning siren starts up. What about the eighth man? He is the piano player, a new recruit (played by the writer William Sansom, who did in fact serve with the AFS), and over the siren's wailing the squad sing one last verse for him. No other two-minute sequence of a 1940s film gives so moving a sense of ordinary Englishmen pulling themselves together via music, and for this purpose, the casual, even amateurish acting and filming, the sense of a production crew larking about with the song just as the firemen lark about with it, seems perfectly right.

The performing of popular music, inevitable as a wartime film technique, was scarcely limited to the war years. Indeed, its greatest period may have been the 1930s, the defining era of English film musicals.[19] Some of these were loosely put together "revue" films like *Elstree Calling* (1930) or *Soft Lights and Sweet Music* (1936); or films set backstage, like John Baxter's *Say It with Flowers* (1934); or film versions of West End shows. By far the most interesting category of musical film, however, and the most obviously English, attempted to fold a variety of music-hall-derived acts, both comic and sentimental, into some sort of plot. These films featured such singing and dancing stars of the halls as George Formby, Jessie Matthews, and above all Gracie Fields, "our Gracie." Fields was famous for singing comic patter and sentimental favorites with equal facility. Appropriately enough, her first record, in 1928, had the funny "Because I Love You" on one side and the serious "My Blue Heaven" on the other. Gracie the comedian is recalled in a scrap of that song which Graham Greene's Pinkie hears at the dance palace with Rose (in the novel *Brighton Rock*, not the film):

> Gracie Fields funning,
> The gangsters gunning,
>   Talk of our love.

Meanwhile Gracie the heart-tugger is audible in that scene of the Merchant-Ivory *Remains of the Day* in which Stevens plays his record and feels the strange potency of music. What he finds so touching is none other than Fields singing "Roll Along, Prairie Moon," one of her biggest romantic hits.

Between 1931 and the outbreak of war in 1939, Fields made a hugely successful new cinematic career for herself by starring in a series of comedy romances, all of them featuring plots constructed around her personality, with ample spaces left in the narratives for musical performance.[20] Among the relentlessly upbeat Fields musicals were *Sally in Our Alley, Looking on the Bright Side, This Week of Grace, Sing As We Go!, Love, Life, and Laughter, Look Up and Laugh, We're Going to Be Rich, Keep Smiling,* and *Shipyard Sally.* In them, Gracie might feature as a singer-waitress in a navvies' caff, waiting for her fiancé to return from the trenches; a manicurist in love with an impoverished songwriter; or a saloon performer trying to reopen a shipyard for her unemployed customers;[21] but whatever the nominal plot, it was always some variant of her own life story which was being projected on the screen. Everyone in the cinema audience knew the outlines of this story— Fields's birth over a chip shop in Rochdale; the mother who scrubbed the stage of the Hippodrome and pushed her talented young daughter into a show-business career; Gracie's temporary work in a cotton mill and her singing for the other mill-girls there; her entertaining of troops in the War; her spectacular success in the revue *Mr. Tower of London* in 1918.[22] Everyone also knew the artistic persona which this story created: working-class, down-to-earth, irreverent, not strikingly beautiful. "Unhampered by the baggage of excessive femininity," as Marcia Landy has observed, Gracie was free "to be an instigator of rebellion, a leader of the group, and a solver of men's and women's problems."[23] A great star, she was still "one of us." In at least six of her films Fields appeared as a character named "Gracie," so little did her celebrity need to be disguised for the scenarios.

The success of the Fields musicals, more marked in the provinces than in London, owed something to the production company which made them, Associated Talking Pictures, which the impresario Basil Dean ran at Ealing Studios in the middle years of the 1930s, and to Dean's (or Maurice Elvey's or Monty Banks's) skills as director. Fields also kept in her entourage an inventive Welsh pianist and composer, Harry Parr-Davies, to provide songs exactly matching her talents. But of course it was those talents themselves—"her gusto and good temper, her candid sentimentality, her readiness to defend herself and her friends against all pomp and privilege"[24]—which chiefly sustained the Gracie Fields films. If her talents were at bottom local, provincial, they were therefore, paradoxically, the more endearing to the nation. Fields sang and mugged her cheerful way through her film vehicles in that "flat but broad-vowelled speech" of Lancashire which could almost be thought the "official accent of music-hall humour." So J. B. Priestley wrote in *English Journey* (1934), his documentary exploration of the nation during the Slump, of English unemployment and industrial decline, of muddling through, of finding ways to cheer everyone up. Priestley added that the accent might

> add no charm of prettiness to a woman's talk, but it can give it flavour, body, character, as it does in the songs and patter of Gracie Fields, who is not only the most popular and most dominating personality of the English variety stage but is also a sort of essence of Lancastrian femininity. Listen to her for a quarter of an hour and you will learn more about Lancashire women and Lancashire than you would from a dozen books on these subjects. All the qualities are there: shrewdness, homely simplicity, irony, fierce independence, an impish delight in mocking whatever is thought to be affected and pretentious.[25]

Priestley was in a good position to make this assessment. Just at the time he was writing *English Journey,* he was also writing the screenplays for *Sing As We Go!* (1934) and *Look Up and Laugh* (1935) and thus making his own considerable contribution to our Gracie's project of bringing Lancashire resilience to the rest of the country.

In the early 1930s Priestley was well launched on his protean career. He had as yet to make his name as avant-garde playwright, cultural commentator, or of course wartime radio broadcaster, but was known to millions as a middle-brow novelist, the author, in 1929, of *The Good Companions.* That bestselling novel was written straight out of Priestley's love for music halls, which he had visited first in Bradford before the War and remembered affectionately throughout life: "a tune from a forgotten operetta, an old music-hall ditty, is my equivalent of Proust's *madeleine.*" The halls furnished the setting for his early literary sketches, one of which, "Secrets of the Ragtime King," an imaginary interview following on a particularly memorable evening at the Leeds Empire, was the young writer's first work to be sold to a magazine.[26] In 1929 the music hall was still alive in England, though under attack from cinemas, and beginning to modulate into new forms, like the radio broadcast or the combined show at the *palais de danse.* Or the abbreviated and genteel form of the concert party, which is what we see from both backstage and front-of-house perspectives in *The Good Companions.*

Concert parties were traveling shows of songs and comedy, often put on at the seaside and opening with a Pierrot number—like that we see being performed by Ida's troupe in the film version of *Brighton Rock*—though the concert-party performers of Priestley's novel, called "The Dinky-Doos," are condemned to a dreary round of inland provincial towns. About to founder, the show is rescued by Jess Oakroyd, a recently sacked Yorkshire mill-worker; Inigo Jollifant, a one-time schoolmaster and brilliant amateur pianist; and Elizabeth Trant, a spinster who suddenly finds herself with a legacy and time on her hands. These wandering, discontented souls happen on The Dinky-Doos by chance and transform them into "The Good Companions." Along the way they overcome obstacles both old-fangled (show-business jealousies and love-affairs) and new-fangled (nasty opposition from the owner of some cinemas), and they turn the show into a great success.

Early on, Miss Trant's insufferable, Oxford-educated nephew lectures her on the principle by which he runs an avant-garde little magazine: "Art has got to be beyond emotion. Life and Art have got absolutely choked up with filthy emotion, and we say the time has come for them to be—what shall I say?—feelingless, all calm and clear." Needless to say *The Good Companions* labors throughout to refute this ideology. For Priestley, the art of a concert party is humane and valuable precisely to the degree that it engages the feelings of an audience, liberates the hearts of its performers, and puts audience and performers together in a common enterprise of good feeling and fun. Jollifant, no less well educated (and sometimes no less insufferable) than the nephew, is made to expound the Priestleyan creed, with an untypical inarticulacy that bespeaks sincere belief:

> "Somehow"—he was in earnest now, saying for once something that was very real and important, felt in the heart . . . "somehow—there isn't too much—er—good companionship left—is there? I mean—people don't sort of—pull together now much, do they? . . . I'd like one or two people to say I was a good companion. That's one of the things that's attracted me about this what's it—concert party; a good crowd sticking together. That's where the fun really comes in, isn't it?"[27]

At this moment he has already started to fall for the Dinky-Doos' pretty ingénue, Susie Dean; in the course of the novel Miss Trant eventually finds love too, while Oakroyd, completing this trio of redemption through good companionship, recovers his self-respect and starts off on a voyage to his much-loved daughter in Canada. Priestley is not the novelist to neglect obvious plot turns, though it might be said in defense of *The Good Companions* that it is not a very plot-driven work. On the contrary, throughout its several-hundred-page length, it is episodic, full of digressions and interpolated tales, mixed in tone, picaresque to a degree: the miscellaneous adventures of characters first tramping the roads of England and then trouping through one small-town concert hall after another. For a book about people pulling together, it is remarkably tolerant of people going their own way, sentimentally or comically—and in this, of course, it participates in a music-hall aesthetic. In the Leeds Empire you could never be sure what was coming next. It might be ragtime, Little Tich's big boot dance, Vesta Tilley singing "Jolly Good Luck to the Girl Who Loves a Soldier," performing dogs, a comedy sketch from Dan Leno, a patriotic effusion, or a memory act like the one Hitchcock put so ingeniously into the opening of *The 39 Steps*. The same now-laughter-now-tears quality in *The Good Companions* makes it stylistically at one with the theatrical milieu it celebrates.

Priestley's novel was almost immediately made into a play, then filmed in 1933 by Gaumont-British, with Victor Saville directing and a likely Jessie Matthews starring as Susie Dean, an unlikely John Gielgud as Inigo Jollifant. The picture strives to show all parts of the country coming together. Just as *A Canterbury Tale* and other wartime films would do a decade later, it opens with an aerial shot of the map of England, first locating the main characters at the corners of the realm, the Industrial North, the rural West Country, bleak East Anglia, then closing in on the central little town at which they encounter the Dinky-Doos and begin their enterprise. The film strives as well to put Jessie Matthews on glamorous display, especially in the big final number, "Let Me Give My Happiness to You," the title of which by itself perfectly represents the spirit of music-hall performance. The "outstanding example of the English picaresque on the screen," a later film historian said of *The Good Companions* film,[28] but Saville's work, in fact tightly plotted and efficient, conveys little of the original's motleyness. This was the achievement instead of Priestley's two screenplays for Gracie Fields.

About these screenplays Priestley said nothing in his autobiographies, nor much about his writing for films in general, which he did most of in the later 1930s, for Hollywood. We do know that Priestley was invited to write for Fields by Basil Dean, who was later to direct several of the dramatist's expressionist works, and who chose Priestley specifically to improve the quality of material for his star.[29] We know besides that Priestley visited Fields at her villa on Capri and got on well with her. No doubt their common devotion to music halls (and their common North Country origins) aided their collaboration. So did their similar view of what the cinema ought to provide: "a bit of glamour, an increased tempo, a touch of the fantastic, people who are more vivid than the ordinary run of folk," as Priestley would write in a 1936 article.[30] Agreement about what films were good for was the more necessary because Fields so disliked the actual process of filming. She missed having a live audience; she did not care for Dean; she hated getting up very early in the morning to report to the studio ("It'll be like going back t' mill").[31]

The first of the Priestley-Fields films, *Sing as We Go!,* is set mostly in Blackpool, and abundantly replicates the dizzying variety of the city— its hodge-podge quality, which the prose of *English Journey* used a list to capture:

> This huge mad place, with its miles and miles of promenades, its three piers, its gigantic dance-halls, its variety shows, its switch-backs and helter-skelters, its array of wine bars and oyster saloons and cheap restaurants and tea houses and shops piled high and glittering with trash; its army of pierrots, bandsmen, clowns, fortune-tellers, auctioneers, dancing partners, animal trainers, itinerant singers, hawkers; its seventy special trains a day, its hundreds and hundreds and thousands of trippers . . .[32]

Nothing in English filmmaking before or after *Sing As We Go!* depicts so well this iconic English place, and for that reason and others *Sing As We Go!* has itself become iconic, a cultural touchstone, something sufficiently well known to be celebrated or mocked. (It is treated in both these ways simultaneously, as we will see, in Alan Bennett's play *The*

History Boys.) And *Sing as We Go!* has received its due of critical attention, from the film historian Jeffrey Richards in *The Age of the Dream
Palace*, and especially from Andrew Higson in his 1995 study *Waving
the Flag: Constructing a National Cinema in Britain*. With great persuasiveness Higson shows how *Sing As We Go!* depends on both the car-
nivalesque spirit of the Blackpool in which it is set and the music-hall
traditions from which it derives. For him, Fields's film, unlike Jessie
Matthews's more up-market and Hollywoodish musical *Evergreen*, constitutes a specifically working-class and English response to the challenge of American musicals.[33]

Look Up and Laugh, in contrast to all this, has been relatively
neglected—a fate it scarcely deserves. The film is as ingenious as its
predecessor in putting music-hall techniques to work onscreen, and
in drawing national meanings out of provincial settings, for both of
which achievements Priestley may be chiefly to thank. That was Graham
Greene's opinion when he reviewed the film in *The Spectator* and commended its "pleasant local flavor," the sense it gave, even while being a
farce, "that a man's observation and experience, as well as his invention, has gone to its making."[34] *Look Up and Laugh* touches offhandedly
on a variety of themes (class struggle, young love versus mature selfless-
ness, the never-say-die spirit) and film genres (knockabout comedy, the
avant-garde documentary) without ever committing itself to any one
theme or genre, yet it still manages to hold together, perhaps more successfully than *Sing As We Go!* And as we will see it makes remarkably
sophisticated use of the popular music at its center.

The star of *Look Up and Laugh*—Gracie Pearson she is called—
enters the picture driving along the highway. She has moved up in the
world. No longer the plucky mill lass of *Sing As We Go!*, she is now a
variety artiste on a visit home to "Plumborough." Priestley's scenario
plunges immediately into song, carrying on as it were from the musical
conclusion of *Sing As We Go!* Meanwhile the final image of the earlier
film, a giant, frame-filling Union Jack, here metamorphoses into the flag
flying from Gracie's convertible. She performs the title song of the new
film from behind the wheel as if car-borne singing with full orchestral
accompaniment were the most natural thing in the world:

> Look up and laugh, be happy, bright, and gay,
> Imagine the sun is shining every day!

This is neither diegetic nor nondiegetic music, but that odd hybrid mode, reserved for movie musicals, in which a performance belongs fictively to the diegesis and simultaneously to the sound stage, where (as everyone in the audience knows, without quite wishing to admit it) orchestra and singer are actually belting it out for the microphones. Gracie carries on with the rising melody lines and fast tempo of the song, then in the bridge section she squeezes the bulb of her car horn in time with the tune, smiling and winking directly at the camera, as if back in the music hall, drawing her audience into the rollicking mood of the number. Of course the audience is literally watching a film on a screen, as now becomes obvious with a cutaway to something that could never appear on the stage of the Leeds Empire—a mildly comic interlude of Gracie the woman driver nearly running over some workmen, then stopping to chaff with them:

> WORKMAN   Can't you see we're trying to paint the road white?
> GRACIE   Can't *you* see I want to get home to paint the town red?

After this broad hint that the film is going to wander freely from tunes to jokes, the song finishes:

> Even though it starts to rain,
> It will soon be fine again,
> All together and laugh your troubles away!

At home, Gracie discovers problems ("Even though it starts to rain . . ."). Her father, the senior stall-holder in the town's ancient covered market, is ailing, while her brother Sidney, played by Fields's real-life brother Tommy, is both in debt and in love. Sidney stammers except when he sings. This is a pleasant conceit in a film which will make so much of the restorative powers of music, and one carried out with real wit in a later scene, where Sidney tries to say gallant things to his girl, runs into trouble, then gives himself a pitch from the piano and delivers the gallantry in North Country *recitativo secco*.

Sidney's girl Marjorie (Vivien Leigh, in her third film role) is the daughter of the overbearing department-store owner Belfer, who wants to close the market down so his own emporium can be expanded, and who has the venal town council on his side. Thus the comic conflict of the film is joined: Belfer versus Gracie, chromium-gilt department store versus homely old market, moneyed Establishment versus little people. The market's age will eventually prove its salvation—the used-book dealer in it produces the original charter of Edward III, stipulating no closure of the market without Royal Assent—but meanwhile Belfer's threat seems serious, or as serious as it can be in this kind of film. If class issues are involved, the market and its customers standing for a certain working- or middle-class ordinariness, cloth caps, local accents, and all, while the department store seems full of over-dressed, bullying pretentiousness, the issues are lightly sketched and taken for granted, or exploited for comic possibilities. Ultimately, of course, they are laughed away in a finale which brings all parties together for a last chorus. Nothing in *Look Up and Laugh* corresponds to the soured class relations we see in the other significant English film about a market stall-holder, Tony Richardson's version of John Osborne's play *Look Back in Anger* (1959), where Jimmy Porter's allegiance to his working-class past and his antipathy to his wife's gentility are both expressed in that sweets stall he holds to so unreasonably.

The market of *Look Up and Laugh* is opened up to the viewer in a long early scene, the starting-point for which is Gracie's near-triumphant entry into the place, greeting and being greeted by old friends, bucking up everyone's spirits. Everyone includes a trio of neatly uniformed sweets sellers, the Jewish goldsmith Rosenbloom with his five pretty dark-haired daughters, the gloomy toy dealer, the elderly modiste with her terrible hats, the fabric seller with his booming voice, the used-book dealer and his granddaughter, and the Chirk brothers, florists, played by Duggie Wakefield and Billy Nelson, two among the crowd of old comedians dragged out of retirement in response to Priestley's "recollection of the halcyon days of the English music hall."[35] In other words the market puts all readily available types together in an appealing setting and finds in their compound eccentricities a cozy version of Englishness, thus anticipating the ethos of *Passport to Pimlico, The Lavender Hill Mob,* and other comedies to be made, on the same Ealing lot as *Look Up and Laugh,* after the war. Like all the Ealing comedies, Fields's film achieves its effects by finding a workable balance between a satiric comedy allowing characters to go their own way into individual skits and a more warm-hearted sentiment drawing them together into ensemble scenes.

Also like the Ealing comedies, *Look Up and Laugh* takes care to extract comic value from its mise-en-scène. The market setting is the achievement of Dean's art director J. Elder Wills, who made in tiny compass something like the "huge mad place" which Priestley called Blackpool. Fantastically detailed, with signage everywhere, a telephone box, multiple flower baskets from the Chirk brothers, multiple watches hung at Rosenbloom's, sheet music cascading from the shelves of Gracie's own stall, cozy niches for Sidney and Marjorie to spoon in, the market gives an idealized view of a prosperous proletarian neighborhood, complete even to street-like aisles crowded with larky passers-by. The effect is far less realistic than that given by the several Blackpool settings of *Sing As We Go!*, which Dean sometimes photographed as if making a documentary, but more expressive. The helter-skelter artifice of the market complements Priestley's helter-skelter plot, as do, a little later in the film, the richly varied departments of Belfer's store, here pianos or gentlemen's hats, there housewares or cooking demonstrations. Whether in the store or the market Dean usually cuts between his short sequences with fancy shaped wipes, adding to the overall impression of speed and variety, of one music-hall turn pushing its predecessor hastily offstage. The music hall is also recalled in the frontal positioning of performers within the sets; they tend to line up as if on a shallow stage, and Dean's camera sometimes frames them as if they were being seen from the front rows of the stalls. This is particularly the case with a gag acted out in the town council chambers. Here, Belfer and his helpers square off with Gracie and her helpers in a municipal debate turned ingeniously into a prizefight. There are ropes around the "ring" where they argue, the mayor keeps accidentally ringing a bell, the helpers act like seconds, spectators cheer, the victorious Gracie has her arm lifted up in the traditional gesture, and so on. It is a moment worthy of Chaplin's visual metaphors, his transforming of X into Y by clever staging and props, and Chaplin, it will be remembered, came from exactly the same English theatrical world as Gracie Fields, and carried into film work the same theatrical skills as she.

The Chaplinesque spirit seems most to preside in the department store scenes of *Look Up and Laugh,* with their air of comics set mischievously loose in a place full of breakable items and disruptable events, of anarchic vulgar energy having its revenge on staidness. Gracie, oddly dressed as a girl guide leader, and three of her market chums, dressed as boy scouts, invade Belfer's during its grand opening celebration, pulling faces at the cooking samples on offer, switching signs, re-dressing fashion displays, and otherwise causing mischief of the sort Chaplin perfected in his Mutual two-reeler *The Floorwalker.* From time to time Gracie winks at the camera, acknowledging the silliness of it all. When she sings she does so comically, displacing the diva Madame Belletrini to guy a florid opera aria, or commandeering the piano showroom for the burlesque number "I'm Anna from Anacapri," wherein she and her pals mock one national style after another ("I'm Heinrich from over the mountains," "I'm Olga the Queen of the Volga"), making lightning improvised costume changes as they do. The significant point about both performances is that they conquer even the stuffy department store. The ladies and gentlemen in the tea-room laugh hard at "Madame Belletrini's" vocal antics, and Belfer's piano salesman not only laughs hard at "I'm Anna from Anacapri" but joins in the merriment, winding up spread-eagled on top of one of the baby grands. This pulling of the audience into the show, this blurring of the distinction between the performer and the performed for, is the third essential element of music-hall style, to go along with the cheerful vulgarity of its comedy and the extreme, fast-changing variety of its acts.

Perhaps including the audience is the most important element. In the central musical performances of *Look Up and Laugh,* our Gracie, the star who belongs somehow to "us," invariably pulls her audience into the fun or the sentiment, like a music-hall star calling out "Are you *with* me, boys?" over the footlights. Gracie's solos turn into choruses for the house, not literally, it may be—though it would be very interesting to find out how many cinema audiences started singing the refrains along with the star—but with onscreen characters deputizing as the "house." One scene with chorusing, for example, begins with the stall-holders locking themselves in the market. The town has turned off the water and gas, and Dean's camera pans slowly over the stall-holders' long faces and dejected postures. It is a shot uncannily like those to be seen in the war-time melodramas (Londoners waiting out a blitz in the Underground, escaping refugees huddled together) of six or seven years later. The market obviously requires cheering up, a duty which Gracie embraces at the cost of walking away from a mild flirtation with a handsome reporter; in the Fields films, communal responsibility always trumps her own romances. Gracie starts her glum listeners off with "Looking on the Bright Side," then when the cry comes "Give us 'Sally,'" she complies, "Sally" being the great hit of *Sally in Our Alley*. Once everyone including an accordion player has joined in, she leaves.

Earlier in the siege of the market, at a peaceful moment of retiring for the evening, something more soothing and romantic is called for. Gracie begins "Love Is Everywhere" as she undresses, then, still singing, wanders in her robe out into the quiet market, a variety-artiste Henry V surveying her troops on the eve of battle. One by one, the stall-holders join in as she moves among them. They are not so much following Gracie's lead as happening to share her mood. The used-book dealer and his granddaughter sing; the modiste adds her tremulous old soprano to the mix as she brushes out her hair. It is a moment to be conscious of the power of music, as the lyrics insinuate,

> Love is everywhere, in the words these lips of mine are singing,
> Even in the dreams the night is bringing,

and as Dean hints when his camera reveals a giant-lettered movie poster on the wall behind his star: "Gracie Fields in *Sing As We Go!*" In that movie then, in this movie now: the indispensability of music could scarcely be more showcased. Eventually a full chorus of voices is sounding the tune, freeing Gracie for a warbling descant. Only Rosenbloom's stall is quiet, the five daughters tucked in for the night, the goldsmith slumbering with his arm curled protectively around the cash register (ethnic stereotypes too are part of the music-hall style, and the blending of visual joke with heartfelt song part of *Look Up and Laugh*'s method). The point having been made, musically, that love really *is* everywhere, and everyone having received a little touch of Gracie in the night, the star finishes quietly by herself, delivering the final words without any instrumental accompaniment, and smiling conspiratorially straight at the camera as she gets into bed.

"Love Is Everywhere" gets a mood across with exceptional cleverness, but of all the musical numbers in the film, the most imaginatively handled is an earlier one, a reprise of the title song. The news of Belfer's assault on the market has been received and Gracie argues for resistance. "Look up and laugh" she tells the stall-holders and, getting the response back "Say it with music, Gracie," begins the cheeky title tune again. The orchestra accompanying her is nondiegetic, as at the film's opening and as with "Love Is Everywhere." After a verse, Gracie jollies the market along in best music-hall style—"Come on, everybody, cheer up! We'll get nowhere if we're miserable. Come on now, let it rip!"— and a few voices join hers, then a few more. The modiste beats time with a piece of sheet music she's picked up—the music for "Look Up and Laugh," in fact, as can clearly be read on the cover: Basil Dean's little joke, his equivalent of a wink at the audience. Musical instruments now appear (we are right in front of the music stall), a tuba, a flute, a drum, a trombone with its slide gone wrong, a violin which the silly-ass Sidney tries to play back-to-front, a jew's harp for Rosenbloom. The instruments are comic props for zanies, but somehow they are also making music, and everyone is now singing and dancing. "Look Up and Laugh" has suddenly become diegetic, as diegetic as "Roll Out the Barrel" in *The Captive Heart* or *Listen to Britain*. The song has been wrested from the studio orchestra to become the property of the market people in the scene, and all are included in the wide shot with which Dean finishes, to the sound of hurrahs and one last rendition of "All together and laugh your troubles away!" It is a preeminent moment of good companionship, of a performer getting everyone to join in a chorus or, as T. S. Eliot once wrote of another great music-hall singer, Marie Lloyd, of getting everyone to feel "not so much hilarious as happy."[36] It is also a theatrical moment, of course, as artificial as could be imagined. And yet the artifice, given the fact that it is Gracie Fields at the center of all the enthusiasm, seems completely convincing. In 1937, one of her biographers records, while Fields was laying the foundation stone for the new Prince of Wales Theatre, she climbed up onto the scaffolding and stopped West End traffic by getting the crowd to sing along with her.[37]

Is there anything really original about *Look Up and Laugh*? In a sense, its charm depends on its utter conventionality, on keeping to the formulaic plot developments and well-understood musical techniques of its genre, or of that genre as refined by the previous Gracie Fields films. But Priestley or Dean or Fields herself was apparently unwilling to make something entirely conforming to type, and at least two sequences of the film deliberately break from convention. One of these moments constitutes the finale. The market is triumphant, if rebuilt (the old one has gone up in a gas explosion), and at the ceremony of rededication the new mayor, a reformed Belfer, speaks; a royal personage speaks; Gracie should speak next, but just as she opens her mouth the band and the crowd plunge into "Look Up and Laugh" one last time. The star has been upstaged by her own number. Nor will the police let Gracie into the now-packed market. All she can do is mumble "thanks" and walk sadly away. Soon of course she shakes herself, joins in the song, and heads off toward her next variety show in Manchester, but there is still an odd melancholy feeling about this exit from Plumborough, the home town which apparently has no further need of her. The feeling is emphasized as she drives by herself (the car now flies *two* Union Jacks, a nice touch) into the distance. This is a *diminuendo* close to a rousing film; a quiet solo at a point where we would expect a big chorus—which the more conventional *Sing As We Go!*, for example, supplies. At the end of *Look Up and Laugh,* all that would be required to complete the likeness to one of Chaplin's melancholy finales, the performer somehow exiled from the happiness he has created, the vagabond's journey continuing into some indefinite future, would be an iris-out on the screen. This, however, Dean fails to provide.

The second and yet odder sequence takes place when town officials arrive to evict the stall-holders from the market. They encounter a barricaded door and Gracie sternly warning them "You can't come in . . . we won't go out." The knocks on the door and the two strongly rhythmic phrases then combine to make the basis of a *Sprechstimme* chorus for the townspeople: nothing sung, just rhythmic chanting to a light, mostly percussion accompaniment. Meanwhile the townspeople are filmed in a series of rapid cuts, usually at canted camera angles and often in extreme close-up. All in all, it is a minute and a half of avant-garde montage no less daring than Britten's score for piano and speaking chorus in the documentary short *Coal Face* from 1935, the same year as *Look Up and Laugh,* or the rhythmic poetic finale of Basil Wright and Harry Watt's *Night Mail.* Just what an avant-garde montage is doing in a Gracie Fields picture is hard to say. Satisfying J. B. Priestley's wish to do new things with the cinema? Showing how up-to-date Ealing could be? Whatever the intention behind it, "You can't come in . . . we won't go out" exploits to the utmost the miscellaneous, anything-can-come-next style of the music halls. As yet another variety turn, it might after all be thought to fit right in to a work which also includes a whist drive, a miniature car race, a helicopter crashing through the ceiling of the council chamber, and a tea cup perched precariously on Gracie Fields's head.

In the years after World War II, comedies like *Sing As We Go!* and *Look Up and Laugh* ceased to be produced. Gracie Fields's film career had gone overseas and in other artistic directions, and most of the music-hall comedians who had been so crucial to her pictures faded from the scene. For that matter, so did the music halls. Glimpses of variety-style performance might still be had, but only in surroundings that confirmed its datedness. In the film of *Look Back in Anger,* for example, Jimmy and Cliff three times improvise music-hall routines: a couple of comic interchanges ("Have you seen Nobody?") and a sung duet ("Don't be afraid to sleep with your sweetheart just because she's better than you") in which, as the direction in Osborne's play says, they "do a Flanagan and Allen."[38] They are trying to bring a little life to proceedings, ginger up Sunday morning in the flat or the rehearsal of Helena's stuffy play by performing something authentically vulgar and working-class, but all that their futile noisy gestures succeed in demonstrating is the desperation of Jimmy's anger. By the date of the film, music halls are a matter for pastiche. They are as lost to the England in which Jimmy dwells as the bright Edwardian uniforms he talks longingly about or the Indian Empire he catches absurd glimpses of in his visit to the cinema. In 1960 Richardson and Osborne would depict the moribund variety tradition more pointedly in *The Entertainer,* the chronicle of the gagman Archie Rice's fall into abysmal failure. Two years later, in John Schlesinger's *A Kind of Loving,* the music hall would appear only as an infinitely depressing relic, a pub singalong where the Alan Bates character, the drunken Vic Brown, completely fails to interest the crowd in "Down by the Riverside." Three years after that, J. B. Priestley might still be thinking of music-hall numbers as his personal madeleine, but he could write about the halls themselves only nostalgically, with Proustian melancholy for *temps perdu*, as he does in his tellingly titled 1965 novel *Lost Empires*.[39]

By the mid-1960s variety was in its absolutely final phase, on television, where it can be glimpsed in the background of the first of the Beatles movies, *A Hard Day's Night*. Richard Lester's film inventively traces the pop group's journey through screaming fans and their manager's fretting to an important broadcast. The Beatles' presence in the film is so dominant as to make it hard to recall that they are sharing that broadcast with a scene from an operetta, a Vegas-style dance number with elaborately costumed chorines, and even an old-fashioned magic act, "Leslie Jackson and his 10 Disappearing Doves." (Paul McCartney's grandfather rubs in the old-fashionedness by telling the magician that he saw the latter's father in the old Empire in 1909.) Just as with the Gracie Fields films of three decades before, the miscellaneousness of the occasion is carried over into the style of the film. *A Hard Day's Night* keeps its plot very loose, alternates its songs with comic bits—

LADY JOURNALIST Are you a Mod or a Rocker?
RINGO I'm a Mocker—

and indulges whenever possible in slapstick or nonsense, or even in the old romantic sentiments which are there to be heard ("If I Fell in Love," "All My Loving") under the newness of the Beatles' musical sound. Nor is variety the only thing *A Hard Day's Night* shares with *Look Up and Laugh*. The two films open in the same way, with artistes journeying and with a performance of the up-tempo title song; they both deride anything self-important, posh, or authoritarian; they both present themselves cheerfully as provincial artifacts and are prompt to offer the cheekiness of Lancashire or Liverpool to the rest of the country. While acknowledging what fun is to be had watching anarchic individuals, both films place value on people coming together: "we're a community," Paul says stoutly (and fairly sincerely) to the shirty old snob who has been giving them trouble in the first-class compartment of their train. On that train the Beatles eventually retreat to the baggage car and start playing cards, but a little audience of giggling schoolgirls pursues them, and a song—"I Shoulda Known Better with a Girl Like You"—appears out of nowhere, at first nondiegetically, as if it were just there in the Beatles' heads, as if just meant to entertain the cinema audience. But in a while Paul begins to mouth the words, then John picks up a harmonica and everyone starts singing. Guitars and Ringo's drum set appear, just as magically as the instruments in the market-hall performance of "Look Up and Laugh." Baggage-car card game has been effortlessly transformed into baggage-car gig, nondiegetic into diegetic music. The point is perhaps to allegorize the unstoppable show-biz process converting four miscellaneous lads into The Beatles, but also, again as in the Gracie Fields film, to reclaim popular music from a soundtrack and put it into the social context where it belongs. The sequence dramatizes and makes viewers sharply aware of the power of music, namely, the power of "I Shoulda Known Better" to pull the four performers, their diegetic audience, and ideally, beyond them, the audience watching everything in a darkened cinema, into a group of good companions.

Three decades after *A Hard Day's Night,* the empowerment-via-music-or-dance movies thickly clustered at the end of the century—Mark Herman's two films *Little Voice* (1998) and *Brassed Off* (1996), Peter Cattaneo's *The Full Monty* (1997), and Stephen Daltry's *Billy Elliott* (2000)—develop this theme of community and music further. Indeed, they develop it to the point of cliché. All the films feature a provincial locality down on its luck, reluctant or held-back singers or dancers, the audition, the hard work of rehearsal, the big opportunity, the diegetic performance, the merging of performers and audience, the redemption of the performers, and the validation, possibly, of their community's values. The Sheffield ex-steelworkers of *The Full Monty* strip for their wives and girlfriends as Tom Jones belts out "You Can Leave Your Hat On." Uncovering, they recover their manhoods and start things afresh in the old rust-belt city. Little Voice looks out over the audience in Mr. Boo's seedy nightclub, sees the apparition of her father there, bonds with him, and launches forthwith into her Shirley Bassey or Marilyn Monroe routines, to everyone's approval, and later to her own emancipation. The miners' band of *Brassed Off* challenges the best of the nation at the Royal Albert Hall and furnishes an opportunity for an attack on Tory callousness about the closure of the pits. In works like these, the cultural authority of traditional or popular music, its infectiousness for the performers and their community, is simply taken for granted—

sometimes to pleasant comic effect, as in the famous scene from *The Full Monty* where the strippers-to-be standing in the dole queue unconsciously begin to roll their shoulders rhythmically to Donna Summer's "Hot Stuff" on the radio. In the empowerment movies, characters may need to be told (in effect) to look up and laugh, but no one needs to lead the way with a song devised for the occasion. The right sort of music is already there, all around the characters, inescapable, just as it is in Sam Miller's disempowerment film *Among Giants* (1998), where in Yorkshire pubs country-and-western songs are always being played, the right sort of wailing to accompany the characters' hard-luck defeats. There is nothing the least strange about the potency of music in this style of film-making. Music is the common currency of the daily life portrayed.

In the earlier films, by contrast, what a musical performance means is *discovered* as it is taking place, not simply presented as a fact of pop-cultural life, and because it is discovered, it can be dramatized with more panache and originality. It is treated that way in the production numbers of *Look Up and Laugh,* in the improvised performances of *A Hard Day's Night,* and in several key moments of a work already touched on and, remarkably, not a musical, *Look Back in Anger.* Richardson's film approaches its exposition of Jimmy Porter and Jimmy's England by way of his trumpet playing. This is a talent made much more of in Nigel Kneale's screenplay than in Osborne's original drama, perhaps because trumpet playing had already been established as a conspicuous and convention-violating activity in the 1950s English cinema, with Kay Kendall famously letting loose on the instrument in *Genevieve* (1953), or John Mills in *It's Great to Be Young!* (1956), playing a jazz-mad music master who leads his pupils to happiness via his trumpet.

Whatever the influences on Kneale and Richardson, they introduce Jimmy's trumpet as soon as their film begins. The setting shown under the opening credits is a jazz club (like the one lovingly photographed by Richardson and Karel Reisz in their documentary of two years previously, *Momma Don't Allow*). Hot jazz is playing. First we see hands clapping, in extreme close-up, so close that they are a little hard to decipher, then a couple of sitting listeners (their heads cut off by the frame) doing a complicated routine of gestures to the beat of the music, and only then a disembodied performer's hand pounding on a bass's strings. After that, another hand strumming a banjo (and the banjo sound comes to the fore at this moment: this is diegetic music), then fingers tapping a beer glass, then dancing legs, then a young woman's cigarette-holding, time-beating hands, then a clarinet being played. All this visual fragmentation makes impossible—pointless—the distinguishing of performers from audience. What we are given here is the general effect of jazz on bodies, or the general making of rhythm, shared out consensually through the smoky room. Even when the camera pulls back a little to reveal Jimmy playing lead, the framing is hardly conventional, since he and the other musicians are generally seen obliquely, through the crowd or over bobbing heads. When Jimmy finishes he takes the applause, but then gets down and mingles easily with the audience, wearing the same clothes as they, picking up and drinking his pal Cliff's beer, glancing at Cliff's girl. Everyone is *together*. In other words, the formation of a tight little group that is accomplished in *Look Up and Laugh* vocally, the star handing melodies over to her followers, is accomplished here instrumentally—and cinematically too, with the aid of special framing and quick continuous editing from shot to shot.

As for the cultural community depicted at this moment of *Look Back in Anger*, it is obviously young people, rather than the working-class provincials of the Fields picture, young people experiencing the pleasure of defining themselves as a group ("It's great to be young!" indeed) and experiencing good companionship, however stodgy Priestley's phrase might seem to them. Richardson's hepcats are also feeling the pleasure of jitterbugging, via American music, away from the feeble tyranny of old England, as soon to be represented by Jimmy's whey-faced landlady or the decrepit codgers whom he and Helena glimpse in a walk in the park. Indeed, Jimmy has to confront old England as soon as he goes out the jazz-club door, which he does at the start of a still more remarkable sequence, an object lesson, if there ever was one, in music's strange potency.

Jimmy stalks through the dark and silent streets—dead streets, he would no doubt say—still hearing in his head the music from the club. He blows his trumpet at random, announcing his presence on the scene as if he were a knight errant blowing his slug-horn before the walls of a castle, or perhaps just trying to awaken some life. Mockingly, one of the riffs he blows is a jazz version of "Rule, Britannia." At this point

Richardson and his music director put something truly odd on the soundtrack, trumpet music coming back at Jimmy from the air or the sleeping buildings. It resembles but is not a literal echo, because the notes are not identical to the ones he's played. Psychology rather than acoustics runs this scene: the non-echoing trumpet, we realize, is the projection of Jimmy's wish. He would like a response, a duet, he would like someone to blare at him as loudly as he has been blaring at the town, he would like to force another group into admiring existence around him; and for all these reasons his auditory imagination creates the sound. Is this nondiegetic music, because it is not actually being performed by the character? Diegetic, because it *is* being performed, in the theater of his mind? However we categorize it, it unquestionably characterizes Jimmy. Simultaneously, it demonstrates what jazz means to him and his friends in the club. What they are all beating time to or playing or hearing in their imaginations is vitality, excitement, effrontery, sex, the approval of everything that is happening at this very minute, the condemnation of everything opposed ("Anyone who doesn't like jazz has no real feeling for music *or* for people," Jimmy will later say), the desire to be together with like-minded others: in short, an "enormous yes." Those two words are how Philip Larkin described a trumpet riff in "For Sidney Bechet," a poem written just four years before *Look Back in Anger* opened. (Larkin had approximately the same relation to New Orleans jazz as Priestley to English music halls.) We read in "For Sidney Bechet" that jazz falls on the poet "as they say love should." It is "greeted as the natural noise of good" and scatters "long-haired grief and scored pity." It is

> Everyone making love and going shares—
> Oh, play that thing![40]

Larkin was rarely so effusive. Films are rarely as articulate as *Look Back in Anger* in demonstrating cinematically the benefits of playing that thing.

DISTANT VOICES, LIP-SYNCHED LIVES

In the long history of English screen work, few *auteurs* can have been as fascinated by music—both musical techniques and the *meaning* of music—as Terence Davies and Dennis Potter. The former's fascination is displayed chiefly in his first two full-length features *Distant Voices, Still Lives* (1988) and *The Long Day Closes* (1992); the latter's in the scripts for three well-known television miniseries, *Pennies from Heaven* (1978) and *The Singing Detective* (1986) for the BBC, *Lipstick on Your Collar* (1993) for Channel 4.

Davies and Potter make a natural pair. To begin with, they are alike in really being *auteurs,* in the original sense of that much-abused term. They are artists with a distinctive point of view and with sufficient creative authority to get precisely that point of view onto film. In all his work Davies has done both the writing and directing. His published screenplays sometimes arrange scenes in an order different from that eventually used in the films but are otherwise a faithful guide to what viewers see, down to the smallest detail: "Track around 180 degrees and crane up from this camera position until the front door [which is closed] is framed" is a typical direction. As he once commented, he goes into production "knowing every shot and camera set-up in the movie as well as what is on the soundtrack at any given point."[41] This sort of advance planning obviously contributes to his creative authority. So does, at least in the case of *Distant Voices, Still Lives* and *The Long Day Closes,* the ability to secure funding from sources (the British Film Institute, Film Four International) unlikely to interfere with a director's artistic control. As for Potter, he could scarcely be such an autonomous agent, given the nature of broadcast television. His working methods were perforce collaborative, as we have seen with *The Singing Detective* and as was even more the case with *Pennies from Heaven,* the first work in which he used songs extensively; at many places in this series Potter drew on the experience of his director Piers Haggard and on the musical enthusiasms of his producer Kenith Trodd. Still, Potter's was always the dominating spirit, even in the first years of his career. In a remarkably brief period he grew skilled at overbearing institutional complexities with the force of his zealous imagination, his belief in himself, and his belief in the power of television drama to alter millions of lives.

As for what Potter's imagination derived from, that was an ever deepening understanding of his own history. In the first episode of *Pennies from Heaven* we hear mention of a Victorian hymn, one of several the derelict Accordion Man plays on his squeeze box: "There is a green hill far away, / Without a city wall . . ." These lines sum up everything needful to say about Potter's lifelong journeying back and forth between the two places essential to him: the city where he wrote film scripts and negotiated the tortuous by-ways of the BBC, the distant beloved Forest of Dean which the best of the scripts are always in some sense about. He and Davies, both unashamedly autobiographical artists, came from humble origins, the coal-mining districts of the Forest and the Irish Catholic backstreets of Liverpool, respectively; both sensed their differentness early; both moved away (Potter via a scholarship to Oxford, Davies via a long process of self-education) and became successful metropolitan intellectuals; both looked back on their origins with a mixture of relief and guilt at having escaped from it. The emotional complications of looking back provide a counterpoint to the workings of their autobiographical plots, or, since "plot" is a word that must be used cautiously with Davies, of the autobiographical situations of their films.

Then finally there is the musical interest. Potter and Davies exhibit the same sort of feeling for and encyclopedic knowledge of Victorian hymns (in Davies's case "Once in royal David's city" rather than "There is a green hill far away"), leftover numbers from the music halls, numbers from American movie musicals, big band tunes, children's songs, folk songs, ballads, pop hits on the radio, old favorites chorused among the glasses in pub singalongs—a world of popular music which would be entirely superseded by rock in the late 1950s and 60s (a process dramatized in *Lipstick on Your Collar*) but which is meanwhile preserved, in museum-like conditions, by Davies's and Potter's curatorial care. For audiences of their work, songs are (at the very least) period markers, "distant voices" marking out the exact distance to the past. At the opening of *Pennies from Heaven* we hear "The Clouds Will Soon Roll By" being sung by Elsie Carlisle, the "Radio Sweetheart Number One," and know instantly that we are in the 1930s. When "Tammy" comes on the soundtrack on *The Long Day Closes* we also know where we are, 1957, and where Davies' pre-adolescent hero Bud has been listening to the song, in some Liverpool cinema showing Debbie Reynolds in *Tammy and the Batchelor.*

For Bud and the other characters of Davies's and Potter's works, songs have of course nothing to do with period atmosphere, everything to do with opening up captive hearts. Songs furnish momentary escape, a fantasy existence greatly preferable to the daily grind, occasional family happiness, gracefulness amid the grit. Music gives inarticulacy a way to be eloquent; in this sense, all of the characters are like our Gracie's brother Tommy, with various kinds of class or familial repressiveness standing in for his stammering. And what do the songs mean, exactly, to Potter and Davies? Answering that question involves some acknowledgment of the differences between them. Their musical tastes are not completely identical. Davies's is more classical and churchy than Potter's, catholic in both senses of the word. Moreover, the two have distinct conceptions of what music on a soundtrack is supposed to do. The songs in Davies's films generally stay at one remove from the action, presiding somberly over onscreen images somewhat as Nat King Cole's song "Mona Lisa" presides over the sad drama of the Neil Jordan film. The songs in Potter's television dramas turn feelings into full-scale performances. That is, Potter follows the musical practice of *A Hard Day's Night,* which greatly influenced *Lipstick on Your Collar,* and of *Look Up and Laugh,* that real 1930s artifact which the period scenes of *Pennies from Heaven* seem to emulate. For Davies, evocation; for Potter, entertainment: crude classifications, admittedly, which will have to be refined in the pages to follow.

It was not easy for Terence Davies to escape, imaginatively, from the traumas and loyalties of his Liverpool upbringing. His autobiographical project began with his very first films, the low-budget, 16mm shorts *Children, Madonna and Child,* and *Death and Transfiguration,* then continued with the two full-length features. In *Distant Voices, Still Lives*—two films, actually, shot two years apart, then joined to make a work long enough to be shown commercially—we observe moments in the life of the working-class Davies family in the 1950s, with brief flashbacks to the war years.[42] Davies himself does not appear. Instead, the sufferings of his much-loved mother, the death and funeral of his sometimes violent father, his older sister Eileen's marriage, the birth and christening of his sister Maisie's baby, and the celebration of the wedding of his older brother Tony are the chief events furnishing the drama, with all these "communal entertainments" amounting to "an idealized alternative commentary to the family's actual stark existence," as the film historian Amy Sergeant observes.[43] In the film, however, family existence is broken up into out-of-chronology vignettes, Davies's master subject being memory rather than character or causality, his organizing principle collage (or "the mosaic of memory")[44] rather than conventional plotting. The father viciously beats both his wife and his daughter and terrifies the children when small (by whipping away the cloth laid for Christmas dinner, for example). And where does all this brutality come from? From drink, being made redundant at work, anger at social injustice, sexual frustration? From any of the textbook causes which kitchen-sink melodramas of the 1950s and 60s would blame for male cruelty? Not at all: the father's monstrousness is just *there*, unexplained and unexplainable, a datum of memory, like the equally unexplainable moments of his loving gentleness.[45] At one moment in *Distant Voices*, the father's voice is heard calling angrily to his wife just as thunder rumbles outside; he really is like the unknowable god of a cruel cosmos, or William Blake's Old Nobodaddy, symbol of furious patriarchal energy. He is certainly not an ordinary character in a film. "No one knows what's going on inside my mind," Eileen's husband Dave spits at her during a fight. No one knows very much about what's going on in the mind of any Davies figure, so resolutely is he turned against the means which other filmmakers have developed to reveal subjectivity and create character. When the as yet unmarried Eileen, on a train, stares moodily out the compartment window, we are not shown (as we *are* shown in *The Singing Detective* and *Brief Encounter*) what the character's imagination puts there.

The mysterious action of memory, catching at certain images and sounds, associating rather than explaining, guides Davies throughout. *Distant Voices* opens out of chronological order, with a brief early morning scene in the mid-1950s, then a flashback to a few years earlier and the family's setting off to the father's funeral in an apparent mixture of grief at his death and stunned relief at no longer having to suffer from his rages. Presumably it is necessary to exorcise those feelings before proceeding to recall others; hence the flashback. Similarly, memory dictates the sequencing of *The Long Day Closes*. Here, with the father dead and family life more benign, Davies stays closer to the recollected experience of one character, Bud, the youngest child in the family and the stand-in for his youthful self. Bud admires and is fascinated by the near-adult lives of his older siblings—a different configuration now, two brothers and one sister—and he worships his mother. There are moments in

The Long Day Closes uncannily like passages in early D. H. Lawrence, *Sons and Lovers* above all: moments showing the mother's devotion to her bright lad or the lad's all-consuming, half-flirtatious, Oedipal devotion to her. As if to underline the resemblance Davies provides the iconic Lawrentian image of a working man's back being washed in the cramped parlor of a working-class home; it is Bud who does the washing, of his brother's back. At other moments Bud is mercilessly bullied at school, suffers from loneliness, is drawn to the glamour of both church rite and movie musical, discovers the first signs of a gay sensibility. Still, all these experiences are glimpsed as elements in a collage, not as stages in a development. *The Long Day Closes* has none of the rites-of-passage forthrightness of, say, John Boorman's *Hope and Glory*, or the child-at-risk plotting of Joseph Losey's *The Go-Between*.[46] "I've never been interested in what-happened-next," Davies once said. "I'm interested in what-happened-*emotionally*-next."[47]

While abstaining from plot, Davies abstains also from conventional cinematic techniques, such as rapid camera movements and standard editing. His takes are extraordinarily long. His pans or swooping crane shots, when provided, are slow. His actors tend to stand or sit stiffly in *tableaux vivants*, centered within frames provided by furniture, windows, doors, or staircases. They face front, symmetrically arranged, looking straight at the lens. They are like statues on altars or figures depicted in stained glass, with the camera taking the worshiper's devotional posture before them. When situated in their cramped working-class interiors these actors also bear more than a passing resemblance to the men and women of Mike Leigh films, who similarly look boxed within or weighted down by the bed-sit or council-house mises-en-scène of their lives; but finally a Leigh character like Cynthia in *Secrets and Lies*, even when photographed inside the frame of a shabby doorway, appears to have all the freedom in the world compared to Davies's characters.

It did not take reviewers of Davies's films long to connect all this abnormal stillness with photographs—photographs in a family album, to be exact, composed and commemorative, with everything extraneous, including any real sense of the surrounding city of Liverpool, cropped out, as David Wilson perceptively suggested.[48] (In *Distant Voices, Still Lives* we actually watch two formally posed wedding photographs being

taken.) An even better analogy, however, would be to the carefully prepared and printed oversize photographs of a gallery or museum exhibition. Davies's desaturated color tones, achieved by the use of a lens filter
and a special process of bleaching, were meant, he later said, to capture
the look of the coal-fire haze of pre–Clean Air Act England,[49] but they
also recall the muted beauty of old-fashioned art photography. Some of
Davies's compositions within his tight frames are undeniably artistic—
for example, the mother down on her knees scrubbing an entryway, for
all the world like a figure in a Bill Brandt photograph from the 1930s.
The viewer of art photographs and the watcher of a Terence Davies film
are essentially having the same experience, an aesthetic one, a meditation on stilled beauty that requires, if it is to be successful, sympathy and intellectual concentration (and patience: one entirely unmoving shot in *The Long Day Closes* shows nothing for more than a minute
but the design on a carpet, with light from a window playing subtly
across its woven texture). The viewer and the watcher are called upon
to be completely absorbed by the framed image, as indeed the young
Bud is repeatedly shown in *The Long Day Closes* to be absorbed, staring
through a window pane—*his* frame—at rain falling in the street or at a
handsome young male form picked out by the light from a Guy Fawkes
night bonfire.

Against the background of such a disciplined visual style, Davies's
music seems to pour out in unruly profusion. Certainly the diegetic
singing in the pub or in a train compartment full of soldiers or out on
the stoop of a terrace house brings to both of the features a welcome vitality. In *Distant Voices, Still Lives* family members let loose companionably with "That Old Gang of Mine" or "Brown-Skinned Girl," a calypso
number of the sort very popular in the 1950s. Eileen, played by an actress with a powerful voice and a commanding presence, Angela Walsh
in her debut role, puts all her married unhappiness and her toughness
into belting out "I Wanna Be Around":

> I wanna be around when somebody breaks your heart,
> Somebody twice as smart as I.[50]

All this singing conveys something other than the stereotypical, kitchen-
sink view of working-class life as drab misery. It conveys good humor,
stoic pride, resilience, and the solidarity of men with men or (especially)

women with women.[51] Those soldiers in the train sing "It Takes a Worried Man to Sing a Worried Song"; they may be drunk, but they are not *worried*. Davies's people make a larger and brighter world for themselves out of whatever materials come to hand—the BBC Light Programme on the radio, the soundtracks of American films, hymnody—a very *constricted* culture, perhaps, as Davies acknowledged, "but a very rich one." He also described popular music as "poetry for the ordinary person,"[52] a phrase recalling the musical eclecticism, the Mass-Observation idealism, of Humphrey Jennings, whose gathering up of evocative noises in *Listen to Britain* does not seem too distant in effect from the soundtracks in Davies's films, both of which might fairly have been titled *Listen to Liverpool*. The Modernist predecessor Davies actually cited as an influence on his work, though, was T. S. Eliot. Davies admired and imitated the poet's fluid handling of memory, drawing on a line from *The Four Quartets* ("a pattern of timeless moments") to explain his purposes in *Distant Voices*.[53] In writing his screenplays Davies may also have remembered *The Waste Land* and its famous pub conversation in Part II,

> Well, if Albert won't let you alone, there it is, I said,
> What you get married for if you don't want children?,[54]

a front-line dispatch from that endless war between husbands and wives which Davies's films report on, in detail. Meanwhile the music-hall songs quoted scrappily throughout Eliot's poem have the same energizing vulgarity as the singing in Davies's pub scenes: cheap music being potent once again.

In one of the flashbacks to the war years, Eileen begins singing "Roll Out the Barrel" during a air raid, not in anything like the stouthearted *Listen to Britain* or *Captive Heart* spirit, but in terror, both of the bombs and of her father. This is Davies making an ironic point with music, something he does frequently. He savors juxtapositions. From the saccharine melody and comfy family feeling of "My Yiddischer Momma," sung by Maisie, he cuts quickly to Eileen just before her wedding, crying out, "howling like an animal" as the screenplay says, "I want my Dad."[55] From Eileen and Maisie both sobbing at the main orchestral theme of *Love Is a Many-Splendored Thing*, on screen at the Liverpool Gaumont, he cuts to a slow-motion shot of a terrible work accident, Tony and a mate falling through a glass skylight. The Gaumont image comes directly from Davies's past ("a visit to the cinema one hot Saturday; my two sisters took me, and everyone was weeping away in the audience"), the cut from his taste for incongruity and mystification: "I wanted to have the irony of the two men falling through the glass roof . . . The idea is that life is much harsher than what you've seen on the screen. And it disorients you, which I think is interesting. You don't quite know where you are."[56] In an even more elaborate counterposing, and a particularly complex bit of out-of-order sequencing, Davies puts Ella Fitzgerald on the soundtrack, singing "Taking a Chance on Love," over three distinct moments. First, in the late 1940s, the mother perches dangerously on a window sill to wash the panes (something that terrifies her little children); then Maisie in a grown-up voice asks "Why did you marry him, Mam?" and gets the answer back "He was nice, he was a good dancer"; and finally in the early 1950s the nice good dancer chases his wife down the hall, beating her relentlessly, so that her screams and then sobs nearly but not quite render the song lyrics inaudible. Taking a chance on love, indeed.

With the Fitzgerald number Davies shifts from diegetic to nondiegetic music. It is the latter category, not individual performances or pub singalongs, which in fact predominates in his films. We get a parade of tunes the characters themselves are not privileged to share: "Taking a Chance on Love," or Nat King Cole (at the opening of *The Long Day Closes*) velvetly crooning "Stardust." At the opening of *Distant Voices* comes Jessye Norman singing the spiritual "There's a Man Goin' Round Takin' Names" and powerfully evoking a mood of sorrow for the dead father. All three of these pieces might have been heard on a record or radio program (like *Look Back in Anger*, Davies's films faithfully record the Americanization of pop-music taste in the 1950s). That is, the pieces, even if unheard by the characters, could arguably be thought to belong to the characters' milieu. The same cannot be said about Benjamin Britten's "Hymn to the Virgin," performed chorally at the moment Maisie gives birth to her child,

> All this world was forlorn
> Eva peccatrice,
> Till our lord was y-born,
> De te genetrice;

or about the ending of Vaughan Williams's Pastoral Symphony, accompanying the mother's weary going to bed after her daughter Eileen's wedding celebrations; or about Peter Pears's performance of Britten's art-song arrangement of "O Waly Waly," accompanying the farewells after Tony's wedding. "O Waly Waly" expresses love's fulfillment, as in

> Give me a boat that will carry two
> Then both shall row my love and I,

lines heard exactly at the moment Tony and his bride get into the taxi carrying them off to their life together. It also expresses love's innocence,

> A-gathering flowers both red and blue
> I little thought what love can do,

and finally love's sorrow,

> O love is handsome and love is fine
> And love's a jewel while it is new
> But when it is old
> It groweth cold
> Then fades away like morning dew.

Davies privileges these last verses when he puts them at the very end of *Distant Voices, Still Lives;* they sound as the wedding guests walk away from the camera and fade into darkness. All this music by Vaughan Williams or Britten is applied from outside, a tribute of heard beauty to the beauty of the photographed diegesis. It is Davies's, not the characters', device for evoking a range of complex emotions, like wistfulness and pleasurable melancholy, romantic longing and romantic disenchantment. In this sense it is very much like old-fashioned film-score music, played *on behalf* of the characters for the audience in the cinema. Or for the audience on the set. According to Pat Kirkham and Mike O'Shaughnessy, the director sometimes arranged for recordings of his soundtrack music to be played as filming was taking place.[57]

Music of various kinds, diegetic and nondiegetic, has a no less important part to play in *The Long Day Closes.* This is a somewhat more straightforward film than its predecessor, with a clearer chronology and a tighter focus on Bud, the filmmaker to be, observed here in a cinematic equivalent to the first chapters of *A Portrait of the Artist as a Young Man,* complete even to scenes of Catholic-school cruelty and epiphanic glimpses of human beauty. Like the Joyce novel, *The Long Day Closes* is in places highly subjective in imagery. Unlike *Distant Voices, Still Lives,* it *does* show a main character, Bud, glancing at a window and seeing there a remembered image, thus inviting us into his thoughts. In a longer classroom sequence it uses melodramatic lighting to isolate Bud at his desk, then follows his turned head to a point-of-view shot of an entirely imagined scene, a sailing ship breasting the seas—the expression of this lonely boy's longing for escape and romance. On the soundtrack at this moment are heard sounds of wind and creaking ship's rigging, and the voice of the great English contralto Kathleen Ferrier in an a cappella rendition of the folk song "Blow the wind southerly." When the film cuts back to Bud, sea-mist is blowing anti-naturalistically in the air of the classroom and his face is wet with spray.

More plausible weather effects occur in *The Long Day Closes* too. Liverpool in the late 1950s seems drowned in melancholy rain, so much so that Davies's film occasionally has the look of Hamer's old crime melodrama *It Always Rains on Sunday.* Bud stands shivering in the downpour outside a cinema, unable to enter the sunnier world the soundtrack has already summoned up via Doris Day's brassy performance of "At Sundown." When Davies's characters sing themselves—as for example the mother quietly going through "If You Were the Only Girl in the World" as she works in her kitchen—they convey something like the pathos of the young girl Vi in *It Always Rains on Sunday,* hopelessly miming the records in an East End shop,

> 'Ow much do I love you?
> I'll tell yer no lie.
> 'Ow deep is the ocean?
> 'Ow 'igh is the sky?,[58]

and reaching out to a larger world in the only way she can.

For Davies himself, the skies are dropping "Hollywood rain," photogenic sheets of studio-produced downpour as seen in *Singin' in the Rain* and other musicals—yet another indication of the extent to which *The*

Long Day Closes and its characters are besotted by the many-splendored cinema.[59] There is less pub singing here than listening to film voices and film music; at parties, one family friend does imitations of Jimmy Cagney. Davies's own trick is to insert an odd sort of aural collage into the film, stray lines spoken by famous stars and heard at intervals on the soundtrack. Among the speakers are Orson Welles in *The Magnificent Ambersons,* Alec Guinness in *The Ladykillers,* and Jean Simmons and Martita Hunt in *Great Expectations.* As for film music, when "Blow the wind southerly" finishes in the classroom sequence, Richard Rodgers's "Carousel Waltz" comes up, replacing the severe beauty of the English folk song tradition with the glamour of Hollywood. Simultaneously with this shift, the backlighting surrounding Bud in a glow begins to flicker, the camera pans slowly, and via a lap dissolve Davies conducts his younger self to the balcony of the Gaumont, where the boy is now backlit by the projector's beams and revealed as being utterly fascinated by what the beams put on the screen.

The culmination of all this film consciousness is an elaborate three-minute set piece in which Davies for once, and appropriately, allows himself some cinematic flashiness. The sequence consists of a prolonged overhead tracking shot, beginning with a straight-down view of Bud idly swinging on an iron bar in the basement area of his house (he has been left alone by his older siblings, who are off on a bike trip). Debbie Reynolds sings about cottonwoods whispering and Tammy being in love. Davies begins a slow tracking from right to left. Dissolve to a cinema and a straight-down shot of the audience in their haze of cigarette smoke. Dissolve—the tracking movement always continuing at the same slow rate—to a church during Mass, the cinema audience transformed into a congregation, facing the same direction, feeling the same complete absorption into a ceremony. By the time we get to the altar and a shot of the celebrant elevating the Host directly towards the camera, two new sound elements have been added to Reynolds's triune repetitions of "Tammy": the tinkling of the Sanctus bell, and Dennis Price's voice (from *Kind Hearts and Coronets*) going on about the special idiocy of the D'Ascoyne son who became a clergyman. Dissolve from the priest to the exactly matching figure of the schoolmaster, and from the church to the classroom; the boys there are formally, ritually dismissed, in the scholastic equivalent of "Ite, missa est." As they leave for home, dissolve finally to Bud's house and its now abandoned iron bar, bringing the sequence full circle.

What this "geography-defying coup de cinema"[60] communicates, besides the obvious—Terence, Terence, Terence's in love with the movies—is something fairly predictable, an understanding of the fundamental sameness of 1950s working-class rites; a perception about the interchangeability of authority figures. These are points of significance to Davies, but they scarcely constitute the meaning of his film as a whole. That meaning, more and more clearly expressed as *The Long Day Closes* moves to its own close, and expressed both musically and visually, is the pastness of the past, or the inevitable surrender of childhood (and other aspects of life) to time. "*The Long Day Closes* is not the *Brideshead* [*Revisited*] of the urban proletariat," John Caughie conceded, but still thought, rightly, that Davies's film was fascinated "with the appearance and the sound of the past, and the melancholy of loss."[61]

This is as much to say that the dominant mood of the film is not nostalgic but elegiac, elegy being distinguished from nostalgia by its greater awareness that the loved thing is after all not there, magically preserved in emotion, but gone. One might say that elegy harps on the distance implied in a title like *Distant Voices, Still Lives*. The mood of loss had been hinted at in the lament for love, "O Waly Waly," which closes Davies's earlier film, and it is hinted at here as well, in lines which come abruptly out of the texture of the script like "Life also co-operates in the work of destruction," a sad admission made during the schoolmaster's science lesson about erosion. Elegy is more directly expressible, however, in music and responses to music—which seems to be why Davies puts so much music into his film. We hear an excerpt from George Butterworth's tone poem "A Shropshire Lad," the rendition in melody of A. E. Housman's elegiac poetry. We hear Bud's mother sing "She Moved through the Fair" to him as she strokes his hair, then falls into melancholy recollection:

MOTHER   (*More to herself*) My dad used to sing that.
BUD   Granddad O'Brien?
MOTHER   (*Her eyes filling with tears*) Yer.
       (*She continues stroking his hair—but crying silently so that* BUD

won't hear her or be disturbed. Hold on both of them as they sit in
the firelight. Silence)[62]

Above all, we hear the piece which concludes the film, a nondiegetic, male-voice choir performance of Sir Arthur Sullivan's "The Long Day Closes." Sullivan is one of that group of classical and intensely English composers on whom Davies relies for the emotional climaxes of his pictures: *his* music, in the sense that "That Old Gang of Mine" is his characters' music. Sullivan's setting is essential to a sequence which, every bit as static as the "Tammy" sequence is dynamic, is nonetheless remarkable. Bud and his friend Albie look out at the darkening sky, perhaps through a window, though the framing is odd and unreal; the sky looks very much like a cinema screen, as Susannah Radstone has observed.[63] The boys see clouds fast-scudding past the moon. A random crackle of radio waves comes at them, "from deep space," according to the published screenplay. A bell tolls, sounding a knell for the picture and for Bud's youth. The singing begins. At an earlier moment Davies gave us the hopeful romanticism of lines from "She Moved through the Fair":

> She stepped away from me,
> And she went thro' the fair.
> And fondly I watched her
> Move here and move there.
> And then she went homeward
> With one star awake
> As the swan in the evening
> Moves over the lake . . .

Now, for three and a half minutes, while the camera holds steady on the sky and the moonlight gradually fades, he provides the sadder verse of Henry F. Chorley, in Sullivan's plaintive Victorian harmonization:

> No star is o'er the lake
> Its pale watch keeping.
> The moon is half awake
> Through gray mist creeping.
> The last red leaves fall round
> The porch of roses.
> The clock has ceased to sound,
> The long day closes . . .

Earlier, Bud spoke of light shining into the sky and going on forever. Now we hear from the choir that

> The lighted windows dim
> Are fading slowly.
> The fire that was so trim
> Now quivers lowly . . .

Earlier, boisterous pub singing was on the soundtrack. Now there is the sung adjuration to

> Sit by the silent hearth
> In calm endeavour,
> To count the sounds of mirth
> Now dumb forever . . .

Exactly as the last chord of Sullivan's music diminuendos into silence the moon finally disappears completely and the screen goes black. This is the comprehensively elegiac farewell to the childhood and to the way of life which Davies's film has been about.

It would be natural to think of Dennis Potter's television dramas as an influence on Davies's work. In fact Davies disdained Potter; "I saw one episode of *The Singing Detective* and I found it unwatchable. They're records of people talking, and I just get bored with that."[64] As far as it goes, "records of people talking" is a tolerable description of Potter's obsessed-with-language dramas. His scripts establish character by way of self-defining speeches, angry confrontations, and throwaway comments, that is, by way of the verbal techniques which playwrights have used for centuries. Once characterized, his figures interact with each other in more or less conventional plots conforming to recognizable dramatic genres ("love story," "drama of adultery," "hospital comedy," "innocent man accused of crime"). In other words, Potter is altogether a more accessible author than Davies. Every moment of his screen work confirms his belief that the audience's understanding matters, and that it does so because *television* matters, because television is the only medium capable of stirring feelings on a huge scale and reshaping contemporary attitudes. Potter's television dramas have in fact achieved widespread success, being popular, if often controversial when first broadcast, popular even now years later in DVD editions.[65] (By contrast, DVD versions of *Distant Voices, Still Lives* or *The Long Day Closes* have only recently become available, and only in Britain.) Obviously, there have been many factors in Potter's success—his emotional openness and the daringness of his imagination, his luck in finding skilled collaborators, his (or his directors') willingness to allow the camera to move, to set up shots in a variety of ways, to keep the pace moving smartly, to edit sequences effectively; Potter's television is simply more watchable than Davies's cinema. What has really given Potter his distinctiveness and his success, however, is music. Beginning with *Pennies from Heaven*, the drama with which we will be most concerned, period songs have been his "chariots of ideas,"[66] the television series themselves as much records of people lip-synching as records of people talking.

Popular music comes in to *Pennies from Heaven* by way of the main character, Arthur Parker, a commercial traveler in sheet-music and later a record-store owner. Plausibly enough, "Roll Along, Prairie Moon"— sung now by Fred Latham with Jack Jackson's Dorchester band, rather than by Gracie Fields—rolls along in his own mind as he makes his sales calls in the west of England. Arthur is a wandering husband, highly sexed himself, frustrated by his wife Joan's frigidity, and he falls hard for a beautiful young schoolmistress, Eileen Everson, whom he encounters by chance in a Gloucester music shop. He follows Eileen to her Forest of Dean home and there makes love with her, genuinely caring about her, but at the same time lying to her and giving her a false address; very little that Arthur says about himself can really be believed. Potter regularly cuts away from this Arthur-Eileen melodrama to scenes with the jealous and lonely Joan in London; he also introduces two denizens of the countryside—the Accordion Man, a hitchhiking rural busker whom Arthur picks up along the road and treats to food and drink, and a young blind girl, whom Arthur meets briefly, addresses with extravagant gallantry ("I think you are the most beautiful young lady I have ever seen!"), and fantasizes about carnally. Eventually the Accordion Man rapes and murders the blind girl, and by the end of the series Arthur is tried, convicted, and hanged for the crime—vicarious punishment, as it were, for his thoughts of wanting to take her knickers off. All these lurid happenings Potter developed from a suggestion by his friend and producer Kenith Trodd, who sent the playwright clippings about a once notorious 1930s murder.[67] In this case, a commercial traveler, married but with several women on the side, picked up a hitchhiker, knocked him out, and incinerated him in his car, hoping to take over his identity and start a new life.[68] It was a case that could not but feed into Potter's fascination with doubles—a fascination carried out here in the strange bond between Arthur and the Accordion Man (the former calls the latter a halfwit, then rushes to embrace him), and expressed much more elaborately in the parasitic and finally violent relation between Philip E. Marlow and his suave creation the Singing Detective.

One of the critics of *Pennies from Heaven* called it "the televisual equivalent of the Victorian novel with, perhaps, *The Good Companions* as the missing link."[69] If so, Thomas Hardy would be the most relevant novelist. Just before writing the script Potter had adapted *The Mayor of Casterbridge* for a seven-part BBC series, and Eileen's introduction to sex is followed by a succession of grimly Hardyesque plot turns. She becomes pregnant with Arthur's child, loses her teaching post, goes off to London, nearly starves, then meets a smooth-talking pimp, who arranges for an abortion and sets her up as a prostitute. Initially ashamed, Eileen soon enters willingly enough into her new life, renaming herself "Lulu" and dropping her school-mistressy dowdiness for urban flash. Perhaps a wish fulfillment more than a character in the usual sense, Eileen embodies the impossibly contradictory female qualities Potter seems to have dreamed about finding throughout his life: the virgin's innocence, the sexually awakened woman's allure; provincial virtue, big-city sin. At one moment in the series Eileen is sacrally backlit and framed under a music-shop tambourine in such a way as to seem haloed (on the soundtrack at this moment, we hear "Never thought I'd see an angel"); at the next moment, her eyes glisten with provocative curiosity as Arthur tells her about a couple having sex in a hotel lift.

Having reunited with Arthur, Eileen shows a growing resilience and spiritedness, enjoys spending her ill-gotten gains, then takes the lead when the police seek her lover for the blind girl's murder. At this point, on the run, Eileen and Arthur seem a little like Karl Hulten and Betty Jones, the criminal couple of the Cleft Chin Murder; John R. Cook has argued that the old 1940s case was an important source of the *Pennies from Heaven* plot.[70] Whether or not this is true, Eileen and Arthur undoubtedly share both a folie-à-deux and a few moments of criminal-domestic happiness, like the couples in *No Orchids for Miss Blandish* or *They Made Me a Fugitive*. Their refuge is the barn of a run-down farm. When the crazed old farmer enters in on their love-making and forces them, with a shotgun, to continue under his voyeur's gaze, Eileen gets the gun away from him and then shoots him dead. This is an *acte gratuit* ("Why did you do it?"—"Because I felt like it") demonstrating her final emancipation from ordinary morality. From this point the plot gathers quickly to a close: Arthur's arrest, his trial and conviction, a last, death-cell farewell to Joan, his execution—and then finally, apparently because Potter's daughter Jane could not stand so harrowing a conclusion to the serial[71]—his miraculous and completely unexplained rescue from the finality of the noose. Eileen has gone to Hammersmith Bridge, that site sacred to Potter's imagination, to commit suicide, as the Accordion Man has previously done (and of course as Philip Marlow's mother does in *The Singing Detective*), but instead meets the resurrected Arthur. The two dance off together into an artificial, indefinite, musical-comedy future, like Gracie Fields at the end of *Look Up and Laugh*. "Couldn't go all through that wivaht a bleed'n 'appy endin' now, could we?" Arthur says with a knowing smile. Lew Stone's "The Glory of Love" plays on the soundtrack.

That *Pennies from Heaven* would involve a lot of music was clear from the start. In thinking about the ways songs might be integrated with television drama, Potter had at least two models, both from 1976: Howard Schuman's *Rock Follies,* for Thames Television, and Max Bygraves's BBC 2 comedy series *I Wanna Tell You a Story.* He reviewed both series favorably. *Rock Follies,* a backstage farce with original music, had according to Potter "gusto, inventiveness, comedy, and sparkle"; in a review parodying the style of Raymond Chandler he complimented Schuman for "making his own language with a kind of music that hoodlums never heard back in Chandler's Bay City."[72] Bygraves, meanwhile, met with approval for the irony of his contrasts: "a glimpse of Hitler and Mussolini is followed not by jackboots but dancing shoes. Leggy girls and spangled backdrops diverted us past the disasters."[73] Schuman-style inventiveness and Bygraves-style ironic divertissements would have their part to play in *Pennies from Heaven,* but the source of the music in the series really lay deeper, in the personal agendas of both Potter and Trodd. The producer brought to the project an aficionado's enthusiasm for and an encyclopedic knowledge of 1930s music, especially big-band arrangements by Lew Stone and songs by Al Bowlly, "a British crooner of the period when popular lyrics implied that dreams were possible."[74] As an undergraduate at Oxford Trodd had written an essay for *Isis,* then edited by Potter, acknowledging "the mixture of gold dust and synthetic treacle" in popular music, but admiring at the same time the songs' capacity to "communicate genuine emotion and capture the atmosphere of their period to a degree which seems to contradict the shoddiness of their raw materials."[75]

As for Potter, he had much the same fondness for Bowlly and Stone—he had used their music exclusively in his early drama *Moonlight on the Highway,* and at one point considered writing a television biopic of Bowlly—and he made the same frank assessment of the old songs' cheapness, their "tink-tink-tink syncopations," and their ludicrous or banal lyrics. He knew the songs were not life, and not current. In an interview, he said that his enthusiasm for them was formed of "the gap, the ache, between Then and Now, and the possibly even greater divide between the real substance of life as it then was at the time and the 'life' depicted in these brief dreams set to music."[76] But like Noël Coward, whose line about the potency of cheap music he approvingly quoted in a 1992 interview with Graham Fuller, Potter fervently acknowledged their energy, the way songs could wrap themselves around an emotion and preserve it. He went far beyond both Trodd and Coward in believing that popular songs could do more than entertain. Rather, they could create a "world shimmering with another reality." For Potter, songs like "Button Up Your Overcoat" or "Down Sunnyside Lane" might reduce everything to the utmost simplicity, but they were nevertheless in a line of descent from the psalms, an expression of the "angel in us," even an opening to the lost Garden of Eden.[77] It was typical of Potter, in 1992, to stand back a little from this psalmody-pop tunes analogy ("I meant that partly ironically"); equally typical of him, in the spring of 1977, when he was writing *Pennies from Heaven,* to invent a musical interlude insisting on it. In the second episode, "The Sweetest Thing," the as-yet-virginal Eileen begins to read Psalm 35 to the children in her Forest of Dean school—Potter's own school, in fact, re-opened for filming.[78] Under her reading, the soundtrack insinuates the Ambrose Orchestra version of "You've Got Me Crying Again."[79] This reveals Eileen's apprehensive fascination with love and hints at troubles with Arthur to come, but it also asserts an equality between the emotional power of

> You make me happy and then
> Somebody new looks good to you,

and the emotional power of the verses spoken immediately after the song dies down,

> And my tongue shall speak of thy righteousness
> And of thy praise all the day long.

Conducted by King David, conducted by Ambrose, Eileen is led along on her search for a place shimmering with a reality other than that of a dusty classroom, cowed children, and an apoplectic headmaster who himself despises "cheap music." The headmaster is Potter's opposite, in the sense that he describes cheap music as what children, as they grow up, have to take as substitutes for their lost visions of the Garden of Eden and its magical, diamond-shaped trees. But this red-faced, angry man is not a pure villain. Potter had the dramatic subtlety, and the human sympathy, to endow him with an understanding of children's wonder and a secret affection for Eileen.

In the schoolroom scene it is not Eileen's voice (the actress Cheryl Campbell's voice) heard singing "You've Got Me Crying Again," but rather the voice of the singer with Ambrose's orchestra, in a period recording. Campbell merely lip-synchs the lyrics. This is the fundamental and defining technical musical technique of the whole series, and of course of *The Singing Detective* and *Lipstick on Your Collar* too: the replacement of filmed musical-comedy-style performance by "miming" (Potter's and Trodd's term) to the sound of old records. Miming or lip-synching was part of the plan from the very start, proposed by Potter in a telephone call to Trodd. What would the producer think, he asked, of a first scene consisting of

> suburban husband and wife waking up, a bleary, dreary Monday morning, he wants to make love, she doesn't, he's got to go to work, she's very

repressed and uptight, it's a dingy room, suddenly we hear music. And maybe the lighting changes, and suddenly the husband is singing "The Clouds Will Soon Roll By" in the voice of Elsie Carlisle.

Trodd volunteered to produce a male-voice arrangement of the song, but Potter responded that he wanted "as much dislocation from the conventional as possible . . ."[80]

With lip-synching, in other words, he would defy expectations, disorient viewers, and strike a blow at the naturalism of television—that aesthetic and moral drabness against which, as we have seen with *The Singing Detective,* he thought his art was destined to strive. As a striking new artifice, lip-synching would emphasize the *strangeness* of the potency of cheap music and prevent viewers from watching a musical routine in the same complacent spirit with which they might have watched, say, a number in a Gracie Fields film. At the same time lip-synching would have certain practical advantages (Bob Hoskins, who took the role of Arthur, was not very talented musically, and could not easily have performed the songs himself), and it would audibly communicate the period feel of the series. That is, the very sound defects of the recordings used, their hisses and cracklings (Trodd accurately described the recordings as "surfacy"), would guarantee a kind of authenticity, just as the visual defects of old documentary films, the speckles and random scratches on worn-out prints, seem to guarantee visual authenticity, the "real" look of the past. (The third episode of the series coincidentally supplies a few moments of documentary footage of London, accompanying Eileen's entry into the city and the singing of "Life Begins at Oxford Circus"; the footage is speckled and scratched.) There would be a stylishness about lip-synched music that would fit in beautifully with the visual stylishness of the series, the carefully chosen poster-style graphics under the credits, for example.

Potter and Trodd said nothing about one other advantage of lip-synching in *Pennies from Heaven,* but it is nevertheless important. This is the affording of a kind of cultural and psychological realism, a way of getting inside characters' minds and revealing exactly what is stored there. In the opening scene of the series, that bleary, dreary Monday awakening, it is Elsie Carlisle's voice which we hear singing

Somewhere the sun is shining,
So honey don't you cry,

because hers is the voice Arthur hears *in his own head.* It is what the 1930s and the radio and the popular-music industry and even a certain emptiness in Arthur ("I'm empty—blank—I've got nothing [taps his heart] here. Nothing at all!" he says despairingly to his wife) have put there, ready for use. If he had more resources within, like one of Terence Davies's working-class characters singing a ballad while she works or entertaining the pub crowd with a defiant "I Wanna Be Around," Arthur might perform "The Clouds Will Soon Roll By" in his own voice, but instead Carlisle's has to serve him, in a kind of vicarious articulacy. If Arthur had the resources of a Jimmy Porter—and indeed the opening situation of *Pennies from Heaven* is close enough to that of *Look Back in Anger,* the husband's angry crudity set against the wife's gentility, class warfare fought out between the sheets—he would play jazz trumpet; but all Arthur has is the sheet music he carries around in his briefcase and in his head ("I don't suppose there's a chap in England who knows more about the songs that sell than I do"). Is Arthur's second-hand singing diegetic? No, in the sense that it is not literally produced from within the diegesis; it belongs to the soundtrack. Yes, in the sense that it genuinely belongs to him, his métier, his moment, his radio tuned to the Light Programme; beyond question it is what is in his ears. As we have previously seen with *Look Back in Anger* and *Look Up and Laugh, Pennies from Heaven* artfully blurs the standard distinction between diegetic and nondiegetic.

Potter once likened the lip-synching of his dramas to karaoke, that late twentieth-century pop-cultural phenomenon made much of in his posthumous series *Karaoke:* "it's also about the world being other than it is," he said.[81] True, but as a technique karaoke is really the opposite of lip-synching. Arthur does not insert his voice and personality into some more glamorous world, but rather welcomes that world, in the person of a recorded performer, into his drab surroundings and unfulfilled sex life. At least, he does so at the hopeful start of the episode. By the end, it is more difficult. He comes home to Joan and lies in post-coital *tristesse* beside her:

ARTHUR You don't like it very much, do you? . . . It's not meant to be a
    duty or anything like that . . .
JOAN Let's get some sleep, shall we?
ARTHUR It's supposed . . . Joanie, angel . . . ? It's—paradise. It's
    supposed . . . like in the songs . . .

But she remains unmoving, and when the title song of the episode, "Down Sunnyside Lane," comes up on the soundtrack, he can mime only the opening words. On the line "Hey-ho, around you my arms would be curled," Haggard cuts from a side shot of Arthur to a frontal close-up, and we see his desperate face, his clenched mouth not succeeding in shaping itself around the words, which Jack Payne and the BBC Dance Orchestra carry blithely on with.

Joan, a more day-dreamy character than Arthur, does sometimes insert herself into the glamorous world, as when in the first episode, reading a woman's magazine ("I wish you knew Gertie Lawrence. She is my ideal of a capable, beautiful and desirable feminine thing . . ."), she succumbs entirely to reverie. Close-ups of the magazine show photos of society girls, all of them Joan, and the introduction to "Blue Moon" starts up on the soundtrack. Only a few lines of this are mimed; Joan's fantasies are more visual than musical, so Potter now arranges for her to be elaborately bejeweled, gowned in diaphanous white, and bathed in "Hollywood midnight blue, dusted with diamonds."[82] As the song continues in its intoxicating way Joan floats gracefully downstairs to do her vacuuming and scrubbing, still in her Gertie Lawrence get-up. Scrubbing her threshold, Joan is framed exactly like the hard-at-work mother in *Distant Voices, Still Lives,* and she wields the same scrubbing brush and bucket, but of course there could hardly be two similar images with more dissimilar purposes. In a particularly brilliant bit of prop design, incidentally, Joan's scrubbing brush is made to glitter with the same light-catching sequins as her gown: so far does her fantasy extend.

This is a moment of pure cinema, of course, the analogue to the sequence in *Brief Encounter* when Laura Jesson projects romantic movies starring Alec and herself onto the window of her suburban train, or to sequences about cinema-intoxication from the English crime cinema, like Betty Jones of *Chicago Joe and the Showgirl* dreaming her way into *Double Indemnity.* Cinematic moments have a rightful place in *Pennies from Heaven,* a series which after all takes its title song from a 1936 Bing Crosby musical and which is set in a period when everyone found escape at the Odeon or the Gaumont. Even Arthur, in a reverie of his own, dances with Eileen in a spotlighted, white-costumed Fred Astaire and Ginger Rogers–style number, "Dancing Cheek to Cheek." Late in the series a youth approaching Eileen says he wants a kiss "like they do in the pictures." Eileen herself, drunk in her pimp Tom's flat, says "Let's pretend we're in the films," very much like the real Betty Jones of the Cleft Chin Murder case and like all of Betty Jones's cinematic descendants; there follows for Eileen and Tom a lip-synched, savagely ironic "When I'm Calling You," the Jeanette Macdonald–Nelson Eddy duet from *Rose-Marie*. Still later, on the run with Arthur, she and he take refuge in a cinema, like Alec and Laura in *Brief Encounter* or Holly Martins and Anna Schmidt in *The Third Man*. We see a few frames of the comedy they watch. All this cinema consciousness follows from Potter's liking for frank artifice, his dislike of television naturalism. It goes along with Piers Haggard's fancy shaped wipes and irises in or irises out, with his canted camera angles,[83] with some of the costuming (in one production number Eileen appears as a demure, straw-bonneted, flower-surrounded shepherdess), with the smoke effect comically overproduced for the singing of "Smoke Gets in Your Eyes," with the characters' occasional mugging straight at the camera, with the song lyrics suddenly appearing on the screen (complete with bouncing ball to help the audience sing along) in "In the Dark" at the end of episode six.

For the most part, however, the performances of *Pennies from Heaven* keep to a more or less realistic aesthetic and stay within the characters' lives and settings, unglamorous as these may be. Take "Roll Along, Prairie Moon," a number so repeated and discussed in the series that it comes to seem emblematic of the whole enterprise (and even of Potter's whole artistic enterprise: it was sung by choir and congregation at the 1995 London memorial service for him).[84] Discussing his business with Joan at the breakfast table, Arthur picks "Roll Along" as the sort of coming hit which shopkeepers are too stupid to buy ("Do they ever dream any sort of dream—or look at the moon?"). Late at night he mimes the song in the Roy Fox version. On the highway, in a scene already touched on, he mimes it in the Jack Jackson orchestra version, smiling and as happy behind the wheel as Gracie Fields is at the opening of *Look Up and Laugh*—but then the shots of Arthur are intercut with a montage of shopkeepers angrily turning down his wares. Throughout *Pennies from Heaven*, escapism and reality conduct an intricate pas de deux. When Arthur mimes "Roll Along" after being smitten by Eileen, it is in the more romantic version of Al Bowlly; the camera is elevated to look down through foliage at our hero as he sings to the night air and assumes a rapt posture, arms extended, hat pushed back. At this point some ingenious graphics work puts a sketched horse under Arthur, then a big full moon in the sky, then cowboy clothes on the salesman. The screen image has become the cover of the sheet music he has been peddling. No sooner does Potter lift us above and away from ordinariness, however, than he drops us back down into it. A close-up of that white moon dissolves to a shot of the Gloucester docks, where in the back seat of his parked car Arthur is making noisy love to a red-dressed tart he has picked up in the pub. The sounds of sex mix with

> Far away shed your beams,
> On the girl of my dreams,
> Tell her too, I've been true,
> Prairie moon,

still being sweetly crooned by Bowlly.

It is not as though this sort of crass juxtaposition cancels out Arthur's romanticism, replacing it with lust. Rather, the two qualities continue to exist side by side in him, along with a lot of other contradictory qualities, like frankness and lying, or energy and laziness. He is a bundle of complexities and changes. If there is one unchanging constant in his life, it is his belief in the songs—not, to be sure, in what they promise about faithfulness, but in their opening a way to a world he *knows* is there, though he may also know (without admitting it) that it is just out of his reach or reachable only at moments. "It's shining, the whole place, *shining*," he declares to three disbelieving fellow salesmen at the breakfast table scene in the second episode. The others have all got "padding" around them, he claims, which prevents them from seeing . . . From seeing what? "It's not the sort of thing you can put into words," Arthur says apologetically, and then he lip-synchs a song ("Yes, Yes! My Baby Said Yes, Yes!"). Music can come closer than words to the meaning he's after. It's "these songs—all these lovely songs"; the sheet music in his salesman's case gives him his only means of looking "for the blue, ennit, and the gold. The patch of blue sky. The gold of the, of the bleed'n dawn, or—the light in somebody's eyes—Pennies from Heaven, that's what it is." Music gives him access to his own heart:

> Everything I've . . . everything I've ever dreamed . . . everything I've ever hoped for—longed for—(*hits his chest as though in pain*)—deep inside—right inside me here, in my heart—Everything![85]

This may be a tissue of clichés, indeed of song clichés, but it is so fervently acted by Hoskins, with just the right clumsy heart-pounding gesture that a man like Arthur would make, that it seems completely convincing. The inarticulate man's apologia for popular songs turns out to be the most articulate thing ever said about music in an English screen work, the most impassioned claim for its meaningfulness. It was perhaps some recognition of this which led to the breakfast scene's also being included in Potter's memorial service, acted by Kenith Trodd and the BBC executives Michael Grade and Alan Yentob.[86]

Eileen is not granted anything like Arthur's song-inspired eloquence. Nor does she suffer from his self-delusions and fecklessness. Like the Ruth Ellis of *Dance with a Stranger,* she is stronger and more intelligent than her lover—one of the reasons so many commentators on *Pennies from Heaven,* Trodd included, have thought Potter wrote himself into her. Her defining song is not something chipper like "Roll Along, Prairie Moon" but the sad ballad "In the Middle of a Kiss," the rough equivalent of Ellis's "Would You Dance with a Stranger?" Eileen lip-synchs "In the Middle of a Kiss," which both Haggard and Trodd identified as their favorite number in the whole series,[87] in the hayloft of the barn where she and Arthur are hiding from the police. It is painfully reflective, a rebuke to Arthur's simple-minded line immediately preceding it ("I want it all to be all right"); it wavers between major and minor tonalities, bittersweet in a way that brings that tired adjective to life:

In the middle of a smile,
We stumbled into paradise,
In the twinkle of an eye,
We lost it again.

These lyrics and the remarkable tune accompanying them gave Haggard and Cheryl Campbell something to work with, a script for understated staging. He kept the actress largely still, looking pensively out a half-door high up in the barn, then turning to her lover; the slow pace of the editing keeps time with the music. Campbell as Eileen looks weary, as she sits on the frame of the door, though there is still some residual authority in her, a glimpse, that is, of the classroom teacher Eileen once was, leading her slowish pupils through some tedious lesson. Haggard cuts abruptly to a perspective from the other side of the half-door, with the camera positioned down low, looking up in a long shot at Eileen perched a little precariously in the opening, like the window-washing mother in *Distant Voices, Still Lives.* Still, the main effect of the cut is to give a visual sense of "paradise." It is made out of the most ordinary materials, spaciousness, sunbeams coming in from the ruined roof, a pair of doves flying up from the floor (they managed to get both doves right in one take, Haggard notes in his commentary on the DVD edition of the series). The camera cranes slowly up and toward Eileen, now in a more resigned, the-hell-with-it pose, and Arthur comes into the opening made by the door frame. Paradise is shrinking for them. The camera finishes its movement exactly on the last line of the song. Arthur reaches over and delicately takes a stray straw out of her hair—again, something ordinary, a throwaway gesture, but as made by Hoskins it expresses a tenderness not yet seen in the character. He may not have heard the lip-synched lyrics, exactly (none of the listening characters in the series seems to do that) but in another demonstration of the strange potency of cheap music, he appears affected by the song nonetheless, by the way it sums up what he and Eileen have had, their workaday domesticity and their sad paradise.

Staying within the characters' worlds, faithfully balancing the tawdry actuality of their lives with the dreams that—via songs—just manage to escape from the tawdriness, is the principle followed even with the title song of the whole series, "Pennies from Heaven."[88] This is given to the Accordion Man to mime, in an unremarkable café where Arthur is treating him to a meal. The Accordion Man is starved, and his hunger leads directly into the opening lyrics, about the best things in life once being free; but because no one appreciated "a sky that was always blue," it was planned that the best things "should vanish now and then, / And you must *pay* to get them back again." This is a tramp's hard-bitten philosophy, one might say. On "pay" the Accordion Man gestures with a bite of sausage impaled on his fork; later, steam from the tea urn billows out to illustrate: "Don't you know each cloud contains / Pennies from heaven?" Similarly ingenious business follows as the Accordion Man moves about the room, turning an umbrella upside down, helping a little old lady with change from the till; it was (presumably) Haggard's brilliant staging decision to have the extras in musical numbers pay a kind of half attention to the strange things going on, interacting blandly with the star performer but essentially going about their own business and so preparing the way for a return to non-musical reality. Not the least of the accomplishments of the series is the seamless integration of music numbers into spoken drama, the rapid and graceful transitions. As the song "Pennies from Heaven" ends, the Accordion Man's lip-synching almost imperceptibly becomes his chewing of his fry up; the last strains of music sound under the clink of cutlery against plates. Elsewhere in the series Haggard dims or alters the lighting for songs—we are given a lurid violet for Eileen's striptease number "Oh You Nasty Man"—but here the director holds back from that, to emphasize the ease and naturalness with which "Pennies from Heaven" comes out of the immediate scene. The song belongs to the space. Hopefulness—"Every time it rains, / It rains pennies from heaven"—blooms for a moment, then fades out into survival.

Staging of this intricacy, the handling of props while "singing," the choreographing of a performer moving among extras, obviously required careful rehearsal, which the BBC of this period was able to provide. As Haggard later explained, for each 75-minute episode he had available three weeks of rehearsal preceding the three days of studio filming. Three days was not a particularly generous allowance, but he could and did use four or five cameras simultaneously to capture different angles on action and give him a lot of material to edit. In keeping with English industry practice at this period, interior scenes were shot on tape, exteriors on 16mm film, so *Pennies from Heaven* lacks the perfect visual seamlessness of *The Singing Detective,* but Haggard put medium fog filters on his cameras to soften the hard edges of videotape and achieve a slight milkiness or haziness, and this consorted reasonably well with exterior scenes shot under gray English skies. *Pennies from Heaven* looks unified enough; what Haggard said of one important number in it ("conceived and lit like a movie") might justly be said of the whole.

As for the literal choreography involved in *Pennies from Heaven* (full-scale dance routines feature in one or two numbers per episode), Haggard gave credit for this to the choreographer Tudor Davies. Unlike the choreographer of the 1981 MGM remake of *Pennies,* who opened his dance performances up, taking full advantage of a Hollywood sound stage,[89] Davies often had to work in very cramped spaces, such as a Gloucester pub or a schoolroom full of desks, where Eileen's headmaster decorously mimes his devotion to her—a performance of the sort Trodd liked specifically because it was "modest" and "British": another way of remaining within the characters' worlds. Joan's suburban sitting room is even more cramped than the schoolroom. In it, she and two friends vent their resentment at their husbands by singing "You Rascal You." The trio gambol around the sofa and armchairs, sometimes still primly holding their teacups. When Arthur's body magically appears, stretched out before them, they stab him and waggle their bloody hands at the camera; once he's nailed into a coffin, Joan does a tap dance on the coffin lid. Haggard called dancing like this "sweet and Thirties," but also "sour and dark."

In exploiting a comedy of incongruous contrasts—housewives versus bloody knives, gentility versus hostility—"You Rascal You" is typical. It is important to note how often *Pennies from Heaven* is funny in this way. A stuffy bank manager, immediately after having refused Arthur a loan, partners a cozy duet ("Without That Certain Thing") with him, in the glare of the footlights with which his office is suddenly equipped. In a split second Eileen's coal-miner brothers and father, speaking the broadest Gloucestershire ("Eileen, where bist?"), are transformed by Lew Stone's "You Couldn't Be Cuter" into a West End dancing and singing chorus line. The condemned Arthur and his two death-cell warders reminisce idly about the Hammersmith Palais, then segue into the cheerful trio "I Like to Go Back in the Evening." The Accordion Man, full of guilt about what he's done to the blind girl, goes to ground in a London doss house, then joins the other dossers in an *apache*-style performance of "Serenade in the Night" (each dosser plays an accordion; the murdered girl appears as well). On the run, abandoned in the ruined barn—Eileen has gone off to try to get food from the farmer—Arthur kicks at straw at first randomly, then in rhythm to Lew Stone's jaunty number "Pick Yourself Up." Miming of the lyrics follows,

> Nothing's impossible, I have found,
> For when my chin is on the ground,
> I pick myself up, dust myself off,
> And start all over again,

together with some funny business with a rake, and then a comedy duet with a dancing straw man.[90] This is Arthur escaping from his troubles, escaping it might be said in a morally questionable way, slipping into that fantasy life which has always offered him such rich satisfactions and gotten him into such terrible trouble; the straw dancing partner seems a particularly shabby replacement for Eileen (who is in no mood to dance), the whole number a bit of frou-frou after the heartbreak of Eileen's "In the Middle of a Kiss." But "Pick Yourself Up" is a cleverly choreographed and entertaining bit of frou-frou, which is really the point. Just as the musical interludes of *Pennies from Heaven,* the comic ones especially, offer characters momentary release from their drab lives or nasty predicaments, they offer viewers release from a grim story, and from standard dramatic techniques as well. If Orwell was right in thinking everything funny subversive, every joke a custard pie,[91] the musical interludes of *Pennies from Heaven* are custard pies thrown in the face of conventional television.

The most incongruously comic, and purely entertaining, interlude of all is the scene of Arthur's trial. Two songs feature here, the first being Harry Roy's "Roll Along Covered Wagon," lip-synched by Arthur in a courtroom transformed into an Old West saloon, with the prosecuting counsel making his entry like a hired gunslinger, cigar smoke wafting throughout, and gambling on the green baize tables—Potter's comment, no doubt, on the chanciness of the justice system. After a brief return to sober reality, counsel offers a metaphor to describe Arthur's absurd attempts to exculpate himself, and this cues "Whistling in the Dark," an Ambrose Orchestra melody given an even more elaborate treatment, a surreal treatment according to Lindsay Anderson.[92] The learned judge performs the solo whistle part while counsel does a soft-shoe routine, a straw boater perched cheekily atop his barrister's wig; then there are tight-rope walking and magic tricks with feathers and colored handkerchiefs, culminating in the manifestation of two grand Union Jacks. All this looks as though it might have been developed from a reading of Leopold Bloom's trial in the "Circe" chapter of *Ulysses,* with its blending of the ludicrous and the threatening, its grotesquerie and its slapstick humor, its extrapolation of comic routines from single phrases. Potter knew something about Joyce,[93] and he was perfectly capable of turning to a writer of Joyce's complexity for inspiration; but his comic imagination might equally have been influenced by Monty Python courtroom routines, especially one from a 1969 broadcast in which fantastic shenanigans during a trial are followed by a song.[94] Whatever its sources may be, though, the interlude when screened seems like nothing so much as Potter's pastiche of the music hall. The multiple turns and lightning-fast changes, Potter's having performers play directly to an audience (here, the oohing and aahing jurors), his combining of music, comedy, and magic, all belong to that venue, as is slyly suggested in the judge's crotchety line after the music has finally died out: "This is a court of law, not a music hall." In 1978, when *Pennies from Heaven* was broadcast, the music hall was a thing of the past. It was characteristic of Potter, like Gracie Fields and J. B. Priestley before him, not merely to invent a new kind of entertainment to take its place, but to fold within that entertainment a tribute to the most traditional and English kind of musical performance.

The critical issue which *Pennies from Heaven* raises may now be apparent, even obvious. It is the proliferation of music in the series, the seemingly endless rolling out of lip-synched numbers, more than five dozen in all. Despite Haggard's ingenuity in staging the songs differently, not to mention the differences between the songs themselves (no two pieces could be more dissimilar than "Down Sunnyside Lane" and "In the Middle of a Kiss"), there is finally a sameness about the multiplied performances. The songs' effects eventually become predictable, the entertainment they offer seems relatively unvarying, an impression of course reinforced when the episodes are seen all at once on DVDs, as they tend to be today, instead of in week-by-week broadcasts, as in 1978. By the late stages of the drama even Arthur has come to be a little wary of the songs. The shining world they promise has been darkened by events, and at the end of the fourth episode he apparently agrees with Eileen when she tells him flatly that the songs won't come true. Standing in the gloom of his failing record shop, he and she decide to run away, first smashing up the records in a little orgy of destructiveness. Dozens of songs, including a lot of numbers lip-synched earlier in the series, eventually lie on the floor, symbolically shattered. At this point, logically, the lip-synching ought to stop and be replaced by reality, but instead it continues, with yet a fourth version of "Roll Along, Prairie Moon" (the record is preserved from the auto-da-fé), performed by Arthur and Eileen on a giant stylized platter spinning in the void, a cowgirl trio assisting. For the characters to be caught in a mechanical device seems appropriate. By this point it is clear that Potter has been caught in a musical-dramatic machine of his own devising, the lip-synching machine. He is so devoted to the technique that he is willing to bend the drama to continue it; much more mimed music follows in episodes five and six.

Lipstick on Your Collar also features a music-machine, the giant juke box of its extremely clever opening credits sequence, in and around the turntable of which three 1950s bobby-soxers lip-synch and frolic to the title tune. The series proceeds from there to the War Office, where a bored language clerk dreams himself into rock 'n' roll escapes from the work of translating Russian army documents. We first hear the Platters' "The Great Pretender" playing in Private Hopper's head, and then the Crewcuts' "Earth Angel" in a fully lip-synched rendition, with Hopper miming his teenage devotion to the apparition of a nude blonde. A great many more lip-synched numbers follow over the course of the first and all the remaining episodes—with the result that the issue of repetitiveness comes up here just as with *Pennies from Heaven*. The music in *Lipstick on Your Collar* tends to be performed on the same set, by the same characters, in the same pastiche style, and to the same ends—whimsical comedy, and the juxtaposing of stuffy militarism with youthful rebelliousness. In this drama set in the Suez Crisis year of 1956, Potter hammers relentlessly away at his central contrast, the Cold War versus hot blood, the call to decisive action versus the lyrics of Anne Shelton's big hit of 1956, "Lay down your arms and surrender to mine." (He had dramatized exactly the same contrast in his 1970 television play *Lay Down Your Arms*.) The songs may be political metaphors, as Potter indicated to the interviewer Lesley White at the time of broadcast ("signals of change and rebellion in a land of furled umbrellas"[95]), but their mode of performance is notably unchanged from that of earlier Potter works. "It's familiar stuff," Martyn Harris said of the songs, in a review generally favorable to *Lipstick on Your Collar*; Max Davidson thought that the miming, which "had started out as a useful shorthand for the discrepancy between people's interior and exterior lives," had become "simply a way of giving the story a bit of variety."[96] The simple truth is that Potter's heart does not seem to be in "The Great Pretender" or "Earth Angel." Rock 'n' roll had far fewer associations for him than had the 1930s songs of *Pennies from Heaven*; he was not at home with it, as Kenith Trodd suggested.[97]

In the White interview, Potter said of *The Singing Detective,* the middle work in his popular-music trilogy and the crowning achievement of his career, that its songs "are chariots bringing in a past [the main character] is trying not to deal with." That is true of some songs in *The Singing Detective*—not, to be sure, of "Dry Bones" as hallucinated in Marlow's hospital ward, but of the several performances going back to the Forest of Dean, where music provides less easy escape, more painful remembering. The preeminence of *The Singing Detective* among Potter's works has to do with its willingness to admit pain, real pain, into the story, and of course with many other things as well: the wit of its allusiveness and the interest of its relation to American detective fiction; the verbal fireworks of its script; the layering in time of its plot; and the deep roots in Potter's life from which it stems—his chronic illness, his childhood history, his knowledge of the way writers habitually distort childhood history. (By contrast, for *Lipstick on Your Collar* Potter was merely remembering the few youthful months in which he served as a Russian-language clerk, felt bored by translating, and listened to the rock 'n' roll.) But the preeminence of *The Singing Detective* also has a great deal to do with its handling of lip-synched music. In *Pennies from Heaven,* as we have seen, Potter was fascinated by the 1930s songs, both by their kitsch and their power, and he created a drama to express his fascination. In *The Singing Detective,* Potter had an urgent story to tell and discovered that 1940s songs would be one way to tell it.

Credit must also be given to the brilliance of the staging and filming in *The Singing Detective.* Working with more resources than were available when *Pennies from Heaven* was shot (and of course with the benefit of experience gained on that project), working with somewhat more freshness than apparently remained for the production of *Lipstick on Your Collar,* Potter and Jon Amiel together assembled musical scenes of a remarkable complexity. These do not exactly culminate the tradition of music in film examined in this chapter. They are too idiosyncratic and Potteresque for that, too dependent on their special technique of lip-synching; and anyway "tradition" may not be the term for the loosely related performances I have been describing. What can be said is that the songs in *The Singing Detective* accomplish the purposes of several different kinds of film music—the releasing of captive hearts audible in the orchestral music of *Brief Encounter* or the singing in Terence

Davies's films, the sheer entertainment value of numbers in *Look Up and Laugh* or *The Good Companions*. Music in *The Singing Detective* strikes inward and sounds outward at the same time.

Consider a sequence of four musical scenes in one of the key Forest of Dean settings, the working men's club. Potter had written about this local institution in his first book, the journalistic study *The Changing Forest*:

> Since it is eight o'clock, the Club is now almost full, clouding rapidly with the drifts of tobacco smoke, noisy with chatter, coughing and laughing, all of which seem half a pitch above the normal. At that time my mother was playing the piano at week-ends, but she doesn't sing as a solo performer any more . . .
>
> It is still too early for community singing in anything but the most spasmodic and half-hearted of fashions, and the piano merely plonks through the talk and the guzzling as the necessary prelude, the reminder of things to come and voices yet to be heard. . . .

Potter quotes fragments of talk—"Yunt that the dress her sister used to wear—well, if it chunt, I'll bet that's somebody else's hand-downs any road"—then describes the arguments, the community announcements, and finally the solo singing:

> . . . there is an attentive, expectant shuffle, with a lot of "sh"-ing across the laden tables, still clinking with glasses and bottles. Some of the songs are the latest that can be bought in the record shops or heard on Juke-box Jury, others are the older, more sentimental and beery kind, sung with a gusto sufficient to remove any spurious nostalgia . . . Both kinds are assimilated into a common type, so that "She Was Only a Bird in a Gilded Cage" or "She Was Only Six-teen, Only Six-teen" sound as though they might have been written by the same person.

At a late stage of proceedings, finally, the singing sounds "as though the music had been rubbed inside the body of an empty, froth-speckled beer glass and then held up to be dried by a hundred throaty blasts."[98]

A great deal of this is replicated in *The Singing Detective*. We see there the Nissen hut packed with cloth-capped miners and their wives and children, the smoky conviviality, Philip's mother at the piano on a raised dais, Philip with a bottle of pop smiling at his father, who in the first of the club scenes is singing "It Might as Well Be Spring," from the American musical *State Fair*. He is *lip-synching* the song, of course (it is actually being performed by Dick Haymes), and since what we are witnessing at this moment of the drama is a musical performance, we might ask if the technique is still necessary. Why not just have the actor, Jim Carter, perform the song? Potter kept to lip-synching for reasons established years before with *Pennies for Heaven*. He liked the period sound, and he liked the access lip-synching gives to the world of the characters. When the listeners in the club hear Mr. Marlow sing "It Might As Well Be Spring," they are really hearing the song as crooned in the cinema, just as later when he gives them "Birdsong at Eventide" they really hear the virtuosic whistling of the Ronalde recording. To "It Might As Well Be Spring" the listeners sing along, initially in the spasmodic and half-hearted way Potter described in *The Changing Forest*, then more enthusiastically: that part of the soundtrack *is* real, presumably, recorded from the voices of the Forest of Dean people whom the BBC had drawn as extras into the production.

All the performances in the club are entertaining, and entertaining partly because of the lip-synching. There is a constant comic contrast going on here—on the one hand, the would-be suavity of Mr. Marlow (and of Raymond Binney, who joins him in duets in the two last scenes), their homespun ease on the platform, their ham-handed gestures and too expressive faces, and on the other, the real suavity of the professionally sung music, the sophisticated sound of the Inkspots doing "Do I Worry?" or the Mills Brothers doing "You Always Hurt the One You Love." For its part, the audience eats up Marlow and Binney, and the director Jon Amiel makes sure that we see the audience as much as the performers. He moves the camera slowly through the crowd and sends extras constantly across the field of view, giving a sense of claustrophobia, of just how tight a little world this is. He also cuts incessantly back and forth from shots of the dais to shots of the floor, from close-ups of the singers to equally lingering close-ups of the remarkable Forest of Dean faces, male and female, middle-aged and old, in the audience. Amiel's presentation is objective except when he conveys Philip's point of view, especially his troubled point of view. And there are opportunities for Philip to be troubled. He sees the casual hand Raymond lets fall on Mrs. Marlow's shoulder or catches Raymond's sardonic look at the cuckold next to him on the platform. "Do I worry? You can bet your life I do!" as the song lyric says. To make these perceptions even more painful—whether for the little boy or for the man he eventually becomes, lying in the hospital and recalling all the times in the club—Amiel darkens the lighting anti-realistically, cants the camera angle, and uses extreme wide-angle lenses to enlarge adult faces into grotesque caricatures. These loom out of the darkness to laugh maliciously at the hoodwinked Marlow and his humiliated son.

If there needed to be one more rationale for lip-synching, it would be that it is a disorienting device, serving the anti-naturalistic function so important to Potter's television work. To have a velvety American baritone emerge from the mouth of a Forest of Dean miner is an impossibility akin to the visual impossibilities of the action in the club scenes, as when Philip glances across the room and notices two drinkers talking intently. One is very small, one very big (the actors Ron Cook and George Rossi, who will later become the two mysterious trench-coated thugs), and when Philip returns to them a second later they have vanished magically into thin air. The most astonishing impossibilities, however, come as "Birdsong at Eventide" reaches its twittering climax, in the second of the club scenes. Amiel sends the camera on a slow pan completely through the rapt audience, ending with a close-up on Philip, but Philip grown up into Marlow, disfigured by his psoriatic lesions and wearing his hospital pajamas. He tries to applaud his father along with everyone else but his gnarled hands won't let him. A man wearing a cloth cap—a recurrent accusatory figure of Marlow's nightmare, his "angel of guilt" as Amiel called him[99]—comes up and accosts him, claiming drunkenly and viciously that he never gave his father enough credit when he was alive. "Are you saying my Dad is *dead*?" Marlow responds disbelievingly, and through the club chatter he tells Cloth Cap how much he desperately wants to speak to his Dad, then calls up to the platform in broad dialect, "Dad! Dad! Over here, ol' butty!" Silence falls, and the camera pulls back to show Marlow in long shot, all by himself in a club room completely emptied of its life, the chairs upside down on the bar, the piano sheeted. Cloth Cap looms up again but speaks now in the educated accents of one of Marlow's doctors: a device for getting us back to the hospital setting and the feverish, hallucinating patient.

This is an exceptional scene. Amiel said that merely reading it in the script made him cry, and his commentary on the DVD edition of *The Singing Detective* speaks eloquently of the labors he and Michael Gambon went through to get it right. But then all the club scenes are exceptional. They confirm the extraordinary power of Potter's imagination, of his (and Amiel's) ability to shock viewers and at the same time help them understand the complex machine for remembering that Marlow is, the in-and-out windings of his guilt, loyalty, and love. They confirm the pleasure that music can give (even the whistling of "Birdsong at Eventide" is an entertainment in itself) while fully explicating the social context that this music belongs to—the club, the club listeners with their longing for something different from and better than daily life, their need to sing and to sing together. Like the opening jazz-club sequence in *Look Back in Anger,* the club scenes in *The Singing Detective* are about what music at a particular place and time *means.* Songs like "You Always Hurt the One You Love"[100] might inherently be cheap— Potter would not necessarily disagree with Noël Coward on this point— but a certain value has been given to them by people who like their melodies and their words. And even cheap music has an artistic value when ingeniously linked to the other elements of filmmaking; when the "cuckoo, cuckoo" of a whistling solo sounds over a shot of the smiling betrayer Binney, or when phrases of a lyric,

> You always take
> The sweetest rose,
> Crush it,
> Till the petals fall,

are matched with a cut to Mrs. Marlow hopelessly banging away at the piano for her husband and her lover, her eyes closing in pain—or remembered pleasure? It is difficult to tell—on "Till the petals fall." In the end, what the club scenes chiefly confirm is the not-so-strange potency of music and images combined.

BY WAY OF TONY HARRISON
AND ALAN BENNETT

What remained to do was to put the poetry I had nurtured in the flames of the family hearth into the cinema.

TONY HARRISON ("FIRE AND POETRY")

RUDGE   I'm keen on a film.
IRWIN   What film?
RUDGE   Well, lots of films, only Miss said to say film not films.

ALAN BENNETT, *THE HISTORY BOYS*

A picture of English screen work might be given in many ways. How I have given it in this book is as a history of interrelatedness—of the various working involvements of filming with writing, and of a series of harder-to-define but no less important affiliations, rivalries, influences, emulations, and mutual understandings and misunderstandings between these two expressions of contemporary Englishness. Arguably, this interrelatedness is something distinctive in world film culture. Over the century or so of its existence, the English film enterprise has with remarkable frequency been defined by acts of positioning itself in the larger national culture. In 1928, for example, when the silent nightclub thriller *Piccadilly* was being shot, it might not have looked like a very home-grown project, with its entirely German creative team (Evald André Dupont as producer and director, Alfred Junge as art director, Werner Brandes as cinematographer) and with the fast-rising Chinese-American actress Anna May Wong as the star. But the scenario the filmmakers were working with was by Arnold Bennett, by far the most esteemed of middle-brow novelists in the 1920s, and an icon of sturdy and successful Englishness. To arrange for Bennett to write *Piccadilly* was to locate its exotic allurements within a familiar context; his understanding of what drama should be (he wrote several successful West End plays) would organize lurid happenings—a Chinese girl dancing ecstatically in the scullery of a nightclub, a shooting in Limehouse, a courtroom confession and suicide—into something like a conventional plot. Thanks to Bennett, *Piccadilly* presents itself as a fantasia on London *luxe* along the lines of his novel *The Grand Babylon Hotel*, a work itself "absolutely perfect" for filming, as Bennett was informed by an eager would-be producer, possibly because Dupont had used the title for a successful German silent of his own in 1920.

As far as we can tell from his journal entries, Bennett was interested in the cinema less as an art form than as a source of quick income and as a glamorous enterprise to be visited, which he did at Elstree during the shooting of *Piccadilly* ("Considerable heat from *terrific blaze of electric lamps*").[1] This would not be the case for later writers. One of the salient long-term trends in twentieth-century English cultural history is writers' steadily increasing interest in and knowledge of screen work, and their respect for it as an art form. Graham Greene, in some ways Bennett's successor as a critically acclaimed novelist with a wide popular appeal, the author of both serious fiction and "entertainments," was in the period of *Piccadilly* just down from Oxford, where he had been a devoted reader of Bryher and Kenneth MacPherson's avant-garde film magazine *Close Up*, and also the self-appointed film critic of an undergraduate journal.[2] From these early enthusiasms he went on to regular film reviewing, to the writing of screenplays, to receiving an offer from John Grierson to produce films (not accepted),[3] to the perfecting of a camera-influenced narrative style, to a career and a livelihood profoundly influenced by the cinema. This sort of fascination with film is notable also in the work decades later of the novelists Kazuo Ishiguro and Hanif Kureishi, David Lodge and Peter Ackroyd, William Boyd and Irvine Welsh, Ian McEwan and Angela Carter—and in the work of the playwright Steven Berkoff (to name only one example), whose stage play *On the Waterfront*, produced in London in 2009, ingeniously adapts Elia Kazan's famous 1954 film. Running alongside writers' fascination with the cinema, meanwhile, is the literariness of prominent English filmmakers. As we have seen, the screen work of Powell and Pressburger, Humphrey Jennings, or Dennis Potter is scarcely imaginable without its basis in literature read, other arts appreciated.

At the end of the twentieth century and the beginning of the twenty-first, interrelatedness has achieved a culmination in the sort of complex sensibility—"the cultivated imagination," as described by Hanif Kureishi in a comment quoted in the Introduction—which moves freely and ingeniously among art forms and media, flexibly adapting what is found there, reaching with equal ease into the various English heritages and into popular culture, and reaching with equal or at least comparable ease into the resources of images and the resources of words. How long and to what extent this newly emergent sensibility will be productive, and productive in specifically English ways, is an unanswerable question. As everyone knows, contemporary culture is constantly changing, is under pressure to change, has defined its very contemporaneity by its eagerness to change; and the growing internationalization of the entertainment industries is rendering old-fashioned the very idea of a national cinema or a national literature. Meanwhile the Internet and like technologies have suddenly furnished, too suddenly for anyone really to understand them, new possibilities for communicating both words and images. What seems certain, however, is that in recent years the interrelatedness of English writing and filming has led to a handful of remarkable accomplishments. We can see these at their most significant in the late-career productions of two idiosyncratic but also representative figures, Tony Harrison and Alan Bennett.

Harrison and Bennett make a natural pair, belonging to the same generation (Bennett was born in 1934, Harrison in 1937) and more or less the same social class, as Bennett has noted[4]—the one the son of a butcher, the other the son of a baker. They are products of the same provincial city, Leeds, from which they escaped via their educations and their relatively early creative successes. (In another sense, which both have repeatedly acknowledged, they have never escaped or wanted to escape from Yorkshire, its landscapes, its buildings, its dialect, its cultural institutions like the music hall.) Both Harrison's poetry and Bennett's plays have been aimed at general audiences. "Popular without being populist," as Richard Eyre has said of them, "they are thoroughly accessible, and thoroughly and unapologetically elitist—if that means believing in the absolute values of good and bad art and refusing to talk down to people from the class you were born into."[5] In the cosmopolitan artistic circles in which Harrison and Bennett now move, they have preserved a certain modesty and directness of manner; in an internationalizing world they have carefully preserved their Englishness. That Englishness they have repeatedly dramatized, with a due measure of irony and criticism, in their works, and as we will see in modes which have inevitably included film as well as the written word.

Like a number of modern poets, Tony Harrison was born into one social class but has done his writing in another. Much more than fellow poets, however—even more than Seamus Heaney, for example—he has made that transit his subject. His poems, and scarcely to a lesser extent his verse plays, are fundamentally about a Yorkshire lad who read omnivorously, learned ancient Greek, and transformed himself. Greek got him through Leeds Grammar School and Leeds University and eventually into a world where his translation of Aeschylus's *Oresteia* would be staged by the National Theatre, his reimagining of a satyr-play by Sophocles, *The Trackers of Oxyrhynchus*, put on at the ancient stadium of Delphi. Nevertheless, the chorus of *The Trackers of Oxyrhynchus* sound remarkably like Yorkshire lads themselves:

> Sniff, sniff
> Sniff at the dung,
> t'devil who did this is gonna get 'ung.[6]

They also do a rambunctious Northern English–style clog dance, as if having strayed into antiquity from the sort of West Riding music hall which J. B. Priestley championed. A typical Harrison work veers unpredictably from Yorkshire to Greece and back again, from mythology to modernity, often modernity in its crassest forms, including obscenity, curses, or graffiti scribbled on brick walls in Bradford. Both a "scholar and a scally," as a reviewer called him,[7] Harrison views things simultaneously *sub specie aeternitatis* and with a sharp Leftist anger about the state of politics in post-industrial Britain, frequently yoking these perspectives together with rhyme.

> This is the *terminus ad quem*
> For bolshy bastards such as them,

he has the villain of his film/poem *Prometheus,* the god Hermes, explain, at the moment when Hermes has taken on the role of tallyman in an about-to-be-closed colliery, receiving from each about-to-be-redundant coal miner his tally (and also a whispered angry "Cunt!"). Hermes then lowers the cage full of miners into the pit while contemptuously intoning, in Greek, lines 944–946 of *Prometheus Bound.* There are still more ingenious rhymes in Harrison—

> Zeus likes to pump his pungent pee
> All over poets and poetry.
> First burst to Aeschylus, then squirt a
> Shower on Shakespeare, Schiller, Goethe[8]

—and all of the rhyming is important, a source of highly energized wit and of a rough cheeky music, like a street ballad's or a music-hall song's, which is audible in even the angriest of his works. Harrison is almost certainly the most accomplished rhymer of all poets working in contemporary Britain.

Prometheus is one of a dozen or so "film/poems." What Harrison's term means requires some explanation, and some history. The poet grew up almost as much devoted to films as to his books. The Introduction ("Flicks and This Fleeting Life") to his recently published volume *Collected Film Poetry* recalls this devotion in loving detail—the evocation of long-closed cinemas in Leeds, the history of his visits there with his mother to see *Snow White and the Seven Dwarfs,* with his father to see James Cagney in *White Heat,* the latter experience one he also wrote a moving sonnet about in *School of Eloquence.* Exactly in the manner depicted in Terence Davies's film *The Long Day Closes,* Harrison the young boy would lurk outside cinemas showing an A-rated film, pleading with adult strangers to take him in. When he was bored in the schoolroom, Harrison would put drawings on the corners of successive pages of his Latin grammar, thus turning the primer into his own flick book. Just after World War II he watched newsreel footage of Nazi concentration camps, a life-changing experience, he comments, and while at Leeds University he saw classic films "from Eisenstein to the GPO Film Unit," and foreign films by the *auteurs* of the 1950s and 1960s.[9]

Surviving the experience of a crude television arts program which "illustrated" with random images a reading of some of his early poems, Harrison went on to more successful involvements with broadcasting, for example a televised performance in 1987 of his controversial poem *V.*, on Channel 4, with direction by Richard Eyre. Meanwhile, with *Arctic Paradise* in 1981, he had begun writing verse specifically tailored to filmed images, following up with the filmed verse drama *The Big H* in 1984, and finally a series of works—the first "film/poems"—directed by Peter Symes: *Loving Memory* (1987), *The Blasphemers' Banquet* (1989), *Gaze of the Gorgon* (1992), and *Black Daisies for the Bride* (1993). From the start these were intensely collaborative projects, in which Harrison went on location with the camera crew, scouting visuals with them. The poet came "notebook under arm," as Symes has said,[10] shaping his verses to fit the images discovered and photographed, while in a corresponding process the director and cameraman sought new images to fit the evolving poem. There would follow prolonged editing sessions to match soundtrack with film as precisely and evocatively as possible. When Harrison started directing the film/poems himself (and shifted from the BBC to Channel 4), with *The Shadow of Hiroshima* (1995), he used essentially the same working methods. *Prometheus,* by far the most extensive of these projects, a full-length reworking of Aeschylus's tragedy set in a journey through a decaying, post-industrial Eastern Europe, followed in 1998. *Metamorpheus,* back on the BBC and with Symes directing, came in 2000.

What makes all the film/poems distinctive, whether they assign Harrison's verse to a voice-over commentary or distribute it among characters in an acted-out drama, is the absolute parity they assert between film and verse. There is never any question of the words commenting on preexisting images (as for example E. M. Forster's prose comments on the wartime sights of London in Jennings's *A Diary for Timothy*), or of images illustrating preexisting texts (as in Jennings's *Words for Battle*). Rather, words and images derive from the same inventive process and in the finished work merge into a single form, a hybrid: collaboration pressed as far as it will go. For Harrison, the "combined prosodies of film and poetry," the "flickering momentum of the flicks" and the "metrical beat of poetry" together depict, perhaps constitute the only way of truly depicting, the sense of passing time, and therefore the shortness of life, and the need to grasp the significant details of life as time ushers them relentlessly by. In *The Blasphemers' Banquet,* which is Harrison's attack on that Islamic fundamentalism which issued the *fatwa* against Salman Rushdie and which subordinates everything to its belief in eternity, the poet's rallying cry is "Oh, I love this fleeting life!"[11] The fleeting life, seen in moving images and simultaneously heard in the verse, is the underlying theme of all the film/poems.

Quirky and innovative these works might be—something widely recognized in reviewers' comments ("the most independent-minded first feature in a long time," "an extraordinarily vivid and original work," "an important experiment," "brave and inventive")[12]—but they have their conventionalities as well, for example their generally straightforward camera work and editing. Far from being experimental cinema, this is filmmaking which has benefited from many decades of experience in how to frame, how to cut scenes, how to draw attention to what matters. Except for its mythological-symbolical subject matter and its bizarre mise-en-scène, *Prometheus* might be a mainline motion picture. As for Harrison's poetry, it is not just conventional but traditional in form, indeed often a carefully managed pastiche or homage. For example, his verse for *Arctic Paradise,* set in the Yukon, imitates the rollicking meter and internal rhymes of Robert W. Service's poems about the Frozen North, while *The Blasphemer's Banquet* adopts the quatrain of that skeptical poem of the East, *The Rubaiyat of Omar Khayyam,* as translated by the equally skeptical Edward Fitzgerald. *Black Daisies for the Bride,* about patients with Alzheimer's Disease, uses among other models the metric of Christina Rossetti's "In the Bleak Midwinter"; the four individual film/poems in *Loving Memory,* which are about cemeteries and memorialization in widely separated places, gain some measure of unity from the eighteenth-century ABAB stanza they themselves commemorate, that of Thomas Gray's "Elegy in a Country Churchyard." In such imitations, not to mention the large-scale adaptation of Greek dramatic form he devises for *Prometheus,* Harrison makes obvious the absorption into the cultivated past which we have seen to be one of the defining characteristics and ongoing topics of English cultural life. Like Kazuo Ishiguro and James Ivory and Ismail Merchant, like Powell and Pressburger, like Kipling, like Dennis Potter, like the Mike Leigh who directed the Gilbert and Sullivan biopic *Topsy-Turvy,* like the Ross Devenish and Arthur Hopcraft who adapted Dickens's *Bleak House,* like Dickens himself, Harrison, however much committed to the travails and controversies of the present day, is a devoted student of everything that has led up to the present day.

In some ways, the most interesting of all the Harrison film/poems is the latest one (2002), *Crossings,* because the past it pays homage to is a specifically cinematic one. *Crossings* is a remake of the classic 1936 film *Night Mail,* produced by Basil Wright and Harry Watt, no doubt one of the GPO documentaries Harrison saw while at university. In 1936, *Night Mail*'s chief purpose was the giving of information. The film depicts operations on the Postal Special train which carries each evening's mail from Euston Station to Glasgow, but as will be remembered it ends with a poetic text by W. H. Auden, chanted to the beat of music by Benjamin Britten, thereby becoming a brief "film/poem," with words and images contrived together to dramatize the essential rhythms of delivering the mail—and beyond that the *value* of the process, its "human situation," to use an Audenesque phrase:

> This is the night mail crossing the border,
> Bringing the cheque and the postal order,
> Letters for the rich, letters for the poor,
> The shop at the corner and the girl next door.[13]

This conclusion, like the whole of the GPO film *Coal Face,* on which Auden and Britten also collaborated, and other English documentary works of the 1930s (Len Lye's for instance), looks and sounds avant-garde, so ostentatiously so that it jars with the documentary earnestness of the rest of *Night Mail.* Graham Greene noted the inconsistency in reviews of *Night Mail* for *The Spectator* ("the demands of instruction and the instinct to create a work of art have conflicted ... too many technicalities for atmospheric purposes ... too few for understanding") even while praising Auden's "visual verses."[14]

Before Harrison set to work on *Night Mail,* it was redone by others in a version not lacking earnestness itself, *Night Mail II,* shown on Channel 4 in 1989. This film straightforwardly depicts how mail is handled five decades after the period of the original (planes and trucks now have a role to play) and in a Labor-friendly way says much more than the original about the lives and attitudes of the postal workers, including an accommodating Post Bus driver on the isle of Barra. The program ends with a voice-over of verses written by Blake Morrison,

> After midnight, down the long platforms
> Spoking outward from the hub of England,
> Away from where we lie coupling and uncoupling,
> The unseen industry goes on, the Night Mail . . . ,[15]

thus exactly copying the format of Wright and Watt's *Night Mail. Night Mail II* is an exercise in filmmaking piety.

As for Harrison's *Crossings,* when it was broadcast on "The South Bank Show" on March 10, 2002, it was set in a similar archival context, that is, preceded by a documentary on the original *Night Mail* (schoolchildren are shown chanting Auden's verses) and a how-we-made-it featurette on *Crossings* ("In film poetry, you can't bunch your imagery because you have a lot of imagery on the screen . . . you've got to be fairly clear, accessible").[16] *Crossings* itself, however, attempts something different; piety about the past is not on its agenda. Harrison opens with a Royal Mail truck which in passing a pillar box changes the image from black-and-white to color: for the duration of the film, we will leave the archived past for the brightly colored if also shabby present. A fairly conventional documentary sequence follows, with shots of the pillar box and truck leading to close-ups of sorting machinery, which in turn lead to "the Lady in Red," the sleek mail train, ready for its journey north, but that is about all the information Harrison cares to supply. His interest, like Auden's, lies in the human situation of the Lady in Red's mail sacks; what he chants on the soundtrack is

> Panic . . . pain . . . pleasure will go through the doors
> of millions of houses. Which'll be yours?
>
> A thin little letter sealed with a lick
> to make you elated, or make you feel sick . . .[17]

In other words Harrison takes the conclusion of *Night Mail* and expands it to fill nearly the whole of his own film, thus largely avoiding
the tonal inconsistencies of the original. He expands it with dramatic vignettes, for example of a homeless, drug-addled Scottish youth shivering in a cardboard refrigerator box under a railway viaduct (the Lady in
Red thunders overhead, waking him) and longing hopelessly for a letter from his family; of a darts player in a pub whose aim is thrown off
by the passing train; and of a farmer ("SUICIDAL YORKSHIRE FARMER"
the printed script says) waiting at a grade crossing, depressed by the
epizootic of foot-and-mouth disease and dreading the arrival of a letter with demands from his bank. From here we proceed to a dog-track
gambler who's just lost a packet,

> The dog I had quids on and seemed a dead cert
> was thrown by that Nightmail and lost me my shirt,

a Geordie girl out on the streets, looking in vain for sex,

> While the mail rumbles over the Tyne viaduct
> we're out on the pull to get worsels fucked,

a lonely widower,

> Still her love letters in slow motion stream
> through his door in the morning but only in dream,

and, at another grade crossing, a middle-aged woman on her cell phone
to a friend, frantic about the soon-to-arrive letter with a report on her
HIV test. After the recital of so much misery, a final sequence featuring a warm-hearted Highlands Post Bus driver offers some modest relief (here, Harrison seems to have taken ideas from the similar sequence
in the 1989 *Night Mail II*), but the film returns to the homeless Scottish lad for its last images, the lad and then a close-up of mail flying
through letter boxes, accompanied by that ominous question on the
soundtrack,

> Millions of letters through Great Britain's doors
> Panic ... pain ... pleasure ... Which'll be yours?[18]

Described schematically like this, *Crossings* must seem unremit-
tingly grim, an exercise in contemporary English miserabilism, as op-

posed to Auden's generally hopeful report. This was the burden of Peter Lennon's review of *Crossings* in the *Guardian* ("The route Harrison leads us through is Hieronymus Bosch rather than Constable") and of Paul Hoggart's review in the *Times*, a review itself rendered in doggerel as a tribute to Auden:

> Tum-ti-tum rhythms
> Still drive the verse,
> But the view of the nation's alarmingly worse.
> Glimpses of misery whiz
> Past and go,
> Commissioned for Bragg
> On The South Bank Show.[19]

Whatever justice there may be in this charge, *Crossings* is redeemed from being *merely* miserable by the pleasure it gives in its artistry. There is skill in its editing, for example in the way one of its sharp simple couplets,

> I'll lay awake anxious, till t'letterbox flap
> bangs afore dawn like the spring of a trap,

is immediately followed by a shot of greyhounds springing free of the banging flaps of their cages at the track; skill as well in the film's cameo performances, by such gifted actors as David Bradley as the Yorkshire farmer and Bill Paterson (in voice-over) as the Post Bus driver. In any case *Crossings* is less significant in its dourness, in what it conveys about the letter-dreading state of the nation, than in the inventiveness and audacity of its method, its bringing together of clever visual verse with photographed images in a way that seems to maximize the expressive possibilities of both art forms.

None of Harrison's film/poems, *Crossings* included, is presently available on DVD, and the poet has ruefully conceded that funding for future projects looks unlikely.[20] In marked contrast, Alan Bennett's screen projects have had ongoing popular success, especially the most recent of them, the two series of *Talking Heads* on television, and the feature-length film versions of his plays *The Madness of George III* and *The History Boys*. What accounts for this success is partly Bennett's greater conventionality (there is nothing in his screen work quite so audacious in form as Harrison's film/poems), partly his greater accessibility, including the sort of accessibility which comes from writing in prose rather than verse, but another factor is involved as well. This is Bennett's place in the national culture.

To put it simply, Bennett is a far more central figure than Harrison. He is more representative in his viewpoints, more predictable in his artistic aims, attuned to English history rather than Greek satyr plays, gifted with the sense of humor the poet (largely) lacks ("I'm more light-minded than Tony Harrison"[21]), skeptical rather than angry about English values, and not always skeptical about those values. If his political opinions follow close on Harrison's in detesting Margaret Thatcher and distrusting Tony Blair, those opinions tend to be privately confided, in his diaries, rather than publicly declaimed. (Admittedly, he has published the diaries.)

Bennett likes English ordinariness and writes about it often, which is to say that his characters, if sometimes painfully suffering, as those in most of the *Talking Heads* monologues do, rarely fall into a category like SUICIDAL YORKSHIRE FARMER. Bennett is a Mass Observer manqué, someone as fond as Humphrey Jennings or George Orwell of the oddities and eloquences of ordinary English talk, which he puts into his writing in multiple voices, as opposed to the "one defiant Leeds voice" (as Bennett has said, somewhat enviously, of Harrison) "to which he subjugates everything he writes."[22] Bennett's own talk employs the conventional English upper-middle-class devices of self-deprecation, understatement, and irony, all of which can clearly be heard in his narration for a 1995 television documentary on Westminster Abbey. That Alan Bennett should have been chosen as the guide to such a national shrine sufficiently indicates his standing in the cultural establishment, as indeed does his role as adaptor, for the National Theatre in 1992, of another icon of Englishness, *The Wind in the Willows*. So does his receiving the offers of a CBE and of a knighthood, both of which he turned down; he did accept an offer to become a Trustee of the National Gallery. All in all, the strange fact is that an "ostentatiously diffident and private playwright" (as Ian Buruma has said) has willingly turned himself into a public act. "Alan Bennett is having a fantastic success playing Alan Bennett."[23]

Being at the center of contemporary English life, or at the Soft Centre, as Bennett says with typical self-mockery,[24] means among other things being in the center of a film culture. This position he has been happy to occupy, as many of his writings make clear. "Seeing Stars," for instance, reprinted in the 2005 collection *Untold Stories,* is his cinema autobiography, recollecting with a fondness exactly like Tony Harrison's the names of Leeds movie palaces, recounting the experience (again exactly like Harrison's) of waiting for an adult to take him into an A-rated picture. Bennett even seems to have seen and been impressed by the same newsreel of the liberation of Bergen-Belsen which so affected the poet.[25]

From "Seeing Stars" it is possible to gather a list of Bennett's favorite films, among them any comedy with George Formby, Olivier's *Henry V, Casablanca,* and *Citizen Kane,* the last two standing out for him because of their less-than-straightforward morality. We know that the young Bennett not only saw but (in *Picture Post*) read in advance about *The Way to the Stars, A Canterbury Tale,* and *A Matter of Life and Death;* in 1987 the older Bennett caught on television two of Harrison's film/poems from the *Loving Memory* series.[26] When early in life Bennett dreamt of making an escape from provincialism, he did so, he has acknowledged, in ways imitated from the myth-making, bettering-yourself-through-education films of the 1940s like *How Green Was My Valley, The Corn Is Green,* or *The Stars Look Down.* The last of these he saw again on television four decades later, as he notes in a diary entry incidentally demonstrating a connoisseur's knowledge of when to tune in ("The best films on TV are often in the middle of the day and at lunch time").[27] Films have furnished Bennett, as they have furnished millions of others, with a cultural shorthand, a way of comprehending and describing experience. When visiting his senile mother in her nursing home, encountering the unflappable and cheerful nurses there, he comments that they seem to belong to a *Carry On* film, whereas he finds himself playing the scene melodramatically, as if it were *Brief Encounter.* Further, the cinema has given Bennett the writer a habitual way of *seeing* in discrete and photogenic images, of setting up actuality as though through a viewfinder:

> On the draining board in the kitchen—which they [Bennett's parents] still called the scullery—there would often be a pan of potatoes, peeled and ready for boiling, and a pan of sprouts and carrots likewise. . . .
> Two such pans would be a revealing shot in a documentary film. The two pans in the kitchen, the two people by the fire. Or one.[28]

All this screen consciousness in Bennett, however routine and however much shared with ordinary people, is something he is far more
than ordinarily aware of and articulate about. He has written perceptively about the differences between staging and filming—"On television the playwright is conversing. In the theatre he is (even when
conversing) addressing a meeting"[29]—and more ambitiously has specu-
lated about the screen's influence on himself and fellow Britons, especially the television screen's influence. The BBC program "A Night in
with Alan Bennett: Looks Like a Chair, Actually It's a Lavatory," broadcast in 1992, is both a history of screen influences on his own work
and an essay on television.[30] From a cleverly designed set—a cliché
intellectual's study, but with the lights and cameras of a working television studio—Bennett holds forth, sometimes mocking the medium in
a High Tory toff's voice ("we don't watch TV very much"), more often
declaring its importance as a life-line, an eye-opener, to most of the
population. In earlier years, Bennett comments, the nation was held
together by the radio and the cinema; now it is television. He warmly
reminisces about television programs important to his development,
comedies particularly (some of them shown later on in "A Night in with
Alan Bennett"), but also Dennis Mitchell's long-forgotten documentary film "Morning in the Streets" (1954), which according to Bennett
signaled the process "unique to television, whereby we began to learn
not only how the other half lived, but how they talked. And so the nation was introduced to itself." The best television, like Mitchell's, could
"get close enough to show how different people were, and therefore how
similar."

Not that television is always at its best. Bennett has nothing but
scorn for much of the current, "consumer-based" medium; the more
channels there are, he points out, the less chance there is for common
discussion the next morning. And he freely concedes that a writer cannot always feel at home in the medium, because a writer's "normal situation is to be of two minds," whereas "doubting and dithering" do not
lead to good television; the public want revelations, not what the writer
holds back. Still, writers of the best television have a chance to accomplish something important. Philip Larkin once wrote about people forever surprising a hunger in themselves to be more serious;[31] television
that educates and reforms—and what could be more educational than
quoting Philip Larkin on national television?—might be like a cultural

supermarket surprising viewers into buying serious items that they did not know they wanted.

Meanwhile Bennett's own writerly engagement with the screen, the origin of all his experience good and bad, and the basis of the cautious praise expressed in "A Night in with Alan Bennett," has been extensive. Throughout his career he has moved easily among films, television, and stage plays, at the start perhaps because films and television could give him a wide exposure and earn him money as a writer, but latterly because his kind of imagination has turned out to be so well suited to the screen, and finally because one of the ordinary realities he has felt a commitment to describe, the film-fascination of contemporary England, seems naturally enough to demand filmed treatment.

The first of Bennett's screen works, the television play *A Day Out*, broadcast on December 24, 1972, follows a 1911 Yorkshire cycling club on an excursion from Halifax to Fountains Abbey. It is a Northern subject, then, and an outdoors, moving-along-the-roads subject, one obviously suited for film treatment—a black-and-white film treatment, indeed, a choice the BBC had to be convinced of, as apt for the period.[32] Bennett had conceived the film as showing "figures in a landscape." Thanks to Stephen Frears, the director, it was somewhat reconceived as "characters in relation to one another."[33] From the start Bennett benefited (like Dennis Potter) from the experience of the skilled film professionals willing to work with him, such as Frears, then just beginning his career, and the BBC producer Innes Lloyd, who later took charge of many Bennett projects, and to whom Bennett later paid generous tribute.[34]

A Day Out sketches the riders as they wheel along—the ladies' man, the misogynist, the snobbish upper-class leader, the retarded son, the cheeky working-class lad—through grim industrial streets to yet another of those hill-top vantage points so beloved on English screens, a place from which to survey the familiar surroundings:

MR. SHUTTLEWORTH   I can remember when all that were fields. It's where my grandma lived.
ACKROYD   There's going to be nought left o't'country if they're not careful. When I were little you could stand on t'steps o't'Corn Exchange and see t'moors. Nowadays there's nought but soot and smoke and streets and streets.
BOOTHROYD   Ay, but there's all this. It'll be a long time before they build up England.[35]

Detail by detail the pre-War period is built up (someone is reading the latest H. G. Wells, a Socialist harangues the group at a pub, the daughter of a great house bravely encounters the boy cyclist with the orthopedic boot), while the ruins of Fountains are duly admired and eventually the club cycles back home. It has all been an idyll, but an idyll under threat from what we know is coming. The film was to have ended with a shot of cyclists wending their way "against the evening sun—country roads, long shadows, lovely light,"[36] but the weather dictated otherwise, and Frears and Bennett substituted an epilogue set on November 11, 1919, the pitifully few surviving club members gathering at the War memorial in Ackroyden Square, Halifax, in the rain, to lay a wreath, sing a scrappy hymn, and remember.

There followed several more Bennett television dramas in this vein, ordinary lives depicted, Northern locations, modest aims, the tracking of the feckless young into casual embarrassments or of the old into their grey declines. (In *Sunset Across the Bay*, from 1975, he literally tracks a retired Yorkshire couple into a dull afternoon's visit to the cinema, where they see Joseph Losey and Harold Pinter's *The Go-Between*, without perceptible effect on their quiet hopelessness.) Bennett gained considerably in cinema knowledge from watching the process of filming these dramas—he has published a number of diaries about his experiences on set[37]—and from acting in screen productions as well, his own or others' (he voiced the Mock Turtle in Dennis Potter's *Dreamchild*, for instance, and took a small role in Christine Edzard's adaptation of *Little Dorrit*). From here it was a natural step to write the screenplays for the cinema features *A Private Function* (1984) and the Joe Orton biopic *Prick Up Your Ears* (1987), and to write screen versions, for television or the cinema, of his stage plays, as happened with the spy drama *A Question of Attribution* (1992) and *The Madness of King George* (1994). The process was reversed for *An Englishman Abroad*, first a television drama directed by John Schlesinger (1983), then a one-act play at the National Theatre in 1988, directed by Bennett himself.

An Englishman Abroad is of particular interest as addressing, along with *A Question of Attribution* and Bennett's earlier play *The Old Country*, the Cambridge Spies scandal, that is, the human situation of Guy Burgess's, Kim Philby's, and Anthony Blunt's betrayal of their country, their "fastidious stepping-aside from patriotism."[38] Burgess, in *An En-*

glishman Abroad, exiled in Moscow and virtually the prisoner of "the Comrades," finds himself trapped between the tatters of his political allegiance to Marxism and his regret for London friends, London gossip, even London suits of clothes. A complex ironist, a player with words, a virtuoso *poseur*—all qualities captured in Alan Bates's portrayal in the film—Burgess welcomes the visiting actress Coral Browne to his shabby apartment with a camp recitation of lines from "The Lady of Shallot." He allows himself the luxury of simple feeling only with music, as when standing with Browne in an Orthodox church, he savors the choral liturgy and the tears stream down his face. Earlier, in the apartment, modulating from Tennyson to Jack Buchanan, he has listened over and over again to the singer's recording of "Who Stole My Heart Away?"[39] The song comes scratchily out from the gramophone, a perfect artifact of its period like all the numbers in *Pennies from Heaven.* Both Burgess and Browne are held entranced by the song, in a framing almost identical to the one used for the gramophone-listening scene between Mr. Benn and the butler Stevens in the film of *The Remains of the Day* (Stevens, like the Lady of Shalott, is another prisoner, and like Burgess the prisoner of a role adopted out of loyalty). At this moment of gramophone listening we see exactly what has stolen Burgess's heart away. It is not Marx, Engels, Lenin, and Stalin, as the opening credits momentarily lead us to think, the famous faces looming boldly against first a Russia-red screen, then a theater façade, while the Buchanan song plays on the soundtrack. What has stolen Burgess's heart away is England, or the lost youth Burgess once led there, or something else wished for and inaccessible, not to be explained in words, only to be savored while the lyrics last. Together with Tony Harrison's *Black Daisies for the Bride,* in which the Alzheimer's patients momentarily recover themselves as they sing or listen to scraps of remembered pop tunes, *An Englishman Abroad* gives the clearest and most poignant demonstration possible of the potency of cheap music.

Along with large-scale projects like *An Englishman Abroad,* Bennett was in the 1980s writing the *Talking Heads* programs for television, as well as acting in one, "A Chip in the Sugar," and making his film director's debut in another, "Bed Among the Lentils," with Maggie Smith as an alcoholic and bitterly ironic vicar's wife. In the way they disclose personal history in a single speaking voice, these monodramas become a twentieth-century analogue to the nineteenth-century dramatic monologue; Bennett is *le* Browning *de nos jours.* In this role, however, Bennett limits himself radically in period color and emotional tone, substituting ordinary English types of the present day for the older poet's vibrant historical personages. *Dull Lives,* Bennett's series was originally to have been called,[40] not a phrase that could ever be applied to Browning's wife-murdering dukes and death-haunted bishops. If what the English call character is "the power to refrain," a claim which Bennett puts into the mouth of Burgess in the stage version of *An Englishman Abroad,* then that sort of character is fully on display in *Talking Heads,* where it takes on varied but always restricted or inarticulate or self-exculpating guises, nationality enacted in refraining from things, a "pathology of the English stiff upper lip."[41] (Julie Walters's character in "Her Big Chance" is an exception: she is an actress with nothing reticent about her.) Formally, the *Talking Heads* monologues are understated themselves, exercises in screen restraint: a single character in a bare-bones set or two, framed conventionally, talking to the (largely fixed) camera, photographed in long takes, sparely edited, narrating in a half hour the crises or non-crises of a life, justifying his or her existence, understanding or not understanding. For this claustrophobic art the small screen of television—"the most patient form of drama"[42]—seems uniquely well suited.

With *The History Boys,* Bennett's most recent screen work, about a group of eight preposterously bright sixth-formers being coached in 1983 for Oxford-Cambridge entrance exams in history, we reach his most ambitious project, something which the minimalist art of television would never have suited. In fact it is a culminating project, in that it encompasses mono- or duodramas in the manner of *Talking Heads* as well as sequences in a much more open, freely cinematic style, and in that it incorporates themes a long time contemplated in Bennett's mind, and situations dramatized in earlier work. Indeed, the history of *The History Boys* goes as far back as Bennett's first play, in 1968, *Forty Years On.*

That extremely funny "ragbag" of a stage work, half allegorical drama and half satirical revue,[43] is also set in a school, and turns partly on a contest between masters, the hopelessly passé out-going Headmaster and his in-coming, more up-to-date replacement. At the comic heart of *Forty Years On,* however, is the device of a school play (*Speak for England, Arthur*), seen in preparation and performance. *Speak for England, Arthur* amounts to Bennett's version of Noël Coward's potted-history play *Cavalcade,* or of the theatrical form *Cavalcade* derives from—the village pageant. Bennett's "village" is London, the history depicted that of home-counties England in the twentieth century; one might say that *Forty Years On* presents a southern pastoral to match the northern pastoral of *A Day Out.*[44] In a series of pastiche vignettes, introduced by a verse declamation which could easily have been scripted by Louis Napoleon Parker ("All our past proclaims the future . . . In this our chosen and our changeless land"), accompanied by period photographs back-projected onto the rear of the set, Bennett takes the audience from Oscar Wilde's era and the heyday of Bloomsbury through World War I and World War II to the present day. The Headmaster's speechmaking is twice interrupted by the roar of jet aircraft, just as the village pageant in Woolf's *Between the Acts* is disrupted by warplanes overhead. In *Forty Years On* the jets are not so much harbingers of coming violence as aspects of modern life, pretentious, purposely materialist, and vulgar: "crass-builded, glass-bloated, green-belted . . . A sergeant's world it is now . . ." The school ("Albion House") finally is seen to stand for England itself, on offer to possible buyers and of "some historical and period interest," though needing also some "alterations and improvements."[45]

Not quite forty years on, Bennett reimagined the school setting for his stage-play version of *The History Boys,* premiered at the National Theatre in 2004, directed by Nicholas Hytner. History remains Bennett's theme, here rendered as classroom lessons rather than as comic vignettes. Again, a contest of masters serves as his plot device, a more effective device than in *Forty Years On* because the dueling personages of *The History Boys* are much better and more antithetically defined. Despising all attempts to prepare the boys for their exams, the old-fashioned humanist Hector wants them to keep on learning Hardy and Housman by heart, or practicing their French in improvised scenes. Like Colpeper in *A Canterbury Tale,* Hector fancies himself a *Kulturträger,* a transmitter of tradition, and again like Colpeper he has a morally dubious side, the groping of boys (while they ride pillion on his motorbike) substituting for the squire's glue-throwing in the dark. Hector's antagonist, the young supply teacher Irwin, has been brought in to polish the scholarship candidates, to give them an "edge." He presses agile sophistry and question-answering glibness on them, all in aid of getting them into their Oxbridge colleges. For complicated reasons not necessary to go in to here, the play ends more or less in a stalemate between these two, neither character seen as purely victorious, neither educational philosophy fully endorsed, though because Hector has poetry to quote and a wicked wit of his own, as well as feelings to be hurt, he eventually seems the more admirable figure.

In a pair of flash-forwards the play informs us that Irwin will eventually leave teaching to become a media celebrity. We briefly glimpse him as a revisionist TV historian like Niall Ferguson or Andrew Roberts (and a little like Bennett himself, of course, guiding viewers around the monuments of Westminster Abbey). In one flash-forward Irwin is being photographed at Rievaulx Abbey for a program on monasticism, part of his series *Heroes or Villains?*—the sort of which-is-it? question *The History Boys* refuses to answer, or even to pose. On microphone at Rievaulx, Irwin indulges his taste for clever paradox ("the monastic life only comes alive when contemplating its toilet arrangements . . . God is dead. Shit lives. . . . there is an increment even in excrement") as he plays his well-rewarded part in a world where culture is now routinely transmitted onscreen. The remarkable thing is that Bennett seems to countenance this world himself, at least to the extent of inserting into *The History Boys* a series of black-and-white video sequences projected on a screen at the back of the stage. Filmed by Ben Taylor, these sequences cover scene changes but also show inherently cinematic moments of action, such as the history boys larking about outside, hurrying past rows of lockers, or (in a classic montage sequence) studying in the library. We also view Hector walking in lonely dignity down a long barren corridor—a setting which Bennett once declared to be his favorite imaginary landscape.[46]

Obviously, the videos bring up-to-date the still photographs back-projected in *Forty Years On*. Constituting a film woven into the texture of the drama, they turn *The History Boys* into something resembling one of Tony Harrison's hybrid forms, or the mixed-media show provided in Tom Stoppard's *Rock 'n' Roll*, with its periodic blaring out of Stones or Pink Floyd hits as psychedelic lettering crawls over the stage scrim.

In their various ways Harrison, Stoppard, and Bennett are all implying that the particular kind of late twentieth-century experience which is their subject can no longer be dramatized by theatrical or literary means alone. Something else is necessary: film, with its capacity for bringing out the visual and kinetic aspects of experience, and for merging image with sound (loud pop music, as in *Rock 'n' Roll,* plays over Bennett's back projections). The videos "help move the action along," Bennett has blandly commented.[47] The truth is that they *are* the action of *The History Boys,* together with the lines spoken and the movements executed by the actors on the stage. The videos turn Bennett into a playwright who at this cultural moment must also be a filmmaker.

While film was running above the stage for the London or New York audiences of *The History Boys,* it was running no less obviously in the minds of the history boys themselves. They are distinguished from their counterparts in *Forty Years On* by being older, more intelligent, more articulate, more literary, and above all more knowledgeable about everything cinematic. Like Bennett, the boys are film connoisseurs, as ready to quote from a George Formby song as from a T. S. Eliot poem. Even Rudge, the relative dullard of the group ("only Miss said to say film not films"), catches on to the social significance of the *Carry On* comedies and expresses interest in seeing *This Sporting Life,* once he discovers that it's about rugger. Meanwhile Posner, together with his friend Scripps the most musical of the boys, performs a verse from Gracie Fields's "Sing As We Go," from the 1934 musical of the same title, and later all the boys, departing heroically for their interviews, exit the stage in a production number choreographed as a pastiche of Fields's "Wish Me Luck as You Wave Me Goodbye." The brilliant success of this moment onstage is the more notable given Bennett's own dislike for Gracie Fields and his puzzlement at movie musicals ("nor did I understand why when she appeared everybody suddenly burst out singing—songs in films always something to be endured rather than enjoyed").[48] Perhaps Hytner was largely responsible for it.

Not far behind the boys in movie connoisseurship, indeed generally running ahead of them, is Hector, who when not quoting *King Lear* or *A Shropshire Lad* in class is playing a cinematic guessing game— "Silly time," he calls it—with the sixth-formers. They enact a brief scene from a film, Hector has to name what it is, and if correct extracts 50p from the boys to be put in a kitty. The kitty is never at risk of being paid out, since Hector can identify everything played before him, even by falsetto-speaking adolescents: the climactic moment from Sidney and Muriel Box's 1945 melodrama *The Seventh Veil*, with James Mason bringing his punitive stick cruelly down on the piano-playing fingers of his ward, or the famous ending scene of the Warner Brothers weepie *Now, Voyager,* with Paul Henreid and Bette Davis sharing noble heartbreak over cigarettes. "It's famous, you ignorant little tarts," Hector says to his pupils as he identifies the film, going on to recite from memory the Walt Whitman lines which furnish the title:

> The untold want, by life and land ne'er granted,
> Now, Voyager, sail thou forth, to seek and find.

(Why *Now, Voyager*? One reason is that it was a favorite film of Bennett's aunts, about whose movie-induced dreams he writes memorably in "Seeing Stars.")[49]

For Irwin, the boys play out an even more famous finale, and a much copied and parodied one—it furnishes a moment of camp humor at the conclusion of Anthony Minghella's *Truly Madly Deeply* (1990), for example—namely, Laura Jesson returning to her husband after bidding farewell to Alec Harvey forever on the station platform in *Brief Encounter.* The high-voiced Posner pipes Celia Johnson's lines about really meaning to throw herself off the platform but not having the courage to do it, while the low-voiced Scripps impersonates Cyril Raymond as her stodgily devoted spouse. With sufficient ingenuity, *The Seventh Veil, Now, Voyager,* and *Brief Encounter,* might all be related thematically to *The History Boys,* their motifs of renunciation or repression linked to those in the play, but the real point about them is that they are simply *there,* part of the texture of the boys' and the masters' lives, things learned by heart, items in that store of useless knowledge which, for all that Hector calls the guessing-game "Silly time," he feels it his serious business to pass on to his pupils.

Some reviewers of the play thought it implausible that the boys should be so savvy about old movies.[50] After all, before DVDs, and with video still an emergent medium, how could sixth-formers of 1983 even see the screen works of the 1940s, let alone remember them well enough to enact them? Should the texture of the boys' lives not rather have included 1980s features like *Local Hero* and *Privates on Parade, Educating Rita* and *Octopussy*? For that matter, should they not have sung the rock music of their own time instead of "Bewitched, Bothered and Bewildered," which in a last demonstration of the potency of cheap music Posner performs for Dakin in the touching simulation of a pre–World War II croon? Bennett might have answered his critics by saying simply that the boys get the old movies from and with Hector, as they get Hardy and Housman and the old songs; that his characters are not media creatures but transmitters of culture; and finally that the chronology and mechanisms of transmittal are less interesting to him than the value of the transmittal itself. Abetted by Hector, the boys here act like the heroine of Mark Herman's *Little Voice* (1998; another play-to-film adaptation), who by a kind of magic channels the singing voices of Cleo Laine and Marilyn Monroe, or like P. E. Marlow in Potter's *The Singing Detective,* who transmits Mills Brothers ballads and Raymond Chandler's shopworn chivalry to an uncomprehending present, or for that matter like Alison the land girl in *A Canterbury Tale,* hearing on her sanctuary of a hilltop the music of long-vanished pilgrims. In its own way, *The History Boys* is a heritage work, the heritage being the sort of film shown at noon on television.

The final stage in *The History Boys* project, predictably enough, given everything we have seen about its cinematic fascinations, was its adaptation for a feature film. Production took place in 2005, with the same cast as in the stage production, during a hurried six-week period dictated by the modest budget which Bennett and the director, again Nicholas Hytner, were given to work with. In his introduction to the published screenplay, Hytner speaks of his early decision not to "try to open out something that worked precisely because it was enclosed," of the play's "dynamic exploration of small worlds that are fully inhabited by large spirits." Elsewhere he has named as his models American play-to-film adaptations like *A Streetcar Named Desire,* which he admires for not straying outside the little world of the originals.[51] Yet *The History Boys* film sometimes does do the conventional thing in moving action outside. In effect, it follows the lead of the videos projected at the National Theatre. That is, it presents away-from-the-schoolroom locales like busy streets for the motorcycle rides, or the boys' individual homes, complete with nervous parents, for the all-important moment of the reception of their acceptance letters.

The film also brings in a new minor character, an art mistress played by Penelope Wilton, and a scene set in an action-filled gymnasium, which Bennett had had to leave out of the original[52]—additions rounding out and rendering more believable the school mise-en-scène. At the same time, the film cuts the play's direct addresses to the audience—ruminations usually delivered by Scripps, the boy closest to Bennett in quality of mind, though spoken on one memorable occasion ("I have not hitherto been allotted an inner voice"[53]) by the tart-tongued history mistress Dorothy, the embodiment throughout *The History Boys* of a smoldering feminism. Hytner shot these direct addresses but then edited them out, as being excessively theatrical, unworkable on the screen. The film may or may not be the definitive version of *The History Boys,* but it is certainly the most highly evolved version, in the sense that it takes full advantage of prior creative experience. It accepts what is useful in the devices of the play, then moves on, using its own techniques.

Some of the film's camera work looks specifically designed to emphasize cinematic freedom. For instance, Hytner (or his director of photography, Andrew Dunn) photographs in a bravura way a class held outdoors, the camera restlessly circling around the seated circle of Irwin and boys as he grills them about the origins of the First World War, then whipping left or right to capture a particular speaker, the cuts between shots accelerating as the boys' answers come faster and faster (none of the answers satisfies Irwin: they are all too predictable). It is a style of filming seemingly designed to assert Hytner's liberation from "the proscenium arch," as he put it in describing his approach to filming *The Madness of King George.* It is also, perhaps, a style meant to simulate the fluency of Irwin's patter (dazzling or dizzying to the boys), or to emphasize the slickness of his intellectual relativism ("what's truth got to do with anything?"), which goes by too fast to be challenged. As a play, *The History Boys* had featured rapid shifts from moment to theatrical moment, fluid action in a sketched-in, highly stylized, and easily changed stage setting. As a film, it presents a much more filled-in, specified world: Irwin and his class are sitting on a perfectly plausible grassy lawn under solid-looking trees, in front of an entirely convincing school building façade—in actuality, the exterior of Watford Boys' Grammar

School; the adjacent Watford Girls' Grammar School was used for interiors. Nonetheless, the film retains the play's fluid action, its sense of shifting hurriedly (there is always time pressure on the boys) from sequence to sequence and from mood to mood. Particularly in the intersections of school corridors the film hands off action smartly from one set of characters to another, in efficiently choreographed transitions which in filming must have taken some time to get right.

That is, the film moves hurriedly except when it focuses on Hector, in the intimate scenes played between him and Dorothy, him and the monstrous headmaster, or him and one of the boys—Posner, for example, in a tutorial on Thomas Hardy's "Drummer Hodge." Hytner's handling of this tutorial, by restrained but perfectly expressive means, is sufficient by itself to refute the astonishing charge (by a *Sight and Sound* reviewer) that the film "has no sense of framing or rhythm."[54]

When the scene begins, Hector has just been informed by the headmaster that his groping has been witnessed and that his retirement will be required; he enters the schoolroom and begins the tutorial in a mood of fatigued defeat. Posner starts his recitation of the poem, Hytner framing him in an extended two-shot with Hector. There is some camera circling here too, but a slow circling, matching the careful deliberateness with which Posner is speaking the verses, until finally we reach a perspective with the full length of a classroom bulletin board stretching between master and pupil. Tacked up on this bulletin board and on its fellow at the other end of the room are hundreds of cut-out photographs and art reproductions, as slowly panned-over by the camera and as revealing as the volumes littering the squire's desk in *A Canterbury Tale*. We see antique Greek heads, views of Italy, film posters for *Gilda* and *Juarez* and *In Which We Serve*, a portrait of Byron, a portrait of Charles Laughton, a portrait of Orson Welles as Kane; all the culture which Hector has thought worth teaching the boys and thus the history of his pedagogic career, the store of adult experience separating him from Posner. Especially prominent is a black-and-white photograph of George Orwell. Mentioned frequently in the play, here in the film he becomes a visual presence, presiding sadly over the discussion of a poem which he did not happen to write about but would have valued.[55]

The first cut in the sequence, to a view of Posner standing silhouetted against the glaring sunlight of the classroom window, comes just as he speaks the last quatrain of Hardy's poem, and from this point on the conversation is rendered in conventional, over-the-shoulder shot-reverse shots. Hytner and his editor John Wilson are keeping out of the way to let the actors get on with their business in close-up, and the business fully communicates the meaning of the lines (Bennett: "it takes the actors to show you what you've written"[56]). Samuel Barnett (Posner) and Richard Griffiths (Hector) act as much with their hands as with their voices. The former's hands clutch together with adolescent awkwardness in front of him, while the latter's hands go to work in a schoolmasterly way, casually gesturing at this or that, driving some point home. Hands are important because of what we know Hector does with his outside the classroom—the groping on the motorbike—as Dorothy, Mrs. Lintott, later emphasizes with an outrageous play on words:

> HECTOR   I gather you knew too.
> *Mrs. Lintott smiles.*
> And the boys knew.
> MRS. LINTOTT   Well, of course the boys knew. They had it at first
> hand.

More movingly, hands furnish a metaphor when Hector tries to tell Posner why books matter:

> The best moments in reading are when you come across something—a thought, a feeling, a way of looking at things—which you had thought special and particular to you. Now here it is, set down by someone else, a person you have never met, someone even who is long dead. And it is as if a hand has come out and taken yours.

Of course the actor extends his hand to Posner as he speaks the last line. He does so somewhat clumsily, as if embarrassed by the action, and Posner hesitantly starts a response. Bennett has said about this bit of business, on his commentary on the DVD edition of the film, that the audience should both want Posner to touch Hector and not want him to. In the event, Posner's hand stops short. This is a moment of refused intimacy like the book scene between Stevens and Miss Kenton in *The Remains of the Day,* and also a moment like many in *Talking Heads,* with gestures started and not finished, with self-knowledge revealed in quiet tones and in extreme close-ups but not in decisive actions. It is in extreme close-up, speaking softly and with lengthening pauses, that Hector lists for Posner Hardy's favorite compound adjectives, "un-Kissed," "un-Rejoicing," "un-Confessed," "un-Embraced," each heartbreaking epithet successively describing his own unloved state, and Posner's state too, Posner the helpless victim of a crush on the rakish Dakin. Earlier, Hector has paused thoughtfully on a line summing Hardy up ("Saddish life, though not unappreciated") as if recognizing how suitable it would be as a summing up for him.

"Freed from the necessity of including nine hundred people nightly into their conversation," Hytner wrote of this scene in the film, "these two marvelous actors played only for each other." He said also that it was *the* scene, its lines almost exactly the same as those in the play, only a little trimmed, which made him happy that *The History Boys* became a film, because onscreen "you're able to get close to them . . ."[57] Coming close—"when you get behind the eyes," in Hytner's phrase—and holding still has of course always been a particular virtue of screen work, the cut-in to an expressive face, the microphone picking up a whispered line, though not more a virtue than the camera's complementary ability to pull back and capture all of an expanded perspective or a fast-moving action, then shift rapidly onward to something else. Here, the Thomas Hardy tutorial closes with the incongruous noise of a motorbike starting up, even while the camera holds for a second longer on Posner's melancholy face. This is a sound bridge, a device repeatedly used in this film, as of course in a great deal of contemporary screen work, and the bridge takes us, over a cut, to Hector in long shot, on that sputtering motorbike, going home by himself up a hillside street. This image in turn moves on to the next via another anticipatory sound bridge, the headmaster's spoken line: "Shall I tell you what is wrong with Hector as a teacher?" The layered visual and auditory ironies here perfectly match the verbal irony in something said later by Scripps, the "bike's melancholy long withdrawing roar"—the parody of a much-celebrated line from Matthew Arnold's "Dover Beach" and one of Bennett's cleverest throwaway literary jokes.

Scripps's line survived from the play into the film, but not all of Bennett's allusiveness did. The filmed *History Boys* is considerably less literary than the stage version, less a farrago of clever boys performing with language and more a study of the boys in their social context and emotional lives. The filmed *History Boys* is also more upbeat, marginally, than the play, in that the fate meted out to the grown-up Posner is softened (he becomes a successful teacher, rather than the mentally-troubled, Internet-haunting misfit of the stage version).[58] Moreover, the film's close-ups make Irwin a more vulnerable and appealing character. "You can actually see what's happening in his head," as Bennett says.[59] In the film Irwin appears nowhere as a media man; both the play's opening, with Irwin offering cynical advice to a group of MPs, and the filming scene at Rievaulx Abbey, are cut.

Of all the substantive changes from play to film, however, the most interesting is a three-minute added scene showing the history boys on an excursion to Fountains Abbey—the replacement, as it were, for the cut scene at Rievaulx. At Fountains the boys chat casually with each other, confirming what we already understand about their relationships (some of the dialogue was improvised by the young actors on the spot) and contributing modestly to the film's disquisition on the meanings of history, here made visible in the Abbey ruins. What the day out at Fountains really does, however, is recall *A Day Out,* Bennett's first film, the cycling club story which followed its characters to exactly the same spot. In his DVD commentary Bennett notes that some of Hytner's camera set-ups at Fountains were the same as Stephen Frears's set-ups in *A Day Out,* not by design, but because the topography of the place seemed to dictate how it should be photographed, then and later. Bennett himself sat in exactly the same place to have his lunch and watch the filming of both scenes, in 1972 and in 2005.

With the two Fountains scenes to guide us we can see how much *The History Boys* owes to *A Day Out,* which is a great deal. Both films are dramas about groups of young men, chafing at but also respecting authority, living in Yorkshire but beginning to negotiate a place in the larger world, gathering or missing the chance to gather romantic and sexual experience—closed-in and self-sufficient groups (Hytner's "small worlds that are fully inhabited by large spirits"), with their own vocabularies and codes of behavior. Both films eventually flash-forward in time to examine what happens to the young men in later life; death becomes a presence in both plots; literature is a presence throughout. So is singing, Posner's performance of "Bewitched, Bothered and Bewildered" being matched by Boothroyd's bike-mounted rendition of "Did You Not Hear My Lady" (music by Handel, lyrics by Arthur Somervell). It would not be an exaggeration to say that essential aspects of *The History Boys* derive from the 1972 film, so that its full history might be schematized as follows:

1968 play (*Forty Years On*) + 1972 film (*A Day Out*)
⇓
2004 play (*The History Boys*) + 2006 film (*The History Boys*)

The flash-forward in *A Day Out*, as already mentioned, is to a commemorative scene at Halifax's World War I memorial. The film of *The History Boys* replicates this in a moment greatly elaborated from the play. This is a moment of Irwin's teaching, again set outdoors. He chooses a memorial to the fallen of both wars as the right setting to stimulate the boys' thinking, or perhaps merely teach them the usefulness of paradox as a rhetorical technique. "It's not lest we forget, it's lest we remember. . . . there's no better way of forgetting something than by commemorating it," he says smugly, standing against the stone-carved names, with the camera moving actively about again (as generally in scenes of Irwin's teaching) to show the statue of a great-coated soldier and the wreath of blood-red paper poppies, not to mention the boys' startled expressions. Irwin's denigration of memorialization will shortly be countered by Hector's championing of that activity in his tutorial on "Drummer Hodge," but at this moment the countering is done by the boys themselves, who come back at Irwin with lines quoted from Philip Larkin's great commemorative poem "MCMXIV," quoted from memory of course, thanks to Hector: "Never such innocence again, / Never before or since . . ." Taken in its entirety, this scene is far more complicated—or less innocent—than its analogue in *A Day Out*. It is a real debate about the value of remembering, rather than a simple display of pathos. We would expect it to be more complicated: Bennett was three decades older when he wrote it. The distance between *A Day Out* and *The History Boys* is measured in a long professional experience with remembering.

Taken in *its* entirety, *The History Boys* is about precisely that, remembering. As much as Tony Harrison's film/poem *Loving Memory* it dramatizes and celebrates individual acts of recollection. Thomas Hardy recalls Drummer Hodge, Posner recalls "Drummer Hodge." With defensive wit Hector resurrects a working-class-drama cliché to announce his disgrace: "Trouble at t'mill." To make plain her contempt for the headmaster, in a passage added for the film, Dorothy goes back to the cinema of the 1940s: "if this were a film . . . he'd be played by Raymond Huntley," adding more ambiguously that Irwin might be played by Dirk Bogarde. Irwin himself digs into the past for facts about monastic plumbing. The boys memorize scenes from movies in order to act them out for Hector (only two scenes, as opposed to the three of the play, but the effect is exactly the same). At the end of their day out at Fountains, boys and masters commemorate the trip with a group photograph, through the taking of which Hector enunciates his educational philosophy:

> Pass the parcel. That's sometimes all you can do. Take it, feel it and pass it on. Not for me, not for you. But for someone, somewhere, one day. Pass it on, boys. That's the game I want you to learn. Pass it on.

These lines will be repeated after Hector's death and the school's service of remembrance for his saddish but not unappreciated life. As the headmaster's eulogy ("he opened a deposit account in the bank of literature and made you all shareholders") sputters to its fatuous end, with the history boys exiting into their various futures and with still photographs of Hector being screened in the hall, in a last reminiscence of the back projections of *Forty Years On,* we hear "Pass it on" once more, in voice-over.

What is the "it" Bennett has in mind here? Literature, certainly, say a feeling for the rightness of the lines from A. E. Housman's "On Wenlock Edge"—

> The tree of man was never quiet,
> Then 'twas the Roman; now 'tis I . . .

—with which Hector responds to his dismissal by the headmaster, only to get "This is no time for poetry" back in return. But in view of Hector's silly-time guessing game with his boys, and still more in view of Bennett's own involvement with films seen, films made, and films remembered, "it" certainly involves something broader than bookishness. The lesson of *The History Boys* in both its versions, and beyond that the lesson of modern English cultural life which this book has explored, is that the parcel to be handed on to posterity includes *Brief Encounter* as well as Housman. It includes *Now, Voyager* and Walt Whitman, Gracie Fields and Philip Larkin, the face of George Orwell in a photograph and the face of Orson Welles on a movie poster, the work of Nicholas Hytner and the work of Alan Bennett, *A Day Out* and *Forty Years On;* English filming and English writing.

NOTES

Introduction

1. Quoted by Kenith Trodd, Introduction to *Pennies from Heaven* (Boston and London: Faber & Faber, 1996), viii.

2. Belsey, *Critical Practice* (London: Methuen, 1980), 104; quoted in *Fires Were Started: British Cinema and Thatcherism,* ed. Lester Friedman (Minneapolis, MN: University of Minneapolis Press, 1993), xvi.

3. As those who have read them can testify, pre-1970s discussions of film make a surprising number of simple mistakes: characters wrongly named, plot turns misunderstood, images misremembered. It is not that critics were careless or impercipient—far from it—but that they had to work from such screenings as were then available, or from memory or perhaps published screenplays. Whatever else videos and DVDs have done, they have made it possible to check and recheck the details of a film.

4. I am thinking of the BFI Film Classics series, and the similar Turner Classic Movie/British Film Guide series from I. B. Tauris.

5. Wollen, "Riff-Raff Realism," *Sight and Sound* 8, no. 4 (April 1998): 22.

6. This was the headline of David Robinson's highly approving review in the London *Times,* for instance: November 15, 1985. For a typical film-studies discussion of the film, highly politicized, minimally aesthetic, see John Hill, *British Cinema in the 1980s* (Oxford: Clarendon Press, 1999), 205–218.

7. Hanif Kureishi, *My Beautiful Laundrette and Other Writings* (London: Faber & Faber, 1996), 3.

8. Kureishi, *My Beautiful Laundrette and Other Writings,* 4.

9. Kureishi, *My Beautiful Laundrette and Other Writings,* 69.

10. John Caughie, *Television Drama: Realism, Modernism, and British Culture* (Oxford: Oxford University Press, 2000), 199.

11. Quart, "The Politics of Irony: The Frears-Kureishi Films," in *Reviewing British Cinema,* ed. W. W. Dixon (Albany: State University of New York Press, 1994), 242; Geraghty, *My Beautiful Laundrette* (London and New York: I. B. Tauris, 2005), 59.

12. Kureishi, *My Beautiful Laundrette and Other Writings,* 5.

13. Shalini Chanda, in a British Film Institute ScreenOnline webpage: www .screenonline.org.uk/film/id/443819/index.html. For a comprehensive study of *Film on Four* and television-cinema links, see "Television Drama and the Art Film: The Logic of Convergence," in Caughie, *Television Drama,* 179–202.

14. Kureishi, *My Beautiful Laundrette and Other Writings,* 3.

15. Deborah Cartmell and Imelda Whelehan, eds., *The Cambridge Companion to Literature on Screen* (Cambridge: Cambridge University Press, 2007).

16. Houston, "British Cinema: Life before death on Television," *Sight and Sound* 53, no. 2 (Spring 1984): 115–116.

17. Quoted in Peter Ansorge, *From Liverpool to Los Angeles: on writing for theatre, film and television* (London and Boston: Faber & Faber, 1997), 62.

18. Williams, "British Film History: New Perspectives," in *British Cinema History,* ed. James Curran and Vincent Porter (Totowa, NJ: Barnes & Noble, 1983), 10–11; Higson, "The Heritage Film and British Cinema," in *Dissolving Views: Key Writings on British Cinema,* ed. Andrew Higson (London: Cassell, 1996), 238.

19. Everett, *Terence Davies* (Manchester and New York: Manchester University Press, 2004), *passim;* Chibnall, *Get Carter* (London and New York: I. B. Tauris, 2003), 14; Christie, *A Matter of Life and Death* (London: BFI Film Classics, 2000), 16; Moor, *Powell & Pressburger: A Cinema of Magic Spaces* (London and New York: I. B. Tauris, 2005), 90–91. Christie also considers the myth of Alcestis as a source for *A Matter of Life and Death* (18).

20. Andrew Motion, *Philip Larkin: A Writer's Life* (New York: Farrar, Straus & Giroux, 1993), 300, 288; Philip Larkin, *Collected Poems,* ed. Anthony Thwaite (New York: Farrar, Straus & Giroux, 1989), 116.

21. Kipling, *Traffics and Discoveries* [1904], ed. Hermione Lee (London: Penguin, 1987), 279. Letter to Walter Creighton (Kipling's co-scenarist), October 10, 1927; see *The Letters of Rudyard Kipling,* ed. Thomas Pinney (Iowa City: University of Iowa Press, 2004), 5: 384–385. Kipling later denied having a hand in writing the script of the finished film; see *Letters* 5: 507.

22. Dyer, *Brief Encounter* (London: British Film Institute, 1993), 38–40.

23. Kureishi, *Sammy and Rosie Get Laid: The Script and the Diary* (Boston and London: Faber & Faber, 1988), 66, 90, 109. The Byron quotation comes from *Don Juan* 2. 186.

24. Kureishi, *Sammy and Rosie Get Laid,* 40.

25. Eliot, *The Waste Land* 368–369; *Norton Critical Edition,* ed. Michael North (New York and London: W.W. Norton, 2001), 17.

26. Kenner, *The Mechanic Muse* (Oxford: Oxford University Press, 1987), 34.

1. Wartime Pageantry

1. "Their Finest Hour" speech, June 18, 1940, reprinted in Churchill, *Blood, Sweat, and Tears* (New York: Putnam's, 1941), 314.

2. Forster, *Howards End* (New York: Penguin, 2000), 142-143. The passage excerpted here goes on for nearly a full page.

3. For early reviews, see William Whitebait, *The New Statesman and Nation*, May 13, 1944, 320; Edgar Anstey, *Spectator*, May 19, 1944, 451; Dilys Powell, *The Listener*, May 18, 1944, 555; Richard Winnington, *Drawn and Quartered* (London: Saturn Press, n.d.), 22; C. A. Lejeune, *Chestnuts in her Lap* (London: Phoenix House, 1947), 121; Peter Burnup, *Motion Picture Herald*, May 13, 1944, 1885–1886; and an anonymous review in *Today's Cinema*, May 10, 1944, 12. For the rehabilitation, see, among others, Ian Christie, *Arrows of Desire* (London: Waterstone, 1985), 49–51; Peter Conrad, "Arrival at Canterbury," in *To Be Continued: Four Stories and their Survival* (New York and London: Oxford University Press, 1995), 22–32; and James Chapman, who in *The British at War: Cinema, State and Propaganda, 1939-1945* (London and New York: I. B. Tauris, 1998), 240–241, puts *A Canterbury Tale* in the context of other wartime "History and Heritage" films. Probably the most comprehensive exegesis of the film is given by Christie in his commentary on the DVD edition (Criterion Collection, 2006).

4. Late in life Pressburger seems to have anticipated David Lean in wanting to film *A Passage to India*. See Kevin Macdonald, *Emeric Pressburger: The Life and Death of a Screenwriter* (London and Boston: Faber & Faber, 1994), 265.

5. Michael Powell, *Million Dollar Movie* (New York: Random House, 1992), 483. Powell, *A Life in Movies* (New York: Knopf, 1987), 92. Powell, interview (September 22, 1970) with Kevin Gough-Yates (London: National Film Theatre, 1971), n.p.

6. Winnington, *Drawn and Quartered*, 22.

7. Raymond Durgnat, "The Powell and Pressburger Mystery," *Cinéaste* 23, no. 2 (1997): 18.

8. Macdonald, *Emeric Pressburger*, 233.

9. Dated June 9, 1940, and written for a wartime exhibition at the Museum of Modern Art in New York. T. S. Eliot, *Collected Poems: 1909–1962* (New York, San Diego, London: Harcourt Brace Jovanovich, 1968), 213–214.

10. Young, *The Island* (London: William Heinemann, 1944), xi, 450.

11. The relation between wartime films and history books is briefly discussed in Jeffrey Richards, "National Identity in British Wartime Films," in *Britain and the Cinema in the Second World War*, ed. Philip M. Taylor (New York: St Martin's, 1988), 43–47.

12. Macdonald, *Emeric Pressburger*, 183.

13. Ibid., 234.

14. Powell, *A Life in Movies*, 437, 447–48.

15. Not Thornton Wilder's *Our Town,* as has usually been said, according to Ian Christie's DVD commentary.

16. Powell, *A Life in Movies,* 433. Esmé Wingfield-Stratford, *The History of British Civilization* (New York: Harcourt Brace, 1938 [reprinting the second English edition of 1930]), 683, 1263.

17. Powell, *A Life in Movies,* 438–444, 446–448.

18. Chris Wicking, "Retrospective: *A Canterbury Tale,*" *Monthly Film Bulletin* 51 (November 1984): 355.

19. Antonia Lant, "Britain at the End of Empire," in *The Oxford History of World Cinema,* ed. Geoffrey Nowell-Smith (Oxford: Oxford University Press, 1996), 369.

20. Powell, *A Life in Movies,* 451; interview with Kevin Gough-Yates, n.p. For a discussion of the two versions of the film, see Antonia Lant, *Blackout: Reinventing Women for Wartime British Cinema* (Princeton, NJ: Princeton University Press, 1991), 214–216.

21. Anstey, *Spectator,* May 19, 1944, 451.

22. See Orwell, *Complete Works,* ed. Peter Davison (London: Secker & Warburg, 1998), 12: 545. Unfortunately Orwell failed to notice the films of the period one would wish, including *A Canterbury Tale.* He tended to address instead (and to despise) American run-of-the-mill entertainments.

23. Powell, interview with Gough-Yates, n.p.

24. Commentary on DVD edition.

25. Macdonald, *Emeric Pressburger,* 234.

26. Interview with Kevin Gough-Yates, November 12, 1970; included in Powell, interview with Gough-Yates, n.p.

27. A typed screenplay in the British Film Institute National Library (Number 13976) supplies a dialogue exchange, never used in the film, which shows that Pressburger thought of the repossession literally, like Kipling: "I wouldn't spend my leave in Canterbury." "Nor would I, ordinarily [Bob Johnson responds]. I promised Maw. Her Maw, my Granmaw, came from there. She'd be 86 next month, but she's dead. She left Canterbury when she was a little girl."

28. See especially Jeffrey Richards and Anthony Aldgate, *Best of British: Cinema and Society 1930-1970* (Oxford: Basil Blackwell, 1983), 53–55.

29. Jeffrey Richards and Dorothy Sheridan, eds., *Mass-Observation at the Movies* (London and New York: Routledge & Kegan Paul, 1987), 256, 269; the second comment was made by a forty-three-year-old Harrowgate housewife.

30. Orwell, *Complete Works,* 12: 508–509.

31. Angus Calder, *The People's War: Britain 1939-1945* (New York: Pantheon, 1969), 315.

32. This excerpt is reprinted in Collie Knox's anthology *For Ever England* (London: Cassell and Co., 1943), 76–77.

33. Vera Brittain, *England's Hour* (New York: Macmillan, 1941), 194–196.

34. An origin ingeniously suggested by Ian Christie, *Arrows of Desire,* 51. The boys here anticipate the larking children of later films: *Hue and Cry* (1947), where

a boys' gang foils some postwar villains, and especially John Boorman's *Hope and Glory* (1987), which depicts children set free, turned into anarchists, by the Blitz.

35. For a different view of these closing sequences, see Gordon Williams, "Propaganda into Art: Wartime Films of Powell and Pressburger," *Trivium* (Lampeter, Wales) 17 (1982): 59.

36. Dilys Powell, *The Listener,* May 18, 1944, 555; London *Times* review, May 10, 1944; William Whitebait, *The New Statesman and Nation* May 13, 1944, 320.

37. On the iconic meaning of these concerts, see Jean R. Freedman, *Whistling in the Dark: Memory and Culture in Wartime London* (Lexington: University Press of Kentucky, 1999), 157–158.

38. Powell interview with Roger Manvell [1946], in *The Penguin Film Review* (Totowa, NJ: Rowman and Littlefield, 1977), 110.

39. British Film Institute National Library, script number 13976, 10–31, 11–43.

40. Dryden, "Imitation of Horace," Book III, Ode 29, line 71 (1685).

41. Powell, *200,000 Feet on Foula* (London: Faber & Faber, 1938); later reprinted as *Edge of the World* (London and Boston: Faber & Faber, 1990). I owe the identification of this book to Ian Christie's DVD commentary.

42. Sydney Duffield, *Rough Stuff for Home Guards and Members of H. M. Forces* (London: Thorson, 1942); Michael Graham, *Soil and Sense* (London: Faber & Faber, 1941); F. Fraser Darling, *Island Years* (London: G. Bell and Sons, 1944).

43. Dilys Powell, *The Listener,* May 18, 1944, 555. Gilbert Adair, "The British Tradition," in *A Night at the Pictures: Ten Decades of British Film,* ed. Gilbert Adair and Nick Roddick (Bromley, Kent: Columbus Books, 1985), 34. For another investigation of Colpeper's psychopathology, see Andrew Moor, *Powell & Pressburger: A Cinema of Magic Spaces* (London and New York: I. B. Tauris, 2005), 97.

44. Macdonald, *Emeric Pressburger,* 236; transcript of 1959 BBC radio interview, reprinted in *Michael Powell: Interviews,* ed. David Lazar (Jackson: University Press of Mississippi, 2003), 23.

45. Scott Salwolke, *The Films of Michael Powell and the Archers* (Lanham, MD, and London: Scarecrow Press, 1997), 116.

46. British Film Institute National Library, script number 13976, 43–119.

47. Macdonald, *Emeric Pressburger,* 237–238. Puck as an antecedent for Colpeper was suggested by John Russell Taylor in "Michael Powell: Myths and Supermen," *Sight and Sound* 47, no. 4 (Autumn 1978): 227, and by Ian Christie in *Arrows of Desire,* 50; see also Andrew Moor, *Powell & Pressburger,* 104.

48. Powell, *A Life in Movies,* 447.

49. Wingfield-Stratford, *The History of British Civilization,* 350. Wingfield-Stratford stipulated that the power of the cinema could be worked only on "the uneducated type of mind."

50. Peter Conrad, *To Be Continued: Four Stories and their Survival* (Oxford: Oxford University Press, 1995), 26.

51. A. P. Herbert, *Siren Song* (New York: Doubleday Doran, 1941), 79. First published in the *Sunday Graphic,* July 28, 1940.

52. Macdonald, *Emeric Pressburger*, 248.

53. Winnington, *Drawn and Quartered*, 22.

54. Parker, *Several of My Lives* (London: Chapman and Hall, 1928), 279, 291–294.

55. Rachael Low, *The History of the British Film 1906–1914* (London: Allen & Unwin, 1949), 95.

56. Parker, *Several of My Lives*, 296–297.

57. Joy Melville, *Ellen and Edy: A Biography of Ellen Terry and her Daughter, Edith Craig, 1847–1947* (London and New York: Pandora, 1987), 209–211, 259; Katharine Cockin, *Edith Craig (1869–1947): Dramatic Lives* (London and Washington: Cassell, 1998), 174–175.

58. P. N. Furbank, *E. M. Forster: A Life*, vol. 2 (New York: Harcourt Brace Jovanovich, 1978), 198; "Pageant of Trees," London *Times*, July 16, 1934.

59. Allingham, *The Oaken Heart* (Garden City: Doubleday, Doran 1941), 296.

60. Powell, *The Military Philosophers; A Dance to the Music of Time*, vol. 3 (New York: Popular Library, 1976), 241–242.

61. Melville, *Ellen and Edy*, 256.

62. Virginia Woolf, *Between the Acts* (New York: Harcourt Brace, 1969), 76, 79–81, 86, 95, 140, 179, 183–184, 188, 192–193.

63. David Lean's *This Happy Breed* (1944) films a series of vignettes chronicling one middle-class family's experiences between the wars, and thus completely domesticates or suburbanizes the pageant. This film, like *Cavalcade*, was an adaptation of a successful Noël Coward stage play.

64. Lejeune, *Chestnuts in her Lap* (London: Phoenix House, 1947), 57.

65. For reports and photographs, see the London *Times*, January 2, 1942; January 2, 1943.

66. On the wartime pageants and their predecessors in the 1930s, see Steve Nicholson, "Theatrical Pageants in the Second World War," *Theatre Research International* 18, no. 3 (Autumn 1993): 186–196; and Mick Wallis, "Pageantry and the Popular Front: Ideological Production in the 'Thirties," *New Theatre Quarterly* 10, no. 38 (May 1994): 132–156.

67. London *Times*, February 22, 1943.

68. For details, see reports in the *Times* for September 23, 1942; September 24, 1942 (an approving editorial); and especially September 26, 1942 (photograph); also Basil Dean, *The Theatre at War* (London: Harrap, 1956), 294–302, 144–145 (photographs).

69. Bennett, "Seeing Stars," in *Untold Stories* (New York: Farrar, Straus & Giroux, 2005), 164.

70. "Michael Powell Directs his New Film," *Picture Post*, February 26, 1944, 20.

71. *Punch*, February 23, 1944, 160.

72. Eliot, *Collected Poems 1909–1962*, 208, 207, 200–201.

73. Eliot, "Ulysses, Order, and Myth," review of Joyce in *The Dial* (1923); reprinted in *The Modern Tradition*, ed. Richard Ellmann and Charles Feidelson (New York: Oxford University Press, 1965), 681.

74. Christie, commentary on DVD edition.

75. For illustrations, see Fiona MacCarthy, *Stanley Spencer: An English Vision* (New Haven, CT: Yale University Press, 1997). The likeness of the Archers' work to Spencer's "magical whimsicality" is brought up in Gilbert Adair and Nick Roddick, *A Night at the Pictures,* 36, but with regard to *A Matter of Life and Death.*

76. For a comprehensive review of Jennings's early life and wartime documentary work, see Peter Stansky and William Abrahams, *London's Burning: Life, Death and Art in the Second World War* (Stanford, CA: Stanford University Press, 1994), 71–125.

77. James Merralls, "Humphrey Jennings: A Biographical Sketch," *Film Quarterly* 15, no. 2 (Winter 1961–62): 31.

78. Jennings, "Prose Poem" published in the *London Bulletin,* June 1938; reprinted in *Humphrey Jennings: Film-Maker, Painter, Poet,* ed. Mary-Lou Jennings (London: British Film Institute and Riverside Studios, 1982), 14. This companion book to the 1982 Jennings exhibition at the Riverside Studios is one of the two most authoritative sources of biographical information on the filmmaker, the other being Anthony W. Hodgkinson and Rodney E. Sheratsky, *Humphrey Jennings—More than a Maker of Films* (Hanover and London: University Press of New England, 1982).

79. *May the Twelfth: Mass-Observation Day-Surveys 1937,* by over two hundred observers, ed. Humphrey Jennings and Charles Madge (London: Faber & Faber, 1937), 151.

80. Many years after Jennings's death the manuscript papers were edited by Mary-Lou Jennings and Charles Madge and published as *Pandaemonium 1660–1886: The Coming of the Machine as Seen by Contemporary Observers* (New York: Free Press, 1985).

81. Dilys Powell, "Films since 1940," in *Humphrey Jennings, 1907–1950: A Tribute* (London: Olen Press, [1950]), n.p.

82. Wright, "Humphrey Jennings," *Sight and Sound* 19, no. 8 (December 1950): 311.

83. Jennings, review of *Surrealism,* ed. Herbert Read; quoted in *Humphrey Jennings: Film-Maker, Painter, Poet,* 14.

84. For a personal account of the stages of Jennings's involvement, see Gerald Noxon, "How Humphrey Jennings Came to Film," *Film Quarterly* 15, no. 2 (Winter 1961–62): 19–26.

85. Gavin Lambert, "Jennings' Britain," *Sight and Sound* 20, no. 1 (May 1951): 25.

86. For a brief discussion of this and other visual links between the Archers and Jennings, see Douglas McVay, "Michael Powell: Three Neglected Films," *Films & Filming* 328 (January 1982): 18–19.

87. Jennings, "Picture: the 'Midi Symphony,'" reprinted in *Humphrey Jennings: Film-Maker, Painter, Poet,* 26.

88. Clive Coultass, *Images for Battles: British Film and the Second World War, 1939–1945* (Newark: University of Delaware Press; London and Toronto: Associated

University Presses, 1989), 89; "National Gallery, 1941," Humphrey Jennings Special Collection Number 7, British Film Institute National Library.

89. The script is reprinted in *The Humphrey Jennings Film Reader*, ed. Kevin Jackson (London: Carcanet, 1993), 24–28.

90. Humphrey Jennings Special Collection Number 7.

91. For an excerpt, see *Humphrey Jennings: Film-Maker, Painter, Poet*, 30.

92. Letter to his wife Cicely Jennings, September 13, 1941, *The Humphrey Jennings Film Reader*, 31.

93. For these and other details on the making of *Listen to Britain*, see Dai Vaughan, *Portrait of an Invisible Man: The Working Life of Stewart McAllister, Film Editor* (London: British Film Institute, 1983), 83–89. Vaughan's book attacks the critics who have neglected McAllister over the years, and makes a sustained case for his collaborative equality with Jennings, yet even Vaughan acknowledges (87) the impossibility of unscrambling their individual contributions to the planning and editing of *Listen to Britain*.

94. Jackson, *Humphrey Jennings* (London: Picador, 2004), 250. Jackson's biography gives a good brief account, and appreciation, of *Listen to Britain*.

95. "Day Report" for March 8, 1941, *The Humphrey Jennings Film Reader*, 13–14.

96. Letter to Cicely Jennings, June 15, 1941, *The Humphrey Jennings Film Reader*, 30.

97. Review of Ministry of Information films, London *Times*, February 24, 1942.

98. *The Lion and the Unicorn: Socialism and the English Genius* (February 1941), reprinted in Orwell, *Complete Works*, 12: 392.

99. Vaughan, *Portrait of an Invisible Man*, 89.

100. Quoted in *Humphrey Jennings: Film-Maker, Painter, Poet*, 37. In this volume (68) the David Mellor essay, "Sketch for an Historical Portrait of Humphrey Jennings," notes that one-day coverage was a regular feature of 1930s and 1940s photojournalism.

101. David Thomson has perceptively analyzed this image in his overview of Jennings's work, "A Sight for Sore Eyes," *Film Comment* 29 (March–April 1993): 56.

102. Jennings, "The Tin Hat Concerto" (August 1941 treatment), *Humphrey Jennings: Film-Maker, Painter, Poet*, 30.

103. The few seconds of filming in the forge gave Jennings the chance to reproduce, in modern terms, an experience of 1830 he had excerpted for *Pandaemonium*: "I went into some of the forges to see the workman at their labours. There was no need of introduction: the works were open to all, for they were unsurrounded by walls. I saw the white-hot iron run out from the furnace; I saw it spun, as it were, into bars and iron ribbands, with an ease and rapidity which seemed marvellous. There were also the ponderous hammers and clanking rolling-mills. I wandered from one to another without restraint. . . ." (from the autobiography of the engineer James Nasmyth); *Pandaemonium*, 172.

104. Anstey, *Spectator*, March 13, 1942, 254.

105. Quoted in Alan Lovell and Jim Hillier, *Studies in Documentary* (New York: Viking, 1972), 79.

106. Ian Dalrymple, reminiscing in *Portrait of an Invisible Man*, 60.

107. "The British Tradition," in Adair and Roddick, *A Night at the Pictures*, 46.

108. Letter to Cicely Jennings, May 10, 1941, *The Humphrey Jennings Film Reader*, 29.

109. Orwell, *Complete Works*, 12: 392–393.

110. Ibid., 12: 395.

111. Ibid., 12: 398–399, 401.

112. "What does seem progressive about these four films [*Millions Like Us, The Gentle Sex, The Bells Go Down, Listen to Britain*] is that they each conjure up a vision of a classless society whose basis is not in the bourgeois patriarchal family but in the 'community,' which depends not upon competition but upon co-operation." Andrew Higson, "Five Films," in *National Fictions: World War II in British Films and Television*, ed. Geoff Hurd (London: British Film Institute , 1984), 22–23.

113. Hodgkinson and Sheratsky, *Humphrey Jennings—More than a Maker of Films*, 138.

114. Malcolm Smith, "Narrative and Ideology in *Listen to Britain*," in *Narrative: from Malory to Motion Pictures*, ed. Jeremy Hawthorn (London: Edward Arnold, 1985), 156. On pages 147–149 of his essay Smith interestingly discusses the structuring of *Listen to Britain* in terms of "micro- and macro-montage."

115. There is some written evidence about how we might interpret the scene. The "Tin Hat Concerto" treatment describes it like this: "It is half-past nine—the children are already at school and the teacher is calling out the orders to a PT class in the playground. Just over the school wall a housewife is washing up the breakfast. The sound of the children comes in through the window. She stops for a moment—looks across to the mantelpiece, to a photo of a boy in a Glengarrie: a great wave of emotion sweeps over her—the sound of the Pipes played not in the hills of Scotland, but in the sand dunes of Syria, where her lad is away at the war. And then she comes back to the washing up, and the kids in the playground go on with their PT" (*Humphrey Jennings: Film-Maker, Painter, Poet*, 30); a post-production script says simply, "A housewife watches her child dancing with others in the school playground below and thinks of the man in a foreign land" (*The Humphrey Jennings Film Reader*, 34). But of course neither of these texts is determinative of meaning in the *film*.

116. Extract from the *Diary of Michael Faraday*, June 1850, entry 260 in *Pandaemonium* (249). Charles Madge describes these words as Jennings's definition of an "image": Institute of Contemporary Art, *Paintings: Humphrey Jennings, 1907–1950* (London, n.d.), n.p.

117. Sansom commented briefly on his work in the film in "The Making of *Fires Were Started*," *Film Quarterly* 15, no. 2 (Winter 1961–62): 27–29.

118. A comment which became iconic itself: it is mocked in the "Aftermyth of War" sketch in Alan Bennett, Peter Cook, Jonathan Miller, and Dudley Moore's *Beyond the Fringe* (1963).

119. The filmmaker Lindsay Anderson captures this Forsterian quality in Jennings in the title and text of his important essay, "Only Connect: Some Aspects of

the Work of Humphrey Jennings," *Sight and Sound* (April–May, 1954); reprinted in the special Jennings number of *Film Quarterly* 15, 2 (Winter 1961–62): 5–12.

120. Charles Madge, interview quoted in Hodgkinson and Sheratsky, *Humphrey Jennings—More than a Maker of Films*, 31.

121. Leonard Woolf, "The Pageant of History," in *Essays on Literature, History, Politics, Etc.* (New York: Harcourt, Brace, 1927), 127.

122. Observation by Lady Forman, formerly Helen de Mouilpied, who worked as a film distributor for the Ministry of Information; quoted in Vaughan, *Portrait of an Invisible Man*, 97.

2. American Gangsters, English Crime Films, and Dennis Potter

1. For details of the Hulten-Jones affair, see Orwell's source, R. Alwyn Raymond's pamphlet *The Cleft Chin Murder* (London: Claud Morris, 1945). *Christmas Holiday* is mentioned on page 15; Hulten and Jones saw two films in their six days together. A more recent review of the affair is Laurence Marks, "The Chicago Affair," *Observer Magazine*, April 1, 1990, 48–50.

2. Steve Chibnall and Robert Murphy, "Parole overdue," in Chibnall and Murphy, eds., *British Crime Cinema* (London: Routledge, 1999), 7.

3. Harrison, "Continuous," from *The School of Eloquence* in *Selected Poems* (New York: Random House, 1987), 143.

4. Geoff Brown, review of *Chicago Joe and the Showgirl, Monthly Film Bulletin* 57, no. 675 (April 1990): 100; Graham Fuller, "Right Villains," *Film Comment* (September–October 1990): 51.

5. Leavis, *Mass Civilisation and Minority Culture* (Cambridge: Minority Press, 1930), 11, 10.

6. Greene, *The Pleasure Dome: The Collected Film Criticism 1935–40*, ed. John Russell Taylor (Oxford and New York: Oxford University Press, 1980), 61, 172, 173.

7. Priestley, *English Journey* (Chicago and London: University of Chicago Press, 1984 [1934]), 300.

8. Orwell, *Complete Works*, 16: 349.

9. Ibid., 16: 350.

10. Ibid., 16: 355, 352.

11. Crippen was still a powerful figure of the popular imagination in 1968, twenty years after Orwell's essay, at least judging by Peter Medak's film *Negatives*. This features a current-day London couple heating up their sex life by role-playing as the murderous doctor and his mistress Belle.

12. Orwell, *Complete Works*, 18: 109, 110.

13. Reviewing *The Lady in Question* for *Time and Tide*, November 30, 1940; *The Gay Mrs. Trexel* for *Time and Tide*, December 7, 1940; *Complete Works*, 12: 291, 304.

14. *Monthly Film Bulletin* 15, no. 172 (April 1948): 47; "C.A.W." in *Today's Cinema* 70, no. 5634 (April 1948): 14; Connery Chappell, "The Picture, the Press, and the Lesson," *Kinematograph Weekly* 2138 (April 1948): 6. For an excellent short survey

of the film and its censorship problems, see Brian McFarlane, "Outrage: *No Orchids for Miss Blandish,*" in *British Crime Cinema,* 37–50.

15. Murphy, *Realism and Tinsel: Cinema and Society in Britain 1939–1948* (London and New York: Routledge, 1989), 188.

16. Cheyney, *Uneasy Terms* (New York: Collier, 1989 [1947]), 12.

17. La Bern, *Night Darkens the Street* (London: Nicholson & Watson, 1947), 86–87.

18. "C.A.W." in *Today's Cinema* 70, no. 5641 (April 1948): 11; W. A. Wilcox in the *Sunday Dispatch,* May 2, 1948, 6. For a different, much more approving view, see the retrospective by Pam Cook, *Monthly Film Bulletin* 52, no. 620 (September 1985): 289–290.

19. For a brief history of censorship of crime films, see James C. Robertson, "The censors and British gangland, 1913–1990," in *British Crime Cinema,* 16–26.

20. Tim Pulleine, "Spin a dark web," in *British Crime Cinema,* 34.

21. Guest's reference to a documentary style comes from his voiceover commentary on a recent DVD recording (Troy, MI: Anchor Bay Entertainment, 2002). For the Shelley poem (Peter Bell the Third: "Hell is a city much like London—A populous and smoky city") see Maurice Procter, *Hell Is a City* (London: Hutchinson, 1954), 148–149.

22. "It gave a sort of internationalism to it," according to Guest on the DVD commentary.

23. Tom Cox, "Get Hodges," *Guardian,* May 28, 1999.

24. For an elaborate consideration of the allusion and the various filmic codes *Richard III* observes, see James N. Loehlin, "'Top of the World, Ma': *Richard III* and cinematic convention," in *Shakespeare, the Movie,* ed. Lynda Boose and Richard Burt (London and New York: Routledge, 1997), 67–79.

25. Hill, "Allegorising the nation: British gangster films of the 1980s," in *British Crime Fiction,* 160.

26. This mural represents "the tyranny of North America," according to Mark Finch's review of the film: *Monthly Film Bulletin* 54, no. 640 (May 1987): 147.

27. Charlotte Brunsdon, "Space in the British crime film," in *British Crime Cinema,* 156; Roger Ebert, *Chicago Sun Times,* May 6, 1988: www.suntimes.com/ebert/ebert_reviews/1988/05/293121.html.

28. Charlotte Brunsdon, "Space in the British crime film," in *British Crime Cinema,* 157.

29. Barrie Keeffe, "Haunting Friday," *Sight and Sound* 6, no. 8 (August 1996): 20; this article is an exceptionally interesting brief memoir of the writing of the screenplay.

30. Keeffe, *The Long Good Friday* (London and New York: Methuen, 1984), vi.

31. David Bartholomew, "The Long Good Friday," *Film Quarterly* 36, no. 1 (1982): 51.

32. "Our Eunuch Dreams," in *Collected Poems of Dylan Thomas, 1934–1952* (New York: New Directions, 1957), 16.

33. Leach, *British Film* (Cambridge: Cambridge University Press, 2004), 178.

34. Murphy, "The Spiv Cycle," in *Realism and Tinsel,* 146–167; Peter Wollen, "Riff-raff realism," *Sight and Sound* (April 1998): 18–22.

35. Wollen, "Riff-raff realism," 22; Murphy, "The Spiv Cycle," 165–166.

36. Wollen connects them, with some plausibility, to the RKO melodrama *None But the Lonely Heart,* directed by Clifford Odets (1944); "Riff-raff realism," 20–21.

37. The sociology-of-crime novel had a marked vogue about this time. Besides La Bern's book, examples are Robert Westerby's *Wide Boys Never Work* (1937), Jim Phelan's *Ten-a-Penny People* (1938), Laurence Meynell's *The Creaking Chair* (1941), Gerald Kersh's *Night and the City* (1946), and James Curtis's *There Ain't No Justice* (1937). *The Creaking Chair* was filmed as *Street of Shadows,* directed by Richard Vernon (1953); *There Ain't No Justice* became a Pen Tennyson film in 1939; and *Night and the City* was the source of Jules Dassin's 1950 film.

38. La Bern, *It Always Rains on Sunday* (London: Nicholson & Watson, 1945), 224, 14, 123.

39. John W. Collier, *A Film in the Making* (London: World Film Publications, 1947), 9. Collier's short book is an interesting and detailed study of all phases of the making of *It Always Rains on Sunday.*

40. Reviews in *The New Statesman and Nation* 34, no. 874 (December 6, 1947): 449; *Spectator* 6233 (December 12, 1947): 741.

41. Richard Mallett, *Punch* 213, 5581 (December 10, 1947), 552.

42. "England, Noir England," *Independent on Sunday,* June 6, 1999, features.

43. Greene, review in *Spectator,* July 3, 1936; reprinted in *The Pleasure-Dome,* 84.

44. Pulleine, "Spin a dark web," in *British Crime Cinema,* 30.

45. Greene, *Brighton Rock* (London: William Heinemann and the Bodley Head, 1970 [1938]), 116.

46. Greene, *The Ministry of Fear* (London: William Heinemann and the Bodley Head, 1973 [1943]), 207.

47. Peter Wollen, "Riff-raff Realism," *Sight and Sound* 8, no. 4 (April 1998): 19, emphasis added.

48. Robert Brown, "Sons and Lovers," *Monthly Film Bulletin* (May 1985), back cover.

49. For more on the resemblances to *Point Blank,* and on the cinematic contexts of the film generally, see Steve Chibnall's British Film Guide volume, *Get Carter* (London: I. B. Tauris, 2003), 5–13. Jonathan Coe, "British Gangsters," *New Statesman and Nation* (August 29, 1997), 40.

50. Quirke, *The Independent* (June 13, 1999), features.

51. Robert Murphy, "A revenger's tragedy: *Get Carter,*" in *British Crime Cinema,* 132.

52. Director's soundtrack commentary on the 2001 Warner Studios DVD recording of the film.

53. Interview with Chris Darke, "From Gangland to the Casino Table," *Independent,* June 4, 1999, 13; interview with Tom Cox, "Get Hodges," *Guardian* (May 28, 1999): 6–7.

54. James Fenton in the *New Statesman* 81, no. 2086 (March 12, 1971): 354; John Russell Taylor in the *Times* (March 12, 1971): 12; Tom Milne in *Sight and Sound* 40 (Spring 1971): 107.

55. Chibnall, *Get Carter,* 50; on Lewis and La Bern, see Robert Murphy, "A Revenger's Tragedy—*Get Carter,*" in *British Crime Cinema,* 125.

56. Lewis, *Jack's Return Home* (Garden City: Doubleday, 1970), 73, 190, 74.

57. Director's soundtrack commentary.

58. Reviews in the *Times,* December 1, 1986; December 22, 1986.

59. Antony Hilfer, "'Run Over by One's Own Story': Genre and Ethos in Dennis Potter's *The Singing Detective,*" in *British Television Drama: Past, Present, and Future,* ed. Jonathan Bignell, Stephen Lacey, and Madeleine Macmurraugh-Kavanagh (New York: Palgrave, 2000), 136.

60. Potter's James MacTaggart Memorial Lecture (1993), quoted in Potter, *Seeing the Blossom* (London and Boston: Faber & Faber, 1994), 55.

61. MacTaggart Lecture, *Seeing the Blossom,* 53.

62. Kenith Trodd, commentary (with Jon Amiel) on the BBC Video DVD of *The Singing Detective* (2002).

63. 1971 BBC radio interview, quoted in Humphrey Carpenter, *Dennis Potter: A Biography* (New York: St. Martin's Press, 1998), 265–266.

64. Interview in the *Sunday Times,* quoted in Carpenter, *Dennis Potter,* 433; Philip Oakes, "A suitable sleuth for treatment," *Radio Times,* November 15–21, 1986, quoted in Carpenter, *Dennis Potter,* 437.

65. Quoted in Carpenter, *Dennis Potter,* 280.

66. John R. Cook, *Dennis Potter: A Life on Screen,* 2nd ed. (Manchester: Manchester University Press, 1998), 348–349.

67. Here and elsewhere the words are taken from the soundtrack of the series, not from Potter's published screenplay (New York: Vintage Books, 1988), from which it occasionally differs.

68. "Skinskapes" is spelled thus in the club's neon sign; it is "Skinscapes" in Potter's published screenplay.

69. Quoted in Joost Hunningher, "*The Singing Detective* (Dennis Potter): Who Done It?" in *British Television Drama in the 1980s,* ed. George W. Brandt (Cambridge: Cambridge University Press, 1993), 244.

70. Vernon W. Gras, "Dennis Potter's *The Singing Detective:* An Exemplum of Dialogical Ethics," in *The Passion of Dennis Potter,* ed. Gras and John R. Cook (New York: St. Martin's Press, 2000), 98; John Caughie, *Television Drama: Realism, Modernism, and British Culture* (Oxford: Oxford University Press, 2000), 173–174, emphasis in original.

71. Cook, *Dennis Potter,* 230–231.

72. Douglas Thompson, "The year of the fedora," London *Times,* August 27, 1986. For a review of the miniseries see Peter Davalle, *Times,* April 27, 1984: it was an example, Davalle thought, of "transatlantic cross-fertilization."

73. BBC note of February, 1984; quoted in Carpenter, *Dennis Potter,* 431.

74. Carpenter, *Dennis Potter*, 436–437.

75. Willie Morris, "The Moviegoer," in "Remembering Dennis Potter 1935–1994," *Voice* (June 21, 1994), 32–33.

76. Chandler, *The Simple Art of Murder* (New York: Vintage Books, 1988 [1950]), 18.

77. In his commentary on the DVD edition of *The Singing Detective*, Jon Amiel comments wryly that this telephone call captures the English "subservience to our American masters."

78. Glen Creeber, *Dennis Potter Between Two Worlds* (New York: St. Martin's Press, 1998), 177.

79. A characteristically acute observation made by R. H. Bell, "Implicated without Choice: The Double Vision of *The Singing Detective*," *Literature Film Quarterly* 21, no. 3 (July 1993): 203.

80. Director's commentary on the DVD. A number of other details in this paragraph are noted by Amiel or Trodd in the course of their commentary.

81. Ron Simon, "The Flow of Memory and Desire: Television and Dennis Potter," *Television Quarterly* 26, no. 4 (1993): 79. Simon quotes the *Casanova* quotation.

82. In a 1976 television review for the *Sunday Times* (October 10), Potter commented with relish on the accidental juxtaposition of and resemblance between two images: a scarecrow put together in a children's program ("wretched, stiff-limbed and blank-eyed") and the posture adopted by the right-wing politician Enoch Powell ("throwing out a rigid arm"), as shown on news reports of the Tory Party Conference.

83. Lodge, *The Practice of Writing* (New York: Allen Lane The Penguin Press, 1997), 217.

84. From *Time Regained*, the last volume of *In Search of Lost Time*; quoted in Roy Armes, *A Critical History of British Cinema* (New York: Oxford University Press, 1978), 13–14.

85. Potter, "George Orwell," *New Society* 279 (February 1, 1968): 157–158.

86. Orwell, *Complete Works*, 12: 133–134.

3. Two Texts to Screen

1. Virginia Woolf, *Collected Essays* (London: The Hogarth Press, 1992), 2: 269. Sharon Ouditt quotes Woolf's line in her essay on the cinematic qualities of *Orlando*: "*Orlando*: Coming Across the Divide," in *Adaptations: From Text to Screen, Screen to Text*, ed. Deborah Cartmell and Imelda Whelehan (London and New York: Routledge, 1999), 146–156.

2. Whelehan, "Adaptations: The Contemporary Dilemma," in *Adaptations*, 17. Whelehan's introduction comprehensively surveys the critical literature on adaptation. Still another contemporary discussion of fidelity is given by Dudley

Andrew, "Adaptation," in *Film Adaptation,* ed. James Naremore (New Brunswick, NJ: Rutgers University Press, 2000), 31–32. Leitch, *Film Adaptation and Its Discontents: From Gone with the Wind to The Passion of the Christ* (Baltimore, MD: The Johns Hopkins University Press, 2007), 20.

3. Peter Ackroyd, *The Great Fire of London* (London: Hamish Hamilton, 1982), 90. Further references will be cited in the text.

4. Dickens, *Little Dorrit* (1857), Chapter XIV; Penguin Classics edition, ed. Stephen Wall and Helen Small (Harmondsworth: Penguin, 1998), 176.

5. Peter Ackroyd, *Dickens* (New York: HarperCollins, 1991), 100. Ackroyd apparently does not read the woman as a prostitute; he merely calls her "disturbed."

6. For details of production, see the profile by Guy Phelps, "Victorian Values," *Sight and Sound* 57 (Winter 1987/88): 108–110.

7. Carey, *Little Dorrit: A Story Told in Two Films* (London: Sands Films, 1987), 5.

8. For a careful analysis and unstinting admiration of the film, see Joss Lutz March, "Inimitable Double Vision: Dickens, *Little Dorrit,* Photography, Film," in *Dickens Studies Annual* 22, ed. Michael Timko, Fred Kaplan, and Edward Guiliano (New York: AMS Press, 1993), 239–282. Another approving discussion is by Christopher Innes, "Adapting Dickens to the Modern Eye," in *Literature in Performance,* ed. Peter Reynolds (London and New York: Routledge, 1993), 64–79.

9. Raphael Samuel, "Dickens on Stage and Screen," *History Today* 39 (December 1989): 46. See the same critic's equally negative "Docklands Dickens," in *Patriotism: The Making and Un-Making of British National Identity,* ed. Samuel (London: Routledge, 1989), vol. 3: *National Fictions,* 275–285.

10. Grahame Smith, "Novel into Film: The Case of *Little Dorrit,*" *Yearbook of English Studies* 20 (1990), ed. Andrew Gurr (London: Modern Humanities Research Association, 1990), 37.

11. Graham Petrie, "Dickens, Godard, and the Film Today," *Yale Review* 64, no. 2 (December 1974): 188–189, 196–197.

12. This dramatization is available in a DVD set: *The Life and Adventures of Nicholas Nickleby* (New York: A & E Home Video, 2002); not a film, of course, but an exceptionally effective filming of a stage production.

13. Peter Ackroyd, "Theatrical Spirits," London *Times,* April 11, 1985.

14. Grahame Smith, "Novel into Film," 45; Robert Gittings and Keith Selby, *The Classic Serial on Television and Radio* (London: Palgrave, 2001), 76; Grahame Smith, "Dickens and Adaptation," in *Literature in Performance,* 61; John Glavin, *After Dickens: Reading, Adaptation and Performance* (Cambridge: Cambridge University Press, 1999), 28. See also the brief mention in Michael Pointer, *Charles Dickens on the Screen: the Film, Television, and Video Adaptations* (Lanham, MD, and London: Scarecrow Press, 1996), 96–97.

15. Dickens, *Bleak House,* Chapters 15, 25; Oxford World's Classic edition, ed. Stephen Wall (Oxford: Oxford University Press, 1996), 224, 375.

16. Quoted by Guerric DeBona, in "Dickens, the Depression, and MGM's *David Copperfield*," in Naremore, *Film Adaptation*, 115.

17. If McKenna needed a guide to his conception of the character, he could have found one in Dickens's comment on another smooth-talker of *Bleak House*, Conversation Kenge: "He appeared to enjoy beyond everything the sound of his own voice. . . . it was mellow and full, and gave great importance to every word he uttered. He listened to himself with obvious satisfaction, and sometimes gently beat time to his own music with his head, or rounded a sentence with his hand" (30).

18. Quoted in Neil Sinyard, *Filming Literature: The Art of Screen Adaptation* (New York: St. Martin's Press, 1986), 110.

19. Raymond Williams, Introduction to *Dombey and Son* (Baltimore, MD: Penguin, 1970), 15.

20. Eisenstein, *Film Form: Essays in Film Theory* (New York: Harcourt Brace, 1949), 195–255. For scholarly assessments of the essay, see Rick Altman, "Dickens, Griffith, and Film Theory Today," *South Atlantic Quarterly* 88, no. 2 (Spring 1989): 321–359; Garrett Stewart, "Dickens, Eisenstein, Film," in John Glavin, ed., *Dickens on Screen* (Cambridge: Cambridge University Press, 2003), 122–144; and Graham Petrie, "Dickens, Godard, and the Film Today," 185–201.

21. Gittings and Selby, *The Classic Serial on Television and Radio*, 76. A strike prolonged the production period of *Bleak House*, but the series would have taken seven or eight months in any case.

22. Herbert Mitgang, "A British Producer Savors the Freedom to Get It Right," *New York Times*, November 24, 1985, sec. 2.

23. Peter Kemp, "Atmosphere of Corruption," *TLS*, June 7, 1985; *Bleak House*, chapter 1, 12.

24. Hazel Hill, "Did Dickens Get a Fair Deal?," *Sunday Times*, May 12, 1985; Susan Elliott (with Barry Turner), *Denholm Elliott: Quest for Love* (London: Headline Book Publishing, 1994), 311.

25. John Wyver, "Falling Apart," *Listener*, April 4, 1985; Byron Rogers, "Lighting Up Time," *Sunday Times* April 14, 1985.

26. Cartmell and Whelehan, "A Practical Understanding of Literature on Screen: Two Conversations with Andrew Davies," in *The Cambridge Companion to Literature on Screen*, 243.

27. Quoted in Gittings and Selby, *The Classic Serial on Radio and Television*, 76–77.

28. "Charles Dickens" (1940), *Complete Works*, 12: 55–56.

29. For a survey of Dickensian adaptations, see Jeffrey Richards, "Dickens—our contemporary," *Films and British National Identity: From Dickens to Dad's Army* (Manchester and New York: Manchester University Press, 1997), 326–350.

30. Ishiguro, *The Remains of the Day* (London and Boston: Faber & Faber, 1989), 47, 50. Further references will be worked into the text.

31. The dramas were broadcast on October 18, 1984 and May 8, 1986 respectively. The text of *The Gourmet,* a bizarre drama about cannibalism, ghosts, and London tramps, was published in *Granta* 43 (Spring 1993): 91–127.

32. "The Novelist in Today's World: A Conversation [between Ishiguro and Oe Kenzaburo]," *boundary* 2 (Fall 1991): 115.

33. Interview with Ishiguro in Allan Vorda, ed., *Face to Face: Interviews with Contemporary Novelists* (Houston: Rice University Press, 1993), 25. For a detailed examination of Ozu's (and other filmmakers') influence on Ishiguro's first two novels, see Gregory Mason, "Inspiring Images: The Influence of the Japanese Cinema on the Writings of Kazuo Ishiguro," *East-West Film Journal* 3, no. 2 (June 1989): 39–52. For Chekhov's influence, see "Maya Jaggi talks to Kazuo Ishiguro," *Wasafiri: Journal of Caribbean, African, Asian and Associated Literatures and Film* 22 (Autumn 1995): 22.

34. David Lodge, *The Art of Fiction* (New York: Penguin, 1992), 155.

35. Leitch, *Film Adaptation and Its Discontents,* 168.

36. Edward T. Jones, "Harold Pinter: A Conversation," *Literature/ Film Quarterly* 21, no. 1 (1993): 7. For a longer discussion of the issues involved, see Jones, "On *The Remains of the Day:* Harold Pinter Remaindered," in Steven Gale, ed., *The Films of Harold Pinter* (Albany, NY: SUNY Press, 2001), 99–107.

37. John Calley, quoted in the commentary on the DVD edition of *The Remains of the Day* (Columbia TriStar Home Entertainment, 2001).

38. "Harold Pinter: A Conversation," 3.

39. Graham Swift, interview with Ishiguro, *Bomb* 29 (Fall 1989): 22.

40. John Pym, *Merchant Ivory's English Landscape: Rooms, Views, and Anglo-Saxon Attitudes* (London: Pavilion, 1995), 20.

41. A point well made by Earl G. Ingersoll in "Desire, the gaze and the suture in the novel and the film: *The Remains of the Day,*" *Studies in the Humanities* (June–December 2001): 44.

42. Recalled in Thompson's clever and interesting diary of the production, later published as "Day by Day," *Premiere* (December 1993): 108.

43. James Ivory, speaking on the DVD commentary.

44. Jones, "On *The Remains of the Day . . . ,*" 103.

45. Thompson's DVD commentary; Thompson, "Day by Day," 143.

46. Quoted in Andrew Higson, "The Heritage Film and British Cinema," in *Dissolving Views: Key Writings on British Cinema,* ed. Higson (London: Casell, 1996), 243.

47. Nicholas Lezard, "*The Remains of the Day,*" *TLS,* November 12, 1993, 21; Mark Steyn, "The remains of the book," *Spectator,* November 13, 1993, 45; Geoffrey Macnab, *Sight and Sound* 3, no. 12 (December 1993): 51.

48. Higson, "The Heritage Film and British Cinema," in *Dissolving Views,* 232–248, which confesses the essayist's personal liking for the heritage films, acknowledges their emotional power, and admits the possibility of divergent inter-

pretations of them. See also Claire Monk, "The British heritage-film debate revisited," in *British Historical Cinema: The History, Heritage and Costume Film*, ed. Claire Monk and Amy Sargeant (London and New York: Routledge, 2002), 176–198.

49. Andrew Higson, "Re-presenting the National Past: Nostalgia and Pastiche in the Heritage Film," in *Fires Were Started: British Cinema and Thatcherism*, ed. Lester Friedman (Minneapolis: University of Minnesota Press, 1993), 109–110, 113, 117–118.

50. Bernard Gilbert, *"Les vestiges du jour:* du roman de Kazuo Ishiguro au film de James Ivory," *Jeux d'Ecriture: le roman britannique contemporain*, ed. Marie-Françoise Cachin and Ann Grieve (Paris: Publications de l'Universite, 1995), 212.

51. Ivory's foreword to Pym, *Merchant Ivory's English Landscape*, 12.

52. Pym, *Merchant Ivory's English Landscape*, 20.

53. The book is Houston Stewart Chamberlain's *The Foundations of the Nineteenth Century*, translated into English in 1911; Chamberlain was a thoroughly Germanified Englishman who married Wagner's daughter and admired Hitler.

54. David Gurevich, "Upstairs Downstairs," The New Criterion 8, no. 4 (December 1989): 77–80.

55. See Alfred Shaughnessy's autobiography, *Both Ends of the Candle* (London: Peter Owen, 1978), 145–150. A far more elaborate history of the series is given in Richard Marson, *Inside Updown: the Story of Upstairs, Downstairs* (Bristol: Kaleidoscope Publishing, 2001).

56. For a plot synopsis and analysis, see Barry Lewis, *Kazuo Ishiguro* (Manchester and New York: Manchester University Press, 2000), 76–77.

57. Mason, "Inspiring Images . . . ," 46.

58. Marson, *Inside Updown: the Story of Upstairs, Downstairs*, 3.

4. The Strange Potencies of Music

1. Ronald Bergan and Robyn Karney, *The Faber Companion to Foreign Films* (Boston: Faber & Faber, 1992), 57, on *Le Bal*; Campaign for Nuclear Disarmament, "CND in the News," http://www.cnduk.org/pages/cnews/042207.html—the latter site one of countless examples.

2. Noël Coward, *Plays: Two*, intro. Raymond Mander and Joe Mitchenson (London: Methuen, 1979), 31–32.

3. Mann is quoted by Graham Greene in *Footnotes to the Film*, ed. Charles Davy (London: Lovat Dickson, 1938), 64; the phrase is from "Tonio Kröger." Powell, *Casanova's Chinese Restaurant*, in *A Dance to the Music of Time*, second movement (Chicago: University of Chicago Press, 1995), 2. Eliot, *The Waste Land*, lines 126–130. According to the Norton Critical Edition of the poem, ed. Michael North (New York: Norton, 2001), 9, "Shakespeherian rag" refers to a 1912 song by Dave Stamper, with lyrics by Gene Buck and Herman Ruby.

4. Coward, *Plays: Three*, intro. Mander and Mitchenson, 197–198.

5. Graham Greene, *Brighton Rock* (London: William Heinemann and the Bodley Head, 1970), 58–59.

6. Music by Giovanni D'Anzi, lyrics by Alfredo Bracchi, tr. Ray Miller.

7. For surveys of pop and rock in contemporary film, see Pauline Reay, *Music in Film: Soundtracks and Synergy* (London and New York: Wallflower, 2004); *Popular Music and Film*, ed. Ian Inglis (London and New York: Wallflower, 2003); Andy Medhurst, "It sort of happened here: the strange, brief life of the British pop film," in *Celluloid Jukebox: Popular Music and the Movies since the 50s*, ed. Jonathan Romney and Adrian Wootton (London: BFI, 1995), 60–71; and especially K. J. Donnelly, *Pop Music in British Cinema* (London: BFI, 2001).

8. For a comprehensive study, see Jan G. Swynnoe, *The Best Years of British Film Music, 1936–1958* (Woodbridge: Boydell Press, 2002). A briskly opinionated survey from the start of the period is given in Kurt London, *Film Music*, trans. Eric S. Bensinger (London: Faber & Faber, 1936), 213–223.

9. Swynnoe, *Best Years*, xiv.

10. Ray, *Our Films, Their Films* (Bombay: Orient Longman, 1976), 144; quoted in *All Our Yesterdays: 90 Years of British Cinema*, ed. Charles Barr (London: BFI, 1986), 9.

11. Maurice Jaubert, "Music on the Screen," in *Footnotes to the Film*, 109; emphasis added.

12. Edgar Anstey in the *Spectator* (April 12, 1946) thought that it followed the over-familiar "tram-route from tears to laughter," and was set "half in the real world and half in a world of theatrical convention" (375); William Whitebait in the *New Statesman and Nation* (6 April 1946) admired only the prison-camp scenes of the film (245).

13. Leach, *British Film*, 20.

14. Barry Day, *Coward on Film: The Cinema of Noël Coward* (Lanham, MD: Scarecrow Press, 2005), 110.

15. This film, which opened a month before *Brief Encounter*, has striking similarities to Lean's film: it is a love story almost turning into tragedy, opens with a failed suicide attempt, and employs an extended flashback structure. Its own orchestral music, by Ben Frankel, is used in conventional, English ways: at the start, the pianist heroine is in a psychiatric nursing home, being treated for a nervous breakdown. She does not—refuses to—speak, and her face is a completely unexpressive mask, so Frankel's music has to bear the entire burden of communicating her despair as she escapes from the ward and runs to the river: the equivalent for the express train which Laura Jesson cannot quite hurl herself underneath.

16. Jaubert, "Music on the Screen," in *Footnotes to the Film*, 109.

17. Forster, *Howards End*, ed. David Lodge (New York: Penguin, 2000), 28.

18. Officially, the "Beer Barrel Polka": original Czechoslovakian lyrics by Wladimir A. Timm and Vasek Zeman; English lyrics by the Tin Pan Alley writer Lew Brown, music by Jaromir Vejvoda.

19. For a history, see Stephen Guy, "Calling All Stars: Musical Films in a Musical Decade," in *The Unknown 1930s: an Alternative History of the British Cinema 1929–39*, ed. Jeffrey Richards (London and New York: I. B. Tauris, 1998), 99–118.

20. Andy Medhurst, "Music Hall and British Cinema," in *All Our Yesterdays*, 174. Medhurst's article (168–188) is a useful survey of the topic.

21. For these and other plot summaries, see Stephen C. Shafer, *British Popular Films 1929–1939* (London and New York: Routledge, 1997), 193–207; also David Bret, *Gracie Fields: The Authorized Biography* (London: Robson, 1995), passim.

22. See, in addition to Bret, Joan Moules, *Gracie Fields: A Biography* (Chichester: Summersdale, 1997); Bert Aza, *Our Gracie* (London: Pitkins, n.d.); and Fields's autobiography, *Sing As We Go* (London: Frederick Muller, 1960), which, however, says almost nothing about her film work.

23. Landy, *British Genres: Cinema and Society, 1930–1960* (Princeton, NJ: Princeton University Press, 1991), 340.

24. Review of *Look Up and Laugh*, London *Times*, August 5, 1935.

25. J. B. Priestley, *English Journey* (Chicago: University of Chicago Press, 1984 [1934]), 190–191.

26. J. B. Priestley, *Margin Released* (New York and Evanston: Harper & Row, 1962), 60, 66. For an extended account of the historical meaning of Priestley's encounter with ragtime, see John Baxendale, "'. . . into another kind of life in which anything might happen . . .' Popular music and late modernity, 1910–1930," *Popular Music* 14, no. 2 (1995): 137–154.

27. J. B. Priestley, *The Good Companions* (New York: Harper & Bros., 1930 [1929]), 58, 277.

28. C. A. Oakley, *Where We Came In: Seventy Years of the British Film Industry* (London: George Allen and Unwin, 1964), 118.

29. Basil Dean, *Mind's Eye: an Autobiography 1927–1972* (London: Hutchinson, 1973), 204.

30. Priestley, "English Films and English People," *World Film News* 1, no. 8 (November 1936): 3.

31. Muriel Burgess with Tommy Keen, *Gracie Fields* (London: W. H. Allen, 1980), 70.

32. *English Journey*, 200–201. The "helter-skelter," an almost too appropriately named fun-fair ride, is "a tower-like structure . . . with an external spiral passage for sliding down on a mat," according to the OED. A "switch-back" is a "railway consisting of a series of steep alternate ascents and descents, on which the train or car runs partly or wholly by the force of gravity, the momentum of each descent carrying it up the succeeding ascent"; especially "such a railway constructed for amusement at a pleasure-resort."

33. Richards, *The Age of the Dream Palace* (London and New York; Routledge, 1984), 169–190; Higson, *Waving the Flag: Constructing a National Cinema in Britain* (Oxford: Clarendon Press, 1995), 98–175.

34. Greene, *Spectator*, August 9, 1935; reprinted in *The Pleasure Dome*, 12.

35. Dean, *Mind's Eye,* 207.

36. "Marie Lloyd" (1922); *Selected Prose of T. S. Eliot,* ed. Frank Kermode (New York: Harcourt Brace Jovanovich, Farrar Straus & Giroux, 1975), 172.

37. Aza, *Our Gracie,* 9.

38. *Look Back in Anger and Other Plays* (London and Boston: Faber & Faber, 1993), 79.

39. In 1986 *Lost Empires* was adapted for an exceptionally well-made Granada television series, adapted from Priestley's novel by Ian Curteis, directed by Alan Grint; "heritage" television, some might say, but in fact a series casting a cold eye on the pastness of this particular heritage.

40. Larkin, *Collected Poems,* ed. Anthony Thwaite (New York: Farrar Straus Giroux and Marvell Press, 1988), 83.

41. Terence Davies, *A Modest Pageant* (Boston: Faber & Faber, 1992), 76, x. This volume contains the screenplays for *Children, Madonna and Child,* and *Death and Transfiguration* as well as for the two features.

42. For an essay situating the film in British film history and the history of working-class cultural representation, see Geoff Eley, "Distant Voices, Still Lives: The Family Is a Dangerous Place: Memory, Gender, and the Image of the Working Class," in *Revisioning History: Film and the Construction of a New Past,* ed. Robert A. Rosenstone (Princeton, NJ: Princeton University Press, 1995), 17–43.

43. Amy Sargent, *British Cinema: A Critical History* (London: BFI Publishing, 2005), 303.

44. Davies, *A Modest Pageant,* 74.

45. David Robinson attributes the father's bullying violence to "mental disturbance": see his review of *Distant Voices, Still Lives* in "Two Cheers," *Times,* October 13, 1988.

46. For a discussion of rite-of-passage films in the 1980s, see Phil Powrie, "On the Threshold between Past and Present: 'Alternative Heritage'," in *British Cinema, Past and Present,* ed. Justine Ashby and Andrew Higson (London and New York: Routledge, 2000), 316–325.

47. Davies interview with David Cavanaugh, quoted in Martin Hunt, "The poetry of the ordinary: Terence Davies and the social art film," *Screen* 40, no. 1 (Spring 1999): 7.

48. For example, David Robinson in the *Times,* October 13, 1988; David Wilson, "Family Album," *Sight and Sound* 17, no. 4 (Autumn 1988): 282.

49. Wendy Everett, *Terence Davies* (Manchester and New York: Manchester University Press, 2004), 25; Wheeler Winston Dixon, "The Long Day Closes: Interview with Terence Davies," in *Collected Interviews: Voices from Twentieth-Century Cinema* (Carbondale and Edwardsville: Southern Illinois University Press, 2001), 190.

50. By Sadie Vimmerstedt and Johnny Mercer.

51. On what singing means to the women characters in particular, see Margaret Walters's review of *Distant Voices, Still Lives:* "Songs of Experience," *The Listener,* October 13, 1988, 39.

52. Dixon, "The Long Day Closes: Interview with Terence Davies," *Collected Interviews*, 187, emphasis in original; Davies quoted in Everett, *Terence Davies*, 208.

53. Davies, *A Modest Pageant*, 74. For a discussion of Davies's debt to Eliot, see Everett, *Terence Davies*, esp. 37–38, 53–55.

54. Eliot, *The Waste Land*, lines 163–164; 10 in the Norton Critical Edition.

55. *A Modest Pageant*, 82.

56. "Familiar Haunts" (Davies interview with Harlan Kennedy), *Film Comment* 24, no. 5 (1988): 16.

57. Kirkham and O'Shaughnessy, "Designing Desire," *Sight and Sound* 2, no. 1 (May 1992): 14.

58. These lines are from Arthur La Bern's novel, rather than the film: *It Always Rains on Sunday* (London: Nicholson & Watson, 1945), 78–79.

59. Kirkham and O'Shaughnessy, "Designing Desire," 14.

60. "Familiar Haunts," 14.

61. Caughie, "Half Way to Paradise," *Sight and Sound* 2, no. 1 (May 1992): 13.

62. Davies, *A Modest Pageant*, 147.

63. Radstone, "Cinema/memory/history," *Screen* 36, no. 1 (Spring 1995): 45.

64. "Familiar Haunts," 17.

65. For a typically approving review, see Dilys Powell, "The sixpenny opera," *Sunday Times*, April 6, 1978.

66. *Potter on Potter*, ed. Graham Fuller (London and Boston: Faber & Faber, 1993), 92.

67. Trodd's introduction to Dennis Potter, *Pennies from Heaven* (London and Boston: Faber & Faber, 1996), xi. Trodd makes the same point in his producer's commentary on the DVD edition of *Pennies from Heaven* (BBC Video, 2004). According to another account, Trodd sent Potter a 1950s handbook on English murders: see Irving B. Harrison, "Dennis Potter: The Why of his Doubles and Devices," www.yorksj.ac.uk/potter/IH_ch6_PFH.htm.

68. The crime took place in November 1930; details of the arrest and trial are given in the *Times* for November 28, 1930, and January 27 and January 30, 1931. The traveler—Alfred Arthur Rouse, a war veteran, as Arthur Parker claims to be—was hanged in Bedford on March 10, 1931, and already by April his wax effigy was being exhibited at Madame Tussaud's.

69. Michael Ratcliffe, "The Pleasing Thirties," London *Times*, March 8, 1978.

70. Cook, *Dennis Potter*, 166. Cook quotes from a Potter interview in which the playwright notes that *Chicago Girl and the Showgirl* derived from the same factual source as he had drawn on for his series.

71. Carpenter, *Dennis Potter*, 356n.

72. *Sunday Times*, December 11, 1977; *Sunday Times*, November 27, 1977. See also Peter Ansorge, *From Liverpool to Los Angeles: on Writing for Theatre, Film and Television* (London and Boston: Faber & Faber, 1997), 66.

73. Dennis Potter, "Bitter-sweet lessons from the memory bank," *Sunday Times*, November 14, 1976.

74. Paul Madden, commenting on *Pennies from Heaven* in *Sight and Sound* 47, no. 3 (Summer 1978): 194.

75. Quoted in the introduction to *Pennies from Heaven*, ix.

76. Quoted in "Parker's piece from Dennis Potter," London *Times*, February 3, 1978.

77. Introduction to *Pennies from Heaven*, x; *Potter on Potter*, 86, 84; interview with Ray Connolly, *Evening Standard*, March 21, 1978, quoted in Carpenter, *Dennis Potter*, 350.

78. Madden, *Sight and Sound*, 195.

79. Lyrics and music by Isham Jones and Charles Newman.

80. Carpenter, *Dennis Potter*, 346, quoting an interview with Trodd. "The Clouds Will Soon Roll By" was written by Harry Woods and George Brown.

81. *Potter on Potter*, 86.

82. Michael Ratcliffe, "The Pleasing Thirties," 9.

83. Canted angles figure in a brilliant pastiche of noir filmmaking at the start of the second episode, when Arthur comes home to the sleeping Joan and menacingly removes his tie, "like at least twenty stranglers in the films," as Potter notes in the published screenplay.

84. Carpenter, *Dennis Potter*, 582. "Roll Along, Prairie Moon" is by Ted Fio Rito, Harry McPherson, and Al Von Tilzer.

85. Screenplay of *Pennies from Heaven*, 68–69.

86. Carpenter, *Dennis Potter*, 582.

87. Commentary on the DVD edition.

88. Words by Johnny Burke, music by Arthur Johnson.

89. For a comparison of original and remake, see David Jays, "In the Night," *Sight and Sound* (September 2000), 20–21.

90. Words by Dorothy Fields, music by Jerome Kern. A demonstration of the system of ironic self-references Potter put into *Pennies from Heaven*, as into all his works: a few minutes after Arthur's performance with the straw man, he is talking with Eileen about his liking for both songs and musicals. He prefers musicals: "like when they can't get anybody to put on their show in a proper theatre. And they put it on in this barn. . . . Like that barn out there. And all the big producers come and see it. It's a big hit. Especially when they dance with a rake and that."

91. "The Art of Donald McGill," in Orwell, *Complete Works*, 13: 29.

92. Quoted by Piers Haggard in the DVD commentary.

93. He lectured on the writer in Dublin during the centenary celebrations of 1982; see Carpenter, *Dennis Potter*, 422.

94. Program Three, "How to Recognize Different Types of Tree from Quite a Long Way Away," broadcast October 19, 1969. Another courtroom routine which might have influenced Potter is from Program Fifteen, "The Spanish Inquisition," broadcast September 22, 1970: here the foreman of the jury acts out "not guilty" in charades.

95. Lesley White, "Dennis the Menace," *Sunday Times*, February 14, 1993.

96. Harris, "Putting Up with Potter," *Spectator*, February 27, 1993, 40. "Privates on Parade," *Daily Telegraph*, February 22, 1993 (quoted in Cook, *Dennis Potter*, 357).

97. Commentary to the DVD edition of *The Singing Detective*.

98. Potter, *The Changing Forest: Life in the Forest of Dean Today* (London: Secker & Warburg, 1962), 127–128, 130–131, 137.

99. Commentary to the DVD edition of *The Singing Detective*.

100. Words by Doris Fisher, music by Allan Roberts.

Conclusion

1. *The Journal of Arnold Bennett* (New York: Viking Press, 1933), 3: 286, 303. See also 283–284, 286. Bennett's original story for the film was published as *Piccadilly: Story of the Film* (London: Readers Library Publishing Co., n.d. [1929]).

2. Greene, *The Pleasure Dome*, 1.

3. Norman Sherry, *The Life of Graham Greene*, vol. 1 (New York: Viking, 1989), 598, quoting a 1936 letter to his brother Hugh.

4. Bennett, "Staring out of the Window," reprinted in *Untold Stories* (New York: Farrar, Straus and Giroux, 2005), 544.

5. "Tony Harrison the Playwright," in *Tony Harrison: Loiner*, ed. Sandie Byrne (Oxford: Clarendon Press, 1997), 43.

6. Sophocles, *The Trackers of Oxyrhynchus: The Delphi Text of 1988* (London: Faber & Faber, 1990), 31. For that matter, in Peter Hall's National Theatre production of the *Oresteia*, the actors speak in North-of-England accents, as recordings of the production make clear.

7. Boyd Tonkin, reviewing *Prometheus*, *The Independent*, November 14, 1998. "Scally" = someone wearing a cloth cap, hence working-class.

8. Harrison, *Collected Film Poetry* (London: Faber & Faber, 2007), 308, 305–306, 335.

9. Harrison, *Collected Film Poetry*, vii–viii, x.

10. Symes, "It's All Poetry to Me," *Collected Film Poetry*, xxxvii.

11. Harrison, "Flicks and This Fleeting Life," *Collected Film Poetry*, xxix.

12. Peter Lennon, reviewing *Prometheus*, in the *Guardian*, November 5, 1998; John Naughton, reviewing *Black Daisies for the Bride*, in the *Guardian*, July 4, 1993; Hugh Hebert, reviewing *Black Daisies for the Bride*, in the *Guardian*, July 1, 1993; Thomas Sutcliffe, reviewing *The Blasphemer's Banquet*, in *The Independent*, August 1, 1989. Even Julie Davidson in the *Herald* (Glasgow), who loathed *Black Daisies for the Bride* for its cooptation of helpless Alzheimer's patients into the program, called it "an artful piece of experimental television" (July 3, 1993).

13. *The English Auden*, ed. Edward Mendelson (London and Boston: Faber & Faber, 1977), 290.

14. Greene, *The Pleasure Dome*, 108, 60.

15. Morrison's poems have apparently not been published; the lines here are taken from the soundtrack of *Night Mail II* (directed by Bob Franklin, produced by Peter Williams); broadcast April 11, 1989.

16. From the soundtrack of the broadcast.

17. Harrison, *Collected Film Poetry,* 405.

18. Harrison, *Collected Film Poetry,* 407, 408, 409, 414. In the published film script, the last lines are "Mail that you'll loathe, or mail that you'll like / or no mail at all because they're on strike!"; but these were cut for the broadcast.

19. Lennon, *Guardian,* March 9, 2002. London *Times,* March 11, 2002. "Bragg" is Melvyn Bragg, presenter on the South Bank Show.

20. Harrison, *Collected Film Poetry,* xxviii.

21. Bennett, *Untold Stories,* 545.

22. Bennett, introduction to *Writing Home* (New York: Random House, 1994), xiii.

23. "The Great Art of Embarrassment," *New York Review of Books* 42, no. 3 (February 16, 1995): 15. For more on Bennett's standing as a central, much-beloved public figure, even as a sort of National Teddy Bear, see Joseph O'Mealy, *Alan Bennett: a Critical Introduction* (New York and London: Routledge, 2001), xiii–xxii, and Alexander Games, *Backing into the Limelight: The Biography of Alan Bennett* (London: Headline, 2001), 226ff.

24. "An article on playwrights in the *Daily Mail,* listed according to Hard Left, Soft Left, Hard Right, Soft Right and Centre. I am not listed. I should probably come under Soft Centre"; diary entry for November 11, 1981; printed in *Writing Home,* 117.

25. Bennett, "Seeing Stars," in *Untold Stories,* 159, 161, 170–171.

26. Diary entry, July 16, 1987; reprinted in *Writing Home,* 159.

27. Entry for August 16, 2004; reprinted in *Untold Stories,* 355.

28. "Untold Stories," in *Untold Stories,* 105.

29. "The Writer in Disguise," in *Writing Home,* 268.

30. Broadcast on BBC 2, July 5, 1992; the odd title refers to the way that television sets used to be closed up in cabinets ("like commodes"). All quotations given here are taken from the soundtrack of the program.

31. Larkin, in "Church Going," *Collected Poems,* ed. Anthony Thwaite (New York: Farrar Straus Giroux, 1988), 97–98.

32. Bennett's production diary; printed in *Writing Home,* 261.

33. *Writing Home,* 263.

34. In a 1991 memorial service eulogy for Lloyd; reprinted in *Writing Home,* 54–58.

35. Bennett, *Objects of Affection and Other Plays for Television* (London: BBC, 1982), 148. *A Day Out* is not available on DVD.

36. Bennett, *Objects of Affection,* 169.

37. See the "Filming and Rehearsing" section in *Writing Home,* 243–290.

38. *Writing Home,* 211.

39. An episode from real life, which Bennett learned about from Coral Browne: see *Writing Home,* 210.

40. "A Night in with Alan Bennett."

41. Steve Lohr, "The Verdigris of Life, as Told (and Lived) by Alan Bennett," *New York Times,* February 9, 1989.

42. Turner, *Alan Bennett: In a Manner of Speaking* (London and Boston: Faber & Faber, 1997), 142.

43. Preface to *Forty Years On,* reprinted in *Writing Home,* 199.

44. Turner, *Alan Bennett: In a Manner of Speaking,* 9.

45. *Forty Years On* (London: Faber & Faber, 1969), 19, 77–78.

46. Bennett, *Objects of Affection,* 7.

47. *The History Boys* [play] (New York: Faber & Faber, 2004), xxix.

48. Bennett, "Seeing Stars," *Untold Stories,* 165–166.

49. *Untold Stories,* 59–61.

50. This is the burden of Rupert Christiansen's pan of the play: "History Boys Is Bunk," *The Daily Telegraph,* July 28, 2004.

51. Alan Bennett and Nicholas Hytner, *The History Boys: The Film* (New York: Faber & Faber, 2006), x; Hytner's commentary on the DVD edition of the film (Twentieth Century Fox Home Entertainment, 2006). In the published screenplay, Hytner and Bennett share writing credit; in the credits of the film itself, which differs in many details from the published screenplay (cuts, mostly), Bennett is listed as the sole writer. Quotations that follow are taken directly from the soundtrack of the DVD.

52. Diary entry, February 10, 2005; reprinted in *Untold Stories,* 342.

53. *The History Boys* [play], 68.

54. Tony Rayns, *Sight and Sound* 16 (November, 2006): 59. A much more favorable judgment ("a profound and nimble film") was rendered by David Jays in the same issue of the journal: "Alan Bennett: A Little Learning," 20. Reviews of *The History Boys* tended to be unfavorable. See for example Deborah Ross, "Too faithful," *Spectator,* October 14, 2006, 72; Ryan Gilbey, "Please, sir, can I be excused?," *New Statesman,* October 16, 2006, 45; Robert Hanks, "Not the Lesson We All Wanted," *The Independent,* October 13, 2006; Cosmo Landesman, "A carry on up the curriculum," *Sunday Times,* October 15, 2006 (a particularly thickheaded attack on the film as so much homosexual propaganda); James Christopher, "Too clever for your own good, boys," *London Times,* October 12, 2006; Peter Bradshaw, "Blackboard bungle . . . ," the *Guardian,* October 13, 2006; and, on the other side of opinion, Philip French, "Mad about the boys . . . ," *Observer,* October 15, 2006.

55. In his commentary on the DVD edition of the film, Bennett remarks that the bulletin-board collage was taken over from the one used onstage at the National Theatre, where the production design was by Bob Crowley. A very similar photomontage appears on the wall of Joe Orton's flat in Bennett's 1987 film *Prick Up Your Ears* (design by Hugo Luczyc-Wyhowski).

56. Bennett interviewed by Nicholas Hytner, *The Daily Telegraph*, June 19, 2004.

57. Introduction to *The History Boys: The Film*, xi; Hytner's commentary on the DVD edition.

58. To balance this, we are informed that Lockwood will meet his death in battle, shot by friendly fire.

59. Bennett's commentary on the DVD edition.

INDEX

A former department chair and director of film studies, **Jefferson Hunter** is the Helen and Laura Shedd Professor of English and Film Studies at Smith College. He teaches courses in modern literature and film. His previous publications include *Edwardian Fiction; Image and Word: The Interaction of Twentieth-Century Photographs and Texts;* and *How to Read* Ulysses, *and Why.* He is a regular reviewer of books on film and of classic films on DVD.